Ina Batzke, Eric C. Erbacher, Linda M. Heß, Corinna Lenhardt (eds.)
Exploring the Fantastic

D1620349

Lettre

INA BATZKE, ERIC C. ERBACHER,
LINDA M. HESS, CORINNA LENHARDT (EDS.)

Exploring the Fantastic

Genre, Ideology, and Popular Culture

[transcript]

© 2018 transcript Verlag, Bielefeld

Bibliographic information published by the Deutsche Nationalbibliothek

The Deutsche Nationalbibliothek lists this publication in the Deutsche Na-
tionalbibliografie; detailed bibliographic data are available in the Internet at
http://dnb.d-nb.de

Cover layout: Maria Arndt, Bielefeld
Cover illustration: Kaleidoscope – Münster, November 2015, private photograph
    by Linda Heß
Printed by Majuskel Medienproduktion GmbH, Wetzlar
Print-ISBN 978-3-8376-4027-4
PDF-ISBN 978-3-8394-4027-8

Contents

Introduction

INA BATZKE, ERIC ERBACHER, LINDA HESS, AND CORINNA LENHARDT

> "'Fantastic,' like its partner 'fabulous,' carries unequivocally
> positive (if imprecise) connotations in common speech. But place
> it in a literary context and suddenly we have a problem. Suddenly
> it is something dubious, embarrassing (because presumed extra-
> canonical). Suddenly we need to justify our interest in it."
> (Armitt 1996: 1)

Roughly twenty years after Lucie Armitt's astute description of the state of research in the literary fantastic as problematic – or even "dubious" or "embarrassing" –, the atmosphere has changed. Scholars researching and writing about the
innumerous varieties of the fantastic no longer have to grapple with arguments
that dismiss it as escapist pulp-fiction, which cannot and should not be discussed
alongside serious literature. Since theoretical debate on the subject was initiated
in the second half of the 20th century, largely triggered by the publication of
Roger Callois' *Au Coeur du Fantastique* (1965) and Tzvetan Todorov's *The
Fantastic: A Structural Approach to a Literary Genre* (1973), research on the
fantastic has become a rapidly developing field of scholarship with great international and interdisciplinary relevance. The field's significance is reflected in numerous scholarly journals, associations, organizations, research projects, and institutions that have focused on and continue to analyze the fantastic. The broad
acceptance of fantastic texts as well as fantastic elements in literature, film, music, digital media, and so forth as relevant objects of study is an enormously ad-
vantageous development. At the same time, this opening-up of the fantastic to
literary, cultural, social, and media studies has created an almost impenetrable
thicket of research foci, methods, aims, and findings. To borrow Armitt's dic-
tion: Suddenly the field appears fantastically messy. Suddenly we have a new set
of problems.

Within the current breadth and diversity of research, one central question has
emerged that seems especially prone to active disagreement: What is the fantas-

tic? While there have been heated debates on how to define and delineate the very subject of research practically ever since the formation of the field, the issue evokes a broader, yet much more interconnected spectrum of answers today than ever before. The traditional polar opposition between narrow, minimalist definitions in the tradition of Todorov and extremely broad, inclusive conceptualizations of the fantastic as any kind of cultural product that juxtaposes an empirically verifiable world to a fantastic alternative is no longer a satisfactory description of the state of research in the fantastic. More recent developments in Cultural and Literary Studies (such as transnational, transcultural, and transmedial approaches) contribute to the field's growing heterogeneity, revealing clearly how significant a place the fantastic holds in contemporary cultures worldwide. At the same time, this proliferation and diversification of the fantastic necessitates an analytical survey and a taking stock of the most important theoretical and textual developments in the contemporary landscape of research in the fantastic.

Exploring the Fantastic: Genre, Ideology, and Popular Culture sets out to address these current developments in Literary, Cultural, and Media Studies. Taken together, the three thematic sections – "Genre," "Ideology," and "Popular Culture" – offer an astute snapshot of the contemporary Anglophone landscape of research in the fantastic and provide new stimuli to theoretical and methodological approaches, its textual materials, its main interests, and its crucial findings. With these subsections, the volume aims at a) contributing innovative research to salient discussions about the definitions, traditions, and boundaries of the fantastic, b) emphasizing a central strategic element of fantastic texts, that is, the critique and subversion of normative ideological constructs, and c) showing exemplarily the broad impact of the fantastic on popular cultural media and texts.

The eleven chapters that comprise the three thematic sections in turn reflect and take part in the most current and urgent debates in the field of the fantastic today. In order to pay tribute to the enormous variety of disciplines and voices involved in these debates, we have included articles from authors of all academic ranks and from a great variety of countries. While some of our contributors are internationally renowned scholars, writers, and experts in the field of the Anglophone fantastic, others have just begun their academic careers and, thus, provide not only innovative perspectives on their subject matters but also attest to the field's continuing vibrancy. Taken together, this volume offers not only an effective stocktaking of the current debates and arguments in the field, but also innovative perspectives, questions, and answers for a truly "fantastic" twenty-first century. In this, "fantastic," of course, might also translate to "Gothic," "magic," "dystopic," or "creepy" – variant aspects of the fantastic that are discussed in depth in this volume.

In the first section, "Genre," four papers engage critically with the key question of how – or whether – the genre of the fantastic can be defined in the twenty-first century. The contributions not only interrogate conventional definitions of the fantastic, its sub-genres, and the fantastic's relationship to "the real," but also engage in innovative re-definitions of the larger genre that take contemporary developments into account. The section opens with Daniel Scott's proposition of a new, grammatical approach to the fantastic that offers a comprehensive definition of fantasy encompassing classic fantasy fiction as well as the works of science fiction and Christian speculative fiction. In "Belief, Potentiality and the Supernatural: Mapping the Fantastic," Scott frames fantastic genres as conditionals, an innovative approach that proposes nothing less than a new framework for reading fantastic literature. Further, the grammatical approach allows Scott to highlight how other models of thought such as theism and atheism have also always been keenly involved in the fantastic, since their narrative stances are accurately reflected in the conditional concepts of fantasy and science fiction. Thus, Scott's method enriches previous research in the fantastic with a new and broadly applicable theoretical perspective.

In "Fantasy without Fantasy: Politics, Genre, and Media in the Fiction of M. John Harrison," Fred Botting presents a performative analysis of the works of British science fiction novelist M. John Harrison that invites readers to actively explore the fantastic and to engage with the different facets of "fantasy without fantasy." Botting takes this phrase, coined by Harrison himself, and – via a reading of Harrison's short stories – develops it into a performative mode of the fantastic that fosters critical engagement with ideology and politics. Zeroing in on the turn-of-the-millennium short story "Suicide Coast" (1999), Botting carefully delineates the narrative layers, modes, and formal features that shape the story's own negotiation of commercial fantasy (a mode aiming at complete immersion). Here, he highlights in particular Harrison's powerful device of the glitch, a formal interruption that irritates the smoothness of commercial fantasy and that tilts the reader's perception. This tilt then creates, as a flip image of commercial fantasy, "fantasy without fantasy" as a new critical lens for reading the contemporary fantastic.

In the subsequent article, Irina Golovacheva asks provocatively, "Is the Fantastic Really Fantastic?" She introduces the concept of "fantastika" alongside the more established notion of "the fantastic" and, thus equipped, tackles two decisive questions: Firstly, is the fantastic present in any genre of fantastika, and secondly, does the presence of the fantastic in the text signify that the latter is an exemplar of fantastika? In a close analysis of these two core concepts in utopian literature and the presumable non-fantasticality of Aldous Huxley's *Brave New World* (1931) and *Island* (1962), she reveals the artificiality of the rigid distinction between such disciplinary genres as scientific writing and fiction on the one hand, and science fiction and utopia on the other.

In the last article of this section, the novelist, poet, and scholar Larissa Lai, too, turns to utopian literature and reflects on how speculative fiction can be social in the 21st century. The implicit paradox in much utopian speculative fiction is that it does its social labor through the contrast between the world it offers and a non-ideal present, and yet seeks to transcend that present, often with an eye to an idealized commons. The question of redress for historical wrongs, however, poses a major problem in relation to that ideal. Lai analyzes speculative texts as "literary experiments" with a utopian edge. Such experiments that provide space for the eruptive potentials in utopian thinking and strive to follow the trail of those potentials, leading us beyond the possibilities of both "the human" and "nature," towards the possibilities of both extra-human and racialized futures.

The second section, "Ideology," discusses the fantastic as a literary genre, with particular regard to its societal and cultural implications. With a clear focus on fantastic texts' critical negotiation of ideology, the four scholars in this section address the question, in what ways fantastic texts reflect, strengthen, or confront cultural ideologies. The specific focus here is on how fantastic texts, on the level of form as well as that of content, participate in questioning normative ideological constructs of nationhood, the environment, the Other, and sexuality.

The section opens with Alfons Gregori's baseline article, "Crossing Impossible Boundaries? Fantastic Narrative and Ideology." In his theoretical and conceptual chapter, Gregori starts out by dissecting the genealogy of both various conceptions of (Marxist) ideology as well as of the fantastic as a mode and genre. Building on this enquiry, he argues for a more liberal and flexible approach to ideology that takes the textual and contextual ambiguities and contingencies of ideological elements in a fantastic text into account. The effect of such a reading of fantastic literature, according to Gregori, is to engage the reader's critical thinking by having to disambiguate not only the fantastic elements but also the potentially shifting ideological meanings of the real and fantastic elements.

In "Questioning Mononormativity: A Future of Fantastic Scholarship in Liminal Identities," Brandy Eileen Allatt investigates the possibilities of science fiction works to critically examine liminal identities in the fantastic by engaging the concept of mononormativity, which implies the idealization of monogamous sexual and romantic relationships in Western societies. While this concept has recently gained prominence as subject of inquiry in the social sciences, Allatt transports it to the field of fantastic literature. Analyzing three works of science fiction, namely Robert A. Heinlein's *Stranger in a Strange Land* (1961), Ursula Le Guin's *The Left Hand of Darkness* (1969), and Vandana Singh's *Distances* (2008), Allatt illustrates the narratives' portrayal of relationships outside the societal norm of two-party monogamy. Her particular focus lies on their subtle or overt criticism of this norm, which resonates with cultural debates of the later 20th century as well as contemporary negotiations of identity and sexuality.

Johanna Pundt's contribution "Organic Fantasy and the Alien Archetype in Nnedi Okorafor's *Lagoon*" considers Nigerian-American author Nnedi Okorafor's contemporary science fiction novel *Lagoon* (2014) and its re-shaping and expansion of established science fiction tropes from a postcolonial perspective. In particular, Pundt examines the author's use of organic fantasy and the archetype of the alien. She analyzes Okorafor's writing of alien arrival, not as a doubling of historical invasion by colonizers, but rather as a countering of colonial forces through the use of organic fantasy as a defamiliarization strategy that allows us to "imagine a Nigeria in which the magical and mythological intersect with science" (176). Ultimately, Pundt illustrates the productive synthesis born of postcolonial sci-fi in *Lagoon* that serves to negotiate not so much a distant future but rather to summon the possibilities of a de-colonial Nigerian present.

Michael Giebel's "Fantastic Struggles: Magical Realism and Superhero Fiction as Manifestations of Cultural Hybridity and Agents of Hegemonic Subversion," presents an investigation into Dominican-American author Junot Díaz' writing, particularly his Pulitzer Prize-winning novel *The Brief Wondrous Life of Oscar Wao* (2007). Giebel illustrates how Díaz gives expression to the cultural experience of the so-called "1.5 generation" by, on the one hand, following the Latin American literary tradition of magical realism, but, on the other hand, interweaving it with a dominant literary mode of the fantastic native to his current cultural context: U.S. America's superhero fiction.

The third section, "Popular Culture," further expands the research into the constructions and deconstructions of ideologies, by highlighting the ubiquitous presence of the fantastic in contemporary popular culture. Discussing a variety of media and genres, the section's three chapters analyze the fantastic and its traces in Anglophone popular culture ranging from the social media phenomenon of "creepypasta" to erotic and romance fiction to Hard SF. Spotlights on fiction, film, television, and Internet memes demonstrate that the fantastic has become a highly effective marketing instrument part and parcel of contemporary mainstream pop-culture. At the same time, the discussions of these chapters also connect to the earlier sections' discussions of genre and ideology, highlighting once again the currency as well as wider significance of the fantastic and its theoretical debates in the twenty-first century.

In "There are no Blank Slates: Relations between the Fantastic and the Real," Sarah Faber argues that the fantastic cannot exist without the real. Based on the assumption that imagination needs references and comparisons to retain meaning and drawing on a variety of pop-cultural narratives, this article explores in how far the fantastic relies on elements of the real world to produce meaningful and relatable experiences for its audience. Fantastic narratives enjoy a comparatively large amount of creative freedom, as they always include elements that contradict our notions of "real" or "realistic." Yet, as Faber shows using examples from the well-known 19th-century novella *Flatland: A Romance of Many Dimensions*, H.P. Lovecraft's writings, and the 2016 Hollywood blockbuster *Deadpool*, even they rely very much on incorporating familiar aspects from our primary reality.

Atalie Gerhard's innovative study "Creepypastas: How Counterterrorist Fantasies (Re-)Create Horror Traditions for Today's Digital Communities" focuses on the pop-cultural significance of "creepypastas" and creates a socio-historical framework for this new genre of communal online horror storytelling vis-à-vis the ideologies fueling the United States' Wars on Terror. In her analysis of the Internet memes "Slender Man" and "Black Eyed Kids," Gerhard, thus, is interested in outlining the genre conventions of creepypastas as the digital age's outstanding contribution to the fantastic literary mode of horror and Gothic writing. Equally central, however, is her focus on understanding the cultural, historical, and social circumstances that contributed to the phenomenon of Internet users collectively weaving legend cycles.

Finally, in "'All the Better to Eat You With': The Werewolf in Romance and Erotic Literature," Alexandra Leonzini turns to the widely popular genres of romance and erotic fiction and focuses on the recent prominence of paranormal creatures, such as werewolves, as romantic protagonists in these texts. Starting her analysis with 19th-century horror fiction before moving to 20th-century films and 21-century romance and erotic literature, Leonzini traces the changes in the construction of the gendered and sexualized body of the figure of the werewolf, arguing that these developments reflect popular cultural tastes and marketing strategies. Particularly in recent years, this has also resulted in the emergence of a large variety of fan fiction that, especially in its erotic explicitness, differs from the publications of established publishing houses catering to the market.

While the eleven articles grouped in the three thematic sections of this volume cannot exhaust the topic, they do create at once an illuminating cross-section and a mosaic of the fantastic now – that is of the fantastic as a genre and as a subject of academic debate in the current moment of the twenty-first century. They show that far from being "dubious," the fantastic has many significant modes that range from the political, the critical, and the philosophical to the playful, the sensual, and the popular. The included articles thus provide new lenses through which to discern the fantastic as well as new impulses for debate, and they connect core issues of the field that have been present since its scholarly emergence to continuing investigations into its future directions. And this future begins in the here and now.

WORK CITED

Armitt, Lucie (1996): *Theorising the Fantastic,* London: Hodder Education.

Genre

Belief, Potentiality, and the Supernatural: Mapping the Fantastic

Daniel Scott

Genre definitions are necessarily problematic in that they attempt to impose rules and boundaries where no tangible ones exist. At the same time, we presuppose genre by default, and disproving genre is certainly as difficult, if not more so, than proving it. In talking specifically about fantasy literature, we are of course intentionally begging the genre question in itself, but it becomes inescapable once we start considering specific genre subcategories and their functions. And despite the many pitfalls that genre discussion contains, it can be rewarding to analyze the connections between the fantasy genre and certain modes of thought. Since my research deals with the intermeshing of theist and atheist thought with fantastic genres, I needed a working genre definition with which to frame the fantastic. It was here that traditional definitions of the fantastic proved to be useful but often ultimately inconclusive, since they could not account for varying viewpoints of the reality from which fantasy derives. This is critical because Christian speculative fiction, an example of theist fiction, shows that our conceptions of fantasy as non-reality do not account for varying epistemic stances of reality, in this case, for the divergence between how atheists and theists perceive the world.

I therefore set forth a broad but hopefully comprehensive definition of fantasy that encompasses "classic" fantasy fiction as well as works of science fiction and Christian speculative fiction. This definition, though it accepts diverging epistemic viewpoints and attempts to avoid bias, is based on an evaluative system that both theists and atheists must necessarily subscribe to: grammar. As I argue, any fantastic text, regardless of its underlying worldview, is effectively a complex conditional construct which can, like a sentence, be sorted according to the same grammatical rules that govern conditional clauses. Doing so allows us to delineate a text's genre according to which kind of modal phrasing is evident in its fundamental assumptions – in short, we can attempt to assign genre on a grammatical basis. Finally, viewing fantastic genres as clauses also opens up new perspectives on the fantastic genres themselves, allowing me to pinpoint an inherent connection between the basic argumentational and epistemic frameworks of theism and atheism with certain fantastic genres throughout modern history.

I begin by taking stock of fantastic genre theory, then move on to the genre problems posed by Christian speculative fiction. After that, I present the conditional grammatical model for genre differentiation and its application to the main fantastic genres. I then explore the model's broader applicability and some of its bolder implications regarding the genesis of the modern fantastic genres before drawing my final conclusions.

1. CONCEPTUALIZATIONS OF FANTASY AND THE FANTASTIC

Any genre discussion regarding the literary definition of fantasy must almost necessarily begin with Tzvetan Todorov's structuralist definition of the fantastic. In his seminal work, *Introduction à la Littérature Fantastique* (1970), Todorov analyzes a wide selection of 19th-century canonical literature and proposes a definitory stratification according to the amount of hesitation a reader encounters with regard to a story's supernatural elements. The resulting genre differentiation runs between the poles of the *marvelous* and the *uncanny*; the marvelous covers texts where the supernatural is used without reservation, such as fairy-tales, *One Thousand and One Nights*, or the modern fantasy genre as it is commonly referred to in publishing (i.e. the kind of fantasy created by Tolkien, Lewis, Le-Guin, and others), but also science fiction. All of these have in common, according to Todorov, that they require us to accept concepts which we unreservedly deem supernatural. The uncanny, on the other hand, refers to fictional texts whose occurrences are deemed strange, but are still considered explicable by rational, non-supernatural phenomena, e.g. the narrator's psychological instability or happenstance. Gothic fiction is particularly prone to this, and Poe's *The Fall of the House of Usher* or *The Raven* can be considered archetypal examples of Todorov's uncanny in that they present a distinctly unusual occurrence (e.g. a talking raven) which can nevertheless still be explained by recourse to other factors (i.e. the narrator's mental state). In between these poles, separated from the other categories by intermediaries (the fantastic-uncanny and the fantastic marvelous, respectively), Todorov pinpoints the fantastic,[1] a liminal area where the reader is unable to decide whether the action of the story was supernatural or natural. In this 'sweet spot', the reader's hesitation allows for a blending of the supernatural and natural, allowing authors to highlight existential ambiguities and uncertainties.

It is here that Todorov's theory, while not inherently or explicitly prescriptive, nevertheless displays a significant judgmental predisposition. In his final chapter on "Literature and the Fantastic," he concludes that like the fantastic, literature itself

"bypasses the distinctions of the real and the imaginary, of what is and of what is not [...] literature contests any presence of dichotomy [...] The nature of literary discourse is to *go beyond* – otherwise it would have no reason for being; literature is a kind of murderous weapon by which language commits suicide." (Todorov 1973: 167)

We can certainly follow Todorov's definitions, we might even readily agree with them with regard to the canonical "high" literature he analyzes. However, Todorov is not being descriptive here, not even of canonical literature, but prescriptive of the way that *all* fictional literature should ultimately aspire to be; after all, literature that does not follow this principle is seen as having "no reason for being." And to say that this grand principle should apply to all kinds of fiction, from *Dracula* and *1984* to *Penny Dreadfuls*, seems at least questionable. While one might not doubt the basic validity of his statement, being that fiction transcends the boundaries of real and unreal, Todorov appears to be subordinating the larger scope of fictional literature to a select portion of "high" fiction. Moreover, in subscribing to this definition, Todorov, like many scholars of his period, is elevating those literatures that conform to this credo above those which do not. This leads him to make statements such as the following:

---

1   The confusion and intermingling of the terms "fantastic" and "fantasy" in academic literature theories require a disambiguation and this study is no different. Unless specifically referencing Todorov's designations, I reserve the term "fantastic" for the general super-genre cluster that encompasses all fiction dealing with the non-real, i.e. science fiction, fantasy, alternate history writing, and similar genres. Fantasy refers specifically to the kind of writing commonly associated with the term, e.g. Tolkien, LeGuin, Lewis, Caroll, and Lovecraft, but also George Martin, Philip Pullman, and Stephenie Meyer.

"The *best* science fiction texts are organized analogously [to Kafka's *Metamorphosis[2]*]. The initial data are supernatural: robots, extraterrestrial beings, the whole interplanetary context. The narrative movement consists in obliging us to see how close these apparently marvelous elements are to us, to what degree they are present in our life." (Todorov 1973: 172, emphasis added)

While according to his own metric, science fiction is generally situated within the marvelous, Todorov implicitly assigns the position of "the best"[3] science fiction to the fantastic or beyond, to the more transcendent area he reserves for Kafka's *Metamorphosis*, which he presents as an example for the literature of the 20th century being "in a certain sense, more purely 'literature' than any other"[4] (ibid: 168). Since the value judgement[5] is not predicated upon anything other than the text's position in this fantastic/transcendent area, it appears that being in this realm confers superiority in and of itself. So while Todorov's differentiation of the marvelous, uncanny and fantastic genres works perfectly without moral or evaluative judgement, the system is clearly geared to serve such an ultimately evaluative purpose. The implied goal for Todorov in differentiating the genres under discussion is to distil from a more general slurry of fantastic literature its supposedly more aesthetically useful, literarily valuable essence.[6] Yet in doing

---

2   Todorov assigns Kafka's *Metamorphosis* a singular position, granting that it seemingly transcends the system he has set up. While like the fantastic, it combines supernatural elements with the transgression of hesitational boundaries, it goes beyond these to occupy a new realm.

3   "les meilleurs textes" in the original French (Todorov 1970: 180).

4   "la littérature du XX ͤ siècle est, en un certain sens, plus 'literature' que toute autre" (Todorov 1970: 177).

5   Todorov follows this statement by saying that it is not in fact a value judgment. I would contend that it is. At the very least, calling one thing more literature than another is openly inviting judgment of that kind, and I can see little other purpose in making such an assessment. Again, it appears that Todorov's phrasing is possibly more problematic than his actual statements.

6   This position is not uncontested. Stanislaw Lem criticized Todorov for, amongst other things, being too egalitarian, and therefore falling prey to his own structuralist preconceptions: "for structural equivalence democratically places the counterfeit on an equal footing with the masterpiece" (Lem 1974: 236). I would contend that Lem is overemphasizing this point somewhat because he disagrees with the structuralist school as a whole. However, I would also say that while they belong to opposing schools of thought, Lem and Todorov are both, in their own way, caught up in the idea that some

so, his approach becomes vulnerable, for if we do not accept the underlying premise that different literatures have different values (in the appraising, valuating, rather than the purely differentiating sense) then the whole reasoning for differentiating the fantastic runs the danger of becoming moot. In this sense the underlying stance also violates a linguistic tenet with which Todorov, as a structuralist, would have been very familiar: that no individual grammar (or language, or langue, or parole) is superior or preferable to another. And while its intentionality does not detract from the system's applicability, it might cast severe doubt upon its usage and overall validity. In the current situation, a system that implicitly assigns values to texts is problematic; once we begin assigning literature values such as "good" or "bad," it is easy to assign the predicate to an entire mode or genre of literature. Literary studies have a long tradition of looking down on certain genres while lauding others; especially the fantasy and science fiction genres long suffered from academic neglect despite (or because of) their more mundane proliferation, simply because they were considered unworthy of scholarly attention. Moreover, in the politically charged context that surrounds some fantasy literature, particularly theist and atheist fantasy, literature is regularly labeled as 'bad' or 'immoral' simply because it adheres to one side or another. Any current study in fantasy fiction, this one included, should avoid using judgmental predications for these reasons alone.

However, despite its evaluative subtext, Todorov's methodology presents a principal advantage: Its metric is broad enough that it is able to encompass the sub-genres of science fiction and fantasy in one single area, the marvelous. It achieves this through a very broad understanding of the supernatural, which at the same time is the basic definition of the fantastic subject matter. This is noteworthy because most scholars after Todorov have concerned themselves with either fantasy or science fiction, as well as the differentiation of the two, or were more interested in other specific or general functions of the texts. As a result, definitions of fantasy and the fantastic have become increasingly 'fuzzy' as the scholarly approaches widened and narrowed simultaneously.

Rosemary Jackson, in *Fantasy: The Literature of Subversion* (1981), deems fantastic writing a method of subverting reality, in a tradition of the Bakhtinian carnevalesque or a Sartrean inverted transcription of the human condition. As such, she also predicates her definition of the fantastic upon the real, pointing out the many reciprocities this implies: fantasy mirrors, deconstructs, and critiques reality, but in doing so also serves to establish and construct it. Unlike Todorov,

---

forms of literature are superior to others, and that it is the obligation of literary studies to prove this superiority. It is with this preconception that I take issue.

Jackson resists the urge to define reality, but in postmodern and constructivist tradition considers reality a social construct upon which fantasy reflects. Kathryn Hume, writing on fantasy as a fundamental impulse of fiction rather than as a genre in *Fantasy and Mimesis* (1984), similarly considers fantasy to be "any departure from consensus reality" (Hume 1984: 28). Since both Jackson and Hume consider fantastic writing from a methodological and functional viewpoint, they apply a very broad definition of their subject. As such, they make no attempt to define a fantastic genre, but instead focus on its societal or narrative functions.

At the same time, other scholars, especially in the emergent studies of fantasy literature, attempted to classify and define the genre or mode of fantasy. Eric Rabkin (*The Fantastic in Literature*, 1976) defines fantasy as being based on reality while being in itself an anti-reality, "reality turned precisely 180 around" (Rabkin 1976: 28). Colin Manlove, in *Modern Fantasy: Five Studies* (1976) similarly defines the fantasy genre as "a dramatic reversal" of our own world, "a fiction evoking wonder and containing a substantial and irreducible element of the supernatural with which the mortal characters in the story or the readers become on at least partly familiar terms" (Manlove 1976: 28). So while all the aforementioned scholars diverge, often strongly, regarding the functions and purpose of fantasy literature, Todorov's assumption that the predication "fantastic" is based in the supernatural is reflected by all of them. Fantastic is seen as a non-reality, one that somehow departs from the consensus reality.[7]

It is when one attempts to differentiate this broad term into more concrete areas such as fantasy, science fiction, and other fantastic genres that it becomes porous. For Todorov, science fiction resided within the same generic realm as fantasy because they both unabashedly deal with something that is not part of our everyday life and therefore fulfill Todorov's broad requirements for dealing with the supernatural without reservation. Many scholars have considered this kind of blanket definition as problematic, like Brian Attebery, who writes in *Strategies of Fantasy* (1992) that "a term broad enough to include both *Conan the Barbarian* and *Cosmicomics* threatens to become meaningless" (1992: 1). While this is certainly an overstatement, it is true that broad definitions, be they Todorov's marvelous, Jackson's subversive fantasy or Hume's conceptual fantasy, all sacrifice precision in order to make more general statements about a wider category that includes both fantasy and science fiction. At the same time, general intuition recognizes a boundary, however frustrating to define, between the different gen-

---

7   However, as I explore in the next section on *Left Behind*, reality is not as consensual as we often make out. What we consider "real" diverges, often starkly, according to cultural, geographical, and, especially pertinently to this study, religious positions.

res of fantasy, science fiction, fairy tale, myth, historical fiction and many other kinds of writing that one would subsume under the fantastic umbrella.

Amongst the scholarly attempts to define these subcategories is John Timmerman's *Other Worlds: The Fantasy Genre* (1983). In differentiating fantasy and science fiction (Timmerman 1983: 15-21), Timmerman delineates three core elements of science fiction: (a) the dependence on technical instruments; (b) a suspension of disbelief in the sense that the science fiction world is considered attainable and (c) a sense of extrapolation in that a science fiction world is deemed to be a possible future of our own, unlike fantasy, which Timmerman sees as a juxtaposition to our real world in the same tradition as Rabkin and Manlove (ibid: 49-50). Whereas these points are somewhat superficial, (b) and (c) highlight varying modalities in the science fiction and fantasy genres which Todorov's system did not account for, namely juxtaposition vs. extrapolation. By defining science fiction and fantasy as opposing modes of dealing with the non-real (or supernatural, as Todorov would have it) in fiction, Timmerman also circumvents the problem of too wide definitions which Attebery criticizes.

However, the problem of attempting to differentiate these genres is where to draw the line between extrapolation and complete disjunction from our reality: Is *A Canticle for Leibowitz* science fiction because it is set after a nuclear war, but without Timmerman's dependency on advanced technology? Is Frank Herbert's *Dune* series science fiction although it includes psionic powers? Is *Star Wars* fantasy because it includes patently impossible concepts like light sabers? Is *Star Trek* not science fiction because it includes utopian elements and faster-than-light travel? In practice, the result is an infinite regress into a myriad of sub-genres, including Space Opera, Hard Science Fiction (but not Soft Science Fiction), Science Fantasy and many others. This, rather than solving the problem of differentiation, merely perpetuates it. Most scholars have meanwhile chosen to bury the debate of fantastic genre differentiation, to the point where Carol Mendlesohn in her *Rhetorics of Fantasy* (2008) makes a point of *not* including any analytic definitions whatsoever, even dedicating her opening lines to that end, writing that "a consensus has emerged" on accepting "as viable a fuzzy set" (Mendlesohn 2008: 1-2) of critical definitions of fantasy.

2. *LEFT BEHIND*: A FANTASTIC PARADOX?

Regardless of whether we follow Mendlesohn's assessment, the definition of fantastic sub-genres would indeed seem futile for the case of theist/atheist fantasy analysis if, like Jackson's, Hume's and Mendlesohn's works, it did not require concrete working definitions of the individual sub-genres in order to function. However, in this particular case, one of the series under analysis, *Left Behind* (1995-2004), reveals a problem that cannot be resolved by a broad definition of the fantastic. The problem is one of epistemic perspective. As the work of two Born-Again Christian Baptists, *Left Behind* is concerned with the coming Christian Apocalypse in the near future, and therefore includes features from the Book of Revelations and the surrounding Millennial mythology, including the Rapture,[8] swarms of demonic locusts, planet-wide earthquakes, rivers of blood, and the Second Coming of Christ. The authors Jerry Jenkins and Tim LaHaye class their series as speculative Christian fiction; to a secular or atheist audience, however, it would be nothing short of fantasy.[9] When assigning it the same broad "fantastic literature" label that covers science fiction and fantasy, one begs the question of what part of the plot exactly constitutes its fantastic element or non-reality. Is *Left Behind* fantastic literature because it contains extrapolations, or because it is a juxtaposition to our reality?

There are three traditional ways of approaching the question, all of which I wish to disregard: First, it is possible to circumvent the conundrum altogether with recourse to auctorial intentionality, constructivism, and/or reader-response theory: While the authors' intention was to write speculative fiction, and their intended and implied readers can be assumed to reflect that intention, an atheist reader is justified in deeming it fantasy literature because as a reader, she[10] can bestow upon a text the meaning she chooses. In this approach, there is no conundrum, because both viewpoints are equally valid and therefore not contradictory. *Left Behind* therefore exists in a dual state of genre assignment, much like *Star Wars* might be considered science fiction by some viewers and fantasy by others. However, unlike for *Star Wars*, the fault lines in *Left Behind*'s case would not run according to taste, but according to religious denomination. Essentially, ac-

---

8   Rapture is a feature of Evangelical Millennial mythology which holds that all believers will ascend bodily to Heaven prior to the seven years of Armageddon; this in turn gives the *Left Behind* novels their point of departure and title, as those who were lacking in faith are left behind on a tumultuous Earth to fend for themselves and find belief in the process.

9   The novel *Good Omens*, in which the atheists Terry Pratchett and Neil Gaiman lampooned the kind of fictional adaptations of Revelations that *Left Behind* represents, is considered fantasy. This classification points to a problematic twist within our perception and definition of the genre.

10 I designate (theoretical) atheists female and theists male for differentiation purposes.

cepting this solution means accepting that our definitions of genre are not simply fuzzy, but starkly divided according to worldview.[11]

The second approach would be to include an exception to the rule, i.e. include Christian speculative fiction (CSF) in the aforementioned long line of subgenres that already dot the fantastic landscape. This approach would allow CSF to exist en par with the other types without the necessity of making it fit any of the already given suppositions. Like the first option, however, this approach concedes that faith-based assessments cannot be reconciled with the systems at hand and demand a new category.

The third possibility is to assume that CSF is not fantastic at all, but somewhere outside the fantastic genre altogether, and therefore not comparable to fantasy and science fiction at all. This would, however, contravene both the intuition of the theist and that of the atheist. It would also pose the question of where to position Christian speculative fiction, if not in the realm that would usually include the speculative fictions.

The three options given above all similarly concede that CSF cannot be covered by existing understandings of the fantastic genre, either because its boundaries (a) only exist in the highly subjective mind of the beholder, (b) need to be expanded in order to accommodate them, or (c) do not apply to CSF at all. In doing so, they expose the frailness of genre definitions as a whole, including the generally acknowledged 'fuzziness' of any given genre definitions, the subjectivity of personal aesthetics as well as the arbitrariness (and therefore interchangeability) of any given value set. Any attempt at overcoming this problem would therefore have to include CSF within the fantastic genre without expanding it or allowing for excessive subjective arbitrariness. At the same time it would still have to accommodate varying assessments according to belief and the necessary 'fuzzy flux' in between the fantastic categories. In the following section I attempt to supply such a definition.

---

11 One might also construct a slippery-slope argument from this approach: If we allow for this kind of "Schroedinger's genre" differentiation, depending on whether we agree with the author's baseline assessment of reality and/or their extrapolation, many or indeed all genre designations might become void. The classification of *1984* as dystopian science fiction might suddenly depend on whether we agree with Orwell's worldview or not.

3. THE FANTASTIC GENRES: A GRAMMATICAL APPROACH

As we have seen, the fantastic as it is generally viewed is that which deals with the supernatural, anti-mimetic, or non-real. This concept, as the example of *Left Behind* illustrates, relies implicitly upon the idea of what we consider to be real in the first place; and many scholars (most notably Rabkin and Jackson) argue that fantasy's purpose is to reflect upon our perception of this reality, often eroding and questioning it. Furthermore it is possible, as Todorov showed, to divide the fantastic realms into individual sub-genres according to the way in which they present us with supernatural concepts. Amongst these, science fiction and fantasy are among those which Todorov would include in his marvelous, i.e. 'extremely fantastic'. This kinship also remains if we do not use Todorov's metric of differentiation according to hesitation, but assume, like Timmerman, that science fiction is the result of an extrapolation from the real and fantasy that of juxtaposition, an assumption that something that cannot be is. Yet despite this difference, both genres are similar in that they take their cue, be it by forecast or inversion, from a certain take on reality. As such they are notably different from other fantastic areas such as gothic fiction, whose departure from reality, as Todorov pointed out, is often more subtle: rather than assuming a reality from which to depart, it intentionally blurs the lines between reality and non-reality.

What all fantastic genres share, however, is that no matter their take on reality or the fantastic, they remain fictional. It is a long-standing staple of both literary studies and logic that fictional texts operate on a different, arguably parallel level to actual texts in that they do not refer to the real world but to a fictional one. As such, while authors create fictional statements, questions, and negations, these cannot be negated, answered or countered by actual utterances. The fictional utterance *Hercule Poirot solved the murder on the Orient Express* cannot be negated by the actual statement *Hercule Poirot did not exist*. While it would be a true, if pointless, actual statement, anyone who tried to use the actual statement to negate the fictional one would cause raised eyebrows because he or she was clearly missing the point, the signified, of the fictional text. Fictional worlds and their texts have resulted in many extended modalities and theoretical complications for linguistic philosophy and literary studies alike. For the case at hand however, I would only like to use one of their simplest assumptions: that it is possible to create fictional utterances which use a grammar that is, for the most part, parallel to that of actual utterances. This means that in writing stories, we create fictional statements, negations, and questions, or more complex clauses.

More generally, we might consider any fictional text or its synopsis to be a more or less complex fictional statement, as in the example above.[12]

However, the fantastic adds a new grammatical layer to its fictional text because, particularly in the area of fantasy and science fiction, it deals in highly modal constructs. This is not immediately visible in the genres' fictional statements, but is an implicit result of their dealing with extrapolation and negation. As Brian Attebery points out: "If we wished to define it linguistically, we might say that the fantastic is the use of the verb forms of reporting for events that in ordinary discourse would require more conditional forms. Rather than saying, 'If only I had wings', the fantastic asserts that I do" (Attebery 1992: 6). While fantastic literature uses the grammar of statements (typically using the past tense), the general implied mode of these statements is counterfactual, which we would normally render in conditional. In fact, as Attebery's own sentence shows, our most basic and intuitive method of conveying distant concepts is by using conditional constructions. The conditional clause accomplishes this by defining a requisite 'starting' reality and postulating a version of non-reality that is contingent upon it. As such, conditional English[13] clauses offer a ready framework for phrasing the extrapolation and juxtaposition systems of science fiction and fantasy by employing different types of if-clause. To use Attebery's example, we could conceive of two fantastic stories: In the first a boy wakes to find he has magically sprouted wings and uses them to fly to the moon (fantasy). In the other, he is the subject of a genetic experiment that allows him to navigate air and space with wing-like mutations (science fiction). While both narrations would take place in the past tense, we could easily construct corresponding conditional sentences:

If a boy woke to find he had wings, he would fly to the moon.
(Counterfactual Second Conditional; Juxtaposition)
If humans are able to create genetic mutations that allow us to fly through space, a boy might fly to the moon.
(Predictive First Conditional; Extrapolation)

---

12 A case might also be made that some texts are not so much statements as questions or negations.

13 Since I am here dealing with American and English literature, and therefore the English language, I am referring to English grammar. This is not to say that other languages do not possess similar or even more refined systems that can be adopted for a grammatical genre approach.

Expressing science fiction and fantasy in this manner allows for a focus on their diverging modal aspect rather than the many outward genre features (genetics or magic) that otherwise lead to sub-genre differentiation: science fiction considers possible realities that might emerge from our own; fantasy creates a reality that is implicitly defined as not correlating with our own, and deals with its implications. This is a different kind of creation than normal fiction; while it would be possible to phrase the earlier Hercule Poirot example as a conditional (*If Hercule Poirot existed, he would solve the murder on the Orient Express*), it is not intuitively necessitated by its founding assumptions in the same way as it would be for a fantastic story. To create a conditional for Hercule Poirot's existence alone seems somewhat excessive, whereas it would seem more appropriate for a boy with wings, or for Tolkien's writings, on account of all the presuppositions that a fantasy world like Middle Earth includes (*If there was an Anglo-Saxon world filled with fantastic beings as well as humans, then in a hole there lived a Hobbit*). Depending on whether such clauses seem more or less adequate, we may consider a given text more or less fantastic. Since this is effectively a question of intuition, it will always be impossible to draw a concrete line at where the conditional clause becomes a necessary addition and therefore at where normal fiction gives way to fantastic fiction. This, however, is to be expected since, as Kathryn Hume famously pointed out, all stories contain fantasy and mimesis to varying degrees. As such, while not ultimately precise, the definition pays homage to the 'fuzzy' boundaries that fantasy, and ultimately any definition within the Humanities, must necessarily exist within.

Finally, the conditional model also allows us to include Christian speculative fiction in the fantastic genre: Since the conditional statements we derive from texts are fictional, they are also self-contained regarding their perception of our current reality. We do not have to agree with the base assessment in the hypothetical clause or with the world that is being postulated in the main clause, but by reading it as a sentence we are implicitly accepting its validity as a fictional construct.[14] Whether we agree with the idea of genetic space-flight engineering being possible or attainable is irrelevant to the function of the science fiction sentence since it merely expresses a fictional conditional (if x is true, then a will/might/can/shall[15] happen). This also allows us to include other kinds of

---

14   This is, effectively, suspension of disbelief.

15   It might even be possible to pinpoint certain narrative modes to the use of certain modal verbs. Dystopias, for instance, tend more toward a strong consequential mode in the sense that they warn of dire consequences of current social realities, and thus seem more affiliated with "will" or even "shall" than with "can" or "might."

speculation that share the same modal construction, such as CSF. *Some of Left Behind*'s core statement could therefore be condensed as follows:

If the Bible is true, then the Apocalypse will be coming soon to cleanse the Earth and usher in Judgment Day.

If the Apocalypse comes, then the Rapture will create a wave of chaos throughout the world.

If the Rapture occurs, those left behind will have to deal with the consequences of not being raptured.

This is modally identical with a sentence we might use to gloss a science fiction text:

If our assumptions about robotics and computer advancements are correct, we will one day develop laws for robots.
(*I, Robot* – Isaac Asimov)

Since CSF's type of modal speculation works analogously to that of science fiction, it demands the same modal classification. Phrasing fantastic stories as conditionals therefore allows for the inclusion of speculative fiction as a whole in the fantastic, irrespective of the worldview that informs the speculations. The only relevant aspect is that they are fictional speculations. Books on conspiracy theory, theoretical physics texts and religious prophecy pamphlets all contain speculations of the "if ..., then ..." type, but are not fictional, and therefore not fantastic. What therefore renders *Left Behind* fantastic is not its content but its particular mode of fictional writing.

Beyond that, the approach offers several new insights. For one, it allows for potential expansion of the fantastic genres according to grammatical rules, as the conditional sentences presented here are in no way the full extent of English grammar's conditional capabilities. Type III conditional sentences, for instance, would allow for us to frame alternate history writing within the fantastic framework, since it allows for formulations of the "if x had (not) happened, y would have (not) occurred" type. Furthermore, the combinability of type I, II, and III conditional sentences can serve to frame other genres, but most of all, the interchangeableness of sentences for some works shows how one text can easily be assigned to several fantastic genres at once: Philip Pullman's *His Dark Materials*, while generally classed as fantasy, contains steampunk (alternate history) and science fiction elements. As such we can frame these plot elements in corresponding sentences:

If Calvin had become Pope in the 16th century, the world might still be dominated by Church Magisteria.
(Type III, alternate history)
If multiple dimensions exist, in line with the many-worlds-theory, then this world might be one of them.
(Type I, science fiction)
If in such a world, souls existed in the form of animals, they would be called daemons.
(Type II, fantasy)

Thus the conditional modal can serve to show how authors like Pullman combine elements from many different genre branches and schools of thought into one system, even to the point that they make different fantastic genres contingent upon each other. By analyzing them in the grammatical system, the modal interdependencies within the texts can be accounted for without giving in to the "tyranny of genre" (Coe 2002: 108).

Altogether, the grammatical approach of the conditional model offers a method of framing not only Christian speculative fiction, but fantastic fiction in general in an intuitively accessible structure that is flexible enough to accommodate varying assessments and beliefs. In this respect it is similar to Todorov's method in that it relies on the structure of a text rather than its outward markers. Unlike Todorov's system, it does not imply any hierarchical evaluation: speculative fictions, be they faith-based or science-based, exist alongside fantasy and other fantastic genres without the need for aesthetic evaluation. Finally, the system takes its cues from the same basic idea that also informed the structuralists, Todorov among them: that fiction is based upon linguistic principles, and can therefore be analyzed and classed according to grammatical structures – the main difference being that whereas the structuralists set out to create a new, specifically literary grammar, this approach attempts to transfer some specific workings of linguistic grammar onto literature. Similarly to grammar, this framework's weaknesses are also its advantages: Since it relies upon a correlation with our intuition, it remains malleable, but also flexible in order to adapt as intuitions change over time. At the same time it attempts to avoid some of the pitfalls which troubled scholars who came after Todorov, whose definitions were either extremely broad and therefore not useful for differentiation, or too fixated upon superficial genre details and therefore became obsolete. Most of all, however, the applicability of the conditional model to fantastic literature opens up new corridors for academic speculations, some of which have an impact on atheist and theist fantasy and are therefore the subject of the following section.

4. IF [WORLD], THEN [FANTASTIC]: THE CONDITIONS OF CONDITIONALS

The conditional model introduced here highlights the way in which fantastic worlds are contingent upon a real world in order to function, be it as a divergence point for the not-world in the case of fantasy or as a basis for extrapolation and assumption in speculative fiction. As the varying perspectives on speculative fiction demonstrate, this reality need not be a consensus reality in the strong sense of a full societal consensus, but merely a reality that is considered real by the ones making the statement, i.e. the author and the intended readership. This departure from the real world is something that the aforementioned types of fantastic fiction have in common. However, I believe this is a trait specific to these kinds of fantastic fictions, and one which they do not share with earlier kinds of writing, the reason being that these types of fantasy fiction are born from a modern worldview in which the world as such is treated as a fixed *known value*.

In his discussion of fantasy fiction, Brian Attebery asks rhetorically, "can any definition [of fantasy] […] accommodate *Alice in Wonderland*, *A Midsummer Night's Dream*, *The Golden Ass*, *The Odyssey*, and perhaps even *Paradise Lost* and *The Divine Comedy*?" (Attebery 1992: 1-2). He goes on to say that the fantastic mode is so vast that even if we tried, we would not include all its examples in the conceptual parameters of our definitions. But his quip highlights a relevant point − namely that of the texts mentioned above, all except *Alice in Wonderland* would likely resist any but the broadest definitions of the fantastic, including the one under discussion. The conditional metric proposed here to describe fantasy, as well as speculative and alternate history fiction, does not seem to apply in the same manner. The idea of subsuming *Midsummer Night's Dream* in a conditional of the type *If there was a fairy kingdom, …* seems either extremely reductive or even plainly wrong. No such assumption seems to be evident in Shakespeare's text in the same way as it would be in Tolkien's. The same would be true of Homer's epic, and certainly of *Paradise Lost* and the *Divine Comedy*. The reason for why these attempts fail is because their authors' worldview was not one where conditional clauses were necessary for fantasy writing. At the time when *A Midsummer Night's Dream* was penned, fairies, magic, and witchcraft were, if not taken for existent per se, far from being considered pure myth. This is certainly one of the reasons why Shakespeare took great care to frame his supernatural plots in foreign or bygone settings, be it the Mediterranean (*The Tempest*), medieval Scotland (*Macbeth*), Denmark (*Hamlet*) or Ancient Greece (*A Midsummer Night's Dream*). Another reason was the constant threat of censorship, but the other was one of simple convenience: European Renaissance thought could accept the existence of fantastic entities in faraway lands as part of its reality simply because its worldview could allow for it. Much like the world map at the time, the Renaissance worldview as a whole contained unknown areas into which the fantastic could still be colored in without appearing out of place. While *A Midsummer Night's Dream* was undoubtedly fantastic, it was operating in an entirely different mode from modern fantasy because it did not need to presume another world in which to take place.

The same is true for *The Odyssey*, *Paradise Lost* and the other examples, whose authors were striving to encapsulate greater truths of being within a mythological context, which, for all intents and purposes, was very real to them. At the very least, Milton, Dante, Homer, and Apuleius were using their mythological narratives in the same way that Shakespeare was using foreign settings: as an acceptable area where the fantastic could occur. This area was neither inside nor outside their worldview because to these pre-modern authors, the world was not yet fully known and therefore could still accommodate the unknown and the fantastic if one knew where or when to situate it. Only later, from the 19th century onward, did geographical, scientific, and historical knowledge accumulate to create a fully-fledged view of a *known world*. The fantastic literature of this intermediate phase is characteristically defined by the Gothic, the liminal, and uncanny where reality and fantastic are no longer easily distinguishable. It is only in 1865, toward the end of this development, that we find Attebery's last example *Alice's Adventures in Wonderland,* which uses a portal into a world distinctly separate from our own in order to tell a fantastic story. Here we find an instance of conditional storytelling, because it is non-real. Before this, pre-modern authors had had no need for a non-reality, and therefore no need of a quasi-conditional mode of storytelling, in order to tell of the fantastic. This is different, not on a scale of magnitude, but in vector of thought, from the later writings of Tolkien, Lewis, and their literary descendants, who were writing at a time when most things in our universe were fixed and known, and not considered a realm for mythological or fantastic narrative to aid in. In turn they required complete mythological abstraction or portals to convey their readers to another more fantastic world. Conversely, one might say that it took the rigid intersubjective obtrusion of modern reality, a dictum of *the world is ...* in order to give rise to a form of literature that could say *what if it were not ...?*

Beyond that, there is a marked parallel between fantasy and religious thought. Scholars and critics alike have noted the correlation that Tolkien and Lewis, the prototypical English fantasy writers, were religious men. The fantasy worlds they constructed served to create mythical reality, in an attempt to return wonder to what they considered a mythless world. This is accounted for in the aforementioned idea of a known world as well as the conditional fantastic frame presented here. However, beyond the search for meaning, there is another reason why the fantastic and fantasy would hold interest for theists in particular, one which the conditional focus helps draw attention to: while the discovery of the world was progressing, the burden of proof for theists was increasing. Secularization, scientific advances and other factors led to theists being increasingly on the defensive, a tendency which had in previous centuries already given rise to Christian apologetics. Now, however, the problem was that the increasingly secular worldview no longer supported arguments for God's existence, e.g. through Creationism. On the contrary, it was increasingly being used as a basis for attacks on theism, such as via arguments from evil, or supporting opposing philosophical worldviews like Empiricism, Existentialism or Modernism.

Against these argumentational assaults, immunization strategies began to evolve. These are argumentational loops which brook no retort or counterattack, usually because they are self-referential or circular. There are many examples in religion, including the appeal to Papal infallibility (Papal dogma states that the Papal decrees are infallible), self-referential justification in religious texts (Sura 2,2 of the Qu'ran which says that the Qu'ran cannot be doubted), or the reference to personal experience or visions, which by definition cannot be examined, doubted or disproven by others. Finally, there is also what Karl Popper refers to as "reinforced dogmatism" (Popper 1964: 215), being of the kind that argues that if you doubt me, then this shows that you are deceived.[16] All of these are problematic from an argumentational viewpoint, but are also ultimately unconvincing due to their more or less obvious circularity.

However, there is another kind of immunization which does not suffer from the same weaknesses; in an effort to escape criticism, it draws the level of argument onto a layer of potentiality. Leibniz's Theodicy, in which he states that this world is the most perfect world to allow for the concept of Free Will, thereby explaining why evil can exist despite a benevolent God, is amongst the most advanced versions of this kind of immunization strategy. Other examples include Pascal's Wager (It is better to believe in God than not, because it is the safer bet) and the proverb that "God moves in mysterious ways." All three share the mark of an immunization strategy, being that they cannot be disproven by logical ne-

---

16 This kind of immunization strategy is also prevalent among less ethical proponents in academic contexts, from Freudian analysis to Feminist and Communist criticism. Practitioners of these fields can counter criticism by pointing out that the critic is clearly in denial (Freudian), or still unwittingly enthralled by the opposed patriarchal or capitalist narrative (Feminism or Communism).

gation or by evidence. More so, they are not obviously circular in the same manner as the earlier examples, but instead appeal to a concept beyond our immediate comprehension, be it the nature of God, the afterlife or possible worlds. In doing so, they all share a common denominator: they appeal to our *imagination*. This represents theist argumentation's final and conclusive retreat in the face of secular criticism, one which atheists have yet to match.

It therefore seems more than simply fitting that in the 1930s, 1940s, and 1950s, when scientific advances had all but conclusively explained most of the known universe, the first wave of modernism was about to give way to the second, and existentialist philosophy was on the rise on the European continent, that a Catholic Tolkien and Protestant Lewis created fantasy worlds like Middle Earth and Narnia in which they could represent a theist worldview without fear of disproval or incongruences. The *argumentational* retreat into immunization strategies thus combined with fiction to become a *narrative* retreat, one that favored potentiality and as such was created upon a conditional II-type supposition of counterfactual juxtaposition. The classic fantasy genre therefore began its existence as a theist retreat. At the same time, the rise of science fiction literature during the same general time frame might be owed to the same factors. For just as fantasy rests upon a theist inversion or denial of a world that no longer reflects its needs, science fiction embraces the current secular worldview and expands upon it. As such it is not surprising that science fiction writing has traditionally been dominated by atheists, be they Stanislav Lem, George Orwell, Isaac Asimov or Douglas Adams.

5. CONCLUDING REMARKS

Framing fantastic genres as conditionals thus proves both congruent with the general state of fantastic research as well as a viable basis in differentiating modern fantasy from its predecessors. The conditional set affords us insight into the founding assumptions that shape modern fantasy, and the accompanying mindsets. The modern fantastic genres therefore stand out from previous forms as distinct conditional narratives that depend upon a fixed worldview in order to spark their narrations. This assessment ties in with earlier findings such as Todorov's, who observes that the fantastic he defined had become extinct with the advent of the 20th century, giving rise to the unabashed marvelous (i.e. fantasy fiction): "psychoanalysis has replaced (and thereby made useless) the literature of the fantastic" (Todorov 1973: 160). His assessment appears to be validated by this model, albeit that we might extend psychoanalysis to modern thought in general. Further, the grammatical approach allows us to highlight how, far from being a recent addition to the genre, other models of thought such as theism and atheism have also always been keenly involved in the fantastic, since their narrative stances are accurately reflected in the conditional concepts of fantasy and science fiction. Thus, far from reinventing the wheel, the grammatical approach aims to enrich previous findings with a new perspective. And now, nearly half a century after Todorov, and seventy years after Tolkien and Lewis, in our attempts at taking stock of the current situation of fantasy literature, I believe it can help us sharpen our understanding of our favorite subject matter.

WORKS CITED

Attebery, Brian (1992): *Strategies of Fantasy*, Indianapolis: Indiana University Press.

Coe, Richard (2002): "Genre Systems: Chronos and Kairos in Communicative Action." In: Richard Coe, Lorelei Lingard, and Tatiana Teslenko (eds.) *The Rhetoric of Ideology and Ideology of Genre*, Cresskill, NJ: Hampton Press, pp. 103-122.

Hume, Kathryn (1984): *Fantasy and Mimesis: Responses to Reality in Western Literature*, New York: Methuen.

Jackson, Rosemary (1981): *Fantasy, The Literature of Subversion*, New York: Methuen.

LaHaye, Tim/Jenkins, Jerry B. (1995): L*eft Behind: A Novel of the Earth's Last Days*, Wheaton, Ill.: Tyndale.

LaHaye, Tim/Jenkins, Jerry B. (1997): *Tribulation Force: The Continuing Drama of Those Left Behind*, Wheaton, Ill.: Tyndale.

LaHaye, Tim/Jenkins, Jerry B. (1998): *Nicolae: The Rise of Antichrist*, Wheaton, Ill.: Tyndale.

LaHaye, Tim/Jenkins, Jerry B. (1999): *Apollyon: The Destroyer is Unleashed*, Wheaton, Ill.: Tyndale.

LaHaye, Tim/Jenkins, Jerry B. (1999): *Assassins: Assignment: Jerusalem, Target: Antichrist*, Wheaton, Ill.: Tyndale.

LaHaye, Tim/Jenkins, Jerry B. (2000): *The Indwelling: The Beast Takes Possession*, Wheaton, Ill.: Tyndale.

LaHaye, Tim/Jenkins, Jerry B. (2000): *The Mark: The Beast Rules the World*, Wheaton, Ill.: Tyndale.

LaHaye, Tim/Jenkins, Jerry B. (2001): *Desecration: Antichrist Takes the Throne*, Wheaton, Ill.: Tyndale.

LaHaye, Tim/Jenkins, Jerry B. (2002): *The Remnant: On the Brink of Armageddon*, Wheaton, Ill.: Tyndale.

LaHaye, Tim/Jenkins, Jerry B. (2003): *Armageddon: The Cosmic Battle of Ages*, Wheaton, Ill.: Tyndale.

LaHaye, Tim/Jenkins, Jerry B. (2004): *Glorious Appearing: The End of Days*, Wheaton, Ill.: Tyndale.

Lem, Stanislav (1974): "Todorov's Fantastic Theory of Literature." In: *Science Fiction Studies* 1/4, (http://www.depauw.edu/sfs/backissues/4/lem4art.htm).

Manlove, Colin (1976): *Modern Fantasy: Five Studies*, Cambridge: Cambridge University Press.

Mendlesohn, Farah (2008): *Rhetorics of Fantasy*, Middletown, CT: Wesleyan University Press.

Popper, Karl (1962): *The Open Society and Its Enemies*, Vol. 1, London: Routledge.

Rabkin, Eric S (1976): *The Fantastic in Literature*, Princeton: Princeton University Press.

Timmerman, John H (1983): *Other Worlds: The Fantasy Genre*, Bowling Green OH: Bowling Green University Popular Press.

Todorov, Tzvetan (1970): *Introduction à la Littérature Fantastique*, Paris: Editions du Seuil.

Todorov, Tzvetan (1973): *The Fantastic: A Structural Approach to a Literary Genre* (Richard Howard, Trans.), Ithaca, NY: Cornell University Press.

Fantasy without Fantasy: Politics, Genre, and Media in the Fiction of M. John Harrison

Fred Botting

Fantasy without fantasy is a phrase adapted from the writer M. John Harrison and used to address the inter-implication of genre and politics. The gesture of subtracting fantasy from fantasy highlights a differential articulation (fantasy-realism/fantasy-reality) which leaves neither pairing clearly separated according to a conventional division of fiction and reality. Furthermore, it engenders questions of fantasy's relationship to language, dream, (ideological) reality, commerce, and a world of simulations. For Harrison, "every act of writing is already a fantasy – if not a wish-fulfilment – if only because the word is not the thing" (2005a). Though the difference between language and the world is crucial to writing, it is not absolute or categorical: fantasy relates to things and commodities, a challenge to generic and commercial classifications. In one interview, describing his novel *Climbers* (1989) as "a fantasy without any fantasy in it," he goes on to call it a "fantasy of reality": excising fantasy from itself demands a reassessment of, rather than a return to, the real (Bould 2005: 328). While *Climbers* appears highly realistic in form and content, documenting, with precise locative detail and episodic colour, the exploits of an odd group of enthusiasts living, working and climbing in the North of England, the emptying of fantasy of itself does not necessitate immediate revisiting of realisms of place, character, time, or solid, rocky realities, even though *Climbers* is very much a novel of the great outdoors. As a "fantasy of reality," its realism is traversed by aesthetic, subjective, and ideological issues: the how, who, and for whom of writing make any unified presentations impossible, partial, and political. Climbing, an activity and metaphor recurring across a number of Harrison's fictions, moreover, enacts at least two countervailing senses of reality and fantasy. In terms of the latter, it is both escape from ordinariness and what, in *Climbers*, is called a "pornography of risk" (glossy magazine photographs of climbers dangling impossibly from perilous ledges); in terms of reality, climbing connotes the solidity of things and a sense of intense singular experience determined by contingency, consequence, and risk (Harrison 1991: 26). "Completely real" but also "a complete fantasy world," climbing announces "a heartfelt and desperate attempt to escape from the circumstances of an ordinary, quotidian sort of life" (Harrison 2005a: 150). Elsewhere, the "fatally real" aspect of climbing forms the basis of "escape from emotional and political demands" (ibid: 150). Consequences, rather than things or causes, enable a distinction: "the difference between fantasy – constructed worlds, virtual worlds and so on – and reality is consequences" (Bould 2005: 328). Given the parenthesis, the distinction seems to have exclusive relevance for generic classification. But the constructed, virtual worlds of fantasy are not simply the friction-free fictions of genre, not distinguished from realism, indeed, but from "reality." Applying to generic and social reality, the statement pertains to the constructed, virtual, and ideological fantasies of daily life and to the intrusive consequences that register a disruptive, critical – and political – experience of reality inimical to a world shorn of risk or responsibility. Harrison is openly critical of contemporary "fantasy culture" with its freedoms of choice and endless consumer opportunities based on outsourcing all the "risk, disorder and poverty" from the "gated community" that is the West, concerned at the way that "internal fantasies" collude with the "public dreams" underlying globalisation and its delusions of unimpeded growth (Mathew 2002). He acknowledges in another interview that writing cannot but be political even if it means simply going along "with the uninterrogated cultural assumptions of the day." In and outside fiction, Harrison takes a critical stance by interrogating contexts and conventions, creating "discontinuities" and collisions of strangeness and normality to thwart easy escapes into fantasy worlds (Varn/Raghavendra 2016). Weird and uncanny modes are favoured as ways of producing destabilising and critical effects. Fantasy, he notes, should also enable critical distancing and interrogative discontinuity, exploiting gaps between desire and possibility, and questioning naturalised assumptions. China Miéville's discussion of weird fiction uses an image offering productive coordinates for distinguishing relations between reality and genre. For him, "[t]he fact of the Weird is the fact that the worldweave is ripped and unfinished. Moth-eaten, ill-made. And through the little tears, from behind the ragged edges, things are looking at us" (Miéville 2011: 115).

Punctures in the symbolic fabric sustaining the web of words and things undo the fantasy of a seamless and unified reality along with the effects of realism.

The holes that appear allow weird fiction to be distinguished as the intrusions of other eyes, other bodies, other powers, impossible according to the assumptions of everyday life. Fantasy fiction moves in the opposite direction, through the holes, to populate the spaces that lie, as it were, 'behind' the woven screen. Uncanny modes register the disruptions of the domesticated unity of the lived and knotted threads binding self and social reality, the holes perceived as interruptions, hesitations or decompositions of habituated patterns of existence. SF acknowledges the holes only insofar as they are unfinished, extrapolating extant rational facts and speculations to challenge, advance or complete the consistency of the weave. But there is a problem: "the arrival of commercial fantasy" aligns itself more readily with consumerism, individual choice, and media-marketed realities (Mathew 2002). This arrival provides good reason to subtract fantasy from fantasy. Like Harrison's political disposition, his fiction is less engaged with forms of fantasy that take reading to another self-contained world, whether it is reached through a portal or creates full readerly immersion (Mendlesohn 2008: xix-xxi). It looks more to those modes – like weird or uncanny fiction – in which strangeness leaks out and intrudes upon comfortable assumptions. Comparing his fiction to "portal fantasies," Harrison makes one difference explicit: in his work "you are not allowed through into the imaginary country." Frustrating smooth transitions or immersion, the aim is to have fantasy "coming off the rails" (Bould 2005: 329).

Fantasy without fantasy, as it develops in Harrison's engagements with genre and politics, cuts a complex relation with prevailing critical notions, articulated diversely with modernism, formalism, materialism, and psychoanalysis. It has elements of Roger Caillois' fantastic as it causes a "bizarre irruption" in reality (1966: 8). It departs from the self-contained structuralism of Tzvetan Todorov, for whom "hesitation" is the defining factor in fantasy fiction. Though fantastic, uncanny or marvelous narratives suspend the empirical and rational assurances governing everyday reality, hesitation leaves the binary distinction of reality and fiction untouched (1975: 25). Structural abstraction from reference and the exclusion of historical conditions, however, are unsuccessful in Todorov: not only does reality furnish "a basis for our definition of the fantastic," fiction "bypasses" distinctions of real and imaginary. Historical changes also have effects, as Todorov acknowledges: by the twentieth century, psychoanalysis has "replaced (and thereby made useless) the literature of the fantastic" (ibid: 167-8). Rosemary Jackson notes Todorov's inability to engage with conditions of cultural production and its attempted preservation of separate domains (1981: 6-8). For her, fantasy is a mode that "interrogates by its difference" the production and maintenance of boundaries between reality and the unreal (ibid: 4). Modernist and formalist techniques engender discontinuities, notably the practice of "de-familiarisation": tired conventions of representation are poetically made strange in order to refresh writing and habitual patterns of perception (Harrison 2005a: 151). The discontinuities Harrison provokes suggest a relationship to the "cognitive estrangement" which, according to Darko Suvin's (1979) deployment of formalist and Brechtian modes, allows science fiction to pose a challenge to the prevailing ideologies and assumptions of particular historical and social conditions of production. Fantasy, from this perspective, is not inimical to or an escape from politics: as China Miéville notes, capitalism is experienced, not in terms of the social relations of production but under the "fantastic form" of the quasi-mystical commodity, so that reality already "*is a fantasy*" (2002: 42). Fantasy, like the imaginary relation to real conditions defining ideology, provides a frame for material existence. Ideology is "an (unconscious) fantasy structuring our social reality" (Žižek 1989: 11). Fantasy establishes the "frame" that guarantees reality, a frame analogous to fictional form: "the structure of a story to be *narrated*" (Žižek 1991: 211). The connection between ideology and fantasy plots how basic distinctions – subject-object, fiction-reality – are constructed and maintained by systems that are internalised, and taken for granted but are rarely directly visible or accessible. Articulations of subjectivity, others and the world, articulations based on patterns of difference and desire, play out within a fantasy-form in which everyday things are not primary: objects do not ground desire or subjectivity because fantasy provides both the "support" and the "screen" in relation to the real that lies beyond symbolisation (Lacan 1977a: 185, 60). In the locus established by fantasy, desire finds "its reference, its substratum, its precise tuning in the imaginary register" (Lacan 1977b: 14). Here, the uncanny can make itself felt, not as hesitation or uncertainty in respect of the difference between real or imagined phenomena, but as a wavering of fantasy form, an "estrangement" disorganising the boundaries imaginarily securing unquestioned distinctions between subject and object. The uncanny registers "imbalance" and decomposition at the limits of subjectivity; it provokes anxiety not at an object or a loss (of self, sense or certainty) but in confrontation with something that has not been made familiar through symbolic processing (ibid: 21; Lacan 2004: 76).

1. COMMERCE OF FANTASIES

"Commercial fantasy" – a term embracing genre and social criticism in Harrison – is also used by Fredric Jameson in discussions of SF. Fantasy is linked to myths and universalised oppositions of good and evil: it constitutes an "ideology" naturalising a specific cultural nexus as a fantasy space in which modernity and its conditions of production are occluded (Jameson 1981: 228). Though fantasy often endorses reactionary positions, Jameson posits a category of "radical fantasy" which, while imagining other worlds, remains cognisant of and attentive to the material contradictions of the form and culture in which it is written. As a genre, radical fantasy neither occults political contradiction nor becomes entranced by its own mythology: it turns on a human element that, though politicised, remains irreducible to history and ideology and offers "a celebration of human creative power and freedom" through forms of "narrative apparatus capable of registering system change and relating the superstructural symptoms of infrastructural shifts and modification" (Jameson 2002: 281). Fantasy and SF, however, remain susceptible to commercial fantasy when market imperatives commodify genre through "gradual penetration of a market system and a money economy" (Jameson 1981: 93). The arrival of commercial fantasy is seen in the flagship fiction of cyberpunk: *Neuromancer* (1984) is situated in "a general period break which is also consistent, not only with the neo-conservative revolution and globalization, but also with the rise of commercial fantasy as a generic competitor and ultimate victor in the field of that culture" (Jameson 2005: 93). Harrison, too, voices similar suspicions. In a review of an influential collection of writings from 1992 (*Storming the Reality Studio*), he notes how the nerds have been elevated into the hacker-prophets of a new global order: "we could perceive the world like the wired, fractured, but – in a neo-Darwinian sense – entrepreneurial creatures we had become." Even the style of cyberpunk fiction operated as "ad, item and shopping mall all at once" (Harrison 2005b: 171). The fantasy announced in cyberpunk's hacker celebration of a world given over to psycho-, bio-, and digital technologies slipstreams new freedoms and imperatives of neoliberal and consumer culture. Its exuberant narratives tell of disembodied users immersed in a neuro-electric "non-space" of information called "cyberspace," accessed through a new – and material – form of portal: the cortex plugged directly into networks of data. An "unlimited subjective dimension" (Gibson 1984: 81), cyberspace imagines commercial fantasy made real: to "go where one wants to go," "be who one wants to be," and "do what one wants to do." In contrast, fantasy without fantasy, as a critical-creative practice, aims to disrupt unquestioning immersion in games, images, and screens, disturbing the techniques of transparency – the "windows" and "portals" – that allow commercial fantasy to proceed undisturbed. Instead of fostering any illusion of seeing through stories or screens, fantasy without fantasy draws attention to the frames in which fiction and reality are opposed and the latter is naturalised. "Egnaro" (1981), for instance, is a story, Harrison glosses,

"about individual human desire where it rubs up against and is hijacked by advertising: the way we are told constantly that we can achieve those internal desires by consuming products. Advertising offers us a trip through the portal which is closed the moment you buy the product. You buy the things that make your life better then find that you're still you. Nothing has changed." (Bould 2005: 330)

Through the "portal," fantasy operates generically and commercially.

Set in a bookshop, "Egnaro" also draws attention to the forms in which fantasy is circulated and sold while refusing any comfortable immersion in a fictional world. On the edges of realism – the grubby backstreets of Manchester with its cheap restaurants and second hand shops – "Egnaro" signifies "a secret known to everyone but yourself," an unvisited land, unknown language, undisclosed universe that "hides itself in interstices" but is intimated in the most banal places: in snatches of overheard conversation, in "an advert for a new kind of vacuum pump," among business papers, in news broadcasts, in misprints from volumes of poetry, or heard in the doorway of a supermarket (Harrison 2004: 93). It could be telling you that the future is Orange. Egnaro's effect is described as "inhabiting two worlds at once" (ibid: 113). It sustains a breach in everyday fantasy for the owner of a seedy second-hand bookshop who lives "between the fantasy on the shelves, which no longer satisfied him, and the meaningless sheaves of invoices floating in gentle pools of cold coffee on the desk upstairs" (ibid: 96). As a disillusioned purveyor of commercial fantasy his subsequent captivation by Egnaro is seen to be a "punishment" for "a life exploiting their fantasies to subsidize his own." But Egnaro itself remains elusive and undefined: "if Egnaro is the substrate of mystery which underlies all daily life, then the reciprocal idea is also true, and it is the exact dead point of ordinariness which lies beneath every mystery" (ibid: 115). The story ends reflectively yet without explanation, between ordinariness and mystery, reality and fantasy, poles articulated by a breach – a "dead point" – with neither assuming precedence nor transparency: a point of non-identification; a site empty of fantasy; a position of discontinuity.

Irresolution and dis-continuity are effects of subtracting fantasy from itself. Providing no comforting answers they provoke critical reflections. While

"Egnaro" engenders interrogative distance, *Signs of Life* (1997) takes a different approach to a context in which commercial fantasy is directly tied to neoliberal deregulation of markets, free enterprise, and consumer culture. It takes place in "Thatcherland," a recognisable yet unreal country determined by an arch "political fantasist" (Harrison 2005a: 152). *Signs of Life* is set in a land of expensive restaurants, designer clothes, and branded goods where a new entrepreneurial ethos thrives in the corporate biotech and medical services sector. Centred on a heterosexual romance, his adventures in entrepreneurial capitalism take second place to her wish to fly (Harrison 2005b: 232). More than a dream or a metaphor of self-fulfilment, her ambition leads her to another lover – a genetic scientist better placed to realise her wish. The genetic modification programme she joins allows her to select the colours, textures, shapes, plumage that will make her a design and technological innovation: "twenty-first-century Transgenic Woman" (ibid: 446). Because she is worth it. Presented in part as an extension of cosmetic surgery, that "fantasy factory stuff," marketing manuals sell individual freedom and potential: "Grow Your Way to Freedom" (ibid: 342, 449). Her desires are realised on computer screens; she spends hours playing with her future form and image: "she loved it. It was as if all along her dream of flight had been a dream of sitting in front of this machine" (ibid: 447). Satisfying as it is, simulation is not the end. Her fantasy of flight, though virtual, is no mere metaphor of self-realisation, transcendence, or personal or sexual liberation: technical and consumable, fantasy and desire are co-opted, shaped and implemented by a convergence of techno-scientific, corporate and consumerist forces. Distinctions between dream and reality collapse as genetic and digital technologies rewrite bodies in accordance with a glossy dream. At a cost, of course. Genetic therapy enables her to grow wings, but not to take off. Her body is covered in sores and bruises and the ragged stubs of carotene and down; her blood is turned into a "junkyard" of proteins (ibid: 456). She undergoes extensive immunological collapse and requires emergency treatment: "intubated and strapped down, she fluttered and thrashed like a sparrow trapped in a room" (ibid: 456). She is a bird, but helpless and flightless. Fantasised freedoms disappear. Reading like a cautionary tale, the ending confronts the reader with a reality that evokes, eludes, and questions fantasy. Desire is disappointed, imagination stripped of its wings, metaphor flapping back on itself. But caution (despite great pathos at her condition and sympathy from her loyal but emotionally exhausted lover) does not call for a return to realism: she still has her scars and stubby feathers, signs of fantasy half-realised. Any warning moves beyond individuals: a parallel narrative about the fantastic amounts of money to be made dumping bio-hazardous materials equates her body (become a "junkyard" of genes, hormones, drugs, and proteins) with the body of the earth and the ruin of another fantasy: a secret wood, rich in childhood associations, is seen strewn with toxic waste and glowing acid-yellow biohazard tape.

2. FLIGHT

Flight remains a metaphor of fantasy, especially in new media contexts: it signals the technical realisation of imagined possibility, transcendence of bodily limitations, thrilling liberation, and immersion. Cyberpunk protagonists enjoy the "bodiless exultation" of the matrix and an ecstatic sense of rapid and unlimited flight through virtual spaces (Gibson 1984: 12). Real users, as Sherry Turkle's documentation of screen experience notes, speak of feeling they are passing through boundaries, using communications technologies that allow unmediated access to other operators and even to programmes (1995: 31). Frames, windows, portals all call on the immersive, interfacial powers of transparency (Galloway 2012: 23). In "Suicide Coast" (1999), a short story engaging with simulation and commercial fantasy, flight is the mode of a crude videogame and metaphor of immersion in screen and narrative. The game's basic geometric form recalls 1980s design: grid patterns, vector displays, and wireframe graphics were basic forms in military training programmes and arcade games as well as providing the visual inspiration for cyberspace in *Neuromancer* (Poole 2000: 127). Gibson's fiction serves as the story's primary point of fictional and historical reference. "Suicide Coast" depicts a similarly hallucinatory virtual space and world in which bodies have been supplanted by machines. But "Suicide Coast" has little of Gibson's technological euphoria. Already archaic by 21st century programming standards, the game is called "Out There" though possessing no innovative features or appealing to any "far out" hacker-surfer-hippie ethos of creative edginess (Rucker 1992). Given the context of the story and Harrison's scepticism about cyberpunk's proximity to commercial fantasy, the lack of technical ecstasy is not surprising. The primary interface used in the game, too, reinforces both connection and difference: "jacking in" to the matrix becomes more banal and brutal as "coring," which leaves a player's body sore, marked by bruises, scarring, and scabs that are the ugly, painful traces of a common surgical procedure. Fusions of body and technology are less affirmative than in cyberpunk, the experience of virtual immersion far less exciting: the near-future of cyberpunk's feverish imagining has ceded to an omnivorous present of mundane regular play. Though transcendence and ecstasy evaporate in "Suicide Coast," the residue of corporeality, Gibson's "meat," remains: semi-catatonic players, barely mobile, sit slumped at consoles. The world of "Out There" is cyberspace degree zero, without elation or sublime overcoming, a relentless absorption, immersion, and repetition without crash, end or exit.

Going to work is as remarkable as coring is commonplace. Not only does the narrator visit his own office, he drives himself there, taking pleasure in being at the wheel of his branded, high-specification German-engineered automobile: roads are now empty, implying how much of daily life and work occurs indoors and online. "No one drives themselves anymore," he remarks (Harrison 1999: 306). Narrator and story are anathema: both make claims on physical space. The office, a converted East London warehouse, is owned by MAX, an online magazine and marketing site specialising in the promotion of adventure sports and equipment. Climbing, the narrator's preferred activity, sits low on the adventure sports industry's list of profitable priorities: its demanding skill-set is not matched by a pressing need for expensive equipment. Despite the predominance of virtual play, commodities are still remunerative: online commercial fantasy spins off into actual goods that are profitable only as little bits of reality held in reserve to guarantee the over-realness of digital activities. At odds with the commercial fantasy that dominates the story from the start, climbing establishes interrogative distance. But judgements from *Climbers* are reiterated in a digitised world marked by a complete change in priorities and values: what the novel dismissively called the "pornography of risk" has become the norm.

The narrator leaves work to visit a friend. In keeping with his old-fashioned appreciation of material reality he chooses to drive himself and visit in person. His friend, Mick, a legend in the climbing community, is now wheelchair-bound, an adventurous career cut short by a car accident. His opinions resonate with the ethos of *Climbers*: "life without consequences isn't a life at all" (Harrison 2004: 394). Mick's position draws an absolute but ambivalent distinction between real life and gaming. The contents of his back room further emphasise real-ness: it is stacked with *used* climbing gear. However, on the desk sits a huge design-spec monitor screen running the program of "Out There": Mick sits in front of the screen, consumed by a single game. If the contrast between active, meaningful, and embodied living and passive, immobile, empty gaming was not already poignant enough, the pattern of consumption and dependency is soon extended with his decision to be "cored." To underline the painful irony of the dramatically reversed priorities, Mick exclaims flatly but distinctly (and with an irony all the more striking for being unmarked): "it's better than living" (ibid: 390). Perhaps it is better than life lived in a chair, but it remains starkly contrasted – so the quiet words and looks between his friend and his partner suggest – to the life he lived before. The signs of his absorption into the commercial fantasy he despised appear in his purchases as well as his coring: on another visit, the narrator discovers a brand new, expensive motorbike outside his house. At dinner – fitting as a result of the neurological trauma attendant on hours plugged in – he leaps from his chair and collapses, exclaiming: "I want to get out of here." To get out of here – his wheelchair-bound barely embodied, almost inactive material existence – requires that he play "Out There," leaving the prison of fleshly limitation to immerse himself further in game activities. Virtual life enhances materiality, supplements bodily failings, and feeds on the gap between physical and fantasised possibility. In two ways: either the playing body functions as the prosthetic "life" of gaming, the deficient condition initiating and sustaining the dominant (habitual and commercial) fantasy filled by virtual images and experienced as better than living (all the while continuing to diminish corporeal powers) or the body signifies the meaty excrescence of game reality in which fantasy gives new form to living (prosthetic life supplanting corporeal existence) with a trajectory aimed "Out There," beyond the horizons of materiality. Mick's position cannot be resolved in one or other way, his body the cleavage of transcendence and abjection. The twists of his fitting body and pained exclamation screams with the bathos of the meat: wanting to get out of here is to be delivered both of wheelchair-bound reality and of online gaming. It screams to regain a life of climbing, a longing for an out there that is no longer accessible. Mick, a subject of tragic loss and corporeal disempowerment, is presented as having become desperately and inescapably bound to a technological logic of incorporation: there is no life for him outside the continuous, uninterrupted, flight of the game. He is an image of meat drained of its information and expectorated by the machine on which he now depends. With life now equivalent to the smooth continuity of projected movement and action that absorbs and captivates him, material differences are discarded in the face of an unending flight of information, an imaginary plane of consumption in which he is the immanence-excrescence of technological becoming: a virtual everyperson, barely mobile amid the images unfolding in and around him, pacifying body and overstimulating his brain.

Mick, however, is not the subject of the narrative. His position, though exemplifying a general condition, is not the point of narrative identification. From the narrator's perspective on game immersion, critical discontinuity looks to the real of climbing (the narrator shortly heads for the practice wall to prepare for a climbing trip). Given that the game is linked to wider working practices and systems of communication (home working; not driving) and part of an online marketing platform, the dominance of a general commercial fantasy in the everyday world of the story is also held at bay: positioned at a remove from the game, outside "Out There," as it were, narrator (and reader) occupy a retrograde critical distance towards the prevailing norms, practices, and fantasies sustaining everyday digitised existence.

3. Dead Perspective

As "Suicide Coast" attends to the fantasy frame of its gameworld, the effects of perspective come into focus. "Out There" is a flight game demonstrating perspective's most minimal and captivating effects. The game is described twice:

"Its visuals were cheap and schematic, its values self-consciously retro. It was nothing like the stuff we sold off the MAX site, which was quite literally the experience itself, stripped of its consequences. You had to plug in for that: you had to be cored. This was just a game; less a game; less a game, even, than a trip. You flew a silvery V-shaped graphic down an endless V-shaped corridor, a notional perspective sometimes bounded by lines of objects, sometimes just by lines, sometimes bounded only by your memory of boundaries. Sometimes the graphic floated and mushed like a moth. Sometimes it travelled in flat vicious arcs at an apparent Mach 5. There were no guns, no opponent. There was no competition. You flew. Sometimes the horizon tilted one way, sometimes the other. You could choose your own music. It was a bleakly minimal experience. But after a minute or two, five at most, you felt as if you could fly your icon down the perspective forever, to the soundtrack of your own life." (Harrison 2004: 392)

With coring, the same experience is delivered, only with the graphics unfolding screenless in his head: "Only the endless V of the perspective. The endless, effortless dip-and-bank of the viewpoint" (ibid: 398). Without the graphic sophistication to dress up the experience as reality itself, the lure of perspectival effects of motion are still strangely addictive (Mick is described as being slumped before the screen looking like a "junkie"). Content, realism or representation are barely relevant to the process: a perpetually fleeing object draws the subject into the illusion of flight. Form is everything here: no things solidify or inhibit the flows of desiring and looking, no object fills up the space or finishes the game, and no boundaries – just a hint of shifting lines and borders – impose any sense of limitation. Virtual movement draws player from things, images, objects – all the trappings of simulated reality – and into an undisturbed sensation of rapid, unimpeded flight, the continuous rhythm of the graphic flying on forever with a playing, looking, desiring subject captivated in its wake. Though this is not the "experience itself" that is furnished by better software, it is gaming degree zero and it exemplifies the basic fantasy form involved in perspective.

Game design draws on various forms of perspective, from pictorial and narrative to cinematic modes (Poole 2000: 141). Noting Gibson's narrative technique, N. Katherine Hayles observes how point-of-view is "abstracted into a purely temporal entity" and "metaphorized into an interactive space" (1999: 39). What Lev Manovich describes as "perspectival machines" – geometric and pictorial representation – split signs and images from the body to frame the subject. The cinematic apparatus, in contrast, offers mobility to a gaze through the camera's positional changes in virtual space while leaving the body immobile (Manovich 2001: 104). Nonetheless, perspective is not static, but involves a "reciprocal relationship" between objects, signs, and subjects: it is "more than just a sign system that reflects reality" but a structuring that "makes possible the manipulation of reality through manipulating signs" (ibid: 167). The frame in which things are arranged, and rearranged, is perspective. But perspective is not reducible to first-person narration or point-of-view in cinema: identification shifts depending on narrative frame or camera position. There are significant differences in media conventions: cinema uses first-person perspective in a limited manner, often to signal a marginal or disturbed subjective position such as hallucination, intoxication or otherness and to evoke an alienating effect, like the machine-optic graphics of James Cameron's terminating cyborg (Galloway 2006: 40, 56). In games, however, point-of-view is more commonly used in the process of sustaining identificatory effects: "where film uses the subject shot to represent a problem with identification, game uses the subjective shot to *create* identification." More important, it makes the connection that provides an "intuitive sense of motion and action" (ibid: 71). Form, frame, and effect have a more dominant role in gaming than the realism or verisimilitude attributed to the visible objects appearing in virtual space. Reduced to little more than a flying "V," the graphic of "Out There" serves well as the site of articulation for a gamer: it is a figure of action and motion in space. Moreover, the spatial field in which it articulates the player is analogous to the manner in which fantasy frames subjectivity in respect of reality. The "V" – itself a perspectival geometric form – also stands as figure of representation in the sense of distinguishing a field for the subject rather than a surface on which images of things are imitated or projected: representation happens "as long as a subject casts his *gaze* towards a horizon on which he cuts out the base of a triangle, his eye (or his mind) for the apex" (Barthes 1977: 69). Representation orientates subjectivity in a visual or narrative field; it forms the perspectival frame in which the subject is positioned as looking, desiring, consuming.

Playing is caught up in an endless and rapid movement of flight, a closed circuit combining identification and the immensity evoked by its blurred borderless flow passing by at speed: ill-defined objects and roughly-lit edges constitute a limited frame to the game fantasy that enhances fantasy's boundlessness: the movement of the graphic in barely delineated space admits nothing other than fantasy flowing without bounds or edges, modulated to a rhythm without disjunction or discontinuity and constantly re-modulating itself in the reflexive action binding "V" of subject to "V" of graphic. It is fantasy degree zero and fantasy operating fully (to the MAX perhaps). It is fantasy, moreover, that admits no other perspective, displays no signs of life outside its own action-movement, offers no other point of identification or reality. There is nothing "out there." Just as commercial fantasy circumscribes material existence in the story, encompassing it technically, economically, socially, and subjectively, so game immersion fills the space it leaves in the reality with commodities of its own design. This is not fantasy without fantasy, that is, a fractured or split perspective, but totalising, continuous immersion. Imaginary fullness, Harrison suggests elsewhere, works like enamoration:

"It's like being in a computer game. One moment you have needs; the next quite suddenly, they're satisfied and sidelined. The field of vision seems empty. Then you detect this faint serpentine flicker as the fractals grow and boil, and new needs have replaced the old. Desire is desire." (Harrison 2004: 429)

Desire is desire is desire … A single line flickers and forms in the space opened by fantasy, absorbing need, desire, and vision: "you can't talk yourself out of it" (ibid: 429). Perspective – fantasy form – constitutes the frame of desiring flickering endlessly and just out of reach, if not out there. In this model, game perspective refuses any outside to fantasy: the lure of any notional space "out there" only reopens gamespace for further immersion in an endlessly shifting movement of an ungraspable "V."

4. REAL THING

The narrative position at the edge of the game maintains a small hold on distance, even if it does not manage – as in *Climbers* – to open a wider breach in perspective, like trying to see out of both sides of a moving train while staring along an empty aisle (Harrison 1991: 173). Climbing, and driving, for the narrator, offers access to some other reality, some meaningful life, "out there." There remains a gulf between the "experience itself" simulated by MAX ware (freed of consequences like sugar-free cola) and the risk that underpins the reality of climbing: "you can't plug in and be a star: you have to practice" (Harrison 2004: 394). Here the narrator takes Mick at his word. He agrees to return the unused and – for Mick unusable – motorbike and then drives back to the office climbing wall to prepare for real activity and experience. Stretching from a painful hold on the wall, muscles straining and aching to the extent that the narrator wonders about the point of it all, his will and concentration are bolstered by images of the rocky outcrop he is planning to climb: there will be no safety net there, nothing to stop an eighty-foot plummet onto boulders, and nothing to help overcome the paralysis preceding a seemingly-impossible move. But conditions of imminent physical danger and real risk – as the scene develops into an immediate and absorbing account of the act of climbing itself – are also the basis of intense experience. From the drive to the site, the glimpse of the boulders below, the awareness of the gaze of other climbers on the narrator's predicament and a feeling of rising excitement, the intensity builds into a continuity of experience different from everyday discrete perceptions. Now rock, idea, body, and action are united: the concentrated involvement in the act is an escape from any concern with daily reality – contracts, business meetings, household bills, emotional problems "mean nothing." The terms in which the story expresses thrill, continuity, focus – explosive tension, "excitement," unimpeded unity of subjective intent, vision, and action ("where you look, you go"), boundless freedom yet complete control ("it's like falling upwards") – directly recalls experience as related in *Climbers*: effortless, magisterial, exhilarating (ibid: 402; Harrison 1991: 50). Unlike game reality and the everyday world of commercial fantasy, climbing is the real thing, experience itself: "this is the other side of excitement, the other pleasure of height: the space without anxiety" (Harrison 2004: 402). Again, distinctions concerning dream, fantasy, and reality are invoked to qualify experiential difference, another reiteration of terms from *Climbers*. "The space without anxiety" refers to a dream of a perfect climb being interrupted by a nightmare moment: from inside a crack in the rock face a hand without body reaches out to grasp and trap the climber (Harrison 1991: 28). The space of anxiety is not the emptiness that contributes to the fantasy of a perfect climb; nor is it the crack that provides the means of movement and connection: anxiety is the sensation of a break in imagined continuity, the moment that fear and self-consciousness reencounter limitation and boundary, a moment that throws the body back on itself and registers the separation of climbing from act. The space of anxiety circumscribes normal distinctions between fantasy and reality as dream-wish and actual world: the space without anxiety – the "other side" of excitement – is the point at which (in defiance of common sense and in cognisance of risk and pain) one makes a move, becomes the move: "suddenly it was no effort"; "suddenly you're moving anyway" (Harrison 2004: 402).

On the point of traversing the space without anxiety the story's narration stalls. Anxiety interrupts the continuity suggestive of real experience, breaking the illusion of present-ness evoked in the prose (its tenses, the details of place and relation of movement and action) as no more than the projection of a climber hanging from a hold on a climbing wall in an East London office. The mode of interruption, however, is significant: "the space without anxiety. The space without anxiety. The space without anxiety. The space without anxiety. The space without anxiety. The space without anxiety. The space without anxiety. The space with-" (ibid: 403). Ironically anxiety, registered as interrupted interruption and repetition, returns, but only technically as a programme malfunction. The commercial fantasy of the game imitates anxiety in repetition at a point (the move in climbing that traverses anxiety as limit and attains sovereign experience) beyond which, as a game, it cannot proceed. The style of repetition, mechanical and homogeneous, marks a particular technical twist in and to the narrative, turning to the other medium of the story:

"you are left with this familiar glitch or loop in the MAX ware. *Suicide Coast* won't play any further. Reluctantly, you abandon Mick to his world of sad acts, his faith that reality can be relied on to scaffold his perceptions. To run him again from the beginning would only make the frailty of that faith more obvious: so you wait until everything has gone black, unplug yourself from the machine, and walk away, unconsciously rolling your shoulders to ease the stiffness, massaging the sore place at the back of your neck. What will you do next? Everything is flat out here. No one drives themselves anymore." (ibid: 402-403)

The narrative ends suddenly and in repetition, but not as a story. The ending is a break in and a displacement of writing that marks a shift in medium: the game presented as an object of written narrative now appears as its primary form; writing becomes subsumed by the disclosure of a "glitch" that brings new technology to the fore. The experience of climbing delivered in writing is disclosed by interrupted simulation as a climbing game. Perspectives and roles alter: the reader now becomes (passive and unwitting) player, subject of a wider dislocation undoing assumptions about identity and medium, distinctions of reality and fantasy and claims about climbing and experience. Though priorities of writing and gaming are reversed (in writing), issues of narrative involvement and game immersion (and, of course, fantasy and fantasy without fantasy) remain in play. A single fantasy frame is fractured, but another takes its place, reflexively opening up interpretative entanglements. You have been reading "Suicide Coast," the title of the story. But nobody reads anymore. You have been playing *Suicide Coast*, a climbing simulation game.

5. GLITCH

"Glitch" is a technical term for a programme malfunction. It is also used by Harrison as a metaphor for the practice of fantasy without fantasy, for the interpenetration of strangeness and normality in fiction and for evoking interrogative discontinuity in narrative perspective (Varn/Raghavendra 2016). In "Suicide Coast," the discontinuity interrupts narrative, exposing the story to the same questions of fantasy and immersion that it poses of gaming and undermining its apparent privileging of real experience over virtual existence. Indeed, written narrative (and the scaffolding of fiction and reality it upholds) seems to be entirely displaced by the revelation that *Suicide Coast* is itself a game. There are continuities amid discontinuity, however: though not the same as the "V" that enables fantasy flight effects, both narrative position and climbing game simulation continue to depend on representational effects that bind the reading or viewing body to the action or movement enjoyed on screen or page. And these effects can be confounded, neutralised by an impossible identification that refuses the subject any secure position: an early scene in Carl Dreyer's *Vampyr* (1932) tracks from cemetery to house but, shot from the position of a corpse, it invites its audience to see through the eyes of a dead man. Rather than completing a naturalised space of representation as uninterrupted unity for the spectator to enjoy, the shot goes to the "extreme limit" of representation by setting out a scene that "has no point of departure, no support, it gapes open" (Barthes 1977: 69). "Egnaro" produces a comparable effect, ending on a "dead point" pivoting uncomfortably between a familiar world and a realm of mystery. "Suicide Coast" closes on blackness: there is no thing and no one to see, nowhere from which to see it. Dead eyes, dead points, dead screens, representation is placed on the same scaffold as Mick's discredited faith in perception and reality. Frustrated by a narrative that is no longer transparent or unified and by a subject position that is both divided and evacuated, a single perspective for reading collapses and attention is shifted to form and medium, to and not through fantasy effects.

Glitch is an apt metaphor, attuned to the content of the story and consonant with its technical and aesthetic ramifications. An error in the functioning of a programme, a glitch can be identified and reduced to a "bug" – then subjected to correction – or, if unknown, can either be ignored or incorporated into subsequent processing: it may even enable analytical or interpretative manoeuvres and, like formal aesthetic reflexivity, it might – "rather than creating the illusion of a transparent, well-working interface to information" – disclose "the machine revealing itself" (Menkman 2011: 27-30). Foregrounding programme and interface also inhibits transparent identification or smooth flow, the viewer "momentarily relocated to a void in meaning" (ibid: 30). Where congruence between expectation and delivery serves to connect information with habitual effects of meaning, the "break" disrupts normal (viewing/reading) processes and signals error, accident or non-sense, an "absence of (expected) functionality" that has both technical and social implications (ibid: 31). Interruptions of flow disclose information's reliance on models of friction-free circulation: simulation's continuity, its "blend" of virtual and physical space producing reality effects that neither jar nor fragment perspective (Manovich 2001: 113). Where modernity's subject is distanced from chaotic reality by the stability of pictorial and cinematic images, the informatic subject "finds peace in the knowledge that she can slide over endless fields of data, locating any morsel of information with the click of a button, zooming through file systems and networks" (ibid: 274). This freedom offers a mobility and fluidity akin to the "transit impermanence" associated with the non-places of supermodernity (ibid: 281). The subject of these movements, at ease amongst flows and in access to information, is not only a creature of surfaces, but a neoliberal user furnished with the greater range of choice, a subject of flight, freedom, fantasy.

Interruptions might briefly frustrate informational desire – drawing attention from window and portal to coding and programme – but they do not bring information processing to a halt. Glitches may allow "scope for creation in unexpected ways" (Fuller/Goffey 2012: 96). An unexpected move, indeed, contributes to system enhancement, offering innovation to a logic of performance optimisation or sites marking the autopoietic self-organisation of all living and cybernetic systems (Lyotard 1984; Maturana/Varela 1980). There may also be a critical practice enabled by glitches, a practice called "counter-gaming," through which transparency and the habitual patterns and assumptions of play are disturbed and challenged by breaks that foreground the medium of information (Galloway 2012: 109). Glitches and counter-gaming bring to the fore the agency of programming itself, indicating the dominance of information in and over the world: a first-person shooter "is not a stand-in for activity" or a vicarious substitute for acting out murderous energies: it "is activity"; no surrogate for activity, it "is information" (ibid: 104). To play is to play informatics and participate in the continuum of information and control – it does not require reference to any reality outside information. Rejecting realism, reference, and mimetic representation, this model of gaming does not forget the player at the console and proposes a notion of "realisticness" which calibrates the effectiveness or pleasure of gaming in terms of a "congruence" or "fidelity of context" between the social reality of gamer and game (ibid: 78). Any gap between social reality outside information and game reality steadily diminishes: the "outside" that emerges in layers of "interface" indicating "the implicit presence of the outside within the inside" (boxes, read-outs, dials, sub-screens) enriches non-diegetic aspects of play to such an extent that it demonstrates how the "outside, or the social has been woven more intimately into the very fabric of the aesthetic than in previous times" (ibid: 42). Social space is no longer confined to material reality but a realm permeated and reprogrammed according to information and code. The encroachment on and recoding of social reality by information, however, has major ramifications for older models of ideology: just as a reference matters less and less to what happens in games, so criticism of the media-political obfuscation of real social conditions or of negative presentations of cultural and sexual identities has less relevance. Identity in the sense that cultural politics worries about it is of no significance to code or programme: what circulates is nothing more than "a datatype" as identity becomes "modular, instrumental, typed, numerical, algorithmic" (ibid: 102).

6. JUST DO IT

In "Suicide Coast," glitch is not only a metaphor of interruption and mark of the interfection of one medium by another. As a break-flow, it disturbs expectations of narrative transparency and draws attention to form and medium. But it cuts two ways. The glitch reveals *Suicide Coast* (the MAX ware simulation) rather than "Suicide Coast" (the short story) to have had an unexpected and powerfully immersive effect, turning an apparently critical tale of new media fantasy into an acknowledgement of the obsolescence of writing. Everything has been subsumed by visual media and digital technology; no one reads anymore; a story called "Suicide Coast" has been replaced by a game called *Suicide Coast*. Yet, by way of the glitch that stops it dead, the narrative line is made to perform in a mode that not only reverses the priorities it seemed to be advocating (inverting and supplanting polarities of fantasy and reality with the prevalence of digital reality): the sudden shift in medium draws attention to hitherto covertly immersive game media and, in the same move, to the capacity of written narrative to engender similar effects. In looking back on what has been written as simulation and forward to suggest that written narrative has been digitally overwritten, it also prompts a different reflection on the form – and medium – of writing. If the story involves remediation (turning an account of climbing into a climbing game experience; or indeed taking the realism of *Climbers* and making it a fantasy game) the polarised trajectory of the glitch also makes the narrative into a remediation, or, rather, a reverse remediation (taking a newer medium and reinscribing it in an older form): it displays, in written form, a narrative performance of the continuous blending of digital simulation; stories can be absorbing, language immersive. Return to the office practice wall, narrator dangling, uncomfortable and wondering just why he puts himself through such painful trials. The reason, as it comes to him, moves him forward, into the flow of a seamless take in which space, time, and motion blend smoothly: while the projection begins in the future tense by imagining driving, Wye valley, space and rock and moss, then imagining the real consequences of a fall, it shifts smoothly to the present: "now all the practice is over. Now …" (Harrison 2004: 401). The climb is underway, people are watching, narrator-climber very much in the moment. Where, in literary terms, the wealth of experience represented in writing would return memory to the present in a Romantic manner (he is climbing in the Wye valley after all), the narrator's experience of the game is made present in a prospective fashion: it is yet to come. Fantasy rather than memory animates the "experience" as something (n)ever-present and always to be enjoyed, flitting on the horizon like the "V" of a flying simulation. This is not quite the fullness-loss in a wider continuity of space, things, concentration, and motion as documented in *Climbers*. The subject of climbing simulation-narration is furnished with a curious self-consciousness that seems to see itself from a position that is neither an ecstatic over-worldliness of sovereign experience nor a frozen, anxious body-consciousness dangling in fear. While a present-ness dominates the description, the narrative sustains a sense of watching through other eyes generated by the use of the second-person singular of language: "your friends look up, shading their eyes against the white glare of the rock. They are wondering if you can make the move. So are you" (ibid: 401). Present-ness is given over to a commentator-coach, a screen or video-real-time voiceover. Like the voiceover of a commercial for sporting goods, it draws the consumer into the scene of fantasy not only with seduction but with a challenge to leap from images to reality. It invokes a "dare," daring the consumer to be who he or she wants to be, a dare to just do it (Goldman/Papson 1998). Like the story's imagined move from practice to act, it bridges fantasy and reality in the manner that a sports psychologist or coach promotes visualisations to enhance performance by removing the inhibitions of self and critical thought that deflect focus from a complete immersion in the act. At stake, more than anything, is experience: the language, and the design of the MAX ware climbing game, is concerned with producing "smooth experience" (Galloway 2012: 104). Flow is the passage to "optimal experience" (Csíkszentmihályi). MAX ware aims to deliver the experience itself. Embracing all forms of technical performance from working to playing to writing, optimal experience appears as the aim of commercial fantasy. In narrative, in games, in the world, commercial fantasy aims to harness the flow that holds consumers in a single-minded focus within its frames. *Suicide Coast*'s invocation of real experience – the sense of challenge, risk, pain – not only manifests the hi-jacking of climbing by the language of advertising and commercial fantasy, it inscribes the transformation, via simulation, of reality from thing to affect: what counts is "experience itself." Climbing, previously offered as the measure of real experience, is eclipsed in this movement (a painful sacrifice given Harrison's investment in the activity): MAX ware provides the "experience itself," without consequences of course, and without the need of any reality other than the commodities that come later. Like perception, it seems, experience has no need of the scaffolding of reality. The only imperative is performance: "you" must live life to the MAX.

7. UNPLUGGED

In the story, the glitch, though rewriting narrative as game and prompting reinterpretation and rereading, does not reassert boundaries between fantasy and reality that were established in the opposition of "Out There" to the consequences of climbing: those distinctions have been displaced, reframed by a technological transformation in which neither pole remains fixed in stable binary opposition. If there is a return of questions of reality, it is minimal. Writing and gaming are not opposed in terms of fiction or reality: both turn on specific fantasy modes. Game effects appear in narrative and language effects in gaming, with the production of reality effects – and affects – displayed through a reflexive glitch in which narrative is seen as a game-fiction performing the smoothness and continuity attributed to simulation and, at same time, introducing into simulation's all-consuming frame, a slight registration of excess, a dead point or blackness interrupting flow. A body unplugs and leaves the computer.

An end or, even, an exit? Or another repetition recalling earlier iterations of "Out There," this time breaking commercial fantasy's incorporation of materiality and embodied activity? Reiteration, however, discloses another dimension of difference, one that neither affirms an absolute separation between fiction and reality nor offers access to a reality "out there": a dynamic differentiation effect, an oppositional alternation between the "artifice" of "Out There" and the "reality" of climbing, forms the basis of the positional and perspectival articulations that gave the story initial credence. Dynamic relations – and realisations – are evident in new digital technologies as modes of reality production: for Hayles, reality becomes an aftereffect of movements between and materialisations of different media layers; for Hansen, the abandonment of orthographical priority and interrelations of media artifice establish reality through affect (Hayles 2002; Hansen 2004). In the first case, reality is an effect of internal variance in media patterns; in the second case, reality is retrospectively constituted through affect as a point where flows are temporarily stabilised in perspective.

In "Suicide Coast," the effect of reality is not assured by the language of the narrative alone, whether it involves the continuity of focus, the use of the present tense, the attention to detail or the invocation of pain or risk since these, it amply demonstrates, can be as artificial and immersive as any simulation. Instead, a dynamic inter-realising differential relation manifests itself in positional and perspectival articulations of familiar differences, assumptions, and mediations: it is a story whose effect emerges from the interplay between two narratives and two games, between Mick's and the narrator's tale, between "Out There" and *Suicide Coast*. Any sense of reality comes from differentiations of the online world of MAX and driving or climbing (reinforced by Mick's statements and predicament). These familiar divisions of world of body and of screen are overturned with the glitch, to leave the reader nowhere: a reality effect of sorts, it discloses the absence of reality in the story, while problematizing the possibility of a reality outside fiction. Almost everything has been given over to simulation: to look for something "out there" is to be embroiled in layers of game reality and to be forced to acknowledge a difference no longer demarcating fantasy and reality but only emerging from the relation between two games. The look out there is pulled back to "Out There," then drawn back further within the trope of game simulation to see only *Suicide Coast*, the game in and for which the other archaic game was no more than a decoy. Out there is a lost possibility, a loss preserved and dismissed in the position of Mick, sadly scaffolded in an obsolete conjunction of perception and reality. One may unplug oneself and "walk away," but where can one go? (Harrison 2004: 403) "Out here" may be different from "out there," but it replays the differential relations between *Suicide Coast* and "Out There": outside "Out There" is also described in the story as a flat place where "no one drives themselves anymore." Does repetition make a difference? Repetition implies another loop in the game, and suggests a reciprocity between outside and inside, a reciprocity subject to the same differential pressures constituting and displacing reality and simulation through an endless recession of the real and a constant flattening of horizons. It also casts doubt on the possibility of ever walking away, of ever exiting the game: narrative repetition performs a gesture of abysmally structured gaming. Games within games within games: gaming plays out to infinity, incorporating, redeploying, and transforming effects of reality along the way. Even the glitch is "familiar" (ibid: 403). A habituated interruption, it further emphasises the absence of any outside-game other than the outsides projected in gaming. The absorption of the outside, of social reality by information, leaves flatness "out here." But if the blankness affecting subjectivity at the repetitive limit of representation intrudes as a moment of discontinuity, if the brief breach of transparency offers a sense of alienation from and dispossession of machinic flows, glitch's sudden interruption of the real works as a guttering and disappearance: flicking off fantasy and fantasy without fantasy, it pivots precariously at a point where commercial fantasy hovers on the verge of unlimited instantiation and where a last glimmer of a radically fantasised outside remains. Turn off, unplug, walk out.

WORKS CITED

Barthes, Roland (1977): *Image Music Text* (Stephen Heath, Trans.), London: Fontana.

Bould, Mark (2005): "Old, Mean and Misanthropic: an Interview with M. John Harrison." In: Mark Bould/ Michelle Reid (eds.), *Parietal Games*, London: Science Fiction Foundation, pp. 326-42.

Caillois, Roger (1966): *Anthologie du Fantastique*, Vol. 1. Paris: Éditions Gallimard.

Csíkszentmihályi, Mihály (1990): *Flow*, New York and London: HarperCollins.

Fuller, Matthew/Goffey, Andrew (2012): *Evil Media*. Cambridge, MA/London: MIT Press.

Galloway, Alexander R. (2006): *Gaming*, Minneapolis/London: University of Minnesota Press.

Galloway, Alexander R. (2012): *The Interface Effect*, Cambridge: Polity.

Gibson, William (1984): *Neuromancer*, London: HarperCollins.

Goldman, Robert/ Papson, Stephen (1998): *Nike Culture*, London: Sage.

Hansen, Mark B. N. (2004): "The digital topography of Mark Z. Danielewski's 'House of Leaves'." In: *Contemporary Literature*, 45/4, pp. 597–636.

Harrison, M. John (1991): *Climbers*, London: Paladin.

Harrison, M. John (2004): *Things That Never Happen*, London: Victor Gollancz.

Harrison, M John (2005a): "The Profession of Science Fiction." In: Mark Bould/ Michelle Reid (eds.), *Parietal Games*, London: Science Fiction Foundation, pp. 144-53.

Harrison, M. John (2005b): "Nerd into Shaman." In: Mark Bould/Michelle Reid (eds.), *Parietal Games*, London: Science Fiction Foundation, pp. 170-71.

Harrison, M. John (2005c): *Anima*, London: Victor Gollancz.

Hayles, N. Katherine (1999): *How We Became Posthuman*, Chicago/London: University of Chicago Press.

Hayles, N. Katherine (2002): "Saving the Subject: Remediation in 'House of Leaves'." In: *American Literature* 74/4, pp. 779-806.

Jackson, Rosemary (1981): *Fantasy: The Literature of Subversion*, London: Methuen.

Jameson, Fredric (1981): *The Political Unconscious*, London/New York: Methuen.

Jameson, Fredric (2002): "Radical Fantasy." In: *Historical Materialism* 10/4, pp. 273-280.

Jameson, Fredric (2005): *Archaeologies of the Future*, London/New York: Verso.

Lacan, Jacques (1977a): *The Four Fundamental Concepts of Psychoanalysis* (Alan Sheridan, Trans.), London: Penguin.

Lacan, Jacques (1977b): "Desire and the Interpretation of Desire in Hamlet." In: *Yale French Studies* 55/56, pp. 11-52.

Lacan, Jacques (2004): *Anxiety* (A. R. Price, Trans.), Cambridge: Polity.

Lyotard, Jean-Francois (1984): *The Postmodern Condition* (Geoff Bennington/ Brian Massumi, Trans.), Manchester: Manchester University Press.

Manovich, Lev (2001): *The Language of New Media*, Cambridge, MA/London: MIT Press.

Mathew, David (2002): "Vital Signs: Interview with M John Harrison." In: *Infinity Plus: SF, Fantasy, Horror*, (Infinityplus.co.uk/nonfiction/intmjh.htm).

Maturana, Humberto R./Varela, Francisco J. (1980): *Autopoiesis and Cognition*, Dordrecht, Holland/Boston: D. Reidel Publishing.

Mendlesohn, Farah (2008): *Rhetorics of Fantasy*, Middletown, CT: Wesleyan University Press.

Menkman, Rosa (2011): *The Glitch Moment(um)*, Amsterdam: Network Notebooks.

Miéville, China (2002): "Introduction." In: *Historical Materialism* 10/4, pp. 39-49.

Miéville, China (2011): "Afterweird: the Efficacy of a Worm-Eaten Dictionary."
In: Ann VanderMeer/Jeff VanderMeer (eds), *The Weird: A Compendium of Strange and Dark Stories*, New York: Tor Books, pp. 113-116.

Poole, Steven (2000): *Trigger Happy*, London: Fourth Estate.

Rucker, Rudy/Sirius, R. U./Queen Mu (eds.) (1992): *Mondo 2000: A User's Guide to the New Edge*, New York: HarperCollins.

Suvin, Darko (1979): *Metamorphoses of Science Fiction*, New Haven: Yale University Press.

Is the Fantastic Really Fantastic?

IRINA GOLOVACHEVA

1. INTRODUCTION

The notion of "the fantastic" is one of the most controversial issues discussed in literary and interdisciplinary studies. The notorious vagueness and elusiveness of the terms "the fantastic" and "fantasy," both of which can be understood at once in the narrow and the broad senses – either as a kind of fiction (a literary quality), a genre, or as an unreal (non-existent) phenomenon, a product of the imagination – results in numerous problems. Often, "the fantastic" is seen as the synonym for "fantasy." The latter, however, is sometimes defined as "a quality of astonishment" (Rabkin 1976: 41), as "an exciting or unusual experience" (*Macmillan English Dictionary for Advanced Learners* 2002: 503), or as an activity of imagining the impossible. Reacting to these definitions, Darco Suvin (2000) claims that interpretations of "fantasy" as a mental faculty are irrelevant. He is adamant in discarding fantasy as a psychological phenomenon or as a quality of the human imagination in theorizing the fantastic.

Terminological chaos has been characteristic of the theory of the fantastic for centuries (cf. Sander 2011). The term "the fantastic" has indeed been applied to a great number of radically different works of fiction. Until recently (that is, before John Clute's 2007 introduction of the new notion, "fantastika"), "the fantastic" had been a blanket term in European and American theory for any fantastic imagery in fiction produced in any historical period. "Fantasy" and "the fantastic" are used interchangeably, as if they were synonyms (cf. Jackson 1981). Attempting to avoid confusion and misunderstanding, some critics choose an alternative term, for example "fantastic fiction," or "fantastic literature," that are, in turn, employed in an undifferentiated way to designate a supergenre, a genre, or a subgenre. I believe that the usage of "fantasy," since it is such a polysemantic word, must be reconsidered in the studies of non-mimetic fiction. Perhaps, we should reserve the capitalized word "Fantasy" to function as a term, as a genre-name for Tolkien and post-Tolkien types of literature. For the same reason, I will also capitalize other genre-names in this paper.

The radically different understandings of the generic history, structure, and mode of fantastic texts result in different approaches to taxonomy. It seems an almost hopeless task to see clearly the use of the terms "the fantastic" or "fantasy," as well as that of much more inclusive ones: "fantastic genre" and "fantastic fiction." It is equally hard to decide which fantastic genre is more general and whether and why we should attest some sets of fantastic texts as forming genres or even supergenres and call other groups of more specific texts sub-genres. Most of the critics suggest that "fantasy" (used as a synonym of "the fantastic") is a genre (or generic area) since it is a part of a larger body of literature (cf. Mendlesohn 2008: xiii). But, there are also those who wittingly claim that "all fiction is, in a sense, science fiction" and that "fiction is a subcategory of science fiction rather than the other way around" (Freedman 2000: 16). Freedman argues that the qualities which are universally recognized in Science Fiction can be found in any work of literature. He provocatively concludes that "it may even begin to appear that ultimately nearly all fiction – perhaps even including realism itself – will be found to be science fiction" (ibid: 16). Some think that Science Fiction is a subgenre of Fantasy, while others claim that it is the other way around. Robert Scholes (1987) treats "fantasy" as literature depicting an internally coherent impossible world in which that tale is possible, whereas Katherine Hume (1984) sees it as a supergenre, synonymous to speculative fiction and including a variety of genres, like Science Fiction, etc. On her part, Cynthia Duncan (2010) uses the term "fantasy" to speak of the works of literature that deal with obviously invented worlds and supernatural beings. When Duncan speaks of "the fantastic," she associates it with fear or anxiety.

The situation is more complicated if either "the fantastic" or "fantasy" are applied to identify and research symbolic elements in modern and postmodern texts that draw special attention of the critics of the fantastic. John Clute, for example, specifies that these literary movements, standing aside from mimetic prose, use elements of "fantasy," but the worlds created by such writers do not invite the readers to co-inhabit the tale the way the authors of generic Fantasy do. For this reason, Clute insists that "to call Fantasy such 'enterprises of Modernism and Postmodernism'" is "to strip the term 'fantasy' of any specific meaning" (1997: 338). In accord with Clute, Darko Suvin claims that non-generic fantastical writings of Modernism and Postmodernism, as well as much self-conscious "high lit" should not be considered within the framework of the fantastic (2000: 216).

There are those who claim that "a single, stable definition of all these concepts is not even desirable" (Percec 2014: VIII). Others argue that the only point of departure for fantastic genre theory can be the individual text itself (cf. Clayton 1987). One of the problems of defining the genres of numerous modern fantastic texts results from their predominant cross-genre nature. Especially challenging for critics like Scholes is the "oxymoronic monster named science fantasy" (Scholes 1987: 5). Yet, as he believes, the blending of Science Fiction and Fantasy was brought about by the presumable need to place "the fantastic" into the strictly positivistic paradigm of science. Such blending, though, endangers not only terminology – this is a minor concern. It also undermines the true meaning of the word "scientific" in the name of the genre. Thus, the magic in Science Fantasy is given a 'scientific' explanation. The fact that the supernatural can be rationalized, however, does not necessarily lead to attributing the tale to Science Fantasy. For example, lycanthropy in *The Twilight Saga* (2005-2008) is explained as a supernatural quality of becoming a werewolf which is passed on genetically. However, the critics never qualify Stephenie Meyer's saga as Science Fantasy, but, instead, many offer a misleading, or empty, genre-name such as "Young Adult Fiction" (cf. Martens 2010; Priest 2013). This fails to reveal the overall generic quality of *The Twilight Saga* which is a contemporary Fantasy whose fantastic elements are only partly rationalized. Glen Duncan's contemporary Gothic Horror novel, *The Last Werewolf* (2011), also rationalizes lycanthropy. Here the disease is represented as caused by a virus and passed on to next generations. However, the fundamental difference between the two stories of shapeshifting lies in the fact that lycanthropy in Meyer's text is reinforced by presumed Native American natural magic rather than by the imagery of a naturalistically explained disease as in Duncan's novel.

It is worth noting, that a new genre needs at least four conditions to start functioning as such: the appearance of the interpretative community (Fish 1980), the coinage of the genre name, the growing awareness of the reading audience of the genre's fundamental differences from the already existing forms, and finally, the critics' understanding of the disruption of historical continuity and of the transformation of genre conventions. As Zgorzelski puts it, "almost every variant is the potential beginning of a new genre; but it is realized as such only when historical continuity is broken by the functional opposition of the variant to its historical roots" (1979: 297). The appearance of a new genre can be seen as the result of "estrangement," as the aesthetic phenomenon of breaching and defamiliarizing the older conventions recognized as genre habituation (cf. Shklovsky (1955 [1917]). One such defamiliarization found in cross-genres is the firm placement of monsters in the modern day with its cars, bikes, schools, colleges, hospitals, and cell phones, as in *The Twilight Saga* or in Neil Gaiman's *American Gods* (2001) and *Anansi Boys* (2005). Another is a comparatively new quality of modern Fantasy whose alternative world is hidden within our own: the world of wizards coexists with—or is actually found within—the world of muggles in J. K. Rowling's *Harry Potter* series.

Cross-genres of speculative literature may be truly entertaining. Yet, when we come across a pseudo-Science Fiction narration which the writer infests with wizards, we intuitively know that the implicit contract between the reader and the writer has been broken. When the two kinds of the fantastic blend, the cognitive dissonance is almost granted. One may even insist, as Darko Suvin (2000) does, that in such cases we get neither valid Science Fiction nor valid Fantasy.

However, hybrids do not make the task of genre definition any more difficult than early Science Fiction did. It took several decades of disputes to arrive at a universally accepted genre name in the 1930s and a more or less consistent definition of Science Fiction had not been established before the 1970s.

At this point in the debate it is feasible to pause and address two questions of fundamental importance: Do we really need the terminological limitations that we voluntarily imposed on ourselves? Why should we define the genres? As Cynthia Duncan remarks, "readers naturally expect critics to provide them with clear definitions that they can apply to the study of specific literary texts, but in the case of the fantastic, they are often left wanting" (Duncan 2010: 3). I believe that clear definitions are needed for the assessment of new writing by both the critics and the reading public. The latter would also, perhaps, be grateful if the former assisted them with very general formulas that would allow one 'to compare like with like' instead of comparing anything with everything – robots with goblins, UFOs with unidentified flying fairies. The regular and devoted reader of "fantastika" wishes to gain expertise, i.e. to be able to base his or her argument on examples. In a way, definitions do help. Despite the fact that they "form a parasitic sub-genre in themselves," as Patrick Parrinder poignantly observed (1980: 2), they offer important guidelines for both the critic who needs a clearly defined framework for the analysis and for the reader who aspires to tell a Science Fiction novel from a Fantasy or a Utopia one in order to evaluate the quality of similar texts. Besides being a truly entertaining and stimulating enterprise, the critical reading of fantastika makes a connoisseur, a Model Reader (in Umberto Eco's terminology); the process of decoding the meanings of a diverse repertoire of speculative fictions is hardly less thrilling than that of solving the "whodunit" problem in detective stories. Using Eco's argument made in *The*

Limits of Interpretation in which he employs Orwellian imagery, we might ask whether "the pleasures of the smart reading be reserved for the members of the Party; and the pleasures of the naïve reading reserved for the proletarians" (1994b [1990]: 98-99). As for critics, we do need established or reestablished terminology and definitions to be able to say certain things about the uncertain mode of narrating uncertain phenomena, to chart the literary fantastic territories or a single terrain by tracing specific fantasticality in order to see both singular and regular phenomena more clearly.

In the following I will (1) revise the basic terminology connected with the phenomenon of "the fantastic," and (2) discuss both the specific qualities and the degree of strangeness in major genres of fantastika with a special emphasis on the fantasticality in Utopia. This will allow me to answer two questions: a) Is the fantastic present in all genres? b) Does the presence of the fantastic in a text signify that the latter is a sample of a fantastic genre text?

2. Approaches to the Fantastic

When discussing a single text containing a "fantastic" element, we do not measure the degree of its fantasticality, such measurement being impossible. Instead, we can assess it pragmatically – whether intuitively or professionally – in relation to the general message, to the intended meaning as perceived in the writer-reader communication.[1] The readers and the critics recognize quite a variety of images as fantastic: Doppelgangers, monsters, time machines, cyborgs, wizards, demons, utopian, or dystopian societies. Are there any common features in the texts representing "the ghostly," "the grotesque," "the magical," "the futuristic," "the scientific," "the fairy," "the ideal," and "the nightmarish"? Is it appropriate that the works highlighting these phenomena are classified as belonging to the unified field of "fantastic fiction"? These questions bring us to the issue of "the fantastic" (fantasticality) proper.

When Roger Caillois (1965) discusses the fantastic in the first chapter, "Première Approche," of his *Au Coeur de Fantastique*, he makes the statement ex negativo by subtracting what is not fantastic from the story and the discourse. So, in his view, the remainder – the fantastic – is anything but the exact, i.e. real-

---

1 Farah Mendlesohn (2008: xv) believes that fantastic fiction is conditioned by genre expectations more than other areas of literature are. The early discussion of the necessity to balance the study of genre's internal construction *and* its function within the text-reader historical relationship is in Zgorzelski (1979).

istic, representation of objects and living beings. In his article "The Natural Fantastic" he qualifies the essence of the fantastic as the intrusion of "the unacceptable" into the trivial, established world, mundane reality: "The fantastic appears as the disruption of a natural order that is deemed impossible to disturb" (Caillois 2003 [1962]: 349). He emphasizes that "the Fantastic presumes a well-ordered universe ruled by the immutable laws of physics, astronomy, and chemistry" (ibid: 349). This means that the intrusion of the strange does not lead to the replacement of the naturalistic world by a totally different one where there is nothing but miracles. The established and acknowledged order of things, its regularity, is transformed by the irruption of the inadmissible.

Rosemary Jackson looks at the phenomenon of "the fantastic," or "fantasy" (she uses the terms interchangeably), from the opposite direction to that of Caillois, claiming that it expresses what is absent within a "dominant 'realistic' order" (Jackson 1981: 25). This is a completely different kind of negation. She underscores the elliptical nature of "the fantastic" that points toward subversion. However, the rich idea of subversion working especially well with the Gothic and Modernist texts, which is exemplified by Jackson's choice of texts for analysis, seems not to be so fruitful if applied to some other genres of fantastic literature, like Hard Science Fiction – "a form of imaginative literature that uses either established or carefully extrapolated science as its backbone" (Steel 1992: 1) – and High (Heroic) Fantasy. Ignoring all Science Fiction in her discussion of *the* fantastic, Jackson explains that "faery, or romance literature" does not reveal strong transgressive and subversive impulses, that it "move[s] away from the unsettling implications which are found at the center of the purely 'fantastic.' [...] [It] defuse[s] potentially disturbing, anti-social drives and retreat[s] from any profound confrontation with existential dis-ease" (Jackson 1981: 9).

Jackson approaches "the fantastic" (or, "fantasy") as an imaginative mode allowing to subvert some forms of reality. She explains the function of "fantasy" as that of tracing "the unsaid and the unseen of culture: that which has been silenced, made invisible, covered over and made absent" (Jackson 1981: 4). Following Jackson, Renate Lachmann (2002) speaks of "the fantastic" ("die Phantastik") as a mode of discourse on alterity, a narration that presents the impossible. I believe, in case we view "the fantastic" as a mode, we can include quite a few mimetic fictions (for example, the modern psychological novel) that contain fantastic elements, thus enriching the whole corpus of fantastic literature rather than limiting it to genre works. I doubt, however, that such an approach would make further discussion easier or more consistent.

"The fantastic" has been regularly characterized as the depiction of "the impossible" (cf. Irwin 1976; Rabkin 1976; Lachmann 2002). There is a notoriously misleading definition of genres offered by Rod Sterling in his role of the narrator of *The Twilight Zone* in the opening scene of *The Fugitive* (1962): Fantasy is the impossible made probable and Science Fiction is the improbable made possible. It is quite easy to discard this formula, since the notion of the impossible is so spectacularly challenged by both modern science and scholarship. Sterling's series itself exposed that he felt free to cross the genre borders, and that he could easily manipulate with both – the impossible and the improbable – indiscriminately and interchangeably in a single episode. Yet, even though the above definition was universally understood as "wrong" by the classics of Science Fiction theory, it is surprisingly echoed in recent works (cf. Wolfe 2004: 222-223). Moreover, we read such paradoxical statements as the following one: "any sufficiently immersive fantasy is indistinguishable from science fiction" (Mendlesohn 2008: 62). Mendlesohn comes to this seemingly illogical conclusion by reasoning that:

"The construction of the fully immersive fantasy requires the construction of concentric shells of belief that allow the reader to exist in a space outside the fictional world, but protected from the outer shell of 'unreality.' The most commonly recognized place to find this concentric construction is in science fiction [...] In that genre [...] the world must be logical and sealed." (ibid: 62)[2]

The notion of "belief" is a helpful tool in discussing "unreality." Indeed, no one can imagine a completely unreal (impossible) world having no connections with our recognizable world (cf. Fredericks 1978).[3] "The fantastic" distorts "the real" in different proportions for various thematic purposes and aesthetic goals as will be shown in the following discussion of fantastic genres. "Fantasy recombines and inverts the real, but does not escape it: it exists in a parasitical or symbiotic relation to the real. The fantastic cannot exist independently of that 'real' world" (Jackson 1981: 20). To sum up, it would be a gross simplification to claim that the presence of "the fantastic" (the impossible or the unreal) is the absence of mimesis.

Still, the notion of the (un)real is, no doubt, crucial for "the fantastic." It is worth noting here, as Wolfgang Iser (1993[1991]) and narratologists (cf. Eco

---

2   Mendlesohn considers China Miéville's *Perdido Street Station* (2000) a typical example of "immersive fantasy."

3   Monika Fludernik (2006) underlines that any narrative is a representation of a possible world.

1994a; Schmid 2010 [2005]) prove, that anything depicted in fiction is "fictive." Such a point of view makes Roger Caillois's ex negativo definition rather inefficient, however keen. If we accept the argument concerning the overall fictivity (or fictiveness) of literature, we can define "the fantastic" as "the superfictive," that is as literature exposing and emphasizing its basic fictitious nature. Indeed, if any piece of imaginative literature is a narration of a fictive story, characters, objects, etc., then the fantastic text is the one that manifests the highest degree of fictivity. Yet, such definition will hardly provide a solution to all the problems and misunderstandings that arise in theorizing the fantastic genres.

3. THE FANTASTIC IMAGERY AND FANTASTIC GENRES

Even a naïve reader can tell the difference between the narratives of robots and cyborgs, on the one hand, and those of ghosts and vampires, on the other. Even inexperienced readers would have no difficulty explaining in what sense *Pride and Prejudice* is different from *Frankenstein* and claim that the novel by Mary Shelley, in contrast to the one by Jane Austen, tells of fantastic discoveries (imparting life to non-living matter) and creatures (the Monster). The experienced (critical) reader would attribute *Frankenstein* either to the Gothic or to the early Science Fiction genre. Some may place it in the borderline genre combining Gothic Horror and Science Fiction. In fact, the publication of Shelley's novel in 1818 marked the appearance of this new genre (or sub-genre). That the generic differences are present in the collective perception is clear from publishing and fandom practice. Generic features are the ones that allow us to identify a fantastic text as Science Fiction, Fairy Tale, Fantasy or Gothic Horror, these being the time-honored terms for classification.[4]

A group of texts is taken to form a single genre if they share characteristics like themes (subject matter), narrative mode, and implied reading audience with a set of its expectations (cf. Stephens 1992). The discussion of the generic nature of fantastic literature is vital because it provides a major instrument of investigation and assessment. It is for this reason that genre taxonomy has been drawing the attention of many critics of speculative fiction including Tzvetan Todorov whose book on the topic became such a breakthrough. Yet, the very first, rather

---

4 Note that unlike the general readership, some critics (cf. Briggs 1977; Griffin/Moylan 2007; Williamson 2015) approach the genres from an evolutionary point of view, that is, they explore a genre's dynamic and diachronic nature. The issue of the evolution of genres, however, will not be discussed in the present paper.

misleading, sentence of Todorov's classic *Introduction à la Littérature Fantastique* illustrates the terminological chaos that still characterizes genre theory: "'The Fantastic' is a name given to a *kind* of literature, to a literary genre" (Todorov 1975 [1970]: 3, original emphasis). Does he equate "the kind" and "the genre"? In the following passages, he seems to be speaking of the fantastic as a supergenre in which he recognizes subgenres defined as "the uncanny" and "the marvelous," the names he adopted from Caillois. The taxonomy proposed by Todorov allowed critics to avoid previously straightforward and naive thematic classifications of fantastic literature. Still, the method suggested in *The Fantastic* turned out to be ineffective: since Todorov saw the "pure fantastic" as a borderline, an intermediary stage of hesitation between alternative explanations of the strange, i.e. between "étrange" and "merveilleux," he excluded an immense corpus of fantastic texts. Because of a very limited number of texts that Todorov chose for analysis, he was heavily criticized by Stanislaw Lem (1974) who discarded the structuralist's immanent single-axis scheme, which, he believed, could not embrace all kinds of fantasticality including Modern Fantasies and Science Fiction.

It is noteworthy that Todorov had to resort to a strictly thematic analysis in the chapters "Themes of the Self" and "Themes of the Other." Writing on "themes of the self," Todorov explored fantastic fiction dealing with metamorphoses, transgression, supernatural beings, and especially with "the transition from mind to matter" (Todorov 1975 [1970]: 114). "Themes of the other" in turn are related to sexuality, desire, sensual temptations, and to the demonic. A thematic approach, no doubt, is fruitful for the analysis of individual texts. However, the total, cumulative effect of these alternative (discursive or thematic) approaches is dubious since it produces hesitation: the critical reader has to choose between alternative – structural or hermeneutical – interpretations of the text. This can readily be tested by Todorov's treatment of Franz Kafka's *Metamorphosis* that seemingly resists the structural approach: neither of the Todorovian genres (the uncanny or the marvelous) is applicable. Besides, no matter how ingenious Todorov's classification is, neither encyclopedias nor the majority of the critics employ it while attributing the genres of individual fantastic texts, to say nothing of groups of texts. Generally, the standard genre-names, such as Gothic Horror or Fairy Tale, are used instead of "the uncanny," "the marvelous," and "the pure fantastic."

A more adequate term than Todorov's "the fantastic" seems to be "fantastika," first coined by John Clute in his address, "Fantastika in the World Storm," given in Prague in 2007 and later elaborated on in his 2011 study, *Pardon This*

Intrusion. The word "fantastika" is a borrowing from Slavic criticism.[5] Clute uses it as an umbrella term to describe "the literatures of the fantastic in the Western World" written approximately since the end of the 18th century "in a consciousness of their generic nature" (Clute 2017: 16). Clute suggests approaching fantastic genres as "centripetal domains for various *forms* of the fantastic" (ibid: 17). The replacement of "the fantastic" with "fantastika" really helps us avoid the vagueness of the former since it points towards different directions, to imaginative texts of every historic period – ancient mythology, folk tales, the Bible, medieval miracle stories, etc.

Apart from terminology, there is another fundamental problem, which is a lack of consensus among the theoreticians of fantastic fiction concerning chronology. We cannot discard the issue of chronology as insufficient since in many ways it is the history of the genre that shapes the framework for speaking about taxonomy. For instance, shall we consider Lucian's and Cyrano de Bergerac's tales of lunar voyages to be early examples of Science Fiction? Carl Freedman discusses the issue in his challenging book, *Critical Theory and Science Fiction*:

"Dante offers plausible scientific speculation as to the geography of hell in relation to that of the earth. [...] One might even argue that Dante and Milton, in the active interest they took in the scientific developments of their own times and places, are considerably more akin to Isaac Asimov and Arthur Clarke than to Wordsworth and T. S. Eliot. [...] It is in this sense of creating rich, complex, but not ultimately fantastic alternative worlds that Dante and Milton can be said to write science fiction." (2000: 15-16)

Freedman, as is clear, further blurs our idea of chronology. To get out of this kind of theoretical maze, John Clute specifies a more or less exact date of the birth of "fantastika": around 1800. So did Caillois who spoke of approximately the same date when, as he claimed, the scientifically minded society emerged and "the fantastic" began to function pragmatically and generically.

Fantastika is not only a handy invention, it seems to be indispensable for our terminological arsenal, since it comprises all fantastic genres, not only the three previously identified in criticism – Fantasy, Science Fiction, and Gothic Horror –,

---

5   The word "fantastika" is an umbrella Russian and Polish (cf. Lem 1970) term for all generic fantastical fiction. Before John Clute, it was used by Birgit Menzel (2005) to speak of Russian Science Fiction and Fantasy. Larisa Fialkova drew my attention to this early usage of the word "fantastika" in European criticism when we were discussing Clute's neologism at "The Fantastic Now" conference in Münster in 2016.

but sub-genres or cross-genres, too. As Charul Palmer-Patel remarks in the first issue of *Fantastika Journal*:

"There are places of overlap, of tangling and disorder. That is not to say that we should not differentiate and define genres within this Fantastika umbrella term [...] There is a scholastic necessity in defining genres: we must do so in order to demarcate the boundaries of our research, in order to say that 'these texts are within my purview because of x reasons.'" (2017: 22)

Despite Clute's confession of his discontent about the established genre-names, being the contributor and the editor of Hugo award-winning encyclopedias on two major fantastic genres – Science Fiction and Fantasy –, he would not initiate any radical change of the terminology (1993; 1995; 1997).[6] Though not revising the taxonomy of genres, he underscores the difference between genre texts on the one hand, and those he calls "fantastical narratives" on the other.

Viewing "fantastika" as a complex of several genre "formula stories" (Cawelti 1976) does not prevent our reconsidering the genre boundaries, which would depend on a synchronic or diachronic approach. No matter how difficult, since they tend to shift, the study of such boundaries must be based on plot structure, the setting, and the functions of the dramatis personae.[7]

4. Fantastika and the Fantastic

Does Clute's coinage of "fantastika" as a kind of non-mimetic and predominantly generic fiction resolve the terminological problems that are hampering our understanding of history, poetics, and pragmatics of the fantastic? The term "fantastika" is convenient for the designation of a specific kind of fiction written ap-

---

6　Clute and other editors of the new *Fantastika Journal* have solved the problem of synonymy in critical terminology by capitalizing genres as proper nouns to differentiate genre names, on the one hand, and emotion, impulse or effect (and mode), on the other. As has been stated in my Introduction, I follow their example.

7　The exemplary classic work that successfully discusses the connection of the plot structure to the functions of the dramatis personae is Vladimir Propp's *Morphology of the Folktale* (1968 [1928]). Another example is John Cawelti's (1976) successful analysis of more or less stable functions and plot structures that resulted in the very illuminating concept of genre formulas in popular fiction.

proximately after 1800 that is pragmatically and functionally different from mimetic prose. Still, I believe, the notion of "the fantastic" is equally indispensable, since it allows us to analyze the ways the writers construct the strange, the alien, the extreme (the excessive or the deficient), the abnormal, the destructive, and the unstable; in other words: anything that challenges the superficial and illusory stability of the world as perceived by a more or less sane individual or society.

The notion of "the fantastic" makes it possible to explore the marginal territories where the fantastic imagery penetrates "the real" as the latter is depicted in psychological, predominately mimetic, prose from 19th-century Romantic fiction on. By reconsidering "the fantastic" on new grounds we may as well pay tribute to Stanislaw Lem who coined two useful terms in 1971, later to be completely ignored by the critical community. Lem maintains that there are two kinds of literary fantasy (used synonymously with "the fantastic"):

"'final' fantasy as in fairy tales and SF, and 'passing' fantasy as in Kafka. In an SF story the presence of intelligent dinosaurs does not usually signal the presence of hidden meaning. The dinosaurs are instead meant to be admired as we would admire a giraffe in a zoological garden; that is, they are intended not as parts of an expressive semantic system but only as parts of the empirical world. In 'The Metamorphosis,' on the other hand, it is not intended that we should accept the transformation of a human being into bug simply as a fantastic marvel but rather that we should pass on to the recognition that Kafka has with objects and their deformations depicted a socio-psychological situation." (Lem 1973: 28)

When Gregor Samsa transforms into a huge insect, his new monstrosity manifests his inner state in "allegorical tenor" (cf. Suvin 2000). This kind of monstrosity is not related to the fantastic "otherness" found in *Frankenstein* or R.L. Stevenson's *The Strange Case of Dr. Jekyll and Mr. Hyde* (1886). The Kafkian beetle image is a "passing fantasy." Another example of an early modernist "passing fantasy" is the Doppelganger who features in Henry James's "The Jolly Corner" (1908), a tale of an immigrant's homecoming. The return of James's Spencer Brydon from Europe to his home in New York seems to set in motion a mental time machine. One day, while wandering around the labyrinth of the house, Brydon feels someone's ghostly presence and soon realizes that, in a sense, he is haunted by an "American version" of himself. His counterpart is not so much a ghost from the past as the visible embodiment of an alternative life in America that was not chosen by the protagonist. He is struggling with himself, or rather, with the part of himself that his mind has to exteriorize (cf. Zwinger 2008; Golovacheva 2013; Golovacheva 2017). This struggle represents a kind of mid-life crisis. Deciding not to wait for a collision, Brydon starts to pursue his "other self" around the house. Finally, Brydon sees the image and rejects it as his double, refusing to have anything to do with him. It is noteworthy that Sigmund Freud speaks of such lack of recognition and rejection in his classic article "The Uncanny" ("Das Unheimliche," 1919). By way of example, Freud describes his own experience: seeing and not recognizing his own reflection in the compartment's mirror – he took his own reflection for a stranger who mistook the door. He felt that he "thoroughly disliked the appearance" (Freud 1955 [1919]: 247) of "the double." Symptomatically, writing this story, James sought after self-knowledge and self-diagnosis, defined an internal conflict (typical of so many transatlantic writers), and cathartically (art-therapeutically) resolved it by shifting the physical episode into the sphere of speculative reality. I believe that this image of the double in James's "The Jolly Corner" is an example of "the fantastic" outside of "fantastika." Indeed, this short story cannot be viewed as a generic text, since the Doppelganger here is a case of a "passing fantasy" signaling the presence of a metaphoric, expressive meaning. One can hardly admire Brydon's double as a "final" fantastic image. Rather, James depicts a peculiar socio-psychological situation.

The distortions and projections found in the realm of "the fantastic" – outside the genre paradigm – reveal its great cognitive potential. Apart from representing the break in the acknowledged order of life, "the fantastic" also depicts phantoms and phantasma, the subversive activity of the human mind; it uncovers the terrible understories of the troubled or alienated self, the strange *lacunae*. It opens the heart of darkness, as is the case in another of Henry James's notoriously labyrinthine tales, *The Turn of the Screw* (1898). Here, the governess's ambition to be the sole guardian of the children and to protect them from the influence of evil spirits may be interpreted either as courageous behavior or as a pathological manifestation of her neurosis. The ambiguous account of the events in the governess' diary allows for controversial views of her mental state – no more and no fewer than those "for" or "against" psychopathological interpretations of *Hamlet*. The governess's cognitive problems are partly based on her two parallel, yet antagonistic, interpretations of what is going on in Bly. No less puzzling are the ghosts – in case they do appear. The issue of the ends and means of Peter Quint and Miss Jessel, the apparitions, is mostly neglected in criticism. If the presumption that the children have secret affairs with the ghosts is true, we have to find an explanation for the fact of their appearance to the governess. Would their invisibility not have been the best protection for the dark affairs? Indeed, by taking such a wrong turn they created a serious obstacle to their secret communication with Miles and Flora. Or, perhaps, it was the right turn – in case the ghosts aimed at driving the governess mad. James's exquisite technique of playing with "the fantastic" – the technique of "adumbration" – allowed him to balance controversial interpretations in order to prevent the reader from taking definitive conclusion.[8]

As the above examples show, "the fantastic," being the result of both fantasizing and discursive strategies, allows the writer to place the strange and the alien into the heart of the trivial in order to challenge the fundamental ontological stability of existence and interrogate the stability and integrity of the mind.

Despite the benefits that the use of both terms – "fantastika" and "the fantastic" – offer, the following questions remain unsolved thus far:

1. Is "the fantastic" present in any genre of fantastika?
2. Does the presence of "the fantastic" in the text signify that the latter is an example of fantastika?

Any kind of "the fantastic" (within or outside a fantastika genre) encourages the reader to reflect on an unknown reality that is open only to presentiment so far. The strange (*étrange*) initiates the process of cognition, of identifying, and explaining the origin and the intrinsic logic of an alternative world or a transformed reality. Are we able to recognize the genres of fantastika mostly because it is "the fantastic" that is different in each of them? I will address and attempt to answer these issues in the subsequent subchapters.

5. THE FANTASTIC IN GENRES: THEMES, MODES, AND TYPES OF COGNITION

As it has been noted in my Introduction, generic definitions are necessary for charting and demarcating the territories of "the fantastic" for research purposes. Let us begin with looking at what is perceived as qualities typically attributed to "the fantastic" in Gothic fiction. Undoubtedly, ghosts and monsters would be named among the primary constituents of the genre, apart from typically Gothic chronotopes, such as castles, convents, and haunted houses. Yet, apparently, monsters or specters as such do not alone predetermine the genre. For example, monsters in Science Fiction are represented to be a part of the natural order. As for ghosts, it is clear that the specter of Hamlet's father and the three witches do not place Shakespeare's tragedies *Hamlet* and *Macbeth* in the realm of Gothic

---

8   There are numerous critical works devoted to *The Turn of the Screw* (cf. Willen 1960; James/ Beidler 2011; Golovacheva 2014: 29-117).

horror. Neither does the devil who appears in the shape of Ivan Karamazov's double in Dostoevsky's *The Brothers Karamazov*. Rather, the latter example proves Todorov's argument that "the fantastic dissolves into the general field of literature" (1975 [1970]: 46). In fact, ghosts, doubles, and monsters often feature in texts that are hardly associated with any genre of fantastika. In Gothic Horror, the radically strange, like ghostly entities, connect the "realistic," that is, pre-dominately mimetically represented world, with the supernatural one. Ghosts, however, play a different role in *Harry Potter* because here they are depicted as regular inhabitants of the magical world. The role of the apparitions in Dickens's *Christmas Carol* differs radically from that of the supernatural visitors (or hallu-cinations) of James's governess in *The Turn of the Screw*, on the one hand, and from the role of Moaning Myrtle in the *Harry Potter* series, on the other. It is clear that such imagery is employed in various genres of fantastika, in Renais-sance drama, as well as in 19th-century psychological novels. These few exam-ples readily indicate that a thematic approach is hardly helpful in genre attribu-tion.

As for monsters, it was Mary Shelley who sanctioned the migration of an-thropomorphous monstrosity from the Gothic to Science Fiction and later to Fan-tasy (cf. Halberstam 1995). Since then, monsters have inhabited all genres – Sci-ence Fiction (*The Strange Case of Dr. Jekyll and Mr. Hyde*, 1885), Fantasy (*The Lord of the Rings*, 1949), and Gothic Horror (*Dracula*, 1897). In recent Fanta-sies, like *The Twilight Saga*, and in contemporary Gothic Horror, like *The Last Werewolf*, monstrosity signals the changing views on natural laws, anthropology, ethnicity, heredity, and transgression in identity and society. As we see, the the-matic type of strangeness as such does not shape the genre.

Maybe it is the analysis of the narrative modes that could provide the instru-ments for the differentiation of fantastic genres? The radically different modes of the fantastic are persuasively discussed in Renate Lachmann's *Erzählte Phantas-tik* (*Discourses of the Fantastic*). They are: "the objective fantastic" ("das objek-tive Phantastische") and "the subjective fantastic" ("das subjektive Phantas-tische") (Lachmann 2002: 22). She argues that the first category, "the objective fantastic," is manifested in Science Fiction and Utopia, both signaling manipula-tion of man through science and technology, through either an institution (state or government), science (technology, medicine), or an alien power (ibid: 8). Lachmann reads Science Fiction and Utopia as depicting an active, often aggres-sive, intrusion. She finds the second mode revealed in Gothic Horror, which speaks of the "indescribability" ("Nichtbeschreibbarkeit") and "immeasurabil-ity" ("Nichtmetrifizierbarkeit") of man (ibid: 8). In such texts, the reader either learns about or suspects the intrusion of ghosts, doppelgangers, or demons as the entities belonging to the supernatural world.

Unlike non-fantastic fiction, which Lachmann considers to be proto-anthropology, fantastic literature ("fantastika" in my terminology) crosses the borders of anthropological norms and can be discussed as meta- or anti-anthropology: "The man in fantastic discourse loses his/her human anthropology, he/she becomes either an agent or a patient of some alternative anthropology which turns him/her into a dreamer, a sleepwalker, a lunatic, or a monster" (ibid: 9).[9] However, I cannot agree with her that all "fantastika" would follow these principles. Insisting that "the fantastic" discards rationality, Lachmann ignores the fact that Science Fiction and Utopia place emphasis on rationality, logic, and positive cognizability, on the presence and "interaction of estrangement and cognition" (Suvin 1974: 255). In my view, the cognition of the marvelous (the strange, the inexplicable) in classic (hard and social) Science Fiction and in Utopia may even be followed by the state of "zero amazement" that results from the primarily logical assessment of how the counterfactual world is constructed.

Carl Freedman reconsiders and revises the notion of "cognition," insisting that we should speak of "cognition effect" rather than of cognition per se:

"The crucial issue for generic discrimination is not only epistemological judgement external to the text itself on the rationality or the irrationality of the latter's imaginings, but rather [...] the attitude *of the text itself* to the kind of estrangements being performed." (2000: 18, original emphasis).

Freedman compares J.R.R. Tolkien's *The Lord of the Rings* and C.S. Lewis's *Cosmic Trilogy*; this is not a random choice since both texts convey similar Christian values. Unlike Tolkien's saga, which Freedman believes to display a "non-cognitive disjunction" from the mundane world, Lewis's trilogy depicts such fantastic images as planetary angels as possible within the authors' actual environment. So, in Freedman's view, *Out of the Silent Planet* produces a cognition effect: "If theology is a science (if, to put it bluntly, Christianity is true) then the powerful estrangements produced by Ransom's adventures on Mars are wholly cognitive" (ibid: 17). Yet, it seems to me that the concept of a "cognition effect" takes us into the realm of the boundless "fantastic" where no genres are

---

9   "Der *phantastische* Mensch scheint seine Anthropologie zu durchkreuzen oder gar zu leugnen – er wird Agent und Patient einer alternativen Anthropologie, in der er als Träumer, Halluzinierender, Wahnsinniger, Monster auftritt" (Lachmann 2002: 9, original emphasis).

identifiable. Indeed, if alchemy is a science then the estrangement (transmutation) in Arthur Machen's "The Spagyric Quest of Beroaldus Cosmopolita" (1923) is cognitive. So is all the magic in *Harry Potter*.

Coming back to Science Fiction for the purpose of improving its definition as the fiction of cognitive estrangement and *novum*, I suggest supplementing it with the notion of "cognitive stability." This addition may be helpful as a generic attribution. Indeed, unlike the non-cognitive genres of Fantasy and the Gothic (with the exception of the "Explained Gothic"[10]), which are not aimed at explaining the irrationalist estrangements, Science Fiction insists on the necessity to explain the *nova*, to give a clue about their origin, to clarify "how we got there from here" (Gunn 2010: 9). Our definition of Science Fiction should by all means underscore the presence of estrangement (consistent strangeness), that is critically and logically cognized, as a dominant feature. Otherwise, if we accept Freedman's idea, we would equate the cognitive effect of such images as cyborgs, on the one hand, with that of elves and werewolves, on the other. The

---

10 In early Gothic fiction, magic or the supernatural sometimes turns out to be an explainable, quasi-magical, or, "staged," pseudo-magic as it is in Ann Radcliff's or Clara Reeves's novels. Her reader eventually finds out that the magic is fake. This type of "the fantastic" is characteristic of "the uncanny" in Todorov's classification. In contrast, the supernatural in Horace Walpole and M.G. Lewis is "accepted," i.e., the reader is not assisted with cognizing (finding explanation of) the nature and the origin of the bizarre event or phenomenon. Instead, he/she is supposed to take these for granted. Such texts are qualified as "marvelous." I have to remark that the latter category appears to me to be most obscure since, according to Todorov, it encompasses both Fairy Tales and Science Fiction, whereas it is evident that the cognition in these two genres cannot be identical or even similar because sane (critical) thinking is supposed to be able to distinguish between fact (invented *novum*), on the one hand, and mythology, on the other. Indeed, does not explanation require rationality? If it does, how can we place Fairy Tale and Science Fiction in the same category (as subgenres)? Todorov does not speak of Fantasy. However, it is this genre that fits his definition of "the marvelous." It works especially well for "immersive fantasy," since, according to Mendlesohn, there "the implied reader, although dependent on the protagonist's absorption of sight and sounds, is not required to accept his or her narrative" (2008: 1). Compare with Todorov: "In the case of the marvelous, supernatural events provoke no particular reaction ... in the implicit reader. It is not attitude towards the events described which characterize the marvelous, but the nature of these events" (1975 [1970]: 54).

horizon of critical evaluation of the genres of fantastika would be lost for us forever.

Freedman suggests defining Science Fiction as "a *recognizable* kind of fiction" (2000: 16). But again, the idea of recognizability can be applied to the imageries in the Gothic Horror, Fantasy, and Fairy Tale. "The fantastic" in Gothic Horror and in such weird tales as Edgar Allan Poe's "The Fall of the House of Usher" (1839) and "Ligeia" (1838) is recognizable but non-cognizable: the strange (the uncanny) almost never gets a rationalistic explanation. In the best Gothic or weird texts, the reader never ceases being puzzled. It is the persisting strangeness that accumulates the effect of horror or terror. Such oddity brings about astonishment that cannot be relieved by rationalistic cognition leading to catharsis and then, possibly, to the state of "zero amazement" (acceptance of the new reality). As for the strangeness found in non-generic, modern, and postmodern fiction, it is much less recognizable, and for this reason we should identify it as fantastic element, or "passing fantasy."

6. THE FANTASTIC IN UTOPIA

In order to address the second question poised in my Introduction – Is "the fantastic" present in any genre of fantastika? – I suggest discussing the genre of Utopia. Indeed, Utopia deserves special attention in my argument concerning fantasticality. Many scholars place Utopia either in the realm of Science Fiction or in its immediate vicinity (cf. Clute/Nicholls 1993). There seem to be good reasons to do so since the texts belonging to either genre depict alternative worlds in a cognitive continuum with our reality: the reader cognizes the *novum* there logically and critically. Still, the differentiation of Science Fiction and Utopia is a vastly disputed issue in the criticism of fantastika genres. The problem is rooted in literary history: Utopia is older than Science Fiction and the territory of Utopia is at once broader and narrower than that of Science Fiction. Indeed, any science-fictional story is a tale of "u-topia" and (or) "u-chronia" – of a non-existing space and time. Science Fiction pointed at and prepared the readers for the birth of the future world which had been previously envisioned in Utopias. Both Utopia and Science Fiction extrapolate the real and imaginary discoveries and inventions. Both genres are nourished by scientific revelations and discoveries. The genealogical closeness of Science Fiction and Utopia is based on the idea of extrapolation in these two genres. This belief still gets strong support (cf. Seed 2005; Parrinder 2000).

Among numerous definitions of Utopia, I prefer the one offered by Kenneth Roemer since it seems to be comprehensive and can be easily tested by examples of a variety of Utopian texts:

"My brief working definition of a literary utopia is: a fairly detailed narrative account of one or more imaginary communities, societies, or worlds. These fictional constructs represent radical, though identifiable, alternatives to the readers' cultures, and they invite iconoclastic and normative evaluations of those cultures." (1996: 393)

Curiously, Roemer does not speak of any fantasticality. The narrative accounts of imaginary community can be found in Science Fiction, in Fantasy, in mimetic fiction, or in non-fiction. So, the story is the only factor that distinguishes literary Utopia from non-literary texts featuring utopianism. Both types are based on some kind of extrapolation, but they can do without a radical *novum* (the impossible and principally unreal). Literary Utopia may or may not expose some strangeness which may be limited to minor exoticism. Consider in this respect Aldous Huxley's *Island*, in which the action is set in an imaginary South-Eastern territory. The oriental setting, though supplied with some exotic flora and fauna (e.g., talking birds – Mynahs), provides hardly more fantasticality than does a mundane rural area, a setting for the imaginary community depicted in another education Utopia, B. F. Skinner's *Walden Two* (1948). Both Utopias extrapolate certain science-based theories and methods. In principle, either educational approach – the one supported by Huxley and the other defended by Skinner – is possible.

In the "Introduction" to *Defined by a Hollow* (2010), Darko Suvin, despite his recent shift to political epistemology, views utopian fiction as a sociopolitical part of science fiction, as he did in earlier writings (cf. Suvin, 1979: 49). Sargent (1994), however, sees it the other way around: Science Fiction is a part (a subgenre) of Utopia.

More important seems to be Suvin's argument in support of utopia's dubious nature, we may say, of its "non-fantasticality":

"However, as soon as the blueprints and beliefs become localized and approach a narrative (as in much of the writing of utopian socialists), there is little delimitation provided by any definition of utopia I can think of. The usual escape clause is that utopia is *belles lettres,* or fiction, while Saint-Simon or Fourier are *lettres* or nonfiction. But that distinction [...], is historically a fugitive one." (Suvin 2010: 40)

Post-modern critical thought has been entertaining the idea that literariness is a common feature of any discourse, that actually there are no special characteristics that distinguishes literature from other texts (cf. Eagleton 2008 [1983]; Miall/ Kuiken 1998). So, apart from the blurring of the boundaries between literary genres, another kind of blurring is now recognized – the one between literature and other narratives (cf. White 1987; Todorov 2007 [1973]). Even though the latter is in many ways a fruitful conception, we should not neglect the existence of the specific pragmatics of the literary objectivity, which differs from that of science or philosophy.

In many cases it is almost impossible to tell whether a utopian text is just a non-fictional product of utopian imagination (as is in the writings of Plato, Marx, etc.), or a literary Utopia. For example, Thomas More's *Utopia* and Tomasso Campanella's *The City of the Sun* have been discussed as non-literary works (cf. Chordas 2010). The problem of searching for the boundaries of Utopia is complicated not only by the fact that they are blurred – there is nothing specific in such transparency of borders which we already discussed in connection with the Gothic, Science Fiction, and Fantasy. The main difficulty arises from the fact that so many Utopias can be realized in the future or even in practice right now. Some actually are. Still we certainly should go on calling them Utopias. But can we also call them "fantastic"? Even if we place them in the realm of "fantastika," we will not be able to discard the fact that the fantastic is not to be found in them. (On the contrary, leafing through the recent issues of *Science* or *Nature* journal, we are certain to discover fantastic predictions and to find the marvelous in a significantly higher proportion.)[11]

To illustrate the stance concerning the non-fantasticality of Utopia, we may look closely at Aldous Huxley's works that reveal the artificiality of the rigid distinction between such disciplinary genres as scientific writing and fiction on the one hand, and Science Fiction and Utopia, on the other. There are numerous correspondences between Huxley's literary discourse and the discourse of con-

---

11 Such, for example, are the papers theorizing the "many interacting worlds" (MIW) hypothesis in quantum mechanics and cosmology. Even well-known quantum mechanical phenomena, like wave-particle duality, or EPR paradox, still seem to be inconceivable, although proven by numerous experiments. In neuroscience, it has been taken for granted that certain cognitive skills, like "theory of mind," are characteristic of humans alone. However, a group of scientists (Krupenye et al. 2016) have advanced a hypothesis that great apes are also able to understand that others' actions are driven not by reality but by beliefs about reality.

temporaneous science. Virtually every *novum* in his Utopias is a reflection of scientific theories or practices.

Huxley called his *Brave New World* (1931) and *Island* (1962) "negative" and "positive" utopias respectively (Huxley 2001 [1963]). I will begin with the novel from 1931. In many respects, *Brave New World* was a response to the historical situation and typical concerns of the late 1920s. The novel reveals the surprising fusion of both Soviet and American realities – Bolshevism and Fordism (cf. Meckier 2001; Golovacheva 2000; Golovacheva 2015). This Russo-American amalgamation shaped the unique imagery of *Brave New World,* which led a few critics to read it as a critical commentary, rather than a future story.

Writing *Brave New World*, Huxley played over a vast and controversial ground of concepts that were entertained in hard and soft sciences. The novel drew from numerous publications and concepts advanced at the time by eugenicists, geneticists, psychologists, physiologists, and demographers. The "borrowings" that allowed Huxley to create his blueprint of a very successful futuristic civilization included Fordism, Freudianism, Pavlovian and Watsonian Behaviorism, Neo-Malthusianism, eugenics, and ectogenesis (cf. Firchow 1984; Baker 1990; Golovacheva 2008). This puts *Brave New World* in the closest proximity to Hard Science Fiction, rather than Utopia. It may even be considered as "only a framework for introducing the scientific concept to the reader" (Parrinder 1980: 23).

Yet, the utopian nature is unfailingly dominant in Huxley's work. It is not by chance that Huxley borrowed Berdyaev's words about utopias found in *Un Nouveau Moyen Âge* (Berdyaev 1927 [1924]) to use in the epigraph to the novel:

"Les utopies apparaissent bien plus réalisables qu'on ne le croyait autrefois. Et nous nous trouvons actuellement devant une question bien autrement angoissante: comment éviter leur réalisation définitive? [...] Les utopies sont réalisables. La vie marche vers les utopies. Et peut-être un siècle nouveau commence-t-il, un siècle où les intellectuels et la classe cultivée rêveront aux moyens d'éviter les utopies et de retourner à une société non utopique moins 'parfaite' et plus libre." (Huxley 1946[1931]): V)[12]

---

12 "Now, indeed, they [utopias] seem to be able to be brought about far more easily than we supposed, and we are actually faced by an agonizing problem of quite another kind: how can we prevent their final realization? ... Utopias are more realizable ..., and towards utopias we are moving. But it is possible that a new age is already beginning, in which cultured and intelligent people will dream of ways to avoid ideal states and to get back to a society that is less 'perfect' and more free" (Berdyaev 1933:187-188). Apparently, Huxley deliberately used the French version for the epigraph, leav-

As is clear from the above passage from Berdyaev and from the fact that Huxley chose these words to precede the novel, the author of *Brave New World* was conscious of the realizability of his blueprint.

Thirty years later, Huxley published his second utopian text where the action takes place in an exotic country. This second Utopia – "positive" by his own classification – is *Island*. This time, Huxley sends his protagonist to the East. The ideal country is placed on the island Pala, somewhere in the Indian Ocean not far from the Andaman Islands. Pala is populated by the descendants of Buddhist colonists who practiced Tantric religion. That *Island* offers a kind of mirror-image of *Brave New World* is well-known. It is curious that in *Island* the happy Palanese do not teach the protagonist, Will Farnaby, Yoga or Tantrism. They treat his neurosis and psychological trauma with the methods developed in the Western humanistic and existential psychotherapy which everyone on Pala, including the children, seem to be acquainted with. Besides, they employ the Ericksonean hypnosis to cure his anxiety disorder. The Palanese healers speak to Farnaby not as Yogins; rather, their speech and methods reveal their awareness of the concepts of Erich Fromm, Carl Rogers, and Abraham Maslow.

Huxley's infatuation with phenomenological psychology as well as with one of the schools of so-called humanistic psychotherapy is proven by the direct borrowings from Gestalt therapy books. In sum, *Island* differs greatly from contemporaneous works of fiction (including from other Utopias) since it deals with personal psychology, interpretations of the functions of the self, and the treatment of the latter's disorders rather than with interpersonal relations or social problems. Moreover, Huxley emphasizes his literary debt by pointing out that he borrowed some of his second wife's, Laura Archera Huxley, ideas for *Island*: "Some of her recipes (for example, those for the Transformation of Energy) have found their way, almost unmodified into my phantasy. Others have been changed and developed to suit the needs of my imaginary society and to fit into its culture" (Huxley 1963: XIII).

Island, unanimously perceived as Utopia, is filled with Gestalt therapy recommendations on training perceptual receptivity. Huxley apparently hoped to show what the basis for a genuinely realistic treatment of the mentally ill should be like. His positive Utopia focuses on the protagonist's obsessive neurosis, his mental history, and therapy. Thus, the author provides his readership with a completely new type of hybrid genre: The Utopian Psychotherapeutic Bildungs-

---

ing out several lines. It is quite possible that by quoting the Russian philosopher in French he intended to underline the transnational significance of his (anti)Utopia, whose message could only be fully grasped by erudite readers.

roman (cf. Golovacheva 2007; Golovacheva 2008: 115-134). The islanders' prosperity is based on a highly developed self-understanding and advanced psycho-therapeutic techniques rather than on social equality or a balanced economy. It is remarkable that despite his general dislike of Behaviorism, Huxley employed some Skinnerian recipes in the novel as well.

The anti-industrial state of Pala was meant to be taken for a possible social construction and a way of life. The novel actually was perceived as instruction, becoming a cult book in the Western world. Huxley must have realized that he supplied the reader with a new and attractive Utopia, which held out the hope of achieving genuine harmony by means of authentic self-understanding and individual as well as group psychotherapy. It was probably the first time that psychology – or, more precisely, its concepts – found itself in the very center of the literary scene. *Island*, as opposed to *Brave New World*, does not contain *novum*, i.e. there is no "discontinuity" that could guarantee such an emotional response as awe or wonder. The alternative world depicted in *Island* – the only fictitious utopian world, perhaps, worth living in – looks achievable not only because it is based on very promising scientific and humanitarian ideas, as well as realizable projects, but because there is nothing "fantastic" in the narrative.

Both Huxley's Utopias, viewed as canonical and exemplary of the genre, show that Utopia is radically different from Gothic Horror, Fantasy, and even Science Fiction, so that I doubt that there are reasons to include it into the list of fantastika genres. Indeed, such a major element as "the fantastic," when present in Utopia, tightly interlocks with both "the real" and "the possible." Moreover, the writer of Utopia strives to construct an alternative reality that lacks fantastic features. It is not the writer's aim to reach the effect of amazement and awe. Rather, he/she aims at depicting a truly plausible reality, be it positive or negative. Utopia, thus, rejects the conventions of fantastic fiction. If we still decide to follow the established critical tradition of including Utopia in the catalogue of fantastika genres, we must specify that it is more than often than not completely devoid of "the fantastic."

7. Conclusion

I have attempted to illuminate several aspects of the critical theory of "the fantastic," some of which arise from an outright terminological chaos. As a basis for further research in this field and for the sake of clarity, I suggest replacing the terms "the fantastic" and "fantasy," still employed interchangeably to denote all varieties of speculative fiction, with the term "fantastika" introduced by John

Clute for all generic literature that is pragmatically and functionally different from mimetic prose. The term "fantastika," besides accentuating the generic nature of such fiction, helps us to avoid the vagueness of the concepts of "the fantastic" and "fantasy" since they point towards different directions, that is, to imaginative texts of every historic period. Unlike these terms, Clute's "fantastika" denotes the texts written in the Western and Slavic world after 1800.

However, the introduction of the new term alone cannot work as a magic wand that would solve other theoretical problems by waving over volumes of speculative fiction. Analyzing generic and non-generic fantastic fiction, I arrive at the conclusion that in order to speak of fantasticality in literature, it is useful to employ both terms – "fantastika" and "the fantastic" – parallelly, and in this way distinguish the historically established genres, on the one hand, and the specific quality and the intensity (or, the degree) of strangeness found in major fantastika genres, on the other. Besides, the term "the fantastic" allows us to explore the specifics of cognition of the strange, the alien, and the extreme in various fantastika genres.

I also hope to have shown that the mere presence of "the fantastic" should not mislead us to label a work of fiction as an instance of fantastika. A brief analysis of two of Henry James's non-fantastika texts has shown how "the fantastic" functions in the marginal territories where it penetrates "the real." Finally, by emphasizing the genre of Utopia, I have supported my argument by indicating that an inherently fantastika text may indeed lack fantastic qualities altogether.

WORKS CITED

Baker, Robert (1990): "Brave New World": *History, Science, and Dystopia*, Boston: Twayne.

Berdyaev, Nikolai (1927 [1924]): *Un Nouveau Moyen Âge. Réflexions sur les Destinées de la Russie et de l'Europe*, Paris: Plon.

Berdyaev, Nicholas (1933 [1927]): *The End of Our Time* (Donald Attwater, Trans.), London, New York: Sheed & Ward.

Briggs, Julia (1977): *Night Visitors: The Rise and Fall of the English Ghost Story*, London: Faber.

Caillois, Roger (1965): *Au Coeur de Fantastique*, Paris: Gallimard.

Caillois, Roger (2003 [1962]): "The Natural Fantastic." In: Laudine Frank (ed.), *The Edge of Surrealism: A Roger Caillois Reader*, Durham/London: Duke University Press, pp. 348-358.

Cawelti, John (1976): *Adventure, Mystery, and Romance: Formula Stories as Art and Popular Culture*, Chicago/London: The University of Chicago Press.

Chordas, Nina (2010): *Forms in Early Modern Utopia: The Ethnography of Perfection*, Farnham: Ashgate.

Clayton, David (1987): "Science Fiction: Going Around in Generic Circles." In: George E. Slusser / Eric S. Rabkin (eds.), *Intersections: Fantasy and Science Fiction*, Carbondale: Southern Illinois University Press, pp. 201-226.

Clute, John (ed.) (1995): *The Illustrated Encyclopedia of Science Fiction*, London, New York: Dorling Kindersley.

Clute, John (2011): *Pardon This Intrusion: Fantastika in the World Storm*, Essex, UK: Beccon Publications.

Clute, John (2017): "Fantastika; or, The Sacred Grove." In: *Fantastika Journal* 1/1, pp. 13-20.

Clute, John / Grant, John (eds.) (1997): *The Encyclopedia of Fantasy*, New York: St. Martin's Press.

Clute, John/ Peter Nicholls (eds.) (1993): *The Encyclopedia of Science Fiction*, London: Orbit Books.

Duncan, Cynthia (2010): *Unraveling the Real: The Fantastic in Spanish-American Ficciones*, Philadelphia: Temple University Press.

Eagleton, Terry (2008 [1983]): *Literary Theory: An Introduction*, Minneapolis: Minnesota University Press.

Eco, Umberto (1994 a): *The Limits of Interpretation*, Bloomington, Indianapolis: Indiana University Press.

Eco, Umberto (1994 b): *Six Walks in the Fictional Woods*, Cambridge, MA: Harvard University Press.

Firchow, Peter (1984): *The End of Utopia: a Study of Aldous Huxley's "Brave New World,"* Lewisburg, PA: Bucknell University Press.

Fish, Stanley (1980): *Is There a Text in This Class?: The Authority of Interpretative Communities*, Oxford, MA/London: Harvard University Press.

Fludernik, Monika (2009 [2006]): *An Introduction to Narratology*, London/New York: Routledge.

Fredericks, S. C. (1978): "Problems of Fantasy." In: *Science Fiction Studies* 5/1, pp. 33-44.

Freedman, Carl (2000): *Critical Theory and Science Fiction*, Middletown, CT: Wesleyan University Press.

Freud, Sigmund (1955 [1919]): "The Uncanny." In: John Strachey (ed.), *The Standard Edition of the Complete Psychological Works of Sigmund Freud.* Vol. XVII (1917-1919): *An Infantile Neurosis and Other Works*, London: Hogarth Press, pp. 217-256.

Golovatcheva, Irina (2000): "A Perfect Psychology for a Perfect Society." In: *"Nature's Nation" Reconsidered: American Concepts of Nature from Wonder to Ecological Crisis.* Abstracts of EAAS Biennial Conference, Graz: Karl-Franzens-Universität, pp. 50-51.

Golovacheva, Irina (2007): "Theories of the Mind and Psychotherapy in the Works of Aldous Huxley." In: Bernfried Nugel/ Lothar Fietz (eds.), *Aldous Huxley Man of Letters: Thinker, Critic and Artist*, Berlin: LIT, pp. 123-139.

Golovacheva, Irina (2008): *Nauka i literatura: archeologija nauchnogo znanija Oldosa Huksli*, Sankt-Petersburg: St. Petersburg University Press.

Golovacheva, Irina (2014): *Fantastika i fantasticheskoje: poetika i pragmatika angloamericamskoj fantasticheskoj literatury*, St. Petersburg: Petropolis.

Golovacheva, Irina (2015 [2014]): "Huxley, Blok and Berdyaev: Observations on the Nature of the Russian Revolution." In: *Aldous Huxley Annual* 14, pp. 125-135.

Golovacheva, Irina (2017): "Bitva alter ego: ot Po do Genri Jeimsa." In: Alexandra Urakova/ Sergei Fokin (eds.), *Po, Bodler, Dostoyevski: blesk i nischeta natzionalnogo genija*, Moskva: Novoje Literaturnoe Obozrenie, pp. 176-188.

Griffin, Michael J./Moylan, Tom (eds.) (2007): *Exploring the Utopian Impulse: Essays on Utopian Thought and Practice*, Bern: Peter Lang.

Gunn, James (2010): "Toward a Definition of Science Fiction." In: James Gunn/ Mathew Candelaria (eds.), *Speculations on Speculation: Theories of Science Fiction*, Lanham, MD: Scarecrow Press, pp. 5-12.

Halberstam, Judith (1995): *Skin Shows: Gothic Horror and the Technology of Monsters*, Durham: Duke University Press.

Hume, Katherine (1984): *Fantasy and Mimesis: Responses to Reality in Western Literature*, Methuen: Routledge.

Huxley, Aldous (1946 [1931]): *Brave New World*, New York: Harper & Row.

Huxley, Aldous (1963): "Foreword," In: Laura Archera Huxley, *You Are Not the Target*, New York, pp. XI-XIV.

Huxley, Aldous (2001 [1963]): "Utopias, Positive and Negative." In: *Aldous Huxley Annual* 1, pp. 1-9.

Irwin, William Robert (1976): *The Game of the Impossible: Rhetoric of Fantasy*, Champaign: University of Illinois Press.

Iser, Wolfgang (1993 [1991]): *The Fictive and the Imaginary: Charting Literary Anthropology, or, What's Literature Have to Do with It?*, Baltimore: Johns Hopkins University Press.

Jackson, Rosemary (1981): *Fantasy: The Literature of Subversion*, London/New York: Methuen.

James, Henry/Beidler, P. G. (ed.) (2011): *The Turn of the Screw: Complete, Authoritative Text with Biographical, Historical and Cultural Contexts, Critical History, and Essays from Contemporary Critical Perspectives*. 3rd. ed., Boston: Bedford-St. Martins.

Krupeneye, Christopher/Kano, Fumihiro/Hirata, Satoshi/Call, Joseph/Tomasello, Michael (2016): "Great Apes Anticipate that other Individuals Will Act According to False Beliefs." In: *Science* 354/6308, pp. 110-114.

Lachmann, Renate (2002): *Erzählte Phantastik: Zu Phantasiegeschichte und Semantik fantastischer Texte*, Frankfurt am Main: Suhrkamp.

Lem, Stanislaw (1970): *Fantastyka i futurologia*. Sv. 1-2, Krakow: Wydawnictwo Literackie.

Lem, Stanislaw (1973): "On the Structural Analysis of Science Fiction." In: *Science Fiction Studies* 1/1, pp. 26-33.

Lem, Stanislaw (1974): "Todorov's Fantastic Theory of Literature." In: *Science Fiction Studies* 1/4, pp. 227-237.

Macmillan English Dictionary for Advanced Learners (2002), Oxford: Macmillan Education.

Martens, Marianne (2010): "Consumed by Twilight: The Commodification of Young Adult Literature." In: Melissa A. Click/Jennifer Stevens Aubrey/Elizabeth Behm-Morawitz (eds.), *Bitten by Twilight: Youth Culture, Media, & the Vampire Franchise*, New York: Peter Lang, pp. 243-260.

Meckier, Jerome (2001): "Aldous Huxley's American Experience." In: *Aldous Huxley Annual* 1, pp. 227-239.

Mendlesohn, Farah (2008): *Rhetorics of Fantasy*, Middletown, CT: Wesleyan University Press.

Menzel, Birgit (2005): "Russian Science Fiction and Fantasy Literature." In: Stephen Lovell/Birgit Menzel (eds.), *Reading for Entertainment in Contemporary Russia: Post-Soviet Popular Literature in Historical Perspective*, München: Otto Sagner, pp. 117-150.

Miall, D. S./Kuiken, D. (1998): "The Form of Reading: Empirical Studies of Literariness." In: *Poetics* 25, pp. 327-341.

Palmer-Patel, Charul (2017): "Excavations of Genre Barriers: Breaking New Ground with Fantastika Journal." In: *Fantastika Journal* 1/1, pp. 21-35.

Parrinder, Patrick (1980): *Science Fiction: Its Criticism and Teaching*, New York: Methuen.

Parrinder, Patrick (ed.) (2000): *Learning from Other Worlds: Estrangement, Cognition, and the Politics of Science Fiction and Utopia*, Liverpool: Liverpool University Press.

Percec, Dana (2014): "Foreword." In: Dana Percec (ed.), *Reading the Fantastic Imagination: The Avatars of a Literary Genre*, Newcastle upon Tyme: Cambridge Scholars, pp. VIII-XIV.

Priest, Hanna (2013): "'Hell! Was I Becoming a Vampyre Slut?': Sex, Sexuality and Morality in in Young Adult Vampire Fiction." In: Deborah Mutch (ed.), *The Modern Vampire and Human Identity*, Basingstoke, UK/New York: Palgrave Macmillan, pp. 55-75.

Propp, Vladimir (1968 [1928]): *Morphology of the Folktale*, Austin: University of Texas Press.

Rabkin, Eric S. (1976): *The Fantastic in Literature*, Princeton, NJ: Princeton University Press.

Roemer, Kenneth M. (1996): "Utopian Literature, Empowering Students, and Gender Awareness." In: *Science Fiction Studies* 23/3, pp. 393-405.

Sander, David (2011): *Critical Discourses of the Fantastic, 1712-1831,* Burlington: Ashgate.

Sargent, Lyman Tower (1994): "The Three Faces of Utopianism Revisited." In: *Utopian Studies* 5/1, pp. 1-37.

Schmid, Wolf (2010 [2005]): *Narratology: An Introduction* (Alexander Starritt, Trans.), Berlin/New York: De Gruyter.

Scholes, Robert (1987): "Boiling Roses: Thoughts on Science Fantasy." In: George E. Slusser/Eric S. Rabkin (eds.), *Intersections: Fantasy and Science Fiction*, Carbondale/Edwardsville: Southern Illinois University Press, pp. 3-18.

Seed, David (ed.) (2005): *A Companion to Science Fiction*, Malden, MA: Blackwell.

Shklovsky, Viktor (1955 [1917]): "Art as Technique." In: Victor Erlich (ed.), *Russian Formalism: History, Doctrine*, The Hague: Mouton, pp. 15-30.

Stephens, John (1992): *Reading the Signs: Sense and Significance in Written Texts*, Sydney: Kangaroo Press.

Suvin, Darko (1974): "Radical Rhapsody and Romantic Recoil in the Age of Anticipation: A Chapter of the History of SF." In: *Science Fiction Studies* 1/4, pp. 255-269.

Suvin, Darko (1979): *Metamorphoses of Science Fiction: On the Poetics and History of a Literary Genre*, New Haven, CT: Yale University Press.

Suvin, Darko (2000): "Considering the Sense of 'Fantasy' or 'Fantastic Fiction': An Effusion." In: *Extrapolation* 41/3, pp. 209-47.

Suvin, Darko (2010): *Defined by a Hollow: Essays on Utopia, Science Fiction and Political Epistemology*, Bern: Peter Lang.

Todorov, Tzvetan (1975 [1970]): *The Fantastic: A Structural Approach to a Literary Genre* (R. Howard, Trans.), Ithaca: Cornell University Press.

Todorov, Tzvetan (2007 [1973]): "The Notion of Literature." In: *New Literary History* 38/1, pp. 1-12.

White, Hayden (1987): *The Content of the Form. Narrative Discourse and Historical Representation*, Baltimore, MD: Johns Hopkins University Press.

Willen, Gerald (ed.) (1960): *A Casebook on Henry James's 'The Turn of the Screw,'* New York: Crowell.

Williamson, Jamie (2015): *The Evolution of Modern Fantasy: From Antiquarianism to the Ballantine Adult Fantasy Series*, New York: Palgrave Macmillan.

Wolfe, Gary (2004 [1982]): "The Encounter with Fantasy." In: David Sandner (ed.), *Fantastic Literature: A Critical Reader*, Westport, CT/London: Praeger, pp. 222-235.

Zgorzelski, Andrzej (1979): "Is Science Fiction a Genre of Fantastic Literature?" In: *Science Fiction Studies* 6/3, pp. 296-303.

Zwinger, Linda (2008): "'*treat* me your subject': Henry James's 'The Jolly Corner' and I." In: *The Henry James Review* 29/1, pp. 1-15.

Insurgent Utopias: How to Recognize the Knock at the Door

LARISSA LAI

I am attuned to the critique progressive people sometimes make, that we are full of a capacity to articulate what is wrong with the world without a plan to set things right. Here, I turn to the concept of "utopia" to see if there is anything it can offer us now in a period that Peter Thompson calls a "Gramscian interregnum in which the old world of the absolute hegemony of capitalism and its ideology is dying, but a new world [...] has not emerged to replace it" (2). Our historical moment is marked by such a strange combination of religious fundamentalisms, the death throes of neoliberalism, the rise of China, the hegemony of the twitter feed, the sinister and biopolitical rule of the secret and not-so-secret police, white backlash, government by troll, but also by the heartening if sometimes unpredictable work of social movements like Idle No More, Black Lives Matter, and anti-rape movements. Committed to a progressive politics and a journey into a better world for humans, non-humans and the planet, I am interested in contemporary drives towards a certain utopian purity, especially as they manifest in certain racialized communities in a Canadian/Turtle Island[1] context. I am specifically concerned with the questions of "how we get there from here," and part of that has to do with what we pay attention to and what we do not, what we push to the foreground and what we relegate to the background. Nevertheless, there is a certain pragmatic realpolitik that I engage in order to recognize the present moment, and to recognize where public discourse stands. I tread carefully because I do not wish to exacerbate the polarization that has overtaken

---

1 "Turtle Island" is the original name of the landmass that Europeans call "North America."

public life in the territories of Turtle Island north of the 49th parallel. What I wish to foreground here are the stances taken by cultural activists in the wake of four recent Canadian/Turtle Island scandals, and specifically what kind of society is implicitly imagined in these stances.

Smaro Kamboureli's concept of "scandal," as a confounding of "fact" with "project" (2009: 89), offers a diagnostic measure of the contemporary. Thinking about Canadian multiculturalism, Kamboureli describes scandal as a "dramatization [...] of conflicts in ways that enact and mobilize the historically and psychologically rooted anxieties of the dominant society" (ibid: 88). The first scandal of this essay's present, then, is the one in which novelist and professor Stephen Galloway, in 2015, was implicitly accused of sexual abuse by the administration of the University of British Columbia, which was followed by a letter signed by many well-known Canadian writers in support of due process, which in turn was followed a counter-letter from a different group of Canadian writers and academics condemning the initial letter for undermining the case of the student complainants against Galloway. The second scandal broke out when Hal Niedzviecki, then editor of the Writers' Union of Canada's magazine *Write* proposed, in the editorial of a special issue devoted to Indigenous writers in 2017, an "Appropriation Prize" for "best book by an author who writes about people who aren't even remotely like her or him" (4). Harkening to older, liberal notions of freedom of the imagination and free speech, that call bumped up against a recognition by many progressive people that a productive understanding of cultural appropriation has its roots in the disjuncture between the liberal ideal of universal access to public voice and the political and historical fact of land theft, genocide and cultural exclusion, primarily against Indigenous peoples. When these critiques were levelled, Niedzviecki resigned his post as editor of *Write* magazine, but not without the appalling secondary scandal of several highly-placed white writers proposing in public to fund the appropriation prize. The third scandal, related to the first, emerged more slowly before rapidly picking up steam as the well-known writer of *Through Black Spruce* and *The Orenda*, Joseph Boyden, came to the defense of Stephen Galloway. Initial queries about the "boys club" looking after its own evolved into a query on how Indigenous Boyden actually was and whether or not he comes by the stories he tells and makes a career of in a good way, or whether he is appropriating stories that belong properly to the communities from which they emerge. Can he, or can he not, claim to speak from those communities? The fourth, and most personally painful scandal, erupted at the conference Mikinaakomins/TransCanadas organized by Smaro Kamboureli and myself, when Rinaldo Walcott queried the absence of Black women on plenary panels. Walcott's critique was valid in that, though we had programmed Black women into keynote, plenary reading and parallel sessions, the Black scholars on the plenary panels were men. Although it involved many Indigenous, Black, Arab and Asian scholars and students, the gathering itself also had many white participants, thus reflecting the demographic of the Canadian state. Nonetheless, the fact that the conference was expressly organized to address issues of land expropriation, disease, genocide, slavery, exclusion, indentureship, residential schools, resource extraction, and the banning of cultural practices, and actively included and held up Indigenous, Black, Asian, and Arab scholars and writers, got bizarrely swept under the carpet. That the conference was implicitly reframed as "white" strikes me as an odd falsification.[2] Lest it seem that, as one of the organizers, I protest too much, I recognize that the conference was far from perfect. I affirm Walcott's broader critique, that at the root of the social, cultural and political life of the Canadian state lies the exclusion, enslavement and death of Black people in all their complexity and multiplicity. The last thing I want to do is play into the hands of a rising white supremacy, which I acknowledge as real and dangerous. I also acknowledge the complexity of Black lives in the Americas through a range of human experience, as well as a long history of relationships both historical and personal through Black and Asian locations. These are largely under-discussed and under-researched, and a remedy for this is deeply necessary.

In this essay, I lay out these scandals not so much to resolve them in their own terms, as others have already written extensively and productively on that front.[3] I believe that action is required, and engage that work through non-textual

---

2   An essay entitled "The Unbearable Whiteness of CanLit" by Paul Barrett, Darcy Ballantyne, and Camille Isaacs in *The Walrus* on the important work of the recently deceased Austin Clarke takes up Walcott's nuanced recognition of Black life as foundational to Canadian Literature, a recognition I would agree with, insofar as I agree with foundations as a way of understanding knowledge formations. However, in the slip between a nuanced essay and the title of the essay, the racial complexity of Mikinaakominis/TransCanadas is undermined. The real and important outrage of Barrett, Ballantyne, and Isaacs gets instrumentalized through the title of the essay as fodder for Twitter. This writer has no way of knowing whether Barrett, Ballantyne and Isaacs composed the title or whether the magazine editors did. Perhaps it does not matter. There is a question of circulation in the era of social media that is seriously in need of address.

3   While this essay does not foreground these scandals, I include a few references to them in my bibliography for readers who are interested. Please see articles and essays by Joseph Boyden, Debra Huron, Marsha Lederman, and Darcy Lindberg. This list is

means. Here, I want to query the implicit imagination of what kind of society is possible in the wake not just of the scandals, but of the histories that produce them, and to locate the modest labor of this essay in its contemporary cultural climate. Specifically, I lay out the role that utopian fictions might play in the move to a better place.

I argue that literature, particularly speculative fiction, has something to show us in relation to the work of eruption, or what John Rajchman (via Deleuze) has called the "knock at the door" (1999: 47), a moment of contingent arrival, not a teleological end, but a double-edged sword that crystallizes hope for an instant, or offers a sign of wonder. Such a knock, or sign, or figure, or eruption is open to co-optation, destruction, bastardization, incorporation, death, or defusal, and yet, when it bursts through, it offers the powerful possibility of critique – narratively or discursively, in its very materiality. The materiality of the rupture is important because it is attached to embodied history. As we drive, for instance, towards the take-down of a publicly posted letter, what is produced in terms of the empowerment of young women? Should our students' vindication be a goal, regardless of what it takes to get there? What is produced as apparent by-product or, better, unexpected flow? I suggest here that the by-products and flows move and shift the interlocking social, ecological, political, and financial systems in which we are all embedded, but not necessarily in just or even ways.

In this essay, then, I remain elliptically attentive to the work of contemporary call-out culture and that phenomenon that Rey Chow described in the 1990s as "the fascist longing in our midst" in which "those who most violently denounce fascism – who characterize others as fascists – may be themselves exhibiting symptoms of fascism" (17). If such remarks strike us as incendiary, perhaps they are. Certainly, we are witnessing a moment in which the work of dialectical movement from thesis to anti-thesis and back again seems to be driving our public intellectual life. It is a dialectics hopped up on the fast-moving qualities of social media – Marx and McLuhan rolled together to produce intense affect. Chow is thinking specifically here of anti-racist activist and intellectual communities in 1990s America; conditions at present have not changed so very much. The programmatic calls in much of contemporary anti-racist community remains troubled by a politics of utopian purity and its attendant idealistic longings. Frustrating though this dynamic might be, we cannot let it go because the work of human and non-human liberation is profoundly tied to these utopian dreams.

---

by no means exhaustive but rather gestures to a long and painful conversation in Canadian/Turtle Island public and private arenas.

Utopian fictions can be useful to give shape to those dreams, and can narratively play them out, illustrating possibilities and pitfalls, but also exceeding and complicating through story the understandings we receive through the discourse of programmatic politics. With the British SF critic Tom Moylan, I contend that contemporary utopian fiction must be understood first and foremost as a critique of contemporary society and culture. His much-cited call to understand utopian fiction not as blueprint but as dream (10) remains of crucial importance in the face of the contemporary violence and the response to it. The "dream" is never perfect. For instance, while Thomas More's *Utopia* offers a fictional respite from the horrors of the Industrial Revolution in Europe, it reveals itself as one that finds hope in what turns out to be European imperialism. Ernst Callenbach's *Ecotopia* (1975) is a green response to 20th-century consumer excess, but one that turns out to be riddled with appalling (and sometimes hilarious) sexism. And my personal favorite, Marge Piercy's *Woman on the Edge of Time* (1976) offers a utopia that is her imagining of the opposite of capitalist patriarchy, in favor of a social and sexual commons that does not erase cultural history but separates it from the bodies who carry that history. It attempts to create a universal experience of motherhood, and a just and even experience of racial difference. The necessity of understanding cultural history as embodied and intergenerational was not an ideal in the moment of that novel's writing as it is now.

Through Moylan's concept of "the critical utopia," I recognize, with him, the necessity in this historical moment for a commitment to ideals, but also the necessity of eyes, ears, and perhaps noses and the skin itself, attuned to the unexpected eruptions that can burst or bubble up from actions taken in the pursuit of well-imagined futures. This is a Deleuzian gesture, taken up by many contemporary critics, writers, activists, and philosophers including the critical geographer David Harvey, who offers us the notion of the "insurgent architect" as a figure who retains a commitment to a certain idealism while attending to the possibilities and gifts that can appear unbidden through the combined action of disparate forces.

Let me explain. We need both aesthetic sensibility and attentiveness to history to recognize the utopian gift when with appears. The philosopher John Rajchman calls upon us insurgent architects to be attentive to "the knocking at the door":

"A 'history of the present' is a history of the portion of the past that we don't see is still with us. Thus it involves a concept of historical time that is not linear and is not completely given to consciousness, memory, commemoration [...] 'Not to predict, but to be attentive to the unknown that is knocking at the door.'" (Rajchman quotes Deleuze in Grosz 1999: 47)

You have to know when the knock comes, and recognize it at such. Further, it is connected to history, though not necessarily in ways we might expect. Vanished in such a model of the future are the planned economies of 20th century socialist states, but also the unfreedom of a Los Chicago Boys-style free market economy in which the economy is idealized as fully self-regulating.

Of course, as Elizabeth Grosz observes, the point of the unpredictable knock is that one cannot pre-arrange it. In moving towards a utopian ideal, there is a gamble involved. The knock at the door could just as easily signal the arrival of the police as the arrival of the ideal society. She writes:

"This is a most disconcerting and dangerous idea: politics seems to revel in the idea of progress, development, [and] movement, but the very political discourses that seem to advocate it most vehemently (Marxism, feminism, postcolonial and anticolonial discourses, the discourses of antiracism) seem terrified by the idea of a transformation somehow beyond the control of the very revolutionaries who seek it, of a kind of 'anarchization' of the future. If the revolution can carry no guarantee that it will improve the current situation or provide something preferable to what exists now, what makes it a sought after ideal? What prevents it from blurring into fascism or conservativism?" (Grosz 1999: 17)

What I want to argue here is that literature, and specifically speculative fiction literature, whether properly "utopian" or not, has a role to play in the unfolding of attention required to recognize the "knock at the door." Indeed, it is attention that is required. If utopia cannot be a total system, if it has limited spatial and temporal qualities, how can we know when it is knocking? Fredric Jameson is useful here in the distinction he makes between two lines of descent from More's Utopia, "one intent on the realization of the Utopian program, the other an obscure yet omnipresent Utopian impulse that finds its way to the surface in a variety of covert expressions and practices" (2005: 3). For him, Utopia is a temporary spatial eruption in time:

"Utopian space is an imaginary enclave within real social space, in other words, the very possibility of Utopian space is itself a result of spatial and social differentiation. But it is an aberrant by-product, and its possibility is dependent on the momentary formation of a kind of eddy or self-contained backwater within the general differentiation process and its seemingly irreversible forward momentum." (ibid: 15)

Further, to enter such an enclave requires a kind of blindness:

"Utopians [...] reflect [...] non-revolutionary blindness as to possible modifications of the power system; and this blindness is their strength insofar as it allows the imagination to overleap the moment of revolution itself and posit a radically different 'post-revolutionary' society." (ibid: 16)

For Jameson, critical spaces of thought are one kind of enclave. But the speculative fiction novel can clearly be another. Indeed, the way in which Jameson describes the utopian enclave bears much similarity to Ursula LeGuin's description of *The Left Hand of Darkness* (1969) as a thought-experiment. In her introduction to that novel she says, "[t]his book is not extrapolative. If you like, you can read it, and a lot of other science fiction, as a thought experiment" (LeGuin 1969: i-ii). I would suggest in fact, that what matters is the work of thought and imagination – the work of "overleaping" rather than arrival. The utopian enclave belongs to a temporality that is always beside us – a self-contained eddy indeed, always moving in multiple directions.

To think of the new utopianism as a kind of insurgency in thought, then, is to think of it as the combined action of idealistic thought, critical thought, and narrative experiment. Writing in the mid-1980s, but looking back on the early 1970s, Tom Moylan articulates the "critical utopia" through the "social" speculative fictions of Russ, LeGuin, Piercy, and Delany. He says, "the new novels negated the negation of utopia by the forces of twentieth century history: the subversive imagining of utopian society and the radical negativity of dystopian perception is preserved; while the systematizing boredom of the traditional utopia and the cooptation of utopia by modern structures is destroyed" (1986: 10). For him the critical utopia is marked by an awareness of the limitation of the utopian tradition. In that moment, however, the critical utopia is still a humanist project. Moylan says:

"The general oppositional vision is challenging corporate and allied state interests. On the terrain of the emerging automated, post-industrial, post-scarcity social order, the choice comes down to the use of that new set of structures and mechanisms for human need and fulfillment or the profit and power of a dominant elite. The new opposition is deeply infused with the politics of autonomy, democratic socialism, ecology, and especially feminism." (ibid: 11)

Obviously, these are all valuable ideals and modes of thinking that the new utopian insurgency does not want to throw out. And yet, they are the values of another historical moment, before the full violence of neoliberal economics has been unleashed, before 9-11, before the rise of China, and before the profound intensifications of our digital lives, which have led to a two-pronged theoretical movement towards the more than human – one located in the new(ish) digital technologies and one that turns to the earth and ecologies to think about how to understand our present and so better imagine the future. In Canada, it is also prior to the success of several apology movements, including government apologies for Japanese Canadian WWII internment, the Chinese Head Tax, and Indian Residential Schools. As their tendency to state incorporation has become evident, these apologies have been followed deeper demands for true historical justice. I would like to suggest that if Moylan's critical utopia needs updating for the 21st century, it is in the arena of how we envision collective social and planetary co-existence and in how we respond to the uneven histories of exploitation, colonialism and imperialism that have brought us to the present moment.

To be sure, these were concerns in the novels Moylan names as exemplary of his critical utopia. I would like to turn at this point to a re-examination of one of my favorite of Moylan's critical utopian novels: Marge Piercy's *Woman on the Edge of Time,* a novel that, incidentally, William Gibson credits as the first cyberpunk novel (Poetry Foundation). This novel was groundbreaking in its moment of publication for the ways in which it took up the real conditions of women's lives. Further, its protagonist is not a bourgeois white woman, but a working class urban Latina who has been diagnosed, possibly unjustly, with a mental health condition. She has been thrown into a psychiatric institution against her will – a prison-like one that routinely conducts violent and de-humanizing experiments on its patients. *Woman on the Edge of Time* belongs to that subgenre of utopian fictions in which it is unclear whether the utopia it conveys is "real" or a figment of the protagonist's imagination. Here, it is the content of Piercy's utopia I wish to take up – an entirely unfair thing to do given my remarks thus far and the forty years that have passed since the novel's original publication. My hope is that this loving unfairness will pay off in terms of illustrating the ways in which the now emergent insurgencies can update the valuable but dated critical utopia.

In the novel's utopia, "Mattapoisett," Piercy does away with racial inequity through one of the very few machines that her utopian Mattapoisettans permit in their society: the "brooder." The brooder stores genetic material for the whole society and gestates children in hanging sacks. Anyone in the society who wants to can be a mother, regardless of gender or fertile capacity. But the child you mother is not a child of your body. It does not share your genetic material, or if it does, you never know it – the new society has done away with genetic continuity as a criterion for familial belonging. Further, though cultures are preserved, the notion of race as it attaches to skin color is not. So, Connie's guide to the utopia of future Mattapoisett – Luciente – described earlier, from Connie's point-of view as "obviously Mexican American" (1976: 28), and later as "moon-faced, black turtle bean eyes" is a Wamponaug Indian (I use Piercy's 1970s language here). So is Bee, described as a "big black man soft in the belly" (ibid: 95). Bee tells Connie: "we broke the bond between genes and culture, broke it forever" (ibid: 96). This is the Mattapoisettans way of ending racism. They do, however, retain cultures and diverse body types. Connie's soon-to-be lover Bee says, "we don't want the melting pot where everybody ends up with thin gruel. We want diversity, for strangeness breeds richness" (ibid: 96). All Mattapoisettans are, then, in 1970s American terms, adopted.

Through her contemporary protagonist, Connie, Piercy does show us what is lost in this utopian imagining. Speaking of her recently deceased contemporary 1970s lover Claud, and Claud's attachment to his blackness, Connie says:

"Claud's delicate pride, like an orchid with teeth. What could a man of this ridiculous Po-dunk future, when babies were born from machines and people negotiated diplomatically with cows, know about how it had been to grow up in America black or brown? Pain had honed Claud keen." (ibid: 96)

In addition to these lines about Claud, Piercy gives us the classed and raced specificity of Connie's life in carefully and compassionately laid out detail through the unfolding of the first quarter of the novel. She is profoundly aware of the material burden carried by the racialized poor in 1970s America. Less well thought through – if only because the novel was written in the early days of the discussion – are the deeper entanglements of history, memory, affect, and em-bodiment, which strike me as of keen importance now, in the wake of so many government apologies for historical wrongs, and as the politics and possibilities of justice present their complications. Also of pressing importance now are two sets of discussions on cultural appropriation, one in the late 1980s and early 1990s, and one contemporary.

Although *Woman on the Edge of Time* is set in the US, the border is a porous thing, and the broad concerns of Piercy's text apply north of the 49th parallel as well, though their racial contours are different. In a Canadian/Turtle Island con-text, we might consider the full range of Indigenous refusals of Canadian citizen-ship. For many Indigenous people, Canadian citizenship constitutes assimilation, and thus complete colonization. If Canadian citizenship is a kind of utopian form, its prior outside, or better, beneath, is Indigenous claim to the land, and by corollary, an imperative to attend to Indigenous epistemologies. Further, the separation of history from the body proves more difficult than Piercy hopes. The question of justice does not necessarily sit well with the model of the commons that remains Piercy's commitment, even as she tries to include in it the work of specificity and difference, and steer it out of the politics of undifferentiated universality and ahistorical sameness critiqued so well by Orwell in *Nineteen Eighty-Four*. If the present moment requires us to open ourselves to non-Western ways of knowing and be accountable for the violence of colonialism and imperialism, then we are in need of a very different set of ideals from the ideals that emerge, for instance, in response to the Industrial Revolution in Europe.

If there is a utopian call in the recent and ongoing Idle No More and Black Lives Matter movements, it is one that demands an attention to the body and calls for forms of social, sexual and racialized arrangement that have not yet been thought, and have not yet emerged in the eruptive sense I have been attempting to articulate, and yet that also recognizes the injustices of the past and present – land theft, slavery, police profiling, residential schools and more. There is a temporal question at work, but is not so much the question of how to get to the idealistic utopia from where we are, but rather, what to want and how to recognize its temporality when that temporality erupts. It is also important to consider who does the work of imagining, in other words, whose creative agency gets materialized – at the level of narrative and at the level of social practice. Also, it becomes imperative to consider how to understand and engage with narratives and imaginings in relation to the communities from which they emerge.

The second issue that demands update in Moylan's commitments is the issue of human/non-human relations, and the question of the more-than-human. If the moment of the critical utopia is one that is concerned with the machinic, over-technologization of human life, ours is one that recognizes human responsibility in the production of technology, our prosthetic continuities with it, and indeed, the recognition that we are it and it is us, as all the cyborg books and movies of the 1980s and 1990s showed us – think especially of *Blade Runner* and *Robocop*. If these films and books illustrate the extent to which the bodies of we signifying monkeys (raced, gendered, and trapped in language) are linked with our technologies, cyberpunk gives us the heaven and the hell of virtual – no longer outer – space.

Kevin McCarron argues that in its celebration of the Cartesian body/mind split, and its ultimate return to a valorization of the human, cyberpunk is a fundamentally conservative genre. For him, its appeal lies on the one hand in a Puritanical dismissal of the body (1995: 262) and on the other, in a dystopic celebration of high capital. He says: "their authors are more than half in love, gazing with rapt fascination at what they hate" (ibid: 270). It is neither a utopian nor a dystopian genre, but rather one saturated with postmodern ambivalence. Its bodies are bodies of money, the economic bodies of high capitalism (ibid: 271). Cyberspace is the smorgasbord of plenty at the end of history, but the cost of dining at this sumptuous buffet is the body itself. It turns out to be a trough at which the mind can stuff itself at the expense of its attached flesh. It engages thus a strange kind of cannibalism, that is, self-consumption. If McCarron is right, and cyberpunk is a celebration of the end of history, then Marge Piercy as its feminist progenitor is the writer whose thought exceeds the limitations of the genre. Piercy's feminist proto-cyberpunk is the rare cyberpunk that values the body's reproductivity (ibid: 270). It is thus now, as neoliberal capital enters its death throes and the clock of the long now resumes its anthropocenic ticking, that Piercy's thinking becomes newly important.

If the 1970s moment, with its attachment to second wave feminism, was concerned with women's reproductivity, new reproductive technologies, and the right to choose, our present moment is a biopolitical one, certainly still about the reproduction of human individuals, but more than that, about the reproduction of both human and nonhuman life from the scale of the nanoparticle to the scale of the planet. It is for these reasons that I think it is important to take up the work of the new materialists on the one hand, and Indigenous epistemologies on the other.

Gayatri Spivak offers us the notion of the planetary, which she describes as committed to actual lives. She opposes it to the global as it pertains to economic globalization: "the imposition of the same system of exchange everywhere" (2005: 72). There is no room for cyberspace in Spivak's notion of the planetary – hers is a distinct return to earth. She writes: "The globe is on our computers. No one lives there. It allows us to think we can aim to control it. The planet is the species of alterity, belonging to another system; and yet we inhabit it, on loan" (ibid: 72). She calls on us as humans to understand ourselves as "planetary subjects" rather than as "global agents," orienting ourselves broadly towards life which she describes as "planetary alterity" that is underived from us, not our dialectical negation, but something that sometimes contains us and sometimes "flings us away" (ibid: 73). With Spivak, Bruno Latour, and others, I propose a relationship to planetary alterity as one that does not place human beings at the center of knowledge or at the center of the reproduction of life, but only as one set of participants among many within it.

Rosi Braidotti (along with many other new materialists) makes a similar shift away from human centrality and human exceptionalism, and stresses instead the self-organizing (or auto-poietic) forces of living matter (3). William Connolly expands this work to argue that neoliberal capital is itself an auto-poietic system, one that impinges, often destructively, on other auto-poietic systems. He writes, "[t]he cosmos consists of multiple, interacting systems with differing degrees of self-organizational capacity. Such a combination helps to make neoliberal capitalism a very fragile order" (2013a: 403). Connolly is highly aware of the multiple speeds and scales of various nonhuman auto-poietic systems and calls for sensitivity on the part of human institutions for such things as the musical capacity of whales, the delicacy of soil processes, and the self-amplifying tendencies of climate change. He wants us to slow down and pay attention to these things, but speed up changes in role definitions, identities, economic priorities, state politics, and international organizations. Rather than offering a utopian endpoint, or the end of history, he offers a practice: "You adopt a problem orientation and trace each emerging problem up and down the scale of the micro, the macro and the planetary as the issue requires" (ibid: 403). The turn towards practice, then, is key. The work of utopia now is insurgent. It is also about labor – the labor of thought, attention, and imagination.

I would like us to remember at this point that the horror of the Anthropocene is the horror of Western capitalism, albeit Western capitalism taken up as globalization in the sense that Spivak delineates. If humans are a destructive geological force, it is not all humans equally – which is a good thing to recognize because it means that there is nothing fated or inevitable about the apocalypse. Rather, like cyberspace, apocalypse is a Puritan nightmare that need not come to pass. If the new materialists give us ground to work with in the Western tradition, then African, Asian, and Indigenous North American traditions can offer us alternate epistemologies that are at the same time alternate ways of imagining our human continuities with the worlds of life and the elements.

Lee Maracle, for instance, in her recent collection of oratories, *Memory Serves,* calls for a return to Sto:lo matriarchy and a world in which story, poetry, and a process she calls "concatenation" is key to the recovery of life and balance. Concatenation requires an active relationship to story and poetry in which the presence of the speaker is as important as the words spoken. Oral poetry for her is not instruction – not blueprint. Rather: "The teaching power of the poem lies as much in its aesthetic beauty as in the poet's philosophical and socio-spiritual logic and her or his ability to achieve oneness with the listeners" (Maracle 2015: 171). For those of us, including yours truly, raised in a secular tradition, notions such as "oneness" and "socio-spiritual logic" are difficult things to grasp. I would suggest that we need to, or better, we need to find genealogical trajectories in the traditions that speak to us so as not to appropriate and not to continue the genocide that lies, always differently, on the conscience of at least some non-Indigenous people.

Location matters. As we must attend to the culpabilities and responsibilities of our human location, so we also must attend to our geo-political, culturally-specific, embodied locations. Maracle writes: "The presence of the speaker [...] [is] as much a part of the [...] [story] as the words spoken" (ibid: 170). What you say depends on where you are, and where you are shows itself in how you speak. So, I recognize, for instance, that in Musqueam territory, where, until recently, I lived and worked, the traditional people use different verbs depending on where the speaker stands in relation to the river (Zandberg 2007).

Maracle's thought is so important here for the ways in which it holds up the importance of Indigenous, and specifically Sto:lo epistemologies. In so doing, it breaks the impasse of human exceptionalism that the new materialists are determined to do away with, while holding up a role for the human, but one outside the Western tradition, and outside the body/mind and nature/culture splits, and the Kantian correlative. While I remain in agreement with the displacements of the (Western) human and the recognition of very large to very small-scale interactivity embraced by writers like William Connolly and Timothy Morton, I want to recognize the productivity of Maracle's work in its delineation of an ongoing role for the human and for Indigenous understandings of human-to-human/"cross-cultural" relations. As the appropriation debates become newly heated, it is more important than ever to attend to body/history relations.

Rafaella Baccolini, quoted by Tom Moylan in his chapter "The Critical Dystopia" in *Scraps of the Untainted Sky* (2000), suggests that this mode might update the critical utopia, in maintaining a utopian core (188), while deploying the dystopian shell narrative to "negate static ideals, preserve radical action, and create a space in which opposition can be articulated and received" (ibid: 188). At the level of form, it is possible to create a locus of hope, while rejecting a conservative dystopian tendency to anti-utopian closure (ibid: 188-189).

What Baccolini describes as a "utopian core" bears much in common with Jameson's notion of the "utopian enclave," except that Baccolini is speaking about texts where Jameson is speaking of the social world. For her, the utopian enclave is a multi-oppositional narrative (Baccolini 2000: 18) within the body of the dystopia that avoids deploying the universalist assumptions of critical utopias (like Piercy's *Woman on the Edge of Time*). Baccolini writes:

"Traditionally, a bleak, depressing genre with no space for hope within the story, utopia (in the sense of utopian hope) is maintained in dystopia only *outside* the story [...] The ambiguous, open endings of [feminist sf] novels [...] maintain a utopian impulse *within* the work. In fact, by rejecting the traditional subjugation of the individual at the end of the [dystopian] novel, the critical dystopia opens a space of contestation and opposition for those groups [...] for whom subjectivity has yet to be attained." (ibid: 18)

Reading the work of Ildney Cavalcanti, Moylan affirms this strategy, proposing that "blank space" in the narrative can function as an anticipation of that which is radically other. By leaving a space for the "utopian object" the writer avoids presenting that object in a compromised, fully-delineated form (2000: 191). This is a useful expansion of his early formulation of the critical utopia. To these productive thoughts, I add the notion that to posit such an enclave in narrative can be productive for the making of relations across cultural difference. In telling a story from my specific location, I do not speak for the one I want to build solidarity with, but leave a utopian enclave in my story, into which, should they choose, their story could enter. The utopian enclave in the dystopian narrative can be a site of relation-making.

I propose a re-turn to utopia – what I will call "insurgent utopia" to update Moylan and others' notions of critical utopia and critical dystopia while remaining in friendly conversation with them. The insurgent utopia can deploy dystopian forms and utopian enclaves as sites for conversation, where attentive listening to the active and positive content of the other is possible. Within the dystopian framework of the nation, for instance, a conference on Indigenous/non-Indigenous relation, while it might at some level fit the incorporative agenda of state multiculturalism, can still produce unexpected eruptions and alliances beyond the capacities of state containment – an insurgent utopia within a dystopian frame.

I find William Connolly's recent work on the general strike and the pluralist swarm in *Facing the Planetary* useful here. Connolly, along with many other new materialists, is interested in the interaction of forces at a range of scales because it is precisely in these interactions that the worst excesses of high capital and (Western) human exceptionalism show themselves. Connolly, Morton, and others argue that non-human forces up and down a range of scales retaliate against anthropocenic excess through micro and macro forms of agency that both exceed and counter human agency in surprising ways. Connolly provides many examples of this. One I find particularly moving (so to speak) is the example of the ocean conveyor system, which flows from the Gulf of Mexico, north to Greenland. It drives downwards in colder regions because Arctic winds evaporate more pure water, so that the liquid water remaining in the ocean is saltier and heavier in the north, but lighter and less salty in the south. Changes in temperature and salt content are what propel the Gulf Stream and enable the wide variety of life forms it supports. Global warming causes the glaciers to melt, so that northern waters are no longer as salty, leading to the danger that the ocean conveyor system may shut down if global warming is not reversed. Worse still, the melting of the glaciers produces an amplifying effect. The more they melt, the slower the conveyor system. The slower the conveyor, the more warmth up north and more glacier melt. While the initial trigger is human, the amplifying effects exceed the human; they are part of a logic that precedes us (Connolly 2017: 102-104). Human action is thus not causal, but rather embedded in larger self-amplifying systems.

No single individual or constituency can single-handedly solve the problems produced through the horrors of the Anthropocene. What is needed, rather, is a "politics of swarming [...] composed of multiple constituencies, regions, levels, processes of communication and modes of action, each carrying some potential to augment and intensify the others with which it becomes associated" (ibid: 125). Connolly holds up, in particular, the "specific intellectual" as figure who understands a lot about a particular location of a phenomenon (ibid: 125). Many specific intellectuals with different knowledges, acting in different ways, are necessary to comprise the work of the swarm. No universality is necessary, rather, a pluralist assemblage of multiple actions may cause the eruption of an event that might trigger a cascade to replace the extractionist cultures we are currently embedded in (ibid: 129). Connolly hopes that several such events might coalesce into a "perfect storm," or alternately that a general strike could be orchestrated, again, comprised of different actors with different knowledges working in different locations at different scales (ibid: 129). Some combination of the intended and the serendipitously unintended might jostle us out from the interior of our dystopian condition to another – a good place or an unexpected place. The knock at the door may come from the inside, break open the door and gush out to encircle the horror. The image then, is of a hatching egg, and a chick that eats the shell from which it has emerged.

Indeed, if what is wrong with contemporary capitalism is that the system of organizing that humans set up to ease exchange within a human frame, and what has happened is that that system has become self-organizing, non-human, in-human and beyond our control, and what exceeds it are the self-organizing systems of the earth itself, it seems only a matter of time before that which capitalism has tried to contain breaks out. The question, of course, is whether the new insurgent earth is friendly or unfriendly, or, as will likely be the case, a little bit of both.

The new insurgent utopian narratives, I propose, take elements of both the critical utopia and the critical dystopia, but re-valence them to make space inside for multiple voices to concatenate as well as for silence and listening. Their promise is that they might work as one force against many to bring a better future eruptively into being. Our job is to recognize such a future when it arrives and continue to act and tell stories to nurture future productive eruptions and hold off the horror of what Connolly calls "the tipping point," that might drive, for instance, the ocean conveyor system, with all the life it supports, to a stop.

In closing, I offer Wayde Compton's recent collection of linked short stories, *The Outer Harbour* (2014), as an example of an insurgent utopia, one that not only illustrates human autopoietic interactions with nonhuman systems, but in fact makes its own autopoietic – and auto-poetic – interaction with human and non-human planetary systems. In light of my Deleuzian arguments about the power of eruption, it would make sense that the subject of Compton's collection is a volcano, or more precisely, a volcanic island that emerges in the Burrard Inlet off the coast of Vancouver. Shaped like a water droplet, it bubbles out of the ocean, and seems hardly solid at all, even as the fiery conditions of its birth coat the mainland neighborhoods around it in ash. There is nothing permanent about it: scientists say it might erode away in a matter of years (2014: 36). It is colonized first by "diaspores" – plant seeds that drift on the wind. One of the protagonists, a young Black woman called Jean, dreams herself as peripatetic, nonhuman life: "She is seagrass. She is bracken and fern. She is thimbleberry. She's a starfish rotating in the untouched shallows, near, but not of, the rippled land, circling around and around it" (ibid: 38). Named after the turn-of-the-century Mohawk poet Pauline Johnson, the island becomes a site of Indigenous activist land reclamation when the Snohomish activist Fletcher together with Jean and several of their friends evade the police in a Zodiac and put up a banner there. In light of Fletcher's Indigeneity, Compton's language is interesting. First of all, he nuances Fletcher's origins: "Fletcher is from Victoria, adopted by whites, had a Snohomish mother from the US, and local father from a band unknown to Fletcher or anyone who might be able to tell him" (ibid: 34).[4] Secondly, he recognizes the necessity of the claim – and specifically of others receiving the language of the claim in order to make it meaningful:

---

4   In offering this level of nuance around Fletcher's identity, Compton points to a complex and unresolved set of debates currently unfolding on Turtle Island around what does and does not constitute Indigeneity, as well as problems of lost memory and history brought about through the violence of colonization including land theft, active genocide, residential schools, and the Sixties Scoop (of Indigenous children from their birth families for adoption into white families).

"The point now is to wait for the communiqué to work its way through the channels of re-
portage and security, all the way to where they are, to the place that makes them illegal by
being there – standing, waiting, thinking, peopling it. Being people where they shouldn't
be. Waiting for time to bring them in." (ibid: 43)

The invocation of illegality in the Vancouver context of Compton's collection,
particularly in light of Compton's writing of another character – Versajna the
"mystery migrant" – calls up the contemporary labor of the activist group No
One Is Illegal, founded in the late 1990s in the wake of the west coast arrival of
three ships full of migrant laborers from Fujian, China. This chain of associations produces Fletcher as simultaneously a migrant and Indigenous in a way
that might be contentious to some modes of Indigenous nationalism. But Compton is both careful and compassionate here. Fletcher's illegality is also the illegality of the blockade and the protest camp, and is thus related to sites like
Unist'oten, Caledonia, Ipperwash, Gustafson Lake, Standing Rock and Oka,
where Indigenous peoples have reclaimed land that was always theirs, taking it
back from presumptive and arguably illegal state appropriation. The question of
"legality," through this logic, becomes about ways of knowing: a question of
whose law gets to count and how we understand what constitutes the law. The
eruptive island is thus both new and ancient. As the lava cools and both physical
and epistemological erosion does its ongoing work, the social and legal status of
the island continues to morph and change.

In placing both Fletcher and Jean on Pauline Johnson Island together, Compton engages a poetic kind of relational work, in which Black diasporic and Indigenous diasporic figures are in a complex conversation with one another. I am
particularly struck by the fact that Jean's dreaming self-as-starfish rotates "near,
but not of, the rippled land" (ibid: 38), a creature, in a sense, of autopoietic solidarity, not attempting to lay claim to this new Indigenous land, but circling in the
water nearby, a dreaming element of the swarm that Connolly invokes.

Lest Pauline Johnson Island appear as on overly idealized site of
Black/Indigenous relations, rest assured that it is not. In the middle of *The Outer
Harbour*, Compton offers a set of fictional flyers that show how Pauline Johnson
Island shifts in the public imagination over time. The first flyer, by the fictional
Anti-Colonial Solidarity Forum to publicize a rally to protest the killing of an
Indigenous political activist – Fletcher – gives the history of Pauline Johnson Is-
land in the aftermath of Fletcher and Jean's attempt to claim it as Indigenous
land. It features the outline of a human figure giving the "Black Power" salute,
superimposed over an image of what is presumably Pauline Johnson Island
(Compton 2014: 103). We learn that the Vancouver Police and the RCMP have

arrested the activists and that Fletcher has been shot. The flyer likens the killing of Fletcher to the factual 1995 killing of Dudley George at Ipperwash by Kenneth Deane, an Ontario Provincial Police officer, when George and other Indigenous activists occupied Ipperwash Provincial Park to assert a land claim over the nearby Stoney Point First Nation reserve expropriated in 1942 to build a military base (CBC, Bryant). In likening the fictional character Fletcher Sylvester to the real world/historical Dudley George, and the fictional Pauline Johnson Island to the real world/historical Stoney Point First Nation reserve, Compton takes a risk, one that offers both sites as eruptive. While Pauline Johnson Island, as a volcano, literally bursts through the ocean floor, the Stoney Point First Nation reserve reveals its emergent properties through both its continuity with the time immemorial of Indigenous presences on Turtle Island, and through its production via treaty process, military expropriation, activist protest, and land claims. There is nothing arbitrary about its emergence; rather it is bound to a complex set of Indigenous and Canadian government actions and to a spatial ethics that recognizes Indigenous priority.

Compton is aware of the historical forces that bring about shifts in spatial imagination and spatial production. The second fictional flyer, for a retrospective celebration of the occupation of Pauline Johnson Island, features the image of a microphone. The image signifies entry into the overtly technological; it is of course, also a device for the amplification of sound, and specifically given the context of the flyer, activist and poetic speech. We see that two other members of the Pauline Johnson Island Four[5] – Alison Bartlett and Jean Martin – will speak. Cross-racial alliance is invoked through the performances of DJ Black Money and Otokuyaku. A speaker called Klatsassin[6] Adams will speak on "new directions in the Indigenous struggle." References to financial concerns –

---

5   The syntax of naming here invokes the name "Squamish Five," a historically existing "urban guerilla" group active through the 1980s in Vancouver. The group is known for three bombings: Cheekye Dunsmuir, Litton Industries, and Red Hot Video. More distantly, the Baader-Meinhof Gang is invoked.

6   "Klatsassin" is the name of a Tsilhqot'in leader who took part in the Chilcotin War of 1864. He and a group of followers killed a ferry worker and attacked a sleeping road crew on April 29 of that year. Along with four other chiefs, the historical Klatsassin was hanged in Quesnel in October 1864 (Stueck). "Klatsassin" translates as "we do not know his name." The choice of such a name and historical figure is a deeply Comptonian gesture, as the presencing of the indeterminate in Compton's work and the play of memory and forgetting form an important aspect of his politics and creative practice.

through the name "DJ Black Money" and through the request for donations for the Fletcher Sylvester Memorial Fund – are important here in light of the material that follows.

The third flyer promotes a demonstration against the re-zoning of Pauline Johnson Island to change its status from that of ecological reserve to incorporation into the City of Vancouver, making it available for private development. The fictive publication – more brochure than a flyer – is an advertisement for "Arrival," a "10-storey residential tower built on Vancouver's newest waterfront." Unlike at Stoney Point/Ipperwash, where the "emergency" state expropriation of Indigenous land was military, at Pauline Johnson Island it is economic. It is neoliberal as opposed to liberal. The subsequent three pages of the brochure offer floor plans for apartments at Arrival.[7] Brilliantly, the last page of the developer's brochure offers a map of the island, and, in fine print, eruption insurance – an old-fashioned utopian guarantee against insurgent unpredictability: "Early detection technology linked to 24/7 evacuation capabilities are included and funded through the strata fee, and eruption insurance options are available" (117).

The story of Pauline Johnson Island, however, is not the dystopian narrative of neoliberal arrival and the triumph of the property developers. We learn in the final linked short story that Arrival has become a prison complex called "The Special Detention Facility" designed to contain three new kinds of subject: ghosts, that is spirits of the dead; composites, that is, machine-generated figures that pull together the features of living activists, but strangely, amalgamated figures that each have their own individual consciousness; and insurgents. These figures may or may not emerge from the ambivalent practice of "Hannibalism" – that is, multi-generational race lightening, while retaining hold on a Black liberation politics – a strategy that Troy, the protagonist of the story "400 FT^3 (11.33M^3)," finds he has been called in to. "The world, now," Troy muses:

---

7   Were Compton less politically generous, he might have attached Asian financing to Arrival. Certainly, within the context of contemporary Vancouver, real estate development like this is tied in the city's imagination to the recent arrival of wealthy Asians from the People's Republic of China and to Taiwan, preceded by Hong Kong investment in the 1980s and 1990s prior to its "return" to China. The Arrival complex might also be understood, however, as an echo of 19th- and 20th-century West Coast immigrant detention centers, like that on Angel Island. Asianness is indeed an eruptive racial force that cuts both ways.

"the world of his coming child, a future world, is an island of growing but unseen debts and consequences [...] The blocks are interlocking, and with them his girl will build a little house on the floor of her bedroom. For her 'babies'. He will watch, transported by pure awe." (Compton 2014: 142)

Alternately, these figures may or may not be the products of series of imaginary arts grants laid out in "Final Report," arts grants that are themselves utopian in the ways their projects escape ordinary state/biopolitical demands for self-documentation and surveillance: The Association for Petrosomatoglyphic Innovation's Clandestine Placement Grant for self-directed projects involving impressions of body parts into the material of the applications choice (ibid: 143); the Logatomic Institute's Angus Nanning Bursary for non-lexical vocalism (ibid: 145); the Society for Creative Intoxication's grant for a performance-based worked depicting the influence of psychoactive drugs in public settings (ibid: 147); the Subjective Joy Foundation's grant for a lifelong simulation of bliss (ibid: 151); or, my personal favorite, the Committee for the Instatement of Paracosmic Arts Committees grant for those with active inner worlds to devise cultural practices for those worlds (ibid: 156). Applicants for this last grant are asked to provide a detailed description of their paracosm, focusing on its artistic and cultural life. They are also required to indicate the kind of government or social form most amenable to housing the committee. The grant, however, is not submittable in the usual way:

"Your application should not be sent. Once completed, it will be sent for; it will be sensed and will attract those within our fictions who circulate, seek, and locate such desires. These agents will smell the yearning your application exudes. They will arrive at the site of your application. They will self-form in your space and appear or filter through or settle there, with you, like moss on a yew or damp on a dockside bollard. These agents will appear according to your abilities of perception – shapes of heavy smoke, ash-light swarms, swallowed laughs with eyes – these will come to collect your proposal [...]
You will know in your heart if your application has been successful.
You will feel it beginning." (ibid: 157-158)

The last iteration of Pauline Johnson Island presented in the book, then, in the final story "The Outer Harbour" is insurgently utopian in the sense that it makes room for history. The neoliberal real estate development "Arrival" has become a prison. But it is a prison that cannot contain its inhabitants. A character known only as "the girl" is dead when we first meet her. But more complicated than that, she belongs to a group of migrants from an unknown country, speaking an unknown language, all with the ability to blink in and out of presence; to move through walls, though not across water. Her companion, a ghost insurgent, who in life may or may not have been Fletcher Sylvester, accompanies her to the mainland, when, from the beach of Pauline Johnson Island, they observe the city on fire. They row there, and rescue a "composite." Like the girl, the composite also blinks in and out, but as a projection of police machinery is able to do so only when in range of the machine. The last miracle of the collection occurs after the girl and the insurgent row the composite out of projector range, and lose him. They land on the Pauline Johnson Island and are about to abandon the boat and push it back out into the surf, when the composite appears, impossibly, seated at the bow. The girl is thrilled by this wonder, and takes pleasure in showing the composite the site of her incarceration, her parents, and the research facilities at the Arrival building (ibid: 193). That the ghost migrant girl and the composite can occupy the same space and keep one another company, stands as a portent of other kinds of new human or nonhuman beings to come, collectively. They are also, in a sense, figures of an insurgent enclave, products of interlocking systems of hope and violence, not fully material and not leading in a linear direction to a better future, but rather, surging in and out of presence, moving in the direction of community, even if it is community that never fully crystallizes.

WORKS CITED

Baccolini, Rafaella (2000): "Gender and Genre in Feminist Critical Dystopias of Katharine Burdekin, Margaret Atwood, and Octavia Butler." In: Maureen Barr (ed.), *Future Females: The Next Generation*, Lanham: Rowman & Littlefield, pp. 11-34.

Baccolini, Rafaella, and Tom Moylan, (2003): "Dystopias and Histories." In: Rafaella Baccolini/Tom Moylan (eds.), *Dark Horizons: Science Fiction and the Dystopian Imagination*, New York: Routledge, pp. 1-12.

Barrett, Paul/Balllantyne, Darcy/Isaacs, Camille/Singh, Chrism (2017): "The Unbearable Whiteness of CanLit." In: *The Walrus* July 6, (https://thewalrus.ca/the-unbearable-whiteness-of-canlit/).

Blade Runner (1982). Directed by Ridley Scott, performances by Harrison Ford, Rutger Hauer, Sean Young, Edward James Olmos, Daryl Hannah, The Ladd Company.

Boyden, Joseph (2017), "My name is Joseph Boyden." In: *Maclean's* August 2, (http://www.macleans.ca/news/canada/my-name-is-joseph-boyden/).

Braidotti, Rosi, (2002):. *Metamorphoses: Towards a Materialist Theory of Becoming*, Cambridge: Polity.

--- (2013): *The Posthuman*. Cambridge: Polity.

Bryant, Michael (2015): "Twenty years after Dudley George's death, land still in federal hands." In: *The Toronto Star* January 22, (https://www.thestar.com/opinion/commentary/2015/01/22/twenty-years-after-dudley-georges-death-land-still-in-federal-hands.html).

Callenbach, Ernst (1975): *Ecotopia*. Toronto: Bantam.

CBC News (2015): "20 Years after Ipperwash crisis, First Nation accepts $95M offer." September 20, (http://www.cbc.ca/news/indigenous/ipperwash-1.3233013).

Connolly, William E. (2013a): "The 'New Materialism' and the Fragility of Things." In: *Millenium Journal of International Studies*. 41/3, pp. 399-412.

--- (2013b): *The Fragility of Things: Self Organizing Processes, Neoliberal Fantasies, and Democratic Activism*. Durham: Duke UP.

--- (2017): *Facing the Planetary: Entangled Humanism and the Politics of Swarming*. Durham: Duke UP.

Grosz, Elizabeth (1999): "Becoming ... An Introduction." In: *Becomings: Explorations in Time, Memory, and Futures*. Ithaca: Cornell UP, pp. 1-12.

Huron, Debra (2017): "Why Joseph Boyden and I need to stop meddling in Métis Identity." *Rabble.ca* August 12, (http://rabble.ca/blogs/bloggers/views-expressed/2017/08/why-joseph-boyden-and-i-need-stop-meddling-métis-identity).

Jameson, Fredric (2005): *Archaeologies of the Future*. London: Verso.

Kamboureli, Smaro (2009): *Scandalous Bodies: Diasporic Literature in English Canada*. Waterloo: WLUP.

Latour, Bruno (2014): "Agency at the Time of the Anthropocene." *New Literary History* 45/1, pp. 1-18.

Lederman, Marsha (2016): "How the Steven Galloway scandal sparked a CanLit civil war." In: *The Globe and Mail* November 15, (https://www.theglobeandmail.com/arts/books-and-media/how-the-steven-galloway-scandal-sparked-a-canlit-civil-war/article33049536/).

--- (2016): "Under a cloud: How UBC's Steven Galloway affair has haunted a campus and changed lives." In: *The Globe and Mail* October 28, (https://www.theglobeandmail.com/news/british-columbia/ubc-and-the-steven-galloway-affair/article32562653/).

LeGuin, Ursula (1969): *The Left Hand of Darkness*. New York: Ace.

Lindberg, Darcy (2017): "Adoption is not a passport to an Indigenous community." *Maclean's* August 5, (http://www.macleans.ca/opinion/adoption-is-not-a-passport-to-an-indigenous-community/).

Maracle, Lee (2015): *Memory Seves: Oratories.* Edmonton: NeWest.

McCarron, Kevin, (1995): "Corpses, Animals, Machines and Mannequins: The Body and Cyberpunk." *Body & Society.* 1/3-4, pp. 261-271.

More, Thomas (1965): *Utopia.* London: Penguin.

Moylan, Tom (1986): *Demand the Impossible.* New York: Methuen.

--- (2000): *Scraps of the Untainted Sky: Science Fiction, Utopia, Dystopia.* Boulder: Westview.

Niedzviecki, Hal (2017) "Winning the Appropriation Prize." *Write.* 45/1, p. 8.

Orwell, George (2008): *Nineteen Eight-Four.* London: Penguin.

Piercy, Marge (1976): *Woman on the Edge of Time.* New York: Ballantyne.

--- (1993): *Body of Glass.* London: Penguin.

Poetry Foundation (2017): "Marge Piercy." In: *Poetry Foundation,* (https://www.poetryfoundation.org/poets/marge-piercy).

Rajchman, John (1999): "Diagram and Diagnosis." In: *Becomings: Explorations in Time, Memory, and Futures.* Ithaca: Cornell UP, pp. 42-54.

"Response to UBCA Dec. 12 Statement" (2016): In: *Open Counter Letter: Steven Galloway Case at UBC* December 16, (sites.google.com/ualberta.ca/counterletter/response-to-ubc-accountable).

Robocop (1987). Directed by Paul Verhoeven, performances by Peter Weller, Nancy Allen and Dan O'Herlihy, Orion Pictures.

Spivak, Gayatri (2005): "Planetarity." In: *Death of a Discipline.* New York: Columbia UP, pp. 85-116.

Zandberg, Bryan (2007): "Reviving a Native Tongue Can a UBC Program Bring Back to Life the Musqueam Dialect?" In: *The Tyee* March 27, (http://thetyee.ca/News/2007/03/23/RevivingANativeTongue/).

Ideology

Crossing Impossible Boundaries?
Fantastic Narrative and Ideology[1]

ALFONS GREGORI

1. INTRODUCTION: IDEOLOGY, MARXISM, AND LITERARY STUDIES

A quite paradoxical fact in literary studies, or humanities in general – definitely a world full of paradoxes –, is the profuse employment of the term "ideology" in their analyses, at the same time as mainstream philosophical and academic trends have heaped the most withering scorn upon this term. After the French revolutionist Destutt de Tracy coined it in 1796 as a sort of science of ideas,[2] the term was undermined by classic Marxist theory. This revolutionary movement apprehended ideology differently, that is, not as some scientific formulation, but as quite the contrary: the misguiding thinking that impedes the triumph of science.[3] At bottom, Marxism identifies ideologies as a set of identifiable political ideas expressive of a political worldview; that is similarly to the conception of ideology as it has been consolidated in contemporary times. However, the original Marxist rejection of ideology did not appertain to this widespread definition

---

1 I would like to dedicate this work to Dietlind Schurak, *in memoriam*. I specially thank Emilia Ivancu for her patient correcting of the text.

2 As a matter of fact, Destutt's conceptualization has firm materialist roots (cf. Hawkes 2003: 60-61).

3 Interestingly, Arendt reasons in a similar way in order to discredit ideologies as scientific artifacts, underlining on the one hand their historical and biased nature, and their ties with totalitarianism on the other: "all ideologies contain totalitarian elements, but these are fully developed only by totalitarian movements" (Arendt 2004: 606).

of the term, but rather to the fact that Marxism needed to establish centralized units for controlling society, in order to eliminate any political contender or adversary to their rule: the sole ideology had to be the socialist-communist one, the power had to lie in the hands of a single social class, while the sanctioned scientific method for surveying social and political phenomena was Marxism itself. Obviously, these elements were not reduced to their ordinary definition: Socialism or communism were not ideologies, but ideals to be followed by humankind to achieve justice and happiness; the proletariat was not a social class, but the rightful majority to build a state free of social classes; and rather than a mere analytical methodology applied to social sciences, Marxism was a consensual equivalent to "Truth," the only authorized approach to reality. It is in this sense that the Marxist view of ideology as "false consciousness" should be understood, as one of the pillars of its classic doctrinal version confronted with the diversity of political options that existed apart from Marxism itself. According to this view, ideologies were nothing else but a layer, a malicious veil covering the real processes of oppression taking place in society. Or even worse: ideologies are phantoms, falsehoods turning up in our lives to deceive people's minds, while materiality would be the only reliable sphere of reality. Thus, ideologies became like ghosts, imaginary entities threatening human beings, or, in other words, nothing that could be examined seriously in literary studies.

The use of the concept of ideology was dogged by controversy because of the extraordinary repercussion of Marxist thought on important approaches to anthropological, sociological or philosophical studies before and after the Second World War, for instance the Frankfurt School of thought or French existentialism. In fact, the term ideology necessarily had acquired a negative connotation very difficult to eradicate.[4] This long-running controversy continued during the expansion of poststructuralist influence on Western social and cultural studies. Certainly, some scholarly proposals related to the Marxist paradigm cast aside a rigid formulation of the materialist determination of the so-called super-

---

4   A very illustrative case of this long-lasting Marxist connotation is Hawkes' identification between ideology and (malicious) untruthfulness: "My main argument … is that the postmodern sign, whether financial or linguistic, is epistemologically false and ethically degenerate. Postmodernism is thus the veritable apotheosis of ideology. I ended the Introduction to *Ideology*'s first edition with the contention that 'postmodernism is nothing more than the ideology of consumer capitalism' … It would be more accurate to say that postmodernism *is* the ideology of globalization" (Hawkes 2003: 10).

structure by the base.[5] However, most of the works ascribed to heterodox Marxism or post-Marxism[6] assumed the term as a bourgeois-related or conservative construct too nebulous and treacherous to be employed in their studies.[7] In other cases, ideology was re-defined in order to be applied with a more precise meaning, but frequently maintaining a gloomy tone.[8] Additionally, the French thinker Michel Foucault articulated a convincing constructivist approach to the notion of power that became capital for examining human relations of subjection and the construction of oppressive social networks, criticizing explicitly and discarding the concept of ideology. From Foucault's point of view, particular "ideological options" were observed as something belonging to each individual (Foucault 1984: 60). Therefore, like other discourses which in themselves are neither true nor false (ibid: 60), they are something to be deconstructed, conformed, and crossed by the same vectors of power-based relations. Ideologies were not considered reliable because of their adherence to a *superior* rational order.[9] In con-

---

5   An example from before the Second World War is the Italian theorist Antonio Gramsci, who left the following assertion in his prison notebooks (though unpublished until the end of 1940s): "The claim, presented as an essential postulate of historical materialism, that every fluctuation of politics and ideology can be presented and expounded as an immediate expression of the structure, must be contested in theory as primitive infantilism" (1971: 407). A much later example is the Swedish sociologist Göran Therborn, who puts science and ideology on the same functional level: "Not all ideology is or can operate as science, art, philosophy, or law, but all these emerge out of ideological configurations and may function as ideologies" (1999: 2).

6   Great thinkers of the 20th century – from Gramsci to the philosopher Slavoj Žižek – fit these descriptions. For further examples and information on their contents, see Hawkes (2003: 117-177).

7   Van Dijk gathered some "commonsense conceptions of the notion of 'ideology'," "as residues of scholarly debates": "(a) ideologies are false beliefs; (b) ideologies conceal real social relations and serve to deceive others; (c) ideologies are beliefs others have; and (d) ideologies presuppose the socially or politically self-serving nature of the definition of truth and falsity" (1998: 2).

8   For instance, the post-Marxist intellectual Ernesto Laclau uses the notion of ideology, though maintaining its traditional negative character as an instance that distorts the truth, because, in his opinion, it involves the concealment of hegemonic discourses (Camargo, 2011: 165).

9   In Foucault's (cf. 1984: 60) reasoned rejection of the notion of ideology, extracted from the English translation of an Italian interview with the author in 1977, the thinker did only take into account its Marxist conception.

temporary times, other voices – not necessarily linked to the Marxist or Fou-
cauldian approaches – denied the appropriateness of the concept of ideology as
an analytical category due to its inconsistency, imprecision, and vagueness when
used in academic surveys.[10]

Nonetheless, the term ideology is recurrently used in literary studies. It is
even one of the practically inevitable words showing up in every study that deals
with political or social aspects of a literary work. This is the very paradox referred to at the beginning of this article. Important introductory works by Marx-
ist-related authors examine the definition and application of the term, yet always
by taking into account the main theory and various trends developing inside
Marxism and post-Marxism – among others, Engel, Lukács, Gramsci, Adorno,
Marcuse, Althusser – and rarely by a deeper discussion of approaches outside
this movement. These theoretical introductions include: *The Concept of Ideology*
(1979), four volumes by Jorge Larraín; *Ideology: An Introduction* (1991) by Terry Eagleton; or *Ideology* (1996) by the latter's disciple, David Hawkes. Despite
these well-known and often-cited reference books, in literary studies, ideology is
not very often used according to the classic Marxist dictate, but simply as a pre-
defined whole of ideas socially shared by the writer, a character, or a group of
characters, regardless of whether ideology constitutes a restraint or a barrier to
know the "real" relationships of domination in society.[11] Ideologies analyzed in
literary studies quite often are specifically labeled as socialist, conservative,
communist, anarchist, feminist, nationalist, etc., but then, occasionally, the
catchall adjective *bourgeois* is applied pejoratively to this kind of approach.

If the present work includes ideology in its title, this is because it may still
constitute a category fully effective when used as an analytical tool. A brief explanation of its relevance is mandatory. First of all, it is not possible to find another term for designating the same meaning that is going to be specified later.

---

10 For instance, Pierre Bourdieu argued as follows: "the concept of ideology has been so
used and abused that it does not work any more. We no longer believe in it; and it is
important, for example in political uses, to have concepts that are efficient and effective" (1994: 266). Another French intellectual, Régis Debray, claims that the existence
of an object called ideology is doubtful, being not a concept but a "hollow word" that
simply poses a false problem (1981: 85, 163, 158). Even if trying to redeem it for the
Marxist analysis, the Mexican philosopher Luis Villoro considers that the term ideology is currently imprecise as a consequence of the disparate meanings assigned to it
by scholars in different contexts (2007: 10).

11 Obviously, the analysis can focus upon the society presented in the text and upon its
metaphorical or allegorical reference in the real world as well.

Second, beside all the criticism directed at it, ideology is still employed both in academic research as well as in institutional or media communication. The third reason is strictly related to the first one: every concept is definable; consequently, it can be applied to any academic framework when appropriately defined, that is, if an academic explanation is provided to make its comprehension possible. Finally, a logical reason reads as follows: the fact that the term *ideology* is present in theoretical discussions that have been held for decades – even if to condemn it as an inadequate concept – makes it deserve its inclusion in an analysis in which many features related to it play an important part.

Yet, research on the ideological aspects of the literary texts should not be a goal in itself. This is a mutilating practice that consists in detaching the social and political features from the artistic whole, often appearing in academic works that deal with literary examples of a realist or fantasy tradition. The deduction of biographical traces in a text that supposedly shows the ideological orientation of the author might have a sociological – sometimes fetishistic – interest, whereas the discovery of a "message" in literary works revealing (presupposed) evidence of a particular ideology may attract historians or political scientists. However, the most important questions that every contemporary cultural and literary scholar should try to answer are missing from these kinds of approaches: how do ideological elements interact with the artistic construction of the work to create meaning in a dialectical way? Moreover, as it has been mentioned above, interest in ideological features in literature has been centered rather on realist and fantasy fiction, neglecting fantastic works, which at first glance might seem peripheral to politic issues.[12] Hence, the central point of this article is to analyze the role that ideological elements play in fantastic fiction, as well as the way the theory of ideology may contribute to analyze this narrative mode in a powerful way, increasing the possible meanings of the literary work. The fixation of this precise goal – inscribed in the hermeneutic perspective – and the adoption of tools developed in literary theory for studying fiction distinguish the resultant academic work from other disciplines that employ different perspectives, methodologies,

---

12 Several exceptions can be traced: thematically, the figure of the vampire; and, from a genre point of view, fantastic gothic fiction. Both coincide with the transition from the feudal system to the capitalist era. Later, zombies – and monsters as an overall notion – have been often approached from a political perspective.

and tools, such as sociology, politics science, psychology or history, among others.[13]

2. FANTASTIC FICTION AND THE INTERPRETATION OF TEXTS

Regarding the analysis of ideology in fictional works, an important question must be emphasized: in wide areas of the Western world, literary studies have only conferred meaningfulness to socio-political conflicts when they were interpreted in realist works. At the same time, the perception of far-reaching ideas in literary texts that present unreal events or phenomena has almost been restricted to artistic expressions previous to the 19th-century Romantic Revolution. Hence, there has been a tendency of reading the literature of the impossible from an allegorical perspective, that is to say, a double, superposed interpretation on which classic works seemed to be focused. This superposition was in consonance with the hierarchical socio-political structure of that era. Indeed, a hierarchy of reading responded to the graphic representation of the power structuration previous to the industrial revolution, a pyramid in which the social estates were stratified.[14] When realism became the hegemonic mode in Western literature in the second half of the 19th century, leaving behind Romanticism, there was a gradual process of identifying unreal fiction with old-fashioned literature, against which the fantastic, the symbolist or (later) the avant-garde authors – among others – reacted. Such a correlation between unreal fiction and old-fashioned literature was reinforced by the signification of the ghost – present in a lot of fantastic short stories and novels – as an anomaly belonging to the past. Unreal fiction, thus, was progressively related to times gone-by, and its impossible entities were interpreted as reminiscences of a finished cultural period that was no longer

---

13 That does not negate the imperative task of an interdisciplinary approach, reposing in applying ideas and notions from other disciplines when it is suitable and fruitful for the carried-out analysis.

14 This part should not be considered a Marxist-based interpretation, because it is not assumed that the cultural phenomenon (a particular way of reading) was a consequence of a material situation (the pre-modern economic order). Nevertheless, eventually, literary effects of economic realities can be perceived in texts under specific circumstances, especially if these economic realities affect some of the actors or relationships of the literary system.

functional.[15] Not only that: they were threatening beings to be gotten rid of in the name of progress. In addition, the growing identification of unreal fiction with youth literature further reinforced the vision of the former as something not related to the present – at least from an adult perspective.

In addition to the controversy around the concept of ideology, the various arguments for or against the use of certain terms or labels used to discuss the literature of the unreal also need to be pointed to. The conflict arena has been represented by many conferences, meetings, and publications on literary theory and literary studies in general. By all means, this is not a question of falling short into the "travesty" ironically denounced by Lucie Armitt in *Fantasy Fiction*, alluding to the critic's or the researcher's obsession with "categorising, classifying, compartmentalising literature into division and subdivision, and arguing over whether the boxes into which these texts are crammed should be labeled 'marvelous' or 'fabulous', 'sword and sorcery' or 'space opera', 'myth or faerie'" (2005: 193). However, divisions and subdivisions make sense when the context, perspective, style, structure, or functionality in which the story is inscribed provide – or help to discover – new meanings and manners of understanding a literary work.

The present attempt to bring fantastic literature face to face with ideology starts by understanding this kind of fiction as an independent narrative mode,[16] separate from surrealism, magical realism, medievalizing fantasy, science fiction, and fairy tales, thus finding its uniqueness in the nature of the conflict that any unreal element has in a fantastic text (cf. Gregori 2015: 23-31). This means,

---

15 Indubitably, science fiction followed a trail under different parameters, having technology and scientific development as main points of reference.

16 Certainly, in the present work fantastic literature is understood as a mode, borrowing the term and the concept from the taxonomy exposed by Fowler (cf. 1982: 106-111) in *Kinds of Literature*. In her book *Fantasy: The Literature of Subversion*, Jackson borrows it with the same meaning from Jameson, but for defining her conception of *fantasy* as a "particular type of literary discourse [that] is not bound to the conventions of a given age, nor indissolubly linked to a given type of verbal artifact, but rather persists as a temptation and a mode of expression across a whole range of historical periods, seeming to offer itself, if only intermittently, as a formal possibility which can be revived and renewed" (1986: 7). Nonetheless, other scholars may use different concepts that correspond to the same conceptualization of mode – depending on how they are defined. Sometimes they adopt terms in order to grasp the fact that the fantastic has exceeded the literary confines, for instance the fantastic as an aesthetic category as postulated by David Roas (2011).

in fact, that the fantastic element – as a motif contrary to the conventional idea of reality – stimulates the main conflict of the narrated story, pushing the development of action and digressive reflections forward. In contrast, most of the above-mentioned modes or sub-genres of fiction such as surrealism or magical realism, though they also contain impossible events and phenomena violating the physical laws and logical order of the world we are living in, do present characteristics that lead to classify them as fiction belonging to the marvelous mode.

Is the fantastic then a mode belonging to a larger category called "fantasy"? Omitting its colloquial use, which is highly imprecise and misguiding, "fantasy" is a term employed for designating the majority of contemporary marvelous literature belonging to both regular and youth fiction. In his seminal study *Introduction à la littérature fantastique* (1970) Todorov distinguished categorically between two different kinds of approaches to the literary unreal; the fantastic and the marvelous. As asserted above, this paper follows this distinction when referring to fantastic literature as an independent narrative mode. However, even authors drawing on Todorov use the terms "fantastic" and "fantasy" in a confusing way.[17] Indeed, even in scholarly works, "fantasy" remains a very broad and diffuse concept. As Armitt admits in her introductory study on this topic, "fantasy" in English can refer to "utopia, allegory, fable, myth, science fiction, the ghost story, space opera, travelogue, the Gothic, cyberpunk, magic realism; the list is not exhaustive, but it covers most of the modes of fiction discussed in this book as 'fantasy'" (2005: 1). However, she distinguishes between fantasy, which would impose "absolute closure," and the "disruptive, open-ended narratives" of the fantastic (ibid: 7).[18] This is a consideration coinciding with the general approach adopted in the present paper. Accordingly, fantasy is understood rather in the marvelous sense of the categorization. In fact, it has been popularly used in

17 For example, Jackson (cf. 1986) translates the French word *fantastique* sometimes as "fantastic," but mainly as "fantasy," even when exposing in her study the Todorovian clue distinction between "merveilleux" (marvelous), "fantastique" (fantasy, according to Jackson [1986: 25]) and "étrange" (uncanny). She argues that Tolkien's, Lewis' or Kingsley's fantasy (prototypical of how it is understood in this paper) "is more properly defined as faery, or romance literature" (Jackson 1986: 9).

18 The inclusion of the Gothic and "ghost stories" in the list partially disrupts its coherence, because, in the case of the Gothic, scholars recognize that the subgenre of the Gothic novel contributed enormously to the constitution of the fantastic in the second half of the 18th century, while most of the ghost stories clearly belong to the fantastic mode, with the exception of those presenting an allegoric character or being a parody, for instance Dickens' *A Christmas Carol* or Wilde's *The Canterville Ghost*.

this same manner, because, as a label in the book market (and not only in English), "fantasy" has been especially used to refer to a sort of literature set in indefinite times, but often making use of a medieval atmosphere, that means, showing elements that could be found (at least) in that period, and including preternatural[19] phenomena and inexistent creatures culturally related to that same period. As it is widely known, Tolkien's *The Lord of the Rings* was the significant boost that consolidated this kind of literature in the market and it gradually became ubiquitous in the Western world's imaginary thanks to the (re)discovery of other authors writing previously, simultaneously or following Tolkien's model. Yet, fairy tales are the most cited of the marvelous, whose characteristics are prototypical of this narrative mode: an uchronic world with the impossible as an inherent and naturalized component of the former in such a manner that the unreal events do not involve a conflict about their own existence or the reality on which the story is focused. That does not mean that these impossible events are completely irrelevant or merely a decoration in marvelous works. Authors and readers usually confer significance and meaning to them, either symbolical, metaphorical or allegorical. However, these kinds of readings allude to a sphere transcending our everyday life and materiality.

For instance, as Roas puts it, Christian marvelous stories are not perceived as fantastic by readers because the preternatural in them corresponds to a theologically codified order, and the referent of this "reality" corresponds with the literary referent – obviously without taking into account whether readers believe in it or not (2011: 51). Having taken elements from both religious fiction and fairy tales, acclaimed literary works of the second half the 20th century achieved the status of bestsellers (as Jackson calls them [1986: 9]) following the model of the medievalizing fantasy. In the "secondary worlds" created by narrators of this marvelous paradigm, magical powers and unreal beings appear naturally, producing, to characters or readers, a surprise similar to what they might experience as when contemplating an extraordinary phenomenon of nature (the Aurora Borealis, a close volcano's eruption, a sperm whale devouring a giant squid, or the abdication of Queen Elisabeth II, among others). The point is that they probably will not take it as an attack on their beliefs in the laws ruling our world, that is, the physical and logical rules that people are usually taught and verify in their everyday existence. In this respect, the other paradigm, which is known as the fantastic mode, goes along with the notion of uncertainty for conceptualizing the

---

19 At least in academic studies, the form "preternatural" is preferable to "supernatural" because the later derives from an ideological conceptualization linked to the Christian hierarchy of the divine creation (cf. Gregori 2015: 31-32).

so-called "fantastic effect," and its connection with an imprecise level of anxiety, fear or horror. This effect involves an uncanny experience, having a metaphysical and intellectual dimension much different from the physical fear felt by readers and characters when immersed in a non-preternatural Gothic novel or in the formidable episode with Smaug in *The Hobbit*.[20]

As a matter of fact, in contrast to marvelous or fantasy texts, the feature identifying fantastic literature is the tendency toward a fragmented state (in an abstract sense), a phenomenon parallel with the process of fragmentation in the modern period. Indeed, since its beginning, fantastic literature has been compiling fragments of motives, themes, and characters belonging to previous literary genres or modes. It has gathered together bits of a declining political regime, rests of an aristocratic world, but also of grotesque spheres, quite alien to *decorum* (social norms, literary constructions, linguistic registers). The fantastic assembled remains of magical worldviews and sometimes made astonishing artifacts of them. This fragmented condition is closely related to the uncanny described by Sigmund Freud in his homonymous essay of 1919 – "Das Unheimliche," originally in German –, and the uncanny itself is inherent in the fantastic effect, as said above. From the historical and political point of view, a parallel with the political evolution in modern times could be drawn: when Western democracies progressed by limiting institutional power in order to allow more individual freedom for their citizens, the fantastic narrative mode flourished as a site of conflicts in which the individual's vulnerability and insecurity were increased. It was the literary mirror image of a different kind of defenselessness with regard to the one reigning in preindustrial times. It was a vulnerability rather connected with fragmentation in Western societies, where the very concept of epistemological legitimacy was gradually eroded, and public powers were clearly segmented.

Apart from this fragmented condition, ambiguity became a notion completely attached to fantastic literature, especially by Todorov's attempt to systematize the divergences between the fantastic and the marvelous. Fantastic works contain ambiguity as any literary text, as long as they implicitly present unexplained aspects: the unsaid, the textual voids leading to indeterminacy (cf. Bouvet 2007). Some of this unrevealed material can increase fantasticality[21] because it refers to

---

20 The distinction between what Roas (cf. 2006) named physical or emotional fear, on the one hand, and metaphysical or intellectual fear, on the other, has been one of his and other scholars' hobbyhorses when working on the theory of the fantastic.

21 This term does not refer to a different sort or understanding of fantastic literature, but to the fantastic condition of a text, in this case according to the assumptions that have

impossible events or phenomena, but obviously the fundamental elements heading to the fantasticality of the text are the unexplainable circumstances pointed out in the story. It is their factual impossibility that makes them unclear: this unfeasibility involves the unclear meaning of the alluded circumstances. On the other hand, the fantastic effect is ambiguous as well, taking into the account the plurality of reactions experienced by characters or readers after perceiving or sensing the transgression of an impossible event or phenomenon. Following Todorov's terminology, in the pure fantastic the unexplained coincides principally with the unexplainable, whereas in the fantastic – marvelous, the unexplainable has been partially explained, though leaving as unexplained a part of it. Therefore, after the implicit acceptance of the vampire's or the ghost's existence, fear and apprehension for the unexplainable moves into the unexplained: How on earth is this unbelievable event possible? Where does the monster come from? Moreover, identity and ideological projections make themselves evident: Who am I if the Other really exists? What are our respective places and the boundaries in-between? How can this amazing phenomenon affect my community, humankind, or me? According to Todorov and his followers, ambiguity is the cornerstone of the fantastic, either through the unexplainable, or through the unexplained, placing the focus on the metaphors and symbols that convey innumerable meanings in literature.

Meanwhile, a less solemn and unhumorous trend shows up in the historical picture of fantastic literature, also being a source of clever debates without leaving the inherent features of its narrative mode aside.[22] In truth, quite often fantastic literary works include parodies of scientific stiffness and more or less subtle apologies of fantastic fiction, revealing an inclination to consider this narrative mode as a way to potentiate freedom of thought, to promote changes of mentality and behavior, and to pay attention to the violence caused by institutionalized confessions and discourses of hatred. For this purpose, the authors use narrative tools that produce uncertainty about definite principles, showing also a propensity for distorting ideas or social convictions that, if presented in a different way, would prove robust and attractive: from the naturalization of traditional religious beliefs through an apparent rationalism of a positivist nature to metafictional

been detailed above. Thus, an increased fantasticality implies the reinforcement of the features through which the concept of fantastic in fiction has been previously defined.

22 Roas (2011: 172-176) convincingly argues that humor does not always prevent or disrupt the fantastic effect. On the contrary, the uncanny may be heightened and deepened when irony and parody are wittily used renewing means, subjects and commonplaces that have been overexploited both in fantastic literature and cinema (ibid: 175).

metamorphoses destabilizing epistemological and ideological assumptions of reality. In the Hispanic literary world of the fantastic, two writers from different times and places, Emilia Pardo Bazán (1851-1921) and Julio Cortázar (1914-1984), are respectively excellent examples of these extremely different tendencies.[23]

On the one hand, ideological and comic elements sometimes boost the uncanny aspects of the texts, developing other meanings in line with approaches like the following one: Irony may be a manifestation of rejecting the banal and the standard, the automatisms of life. This is a typical bourgeois attitude from a leftist perspective. However, at the same time, it is a typical attitude of the working class or the peasantry from an elitist and right-wing position. This intrinsic ambiguity of ironic formulations can underline fantasticality, especially when offered by the agency of misty inexactitudes and imprecisions. On the other hand, it is the uncanny aspect that occasionally confers a preternatural aura to ideological aspects of the story. In both cases, the interweaving of comic, ideological and uncanny factors conduce to the confusion of readers on the subject of political conventions and convictions that are deep-rooted in the social imaginary. Actually, Ismail Kadare (1936), the Albanian writer,[24] effectively applies both techniques in several of his novels, for instance in *The Ghost Rider* (1980) and *Spiritus* (1996).[25] Moreover, fantasticity and metafictionality constitute a very

---

23 In Pardo Bazán's short story "El talismán," the power of traditional Catholicism and common sense – implicitly identified with positive rationalism – are subtly used for discrediting preternatural beliefs. On the other hand, many short stories by Cortázar exemplify the metafictional metamorphoses that destabilize epistemological and ideological assumptions of reality, among many others "Carta a una señorita de París" ("Letter to a Young Lady in Paris") or "Axolotl."

24 For many lovers of fantastic literature, Kadare is still an unknown author of splendid novels (both fantastic and realist), though he has been mentioned ever and again as a candidate to the Nobel Prize in Literature. Some of his works were censured by Hoxha's communist regime, becoming a committed author that showed a deep devotion to Albanian history and traditions. Two important reasons of his lack of popularity are the tenacity with which he continued writing in his mother tongue and the small size of Albania, a country that not only was behind the iron curtain when Kadare started his career, but was also on the periphery of the communist orbit. However, he has received prestigious awards, like the Man Booker International Prize in 2005 and the Prince of Asturias Award for Literature in 2009.

25 The former novel's first English edition was published as *Doruntine*. *Spiritus* remains unpublished in English.

effective duet in damaging any attempt of hegemony by a group or ideology in textual representation.[26]

3. THE FANTASTIC GOES INTO POLITICS

Bourgeoisie, subversiveness, and reason: The Marxist approaches to the study of ideology in fantastic literature

Concerning the introduction of political ideas in literary analyses, the fact that ideologies condition the different conceptions of fantastic fiction should not be forgotten, because theories are definitely not neutral. For instance, in literary theory of the fantastic there is a tendency of using terms belonging to the legal and political spheres (legality, status quo, etc.) or structuring ideas in accordance with underlying ideological assumptions. Todorov's ambiguity is also inscribed in a framework of contemporary art thinking that is not detached from the moral issues that were a source of worry for the Western Christian institutions when observing the tearing apart of their ideological system,[27] operating originally from the Middle Ages thanks to the triumph of Christianity. In the same line, classifications and definitions of fantastic theoretical key terms can be understood from a perspective related to certain political orientations: among others, the Freudian concept of the uncanny, the ethical proposals extracted from the medievalizing marvelous (or fantasy), like Tolkien's concept of consolation,[28] or the escapist argument against non-realistic works. In this respect, all the mentioned concepts become full of meaning – the meaning currently shared – if they work inside the parameters of a certain ideology. How is it possible to apprehend

---

26 For an analysis in English of the ideological use of metafiction in the fantastic fiction of a contemporary Catalan author, Jesús Moncada, see Gregori (2016).

27 This source of worry for the Western Christian institutions came from the breakthrough from the paradigm of the preindustrial era to the paradigm of modernity, which too often appears in literary studies as a quick and sudden move radically changing Western mentality. In reality, this change of paradigm has been a long and controversial process, not concluded if taking into account the existence of supernatural beliefs in Western countries. For a comprehensive analysis of this phenomenon, see Berger (2014).

28 In his essay "On Fairy-Stories," Tolkien described it as follows: "The consolation of fairy-stories, the joy of the happy ending: or more correctly of the good catastrophe, the sudden joyous 'turn'" (1966: 85-95).

them isolated from the ideological context in which they were created? That is, how is it possible to apprehend the uncanny without the belief in the primordial animism assumed by Freud, or the consolation without Tolkien's mythicized Christian symbolism, or a type of animosity towards the notion of escapism that is being developed as a result of the philosophy of the "Art for Art's" sake?[29]

Rosemary Jackson's *Fantasy: The Literature of Subversion* (1981) and José M. Monleón's *A Specter is Haunting Europe: A Sociohistorical Approach to the Fantastic* (1990) are the most significant studies on the function of ideology in fantastic works.[30] They are additionally immensely suitable for the present article because both scholars are interested in fantastic fiction as it has been exposed previously, that is, as literary texts focusing on the conflict that is caused by the contrast between the unreal element and the conventional idea of reality; moreover, this conflict pushes the development of action and digressive reflections forward. Indeed, Jackson and Monleón have in common their post-Todorovian stance, containing interestingly argued reflections on the cultural, social, and political aspects that influence fantastic writing. They stress their preference of the narrative mode that is here called "fantastic" over the marvelous literature. Indeed, while rightly calling it "naive to equate fantasy with either anarchic or revolutionary politics" (Jackson 1986: 14), Jackson takes a political position that condemns the medievalizing marvelous as a result of its allegorical and religious-like character, reproducing the location of good and evil outside the human dimension and displacing human responsibility to the level of destiny. According to her, this narrative mode simply lacks the disruptive character of the fantastic texts, becoming thus conservative tale such as: "those romance fictions produced by Lewis, Tolkien, T.H. White and other modern fabulists, all of whom look back to a lost moral and social hierarchy, which their fantasies attempt to recapture and revivify" (ibid: 95). She puts them all in the same category of "liberal humanism" (ibid: 155).

---

29 During post-war times, many academic apologies of literary commitment criticized the "escapist" tendencies of fantastic or fantasy writers. In fact, this literary commitment and the idea of the "art for art's sake" can be described as two sides of the same coin.

30 We could also take into consideration Irène Bessière's *Le Récit fantastique: la poétique de l'incertain* (1974), which constitutes an essential link between Todorov's and Jackson's approaches, and more recently David Sandner's *Critical Discourse of the Fantastic (1712-1831)* (2011), which despite the bygone period of the title proposes an original distinction between different expressions of the unreal in contemporary literature, touching on ideology as well.

As it was said, Jackson essentially considers a text to be more "fantastic" if read-ers can find potentially troubling and antisocial impulses in it. The author seems to consider 19th-century realist fiction a platform for sustaining the ideology of the bourgeoisie. Her perspective combines a psychoanalytical approach (both Freudian and Lacanian) and an influence of both classic[31] and post-Marxism.[32] In this sense, while she asserts that the formal and thematic features of fantastic fic-tion are determined by the (unattainable) attempt to find a language for desire (Jackson 1986: 62), she also postulates that "the most subversive fantasies are those which attempt to transform the relation of the imaginary and the symbol-ic," particularly when "suggesting, or projecting, the dissolution of the symbolic through violent reversal or rejection of the process of the subject's formation" (ibid: 91). As Jackson herself puts it alluding to Bessière's study on the fantas-tic,[33] when readers get into this kind of disturbed state of mind, the subversive character of the story is confirmed.[34] Consequently, this state of mind may be identified with the anxiety or apprehension experienced by fantastic readers ac-cording to Roas, specifically with his premise about a metaphysical or intellectu-al fear felt by readers when immersed in this narrative mode. In short, subversive ideology in Jackson's view is related to a specific type of the fantastic – which she and other scholars mention as the classic sort from the 19th century – and to a

---

31 The following quotation confirms this affinity with the classic Marxist mainstream: "Like any other text, a literary fantasy is produced within, and determined by, its so-cial context. Though it might struggle against the limits of this context, often being ar-ticulated upon that very struggle, it cannot be understood in isolation from it. The forms taken by any particular fantastic text are determined by a number of forces, which intersect and interact in different ways in each individual work. Recognition of these forces involves placing authors in relation to historical, social, economic, politic and sexual determinants, as well to a literary tradition of fantasy" (Jackson 1986: 3).

32 Conforming to this post-structuralist synthesis, she even offers her own definition of ideology, which she describes as something "profoundly unconscious": "Ideology – roughly speaking the imaginary way in which men experience the real world, those ways in which men's relation to the world is lived through various systems of mean-ing such as religion, family, law, moral codes, education, culture, etc." (Jackson 1986: 61)

33 See footnote number 30.

34 "Fantastic texts which try to negate or dissolve dominant signifying practices, espe-cially 'character' representation, become, from this perspective, radically disturbing" (Jackson 1986: 90).

psychological approach that establishes a narrative mode in line with a certain readers' responses.

José B. Monleón, a more traditional Marxist researcher, wrote his *A Specter is Haunting Europe* by adopting an approach based mainly on Lukács's contributions and their developments by the Frankfurt School of thought. Strongly suggesting Monleón's ideological orientation, the title is an allusion to the introduction of *The Communist Manifesto*: "A Specter is Haunting Europe." As a matter of fact, the main actor to be analyzed critically in this book is – again – the bourgeoisie. Nonetheless, the author also applies a pertinent psychological distinction between two sides or concretions of the disturbance mentioned above: On the one hand, irrationalism, which may have led to expand the boundaries imposed by the bourgeois policy, because the introduction of the irrational in literary texts – through monsters, for instance – fought the model of reason that this class tried to impose; on the other hand, unreason, which contributed to maintain the status quo and the ruling economic order because it allowed the arbitrary power to oppress the weakest and the underprivileged (Monleón 1990: 139).[35] It was through unreason that fantastic literature on the whole played a conservative role for preserving social inequality: "If anything, it served precisely to help modify hegemonic discourse in order to justify the survival of bourgeoisie society, a fact that also explains why the fantastic appeared only after the bourgeoisie had consolidated its power." (ibid: 14) In such manner, Monleón disagrees with Jackson, who thinks that fantastic fiction very often questions the dominant social postulates. Monleón (ibid: 101) argues that the fact of questioning these postulates in or through the text does not imply an ideologically progressive subversion, because in his opinion "reactionary" forces can raise likewise objections against the bourgeois social order.

Indeed, these two paradigmatic examples show the considerable magnitude of a Marxist ideological tradition in Western literary studies. This tradition, however, is not uniform. Dealing with ideology in literature or in the humanities in general, frequent concepts can be found that were forged by left-wing thinkers

---

35 Monleón argues that during the 19th century the lower classes were dehumanized by dominant culture, imposing upon them an image of monstrosity: "By losing his humanity, the proletarian entered the universe of unreason; from there, he became a threat" (1990: 78-79). Besides, unreason was gradually occupying spaces in artistic works, making meaning inapprehensible and preventing from distinguishing between otherness and the self (Monleón 1990: 99). According to the scholar's Marxist postulates, these processes allowed the dominant ideologies to abolish the proletarian instruments of making claims.

belonging to distinct currents of Marxism – including naturally Marx and Engels
–, such as, among others, false consciousness, reification of work, dominant
class, hegemony, or Ideological State Apparatuses (ISA). They are still useful
tools for interpreting a considerable amount of literary works, since numerous
writers of fantastic narratives have been educated in a cultural paradigm in
which these Marxist premises were (and still are) almost inevitable, creating thus
a shared worldview. These writers were either active members of left-wing parties or campaigned for Marxist ideals. Nonetheless, the present proposal moves
rather away from those Marxist concepts – though using and analyzing them
when necessary –, in order to offer a renewed concept of ideology that should fit
research methodologies and perspectives for the analysis of the complex ideological phenomena taking place in contemporary times and fantastic fiction.

Ambiguity and interpellation: Some renewed approaches

In this reorientation of the ideological analysis of the fantastic and literature in
general, the assumptions of the political scientist Michael Freeden shall be taken
into a particular account. They are argued and detailed in his book *Ideologies
and Political Theory* (1996), in which ideology is considered as a manifold phenomenon irreducible to (tendentious) simplifications:

"First, ideologies are importantly attached to social groups, not necessarily classes. Ideologies are produced by, directed at, and consumed by groups. Second, ideologies perform
a range of services, such as legitimation, integration, socialization, ordering, simplification, and action-orientation, without which societies could not function adequately, if at
all. Third ideologies are ubiquitous forms of political thinking, reflecting as they do varie-
gated perceptions, misperceptions, and conceptualizations of existing or imagined social
worlds [...] Fourth, ideologies are inevitably associated with power, though not invariably
with the threatening or exploitative version of power." (Freeden 1996: 22-23)

Moreover, specific and fundamental ideologies like conservatism, liberalism, an-
archism, socialism, nationalism, or feminism do not stand as a solid block, but
rather as a network of non-identical features in different countries and historical
periods. Consequently, we should talk about socialisms, feminisms, national-
isms, and even anarchisms or liberalisms, and that must be reflected on the analyses of manifestations of ideology in literary texts.

The core of Freeden's theory is understanding ideologies not as a set of immutable ideas, but as complex arrangements whose analysis is in debt to premises related to contemporary linguistic theories. Ideologies cannot be monolithic

entities that would fit any model of our interconnected and wealthy Western world in modern times. As Göran Therborn argued in 1980: "Particularly in today's open and complex societies, different ideologies, however defined, not only coexist, compete, and clash, but also overlap, affect, and contaminate one another" (1999: 79). As for Freeden's vision, ideologies are socio-political constructions made of political concepts. These political concepts combine and form singular configurations according to the time and space in which they are inserted. Another key idea about that is what Freeden calls the contestability of political concepts, that is the capacity of getting their meanings modified or distorted due to their ambiguity: "essential contestability provides the manifold flexibility out of which ideological families and their subvariants are constructed"[36] (1996: 3). These political concepts are indefinite terms, floating signifiers always in discussion by socio-political agents of different ideological orientations, with the possibility that they get their meanings modified or distorted due to their ambiguity. Therefore, specific senses of political concepts must be disambiguated in a network of contested meanings, and ideologies are groups of disambiguated political concepts in a defined period of time.

Consequently, ambiguity becomes a central issue in the conjunction of ideology and fantasticality. Disambiguation consists in conferring specific meanings to the set of political concepts taken into account in defined ideologies, not only by means of the discursive tradition transmitted across history or the wide range of cultures in which these concepts have been developed, but through their particular position in the concepts' constellation as well. In this sense, what is interesting about the presence of ideologies in fantastic literature is the co-existence of ambiguities, particularly the overlapping or crisscrossing of the ambiguity created by the preternatural event and the ambiguity related to the ideological aspect. Both ambiguities need the observer's gaze in order to get determined. That means that, when interpreting the ambiguous ideological meaning of certain elements in the text, conforming to a network that place them into the orbit of one or several of the ideologies in question, readers should simultaneously reconstruct what has remained unexplained in the fantastic story and should imagine what is unexplainable as something essential to that fantasticality. Further-

---

36 It must be said that, he himself being a product of his times and context, Freeden sustains his argumentation with the notion of contest, which itself represents a deepseated form in the liberal Anglo-Saxon tradition: he displays conceptual plurality as a market ruled by concurrence laws, but not as a struggle between actors with their own class interests, as Marxism does.

more, the singular fantastic condition of the literary work may influence its readers' perception of the ideological aspect present in it.[37]

Apart from that, when applying Freeden's concept of ideology to the analysis of fantastic works, their fantasticality provides subtle nuances contributing to outlining renewed meanings, as well as challenging ideological idealizations stemming from historically and politically legitimated discourses. This kind of analysis makes sense especially if the examined works are not simple reproductions of genre structures with slightly modified stories and different names for the characters. Since literary complexity allows deep interpretations under the sign of how ideological aspects function within their frame, it is much more convenient for the analysis to select texts in which narrators are able to break the horizon of expectations. That concerns fiction constructed for establishing a fertile and valuable dialogue with the reader, implying, if possible, interesting philosophical, cultural, and ethical reflections. The literary analysis of the ideological component depends on its visibility in the text. In order to disambiguate each relevant term in the interpretation, we should take a logical and reasonable path: the principle of following an isotopic interpretation making sense built on the main line of meanings, according to rationally chosen semantic fields deduced from the text. This coherence principle helps us not to get stuck in an isolated detail or an anecdotic word, although it can consist in a network of calibrated silences as well. Nonetheless, the isotopic interpretation may collide with the antinomic or paradoxical nature of the fantastic, as an artistic form based on contradictions and irresolvable conflicts. Everything in the analysis is significant.

Even the represented reality in the fantastic works is significant, not only as a bare background against which the impossible is outlined. Hence, as for the factor of the real in all this argumentation about ideology in fantastic fiction, ideologies may be considered as part of reality, of our world. On the one hand, this question is linked to the fact that in modern times aesthetic and political ideologies have been reflected on more consciously than in the past. Besides, this *discursive* reality is also communicable or representable in literature, as a political-oriented voice or from a meta-ideological point of view, that is, as a reflection on ideologies in literary works. On the other hand, the fantastic works by means of some conventionalized figures or formulas, like ghosts or vampires, but still by means of hard-to-believe formulas that really break the readers' horizon of expectation. These disrupting options can be so unconventional that they would not be considered as fantastic but rather as something mystifying, absurd, or acci-

---

37 For instance, the gender and national or political questionings of Woolf's *Orlando* can
be undervalued because of its fantastic representation as something inconceivable.

dental, maybe the product of a disturbed mind. Instead, the ideological aspect generally depends on credible manifestations that usually do not break that horizon of expectation.[38] In relation to that, in the postmodern literary framework it is probable (credible) that a vampire devotes himself to get breastfed by young mamas' milk, than that an old, elitist, and foxhunting English lady collects Stalin's photographs while she writes down Leninist speeches in support of striking miners.[39] The first would be considered an original recreation of the vampire's myth, while the second would be received as an absurdity caused by the lady's madness. From this point of view, the ideological component most of the times functions as a benchmark in represented reality in order to avoid the fantastic story to become something else, entering the category of the absurd. As scholars have frequently repeated in studies about the theory of the fantastic, this narrative mode needs (a conventional idea of) reality to be contrasted with the unreal event happening in the story. Precisely the manifestations of ideology add this component of reality to literary texts, helping categorize them as fantastic fiction. The marvelous and the absurd are categories that, for different reasons, lack solid links to the conventional idea of reality.

After this reflection on ideology's ties with reality, it is worth paying attention to a significant concept of Louis Althusser, one of the most influential French critics for the renovation of critical discourse about ideology in the Marxist circles. He is the author of a relevant essay, "Ideology and Ideological State Apparatuses" (1970), which curiously appeared in the same year as Todorov's original French edition of *The Fantastic* (*Introduction à la littérature fantastique*). Althusser opened the door to the identification of socialism or communism as ideologies from a Marxist point of view, because he asserted that every person is subjected to an ideology, which is precisely the instance conferring subjectivity to everyone. Ideology turns individuals into subjects, in both senses of the term. In this way, it consists in the process by which ideology constitutes an individual into subject, in the double sense of this word, meaning on the one hand subjection to the power that dictates that ideology, and on the other hand, the process of acquiring a subjectivity.[40] In contemporary times, Althusser

---

38 That means the horizon of expectation of citizens more or less conscious about how their society is organized.

39 These examples have been invented by the author of this paper.

40 Etymologically, the term "subject" refers to the fact of being subjugated ("subiectus") to someone or to some powerful body, while its meaning emphasizing a person's individuality and autonomy is the current one nowadays in Romance languages like French, Spanish or Catalan, for instance.

(1995: 274, 280-282) proposes the label of the "Ideological State Apparatuses"[41] (ISA) for designating the institutional means by which the individual gets subjected/subjugated to the dominant ideology. Being a system of representations with a practice-social function (Althusser 2005: 231), the dominant ideology all at once pertinently keeps these apparatuses attached and undivided (Althusser 1995: 286).

People become subjects under an ideological shield that penetrates them. Hence, there are two parallel processes taking place in an individual when he or she is socialized: a process of psychological and legal subjugation, and a process of qualification, allowing this person to play a set of roles conferred by society. This constitution of the individual into subject is due to the ideological effect that Althusser called "interpellation." If ideology is understood as a component of reality in the literary text, that means, a technique for subjecting characters to the real world fictionally represented in the story as a convention, accordingly Althusser's ideological effect can be related to the fantastic as a narrative mode. Thus, a strong opposition could be easily remarked here between ideology, which generates subjects, and the fantastic effect, which tends to raise serious doubts about the subject's own identity as we have seen before. In other words, while ideologies interpellate the individuals into subjects, the fantastic "disinterpellates" the subject for keeping him in a bewildering state of mind, looking for interpellation.

4. CONCLUDING REMARKS

As a theoretical examination of the problem stated in its title ("Crossing Impossible Boundaries? Fantastic Narrative and Ideology"), this study displays that, in a rigorous ideological analysis of literary works, it is necessary to combine the profuse Marxist tradition with its renewed versions or brand-new approaches to

---

41 The French thinker gathers in this concept the different churches, the educational system, the family, some other institutions of the legal and political order (parties, trade unions, professional colleges, etc.), as well as media and cultural institutions like the arts, sports, and so on (Althusser 1995: 282). On the other hand, Althusser's approach contributed to generalizing ideology almost everywhere as a structural whole, emptying it from any distinctive meaning and, consequently, weakening its pertinence as an analytical category. It is worth pointing out that Foucault studied under Althusser at the French École Normale Supérieure, though very early in his career he rejected Marxism as an academic methodology.

the concept of ideology. Subtle allusions to political facts or orientations appearing in a text permit complex and more interesting literary analyses when those allusions are displayed in a plot where the fantastic is not only an ornament to satisfy fans of unreal effects. However, it would be wrong to disregard stories denouncing in a rather obvious way offences or political injustices, especially those targeting the ISA, for instance an imperialist, totalitarian or corrupt state, the church as a forbidding institution, or the family as a patriarchal redoubt. Following the same spirit of openly blaming the enemy, conflicts between different nations do not go unnoticed in some literary works, sometimes accompanying an ecologist perspective and an evil-shaped spectrum of capitalism, sometimes reviving the past that has been deformed by the ruling power. Indeed, in some literary works the specter of an evil force that can only be identified as capitalism devastates everything, challenging that other messianic specter announced by *The Communist Manifesto*.

In a dichotomy à la Tolkien, Sandner (2011: 29-30) summarized the effects of the two narratives modes that have been historically opposed by critics: the helplessness caused by the fantastic uncanny on the one hand, and the consolation provided by marvelous stories on the other. However, we have seen that this helplessness, the different forms of shaking human identity and our meaning of life, could develop the skills for the readers' critical thinking: disambiguation of a manifold combination of ideological and fantastic referents can achieve it. This is a capacity often identified with Modernity or Postmodernity, as the high point of the Western idea of the subject and his or her possibility of choosing – the very link between Todorov's first systematic categorization of the literature of the unreal and Freeden's pro-liberal approach to the concept of ideology. Furthermore, critical thinking should be considered a positive element contributing either to the setting-up of a new reality better than the previous one (the utopian perspective), or simply to the improvement of the state of affairs in society (the possibilist option). As for this dilemma, whatever the preference is, the point lies in the expansion of knowledge by imagination, being one of the major basis of human evolution, the crossing of boundaries viewed often as impossible, unwieldy or inappropriate, like those of compartmentalizing ideology and fantastic literature.

It should be concluded that the imperceptive criticism that intended to invalidate the terms "ideology" and "fantastic" as analytical categories has failed, namely it has failed to invalidate their epistemological effectiveness as long as they both are maintained in academic and social use, quite rightly if the arguments that have been exposed are convincing. Accordingly, it should be assumed that the terms "ideology" and "fantastic" are not only profitable and appropriate to study literary texts, but necessary to put light on the gloomy domains of the kind of literature that explores the unreal.

WORKS CITED

Althusser, Louis (1995): "Idéologie et appareils idéologiques d'Etat." In: Jacques Bidet (ed.), *Sur la reproduction*, Paris: Presses Universitaires de France, pp. 269-314.

Althusser, Louis (2005 [1965]): *For Marx*, London/New York: Verso.

Arendt, Hannah (2004 [1951]): *The Origins of Totalitarianism*, New York: Schocken Books.

Armitt, Lucie (2005): *Fantasy Fiction: An Introduction*, London/New York: Continuum.

Berger, Peter L. (2014): *The Many Altars of Modernity: Toward a Paradigm for Religion in a Pluralist Age*, Boston/Berlin: De Gruyter.

Bessière, Irène (1974): *Le Récit fantastique: la poétique de l'incertain*, Paris: Librairie Larousse.

Bourdieu, Pierre/Eagleton, Terry (1994): "Doxa and Common Life: An Interview." In Slavoj Žižek (ed.), *Mapping Ideology*, London/New York: Verso, pp. 265-277.

Bouvet, Rachel (2007): *Étranges récits, étranges lectures: essai sur l'effet fantastique*, Quebec: Presses de l'Université du Québec.

Camargo, Ricardo (2011): *El Sublime Re-torno de la Ideología: de Platón a Žižek*, Santiago de Chile: Metales Pesados.

Debray, Régis (1981): *Critique de la raison politique ou l'inconscient religieux de la politique*, Paris: Gallimard.

Foucault, Michel (1984 [1977]): *The Foucault Reader*, Paul Rabinow (ed.), New York: Pantheon Books.

Fowler, Alastair (1982): *Kinds of Literature: An Introduction to the Theory of Genres and Modes*, Oxford: Clarendon Press.

Freeden, Michael (1996): *Ideologies and Political Theory: A Conceptual Approach*, Oxford: Clarendon Press.

Freud, Sigmund (1985 [1919]): "The Uncanny." In: *Art and Literature*, Albert Dickson (ed.), (James Strachey, Trans.), Harmondsworth: Penguin Books, pp. 335-376.

Gramsci, Antonio (1971): *Selections from the Prison Notebooks of Antonio Gramsci*, New York: International Publishers.

Gregori, Alfons (2015): *La dimensión política de lo irreal: el componente ideológico en la narrativa fantástica española y catalana*, Poznań: Wydawnictwo Naukowe UAM.

Gregori, Alfons (2016): "A head game or a debate about saints? Fantasy and references to republican ideology and policy in Jesús Moncada's short stories." In Emili Samper (ed.), *The Myths of the Republic: Literature and Identity*, Kassel: Reichenberger, pp. 223-236.

Hawkes, David (2003 [1996]): *Ideology*, London/New York: Routledge.

Jackson, Rosemary (1986 [1981]): *Fantasy: The Literature of Subversion*, London/New York: Routledge.

Monleón, José B. (1990): *A Specter is Haunting Europe: A Sociohistorical Approach to the Fantastic*, Princeton: Princeton University Press.

Roas, David (2006): "Hacia una teoría sobre el miedo y lo fantástico." In: *Semiosis* II/3, pp. 95-116.

Roas, David (2011): *Tras los límites de lo real: una definición de lo fantástico*, Madrid: Páginas de Espuma.

Sandner, David (2011): *Critical Discourse of the Fantastic (1712-1831)*, Farnham/Burlington: Ashgate.

Therborn, Göran (1999 [1980]): *The Ideology of Power and the Power of Ideology*, London/New York: Verso.

Todorov, Tzvetan (1975 [1970]): *The Fantastic*, Ithaca: Cornell University Press.

Tolkien, J.R.R. (1966): *The Tolkien Reader*, New York: Ballantine Books.

Van Dijk, Teun A. (1998): *Ideology: A Multidisciplinary Approach*, London/Thousand Oaks/New Delhi: Sage.

Villoro, Luis (2007 [1985]): *El concepto de ideología y otros ensayos*, Mexico: Fondo de Cultura Económica.

Questioning Mononormativity: A Future of Fantastic Scholarship in Liminal Identities

BRANDY EILEEN ALLATT

Fantastic literature has long been a bastion of exploring ideas that might cause a negative reaction on the part of the reader, by placing them in a fictional setting which allows for an exploration of ideas while also distancing the reader from the sense of 'otherness' that might be rejected in a real-world setting. Thus, the fantastic has historically questioned a number of patriarchal ideologies concerning heteronormativity and the gender binary. As Western society begins to more openly discuss liminal identities, non-normative identities that are considered as existing on the edge of society, opportunities arise to address the critical examination of identities that have yet to be explored within fantastic scholarship. This chapter proposes that a new branch of critical scholarship can be found in examining the ethically non-monogamous relationships represented in fantastic literature.

As early as the 1960s, the fantastic has occasionally dealt with relationships that do not subscribe to the Western ideological construct of inherently patriarchal monogamous relationships that subordinate the sexual expression of women and other non-males, while upholding the 'ownership' of a person by another. This chapter will briefly examine the context of consensual (or ethical) non-monogamy in fantastic studies by discussing the growing interest in, and critical discourse on, these consensually non-monogamous relationship structures. Then, it will provide a close reading of three selected works of science fiction which book-end the fantastic between the 1960s and current times in order to show how ethical non-monogamous relationships are represented in fantastic (in this case, science fiction) texts: Heinlein's *Stranger in a Strange Land* (1961), Le Guin's *The Left Hand of Darkness* (1969), and Singh's *Distances* (2008). Please note that while this chapter is about the fantastic as a whole, the scope of this inquiry is largely limited to a discussion of science fiction as an exemplar. In the conclusion, this chapter will return to the discussion of the academic discourse on ethical non-monogamy, this time within the context of critical scholarship in the fantastic, tying in examinations of the literature produced by fiction writers with the critical scholarship produced by academics. Through this approach and considering the inherency of liminal identities in the fantastic due to its distanced positioning of 'otherness,' this chapter intends to show consensual non-monogamy as one of the liminal identifiers of upcoming importance in scholarship on fantastic literature as public interest in non-monogamous relationships models grows.

WHAT IS ETHICAL NON-MONOGAMY?

The concept of consensual, or ethical, non-monogamy, is widely regarded by those within communities focused on exploring ethical non-monogamy to be an anti-patriarchal, feminist, and egalitarian relationship model suitable for all genders and all sexual orientations.[1] As stated by Tristan Taormino in *Opening Up: A Guide to Creating and Sustaining Open Relationships*, "[i]t's no coincidence that many of the people who are living in open [ethically non-monogamous] relationships have defied societal norms in other ways. Confronted with binary choices such as gay or straight, male or female, husband or wife, they literally or figuratively choose 'other'" (2008: 297). Ethical non-monogamy is not the unequal and heteronormative polygyny often found linked to religious beliefs that allow one gender to have multiple spouses, each of whom are only allowed the same, singular spouse. In various forms of ethical non-monogamy, the central tenet is that it is openly and honestly discussed and, most importantly, consented to by all participants involved. This is not to say that patriarchally-linked polygyny is necessarily not a choice for those involved, but merely to acknowledge that one must question how much agency a devout religious adherent feels in their choices, with respect to how closely they uphold their religion's tenets. According to Dossie Easton and Janet W. Hardy in the second edition of their book, *The Ethical Slut: A Practical Guide to Polyamory, Open Relationships & Other Adventures*, consent means "an active collaboration for the benefit, well-being, and pleasure of all persons concerned. If someone is being coerced, bullied, blackmailed, manipulated, lied to, or ignored, what is happening is not consen-

---

1   A succinct overview of ethical non-monogamy and its history, discussed as "polyamory," can be found in Olga Khazan's 2014 article in *The Atlantic*, "Multiple Lovers, Without Jealousy."

sual. And sex that is not consensual is not ethical – period" (2009 [1997]: 21). While ethical non-monogamy can take many forms – from 'swinging' freely between sexual partners for pleasure, to polyamorous relationships centered on sex as an expression of love or affection, to relatively 'closed' polyamorous relationships where the participants are monogamous as a group, and untold numbers of variations between – the central tenet in all of these relationship structures is that those involved have an equal say and equal consent in how the relationship is constructed. Some ethical non-monogamists make use of more than one relationship model. For instance, Person A might be in a polyamorous 'vee,' a relationship model that would look like the letter 'V' if one to draw it on paper with lines to dictate committed relationship dynamics, where they are in a committed partnership with Persons B and C, but might still occasionally engage in a sexual liaison outside of the 'vee' with another party for the purpose of pleasure and without the interest in or capacity to sustain another committed partnership, with all parties fully knowledgeable of and consenting to such an arrangement. It is such open honesty and knowledgeable consent that is the foundation of ethical non-monogamy.

Proponents of ethical non-monogamy argue that, under such a relationship model, women are freed from the patriarchal ideology that casts them as 'tainted goods' if they freely explore and express their sexuality, while men are freed from the patriarchal urge to claim women as property for their exclusive pleasure. In the same vein, those who do not conform to gender and/or sexuality binaries can claim the freedom to explore all facets of their genderedness and sexuality, including the spectrums of sexual and/or romantic interest seen nonnormative identities such as asexuals and aromantics, as well as the individual spectrums of genderedness seen in genderqueer and genderfluid identities. Inherently, consensual non-monogamy challenges many patriarchal concepts such as gendered roles in societies, women as property, and the double standard that allows only men to freely enjoy sex; and promotes the feminist ideology that all genders should be allowed equal access to sexual pleasure, equal consent in a relationship, equal ownership in one's own pleasure through communication with one's partner(s) about one's desires, and equal responsibility for the reproductive and sexual safety of all those concerned.[2] As such, ethical non-monogamy stands

---

2 For further reading on these fundamental concepts within ethical non-monogamous communities, Deborah Anapol's *Polyamory: The New Love Without Limits* (1997 [1992]) proposes many of these general benefits to practicing ethical non-monogamy [ENM]. Anapol's concepts are further expanded by Franklin Veaux and Eve Rickert's *More than Two: A Practical Guide to Ethical Polyamory* (2014), as well as Dossie

in stark opposition to the ideologies that underlie patriarchal practices, such as religion-sanctioned polygyny. To put it simply, where society dictates the 'one size fits all' relationship model of monogamy as the only culturally acceptable norm, ethical non-monogamy stands as a 'choose your own adventure' relationship model based on the equal consent and freedom of all parties involved.

A THEORETICAL REVIEW OF DISCOURSES ON ETHICAL NON-MONOGAMY

Although public interest in ethical non-monogamy rose and then promptly died down in the mid-20th century, ethical non-monogamy has recently seen a resurgence of interest, both in the form of academic discourse across much of the social science spectrum and in public discussions of popular culture. While ethical non-monogamy briefly came to light in the 1960s 'free love' culture, it was dismissed from Western social consciousness along with 'flower power' and bell-bottoms. As psychologists Meg Barker and Darren Langdridge write, "[n]early a decade ago, Roger Rubin's (2001) article [...] bemoaned the lack of popular and scholarly consideration of 'alternative lifestyles' since the 1960s and 1970s, within which he included non-traditional family forms, multiple and open relationships" (Barker/Landridge 2010: 748). Yet, by contrast, "[t]he last decade has seen an explosion of interest in consensually non-monogamous relationships" (ibid: 748). This interest is seen across the cultural spectrum: on bookshelves, with the release of self-help-style books like Tristan Taormino's *Opening Up: A Guide to Creating and Sustaining Open Relationships* (2008), and more academically inclined non-fiction titles such *Sex at Dawn: The Prehistoric Origins of Modern Sexuality* (2010) by the psychologist/psychiatrist team Christopher Ryan and Cacilda Jethá; on television, as in Showtime's series *Polyamory: Married and Dating*, which first aired in 2012; and in news stories about celebrities who

---

Easton and Janet W. Hardy's *The Ethical Slut: A Practical Guide to Polyamory, Open Relationships, and Other Adventures* (2009 [1997]), and Tristan Taormino's *Opening Up: A Guide to Creating and Sustaining Open Relationships* (2008), both of which feature interviews from practicing ethical non-monogamists that cite some of these concepts as rationale for ENM. Furthermore, many of these reasons are echoed in Christopher Ryan and Cacilda Jethá's *Sex at Dawn: The Prehistoric Origins of Modern Sexuality* (2010), which argues that humans evolved to be non-monogamous, and that monogamy came about with the rise of agriculture and fixed communities concerned hereditary estates and paternity certainty.

are rumored to have open relationships, like Jada Pinkett Smith and Will Smith (Marcus 2015).

Barker and Langdridge note, "[i]n terms of popular interest, consensual non-monogamies have become a sexual story of intense public fascination (Plummer, 1995) attracting a new burst of commentaries and debates every few months" (2010: 749). This interest is not limited to popular culture, however:

"[T]here has been a recent proliferation of research on nonmonogamies from disciplines across and beyond the social sciences, as well as moves towards researching diverse family forms (as well as relationships) [...] Another current trend in the research [...] has been a turn towards theoretical work exploring what more explicitly non-normative relationships might look like [...] Such work primarily draws on poststructuralism and queer theory to trouble and collapse hierarchical dichotomies [...] between different forms of non-mono-gamy, love and sex, love and friendship, inside (the relationship) and outside, private and public." (Barker/Landridge 2010: 61)

These theoretically-based approaches are, of course, central in literary scholarship and academic discourse concerning liminal identities, and form the backbone of much of queer studies within literature.

While such theories are used widely in literary scholarship, they are particularly useful in close examinations of fantastic texts, texts which use a technique of estrangement to posit worlds unlike our own and therefore worlds which are inherently much more likely to be non-normative in comparison to other types of fiction. These theories are therefore suitably applicable to explorations of non-monogamy in fantastic texts. As Roberts writes, "[m]any works of feminist SF provide [a] synthesis of feminist and post-structuralist theory" and that "[i]n the 1960s and '70s, [...] for presenting alternatives to contemporary society, SF provides a wider range of possibilities that women writers can use to criticize patriarchy" (1990: 137). Veronica Hollinger notes that, frequently, "heteronormativity is embedded in both theory and fiction as 'natural' and 'universal,'" and "remains unquestioned and untheorized" (2013: 23-4). If SF is, as Hollinger puts it, "ideally suited, as a narrative mode, to the construction of imaginative challenges to the smoothly oiled technologies of heteronormativity," then the same is equally true in the context of challenging the patriarchal, rarely questioned, and seemingly 'universally natural' construct of what sociologists Marianne Pieper and Robin Bauer term "mononormativity." Barker and Langdridge define mononormativity as "refer[ring] to dominant assumptions of the normalcy and naturalness of monogamy, analogous to such assumptions around heterosexuality inherent in the term heteronormativity" (Hollinger 2013: 24; cf. Barker/

Langdridge 2010: 750). Furthermore, if the works of queer theorists such as Judith Butler, Sue-Ellen Case, and others show that "heterosexuality comes to acquire a certain exoticism as an object of estrangement and we are invited to consider it, not as natural and universal, but – to a large extent – as both learned behavior and a network of forces embedded in the very fabric of culture" as a real-word social construct, then it is equally true that mononormativity might also be reflected as a social construct in opposition to fantastic literature's representations of ethically non-monogamous relationships (Hollinger 2013: 24). In the following readings, I will show how the authors eschew mononormativity in such a way, by highlighting relationship structures in their works that fail to uphold the seemingly universal notion of monogamous relationships as normative. While this approach would work well with a number of texts, this paper focuses on two well-known texts from the 1960s, a time when open relationships were more culturally visible than the later decades of the 20th century – Robert A. Heinlein's *Stranger in a Strange Land* (1961) and Ursula Le Guin's *Left Hand of Darkness* (1969) – and one more recent offering, Vandana Singh's *Distances* (2008). As discussed in detail below, *Stranger in a Strange Land* offers up a form of group marriage (the "Nest") for exploration, *The Left Hand of Darkness* is set in a society in which monogamy and non-monogamy are equally normative, and *Distances* showcases a pentad or five-member household.

STRANGER IN A STRANGE LAND'S NON-MONONORMATIVE "NEST"

The relationship structure that emerges in *Stranger in a Strange Land* is more prominently placed and central to the story, and develops much later in the narrative, when compared to the two other texts discussed in detail in this chapter. Mike, a human born on Martian soil and raised by Martians, spends the majority of the story learning what it is to be human, and ultimately rejects a number of human tenets that conflict with the Martian philosophy within which he was raised. Martians, as pictured by Robert A. Heinlein in his novel, do not reproduce in a fashion similar to humans, so Mike develops his own ideas of how a relationship should function. In the narrative, the sharing of water marks the "water brotherhood" bond between two humans, and is ultimately the basis of the family and "Nest" that Mike builds (Heinlein 1991: 352, 436). The Nest itself is featured in great detail within the novel, and much of the end of the narrative is located within the Nest. Heinlein explains how the Nest is constructed through explanatory dialogue between characters, and goes to great lengths to fully develop it for the reader to imagine. The basic structure of the Nest is shown as a larger family group, where all are equal and everything is shared – even sexual partners – out of love for one another.

One is brought into the Nest, as mentioned earlier, through a "sharing of water," as seen when Mike and Jill, a nurse and Mike's first "water brother" (a Martian and therefore monogendered term and concept), bring Patty, a heavily-tattooed member of the Fosterite religion, into the family (ibid: 352). While Patty is not the first water brother to be gained by Mike, it is the first time the family structure and egalitarian sharing is highlighted, with Mike noting to Patty that "[i]f we've got it, it's yours" (ibid: 367). Though this exchange takes place before the Nest is conceived of, it is the beginning of the reader's introduction to the philosophy that later gives rise to the Nest. Later, after the Nest is established, Ben, a reporter and Jill's friend who convinced her to sneak into Mike's hospital room at the beginning of the narrative, visits it and much of what he sees is in conflict with the mores of the larger human society in the novel, which is similar to Western society today.[3] Ben is particularly disturbed by the openness and sharing of sexual encounters and notes to Mike's father figure, Jubal, that "so help me, they were going to it [having sex], with myself and three or four others in the room at the time" (ibid: 443). It is this openness and sharing that directly informs most of the Nest's construction, but the sharing of sexuality seems to be the tenet that most directly conflicts with 20th-century Western mores.

In the Nest, everyone shares everything, which undoubtedly is made easier by the fact that Mike is wealthier than is easily imaginable, being the sole heir to all members of the original mission to Mars. Having dispatched with financial concerns and greed as factors that do not impact the Nest, Heinlein focuses on the sharing of selves within it. Mike realizes that reproduction is "not the primary purpose [for sex] at all [...] only three or four or a dozen times in a woman's life is a baby quickened in her [...] out of thousands of times she can share herself – and *that* is the primary use for what we can do so often but would need to do so seldom if it were only for reproduction" (ibid: 496-7). Sex "is sharing and growing closer, forever and always." Mike shares sex "directly with those fe-

---

3   That is, with the notable exception of the Fosterites. The Fosterite religion is hedonistic Christian faith in which gambling, drinking alcohol, and otherwise sinful activities are condoned within the Church. As such, a Fosterite does not sin when drinking Fosterite alcohol, or playing Fosterite games of chance while at church. However, the overt commercialization of religion in *Stranger in a Strange Land* is beyond the scope of this chapter.

male, indirectly by inviting more sharing with those male" (ibid: 508). There are even indications that Mike might be the biological father of two children born to two legally-married couples within the Nest, with no jealousy or bitterness, only pride, on the part of all concerned (ibid: 461). The result is a collective family in which all "get along together – you've seen us, you've shared – live in peace and happiness with no bitterness, no jealousy" (ibid: 507). While everyone in the Nest is ultimately in a group marriage with their Nest-mates, they all tend to find themselves "in [working] twosome partnerships inside the larger group […] this pairing of partners needn't even be between man and woman. Dawn and Jill for example – they work together like an acrobatic team" (ibid: 488). To be clear, these partnerships are functional, rather than sexual, although there is certainly plenty of sharing of sex between Nest-mates. Heinlein writes from a 1960s mindset that clearly denounces homosexuality as aberrant and such cultural homophobia is reflected in some parts of *Stranger in a Strange Land*. It is the openness and sharing between Nest-mates that directly informs most of the Nest's construction, but the sharing of sexuality is perhaps the tenet that most directly conflicts with 20th-century Western ideologically-bound sexual mores that have persisted into the 21st century.

Heinlein seems to have no problem denouncing social mores of his time, especially those concerning sexuality (except male heteronormativity), and this is seen within the novel. Jubal compares the Nest to the historical example of the "Oneida Colony [which] was much like Mike's 'Nest'; it managed to last quite a while […] There have been many others, all with the same sad story: a plan for perfect sharing and perfect love, glorious hopes and high ideals – followed by persecution and eventual failure" (ibid: 448). Jubal further opines:

"I can see the beauty of Mike's attempt to devise an ideal human ethic and applaud his recognition that such a code must be founded on ideal sexual behavior, even though it calls for changes in sexual mores so radical as to frighten most people […] Most moral philosophers consciously or unconsciously assume the essential correctness of our cultural sexual code – family, monogamy, continence, the postulate of privacy that troubled you so, restriction of intercourse to the marriage bed, et cetera." (ibid: 449)

Ultimately, the ever-cynical but sympathetic Jubal finds the whole philosophy that underscores the Nest to be a "proposition [that] is so naive that it's incredible" (ibid: 450). He follows this opinion with a story of real-world, "pre-

civilization Eskimos"[4] that enjoyed consensual non-monogamy until Western colonial dominance infiltrated their culture. Heinlein further acknowledges the
problematic nature of the Nest for Western civilization, as Sam notes that "[o]f
course we've had trouble; we'll go on having trouble – because no society, no
matter how liberal its own laws may appear to be, will allow its basic concepts to
be challenged with impunity. Which is exactly what we are doing. We are challenging everything from the sanctity of property to the sanctity of marriage"
(ibid: 486). In explicitly discussing the challenges that face non-mononormative
relationships, Heinlein directly confronts the reader with the 'otherness' of ethical non-monogamy in a way that clearly shows it as an ideological construct.

The challenges Sam refers to are not confined to the novel, as seen in its
characters' dialogue as well as in contemporary scholarly criticism of the novel.
Tim Blackmore writes that "Heinlein was, inadvertently, part of a stream of artists who synthesized and reified beliefs and desires that were in a sort of colloi-
dal cultural suspension around them" (1995: 140). The non-mononormative ideology the Nest is based on partially mirrors the historical Zuni tribe, according to
Shaun Reno. He notes in his comparison of the Zuni people and *Stranger in a
Strange Land* that the Nest's "culture and society is held together by group sex,
which is used not merely for the pleasures of eros, physical pleasure, but also for
'growing closer' as in the term agape, love of the soul or mind. Marriage is still
routine, but all members of their society share love, both physical and spiritual"
(Reno 1995: 154). He even finds similarities between the water-sharing ceremony in *Stranger in a Strange Land* and Zuni water rituals between sexual partners
(ibid: 155). "Moreover, [Mike] Smith's teachings are also like the Zuni's – promoting realization of the Self as part of the universe" (ibid: 157). In stark contrast to the other two novels used in this paper, not only is the non-monogamous
relationship structure more central to the story, but the real-world analogues are
also more transparent. Including it with the other novels in this chapter allows

---

4   Editor's note: The *American Heritage Dictionary* notes the following on the usage of
    the terms "Inuit" and "Eskimo": "The preferred term for the native peoples of the Ca-
    nadian Arctic and Greenland is now *Inuit*, and the use of *Eskimo* in referring to these
    peoples is often considered offensive, especially in Canada. *Inuit*, the plural of the In-
    uit word *inuk*, 'human being,' is less exact in referring to the peoples of northern
    Alaska, who speak dialects of the closely related Inupiaq language, and it is inappro-
    priate when used in reference to speakers of Yupik, the Eskimoan language branch of
    western Alaska and the Siberian Arctic." Heinlein's term is outdated, but his novel, of
    course, precedes the contemporary understanding by several decades.

for a broader look at authorial challenges to mononormativity, from the very subtle treatment offered by Singh to Heinlein's nearly didactic and utterly bold foregrounding of non-mononormativity. While Heinlein's textual denunciation of mononormativity may seem to work against the distance provided to the reader through a futuristic setting, these bold discussions happen well into the narrative and occur well after the reader has been introduced much more subtly and informally to otherness that characterizes the Nest.

THE INHERENT NON-MONONORMATIVITY OF *THE LEFT HAND OF DARKNESS*

Ursula Le Guin's *The Left Hand of Darkness* (1969) is a seminal work in feminist science fiction. It is set on Gethen, a planet which is inhabited by people who lack gender unless they are in estrus (reproductively fertile), which they refer to as "kemmer." While the lack of gender in daily life is an integral part of the novella, most of the information about how relationships are structured is background information about Gethen, rather than a focal point of the narrative. Furthermore, while the entire planet's population shares a lack of predetermined gender, the two main countries that serve as locales for the story, Karhide and Orgoreyn, have variations in societal customs for relationships. In the novel, therefore, the picture of relationships on Gethen is incomplete, and only fragments can be pieced together from a close reading of the text. That being said, close readings often provide enough information to glean a nuanced understanding of a liminal subject in literature, particularly within the fantastic where the 'otherness' of a subject is frequently distanced from the reader within the text.

Before going into details about the kinds of relationships in this largely genderless society, the term kemmer needs explanation. Kemmer, unless inhibited through chemical castration, occurs once a month. When a Gethenian comes into estrus, they develop characteristics of a man or a woman, though which gender presents itself varies from cycle to cycle. At this point, sexual intercourse is possible, and biochemically encouraged through the development of sexual desire. Should a Gethenian in kemmer as female become pregnant, they stay female until the child is born and weaned. Furthermore:

"Kemmer is not always played in pairs. Pairing seems to be the commonest custom, but in the kemmerhouses of towns and cities, groups may form and intercourse take place promiscuously among the males and females of the group. The furthest extreme from this practice is the custom of *vowing kemmering* (Karh. *oskyommer*), which is to all intents and purposes monogamous marriage. It has no legal status, but socially and ethically is an ancient and vigorous institution. [...] [I]n Osnoriner there is divorce, but no remarriage after either divorce or the partner's death: one can only vow kemmering once.

Descent of course is reckoned, all over Gethen, from the mother, the 'parent in the flesh' (Karh. *amha*).

Incest is permitted, with various restrictions, between siblings, even the full siblings of a vowed-kemmering pair. Siblings are not however allowed to vow kemmering, nor keep kemmering after the birth of a child to one of the pair." (Le Guin 2010 [1969]: 98)

While there is the social convention of vowing kemmer, which acts as a monogamous marriage bond, there is little indication that this is particularly common or uncommon, but a Gethenian may only vow kemmer once in their lifetime. Those who lose their kemmer-mate can choose to keep kemmer for a cycle with one or more other Gethenians, but they may not vow kemmer with them. It is clear in the text that kemmerhouses afford Gethenians the chance to be promiscuously involved in group sexual encounters as well as in pairings, so the custom of monogamy seems to exist only within the confines of an avowed kemmering pair.

The most common household structure seen in the novel is the Clan-Hearth, or Clan-House, where individuals have their own rooms but otherwise live communally. In Karhide's urban areas, a Karhosh is like a Hearth without the shared familial basis of a Hearth. It is described as "an urban adaptation of the fundamental Karhidish institution of the Hearth, though lacking, of course, the topical and genealogical stability of the Hearth" (ibid: 10). Each parent in Karhide seems to raise the children of their flesh without necessarily receiving any help from the other parent, though it seems likely that other adults in the Clan-House would help with parenting. Clan-Houses and Domains are constructed differently in Orgoreyn, where they "though still vaguely discernable in the Commensal structure, [were] 'nationalized' several hundred years ago in Orgoreyn. No child over a year old lives with its parent or parents; all are brought up in Commensal Hearths" (ibid: 124-5). And while "[t]he whole structure of the Karhidish Clan-Hearths and Domains is indubitably based on the institution of monogamous marriage," there is no indication in the text that not being in a vowed-kemmering pair is in any way seen as being othered (ibid: 98). There is also no evidence that having a different partner or many different partners for each kemmer cycle is aberrant. Thus, the text shows a society where monogamy is far from the only culturally accepted norm.

Instead, what is sexually aberrant or deviant on Gethen is limited in scope, at least within the text. It is noted that "Karhiders discuss sexual matters freely" but "are reticent about discussing perversion" (ibid: 67). The one perversion that is seen clearly and referred to repeatedly is "[e]xcessive prolongation of the kemmer period, with permanent hormonal imbalance towards the male or female," which is "not rare; three or four percent of adults may be physiological perverts or abnormals" (ibid: 67). While not ostracized, such "perverts" are "tolerated with some disdain, as homosexuals are in many bisexual societies" (ibid: 67). Indeed, it is seen in the text that while "tolerated," when discussing the rest of the worlds in that universe where everyone has one gender expressed permanently from birth, these off-worlders are seen as "in permanent kemmer" and as a "society of perverts" (ibid: 38). In Orgoreyn, Genly (who is from a different planet, and is permanently male) is suspected of being a "Karhidish agent" for one "can see he is a sexual deviant of a type that in Karhide, due to the influence of the Dark Cult, is left uncured, and sometimes is even artificially created for the Foretellers' orgies" (ibid: 170). He is sent to a prison, based on this suspicion, where his "nickname among the prisoners and guards is, inevitably, 'the Pervert'" (ibid: 196).

In a Western 20th and 21st century society where monogamous nuclear relationships and families are the only accepted relationship norm, some remarks by Le Guin and others are relevant to this reading of *The Left Hand of Darkness*. As an early work in feminist science fiction, *The Left Hand of Darkness* is not without flaws, as seen and discussed by scholars and Le Guin, herself. Most of those cri-tiques revolve around her attempt to construct a genderless world with words from a highly gendered world, and therefore are not particularly relevant to a discussion of ethically non-monogamous relationship structures in fantastic texts. What is relevant is the text itself, which shows a society where monogamy and nuclear households are not the only culturally accepted norm. In Le Guin's introduction, she notes that the book is a sort of "thought experiment" and that it is "not predictive; it is descriptive" (ibid: xiv-v). She writes that she is "merely observing, in the peculiar, devious, and thought-experimental manner proper to science fiction" what "we already are" (ibid: xviii). Le Guin describes writing science fiction as "offering an imagined but persuasive alternative reality, to dis-lodge my mind, and so the reader's mind, from the lazy, timorous habit of think-ing that the way we live now is the only way people can live" (qtd. in Lothian 2006: 282). Le Guin sees a "struggle for dominance" in the "dualism of division that destroys us" (qtd. in Marcellino 2009: 205). Such dichotomies, she writes, "might give way to what seems to me, from here, a much healthier, sounder, more promising modality of integration and integrity" (ibid: 205). Some of the gender and feminist studies criticism about *The Left Hand of Darkness* can be read as relevant to a discussion of the division between monogamy and ethical non-monogamy. Marcellino's essay is highly relevant in this way. He writes that "LeGuin's gender interdependence [...] challeng[es] the reader to imagine creative solutions to gender oppression that still allows for gender existence" (2009: 210). Furthermore, "LeGuin's utopian works do not remove cultural or gender differences, or posit separation, but generally posit interdependence wherein these differences enhance and mutually support each other in society" (ibid: 211). Through a close reading of *The Left Hand of Darkness*, one sees a world where relationships are constructed in a number of ways without being seen as perverted or othered – be they vowed kemmering pairs, group sex in kemmer-houses, taking a new kemmering partner (or partners) each cycle, or kemmering however one wants, so long as one does not vow kemmering with a full-sibling, or kemmer with them past the birth of a child to the full-sibling pair. In this sense, Le Guin's *The Left Hand of Darkness* shows a society of relationship variety, where everyone accepts their differences in relationship structures in a way that "enhances" and "mutually supports" the society, to borrow Marcellino's words, without "oppression" of some of these structures and in a way that allows for the "existence" of all of these arrangements.

THE PENTAD OF *DISTANCES*

Separated in publication date from the other two novels examined in this chapter by a handful of decades, Vandana Singh's *Distances* (2008) features a protagonist who lives in a five-member family, a pentad. Like information about relationships on Gethen in *The Left Hand of Darkness*, *Distances'* pentad is largely in the background, but the relationship structure itself is explained clearly in a manner similar to that seen in *Stranger in a Strange Land*. When the protagonist, Anasuya, comes to the City, "she was alone" but met Palanik and became a member of his house "'[b]y joining [it],' Palanik [...] took her away from her dry, cell-like dormitory to his own made-house, where she met his mates and at last became part of something: a pentad" (Singh 200: 48). Thus, Anasuya gains "the love of four people when some had none," as Singh describes it, hinting that Anasuya's world contains more than just the pentad showcased in Anasuya's household (ibid: 15). "Palanik, Marko, Parul, and Silaf [are] her mates. They had given her shelter, respite from loneliness, and love" (ibid: 51). While all five are in a pentad together, and share love and intimacy with one another, Silaf "made love only with Parul; her bond with Marko and Palanik was as innocent and artless as the love between siblings. She had (as yet) no bond with Anasuya that the latter could understand" (ibid: 50).

Anasuya alternates spending her time at the House, with her pentad, and at her place of work, where she often stays for extended periods. The House is held together through an orgiastic sharing of food and sex, known as a joran. Orgies seem to have a spiritual basis, as seen in the tale of "the two Lovers [Ekatip and Shunyatip] and the god of air and fire [who] cavorted in a fine orgy with the [...] Nameless Goddess" (ibid: 75). The joran seen in Anasuya's pentad begins after Anasuya has been away for "fifteen days" (ibid: 52). The joran involves everyone preparing a group meal, each doing their part to put it together. As they all sample the food, "Marko's lips were against the back of [Anasuya's] neck" and Parul feeds Palanik "with her lips" (ibid: 55). "The ladle is taken around from person to person: food is sacred, its preparation and its feeding is what binds one soul to another [...] While the cauldron simmers, [...] the lovers couple in all combinations save one [...] Silaf will caress the others but mate only with Parul. Their mutual pleasure is what catalyses the rest of the group" (ibid: 56). Then, "[w]hen the joran [i]s over, it [i]s as though they had suddenly fallen back into their bodies from another place" (ibid: 57-8).

While there is every indication that a pentad is a typical and normal household arrangement and relationship structure in the City, which is the only name given for the location containing Anasuya's household, Anasuya's pentad is different. As explained in the novella:

"A joran was a rare event because the members of Anasuya's pentad were not always at home at the same time. In traditional pentads, the members traveled together if they traveled at all, and the joran was held on a regular basis, with all due ceremony, with one person, the kendr, as catalyst and initiator. The kendr was the hub around which the wheel turned [...] Anasuya's pentad was not traditional; there was no kendr, and matings were more often couplings or threesomes, depending on mood and availability as much as anything else." (ibid: 58)

Nonetheless, Anasuya's pentad is not singled out as perverse or otherwise socially unacceptable, even though it is not traditional. Instead, what emerges is a portrait of a tightly-knit House, which privately and publicly supports Anasuya. When she is lauded by the City for her work, "Anasuya's mates came, all but Silaf, who rarely left home, and were duly awed and proud" (ibid: 91). Even when Silaf leaves, and the "pentad that had not been broken by Anasuya's neglect was in pieces with Silaf's departure," the remaining members of the pentad comfort and console one another (ibid: 148). Anasuya "saw then that Silaf had been what kept the pentad together, by her caring, her strangeness, her need to be part of something." Thus, the pentad is seen as a complete working family, so long as it stays intact, with Silaf revealed to be its probable kendr only when she leaves to follow her former lover's people.

As noted earlier, Singh's *Distances* is a much more recent work, and thus academic scholarship on it is limited. This lack makes it difficult to put this discussion into a critical literary context. The few resources that discuss *Distances* tend to focus broadly on Singh's work or focus on post-colonial discourse. However, taking some liberties in broadening the existing critical discussion from strictly post-colonial criticism to include the liminality of ethical non-monogamy in fantastic literature provides some insights relevant to a discussion of non-mononormativity within the fantastic. Suparno Banerjee writes that, "[a]lthough postcolonial science fictions sometimes create fantasies of escape, more often than not these works genuinely question *all* ideologies of domination, including those of colonial, neo-colonial, and nativist origins" (2012: 284; emphasis added). As mononormativity is an ideology inherent in Western civilization, this remark makes clear that post-colonial science fiction narratives such as Singh's *Distances* question the dominant ideology of monogamy alongside more readily-seen post-colonial issues involving the enforced supremacy of the colonizer's culture upon the colonized. In Banerjee's discussion of the completely normalized (within the context of Anasuya's life in the City) pentad House, he notes that Singh's "narratives seek alternatives [...] probably suggesting that only a radical shift in social consciousness can engender hope for the dis-alienation of these marginalized subjects" (ibid: 302). While Banerjee is writing of "negative states of existence," with respect to "estranged identities" within the novella, the impact of Anasuya's pentad on a marginalized reader who longs for an alternative to the Western-dominant ideology of monogamy would, indeed, offer a glimpse of the possibility of their real-world "dis-alienation" through a major cultural and social shift in Western consciousness (ibid: 301). I doubt that either Singh or Banerjee had mononormativity in mind when they wrote, respectively, the novella or the cited article, but I hope that I have made clear that even unintentional links between the textual normalization of ethical non-monogamy in the post-colonial novella and real-world liminalization of such relationships exist, and are ripe for critical exploration.

BRIEFLY REVISITING THE SOCIAL SCIENCES ON NON-MONONORMATIVITY

Rather than lump all the social science discourse together at the beginning of the paper, or attempt to tie it into each of the fictional works when discussed above,

I have opted to introduce the social sciences' discourses in broad context with critical examinations of fantastic literature at the start, and to close here by discussing the intersectionalities between the scientific discourse and the specific works. In doing so, I hope to reduce the confusion that may be caused by discussing the social sciences' discourses on ethical non-monogamy in what is, ultimately, a discussion of fantastic literature. It should be noted that "[t]he fact that a huge gap exists between public morality and actual intimate behaviour is common knowledge, thanks to studies by Bornemann, Hite and others. Studies show that in fact, from a statistical viewpoint, sexual infidelity is much more usual and widespread than sexual faithfulness" (Sartorius 2014: 82). I feel this is important to emphasize, lest one be tempted to think that mononormativity is somehow inherently more 'natural' or 'universal' than heteronormativity. Much as the divide between the private practice of same-sex sexual encounters and a public display of heteronormativity was once (and, for some, still is) the standard, it is hard to deny that deceitful infidelity often occurs within otherwise mononormative relationships. Certainly, in "questioning whether conventional monogamy is really monogamous that attention has turned to consensual non-monogamies. Discourses of sexual citizenship and identity politics agendas have also increased the visibility of some forms of consensual non-monogamy (notably polyamory) as people have claimed it as an identity-label rather than a practice and have called for rights and responsibilities on the basis of this" (Barker/Landridge 2010: 752). Thus, it is clear that mononormativity has been and is still being challenged in a real-world context, and I have shown how mononormativity is questioned in the three fictional works examined above. Whereas Heinlein is clearly making a point of consciously questioning mononormativity in *Stranger in a Strange Land*, with its references and ties to real-world ethically non-monogamous groups, it is less clear that there is any conscious intent to directly question mononormativity in *The Left Hand of Darkness* or *Distances*. Nonetheless, Le Guin's work features both monogamous and non-monogamous sexual pairings as equally normative on Gethen, while Singh showcases only the pentad as a societal relationship norm in the City. As a result, whether the authors intend to or not, they dispel any notion of mononormativity in their fictional worlds.

LOOKING FURTHER IN THE FANTASTIC FOR NON-MONONORMATIVE REPRESENTATIONS

These three works do not exist in a vacuum, and this examination has implications that resonate into the non-academic world. On Gethen, it is those who prolong kemmer who are perverts and are marginally tolerated, but as Sheff and Hammers write, Western "[c]onventional society [...] generally classifies as perverts people who have multiple and concurrent romantic and/or sexual relationships, engage in group sex and/or openly espouse non-monogamy. Polyamorists are thus defined as perverts by the popular imagination, even if they themselves do not identify as such" (2011: 199). Furthermore, in our society, "[b]eing accused of being a pervert can have detrimental consequences, and [...] everyone involved in 'perverted' sex risks social censure" – a statement that anyone in Western society would be hard-pressed to argue against, regardless of context (ibid: 198). Annina Sartorius, a psychotherapist writing about polyamory in a real-world context, finds that "[t]he future belongs to diversity in family structure," from blended families to group marriages, like those seen in Anasuya's pentad and Mike's Nest: "[g]roup marriage is a relationship structure with lasting and intense emotional, mental and sexual exchanges and which includes three and more partners" (2004: 83-4). As much as "[i]t is likely that there are multiple understandings and practices in play in consensually non-monogamous relationships, and that [non-monogamous people] will employ conflicting discourses and tell different stories at different points as they navigate the kinds of tensions we have outlined and work to accomplish different aims," it is probable that one will see many different sorts of non-monogamous structures, and discourses regarding those structures, in speculative fiction literature as it negotiates and navigates societal and individual tensions surrounding mononormativity (Barker/Landridge 2010: 757).

As noted in the introduction above, the social sciences and popular culture alike have recently begun exploring non-mononormativity through academic and public discourse. One might be tempted to think the three works examined in-depth here are outliers, but they merely serve as literary book-ends for the advent of the modern fantastic and the more contemporary post-human fantastical texts being published now. Internet searches for terms relating to consensual, or ethical, non-monogamy (polyamory being the most widely discussed) result in many links to discussions being held in the public sphere about non-mononormativity's presence in the fantastic. Only a few will be discussed herein, in order to highlight that these inquiries and such discourse is already widely and publicly engaged in outside of academic literary criticism.

Brit Mandelo, an author, editor, and critic in speculative fiction and queer literature, often looks at ethical non-monogamy in literary texts in their publications on *Tor.com*, an online magazine by science fiction and fantasy publishing company, Tor Books. In their review of Malinda Lo's *Inheritance*, they write that the sequel to Lo's *Adaptation* is "concerned with the developing and complicated relationships between Reese, David, and Amber," the triad at the center of the novel [2013]. Mandelo discusses the triad briefly, remarking that the journey for the characters to solidifying their triad "takes a lot of thought and struggle first. That's possibly the most believable part, and the part that [Mandelo] loved the most, about their relationship-narrative: it takes work, and compromise, and the shifting of beliefs to accommodate greater possibilities." While they write with some apparent glee that "it's a queer poly YA novel!," Mandelo also notes that "the infamous love triangle" seen in popular YA novels (which are also often fantastic texts) regularly turn into a "choose-one-partner narrative." Even though it is common for YA texts within the fantastic to uphold mononormativity in their resolutions, one can often find deep, thought-provoking internal discussions that question mononormativity within the very same texts. A prime example can be found in the popular *Hunger Games* trilogy by Suzanne Collins, where Katniss, the protagonist, internally monologizes over why it is that she must choose between Peeta and Gale. Katniss ultimately ends up with Peeta, but the internal critique over the need to choose only one of her two suitors starkly interrogates the mononormativity found elsewhere in the trilogy. It is precisely the concept of mononormativity introduced in the context of the three close readings earlier in this chapter which allows for a nuanced discussion of questioning mononormativity within an otherwise mononormative literary landscape, and it is for scholars and writers such as Mandelo that the social sciences' term, "mononormativity," and its related concepts will likely hold the most interest as the fantastic is a natural home for narratives that question socially normative ideologies, whether in the YA or adult fantastic.

In one installment of their regular *Tor.com* column, "Queering SFF," Mandelo titularly asks their readers "Where's the Polyamory?" Mandelo discusses in some detail the placement of polyamory within adult speculative fiction. They note that "[t]he multiple-partnered relationship is inherently queer even in occasional circumstances where the attraction and involvement is predominantly heterosexual: they're outside the social norm and unwelcome in that norm. They're treated as Other, legally and socially" [2010]. As a whole, Mandelo is quick to criticize the lack of obvious non-mononormativity in genres where the normative is regularly interrogated and questioned, writing that "in adult speculative fiction, there have been a few stellar examples of stories with moresomes." Mandelo notes a few examples of non-mononormative SF texts, such as "Catherynne M. Valente's Hugo-nominated *Palimpsest* [(2009), which] features a poly-amorous romantic unit in an erotic world where sexuality as a whole is much more fluid than in most novels." Also included is Piercy's *Woman on the Edge of Time* (1976), which Mandelo notes "deals with different family units and rela-tionship structures." And, while it is hard to argue with Mandelo's seemingly low opinion of the literary value of Laurell K. Hamilton's ongoing *Anita Blake* fantasy/horror series, the first of which was published in 1993, "one thing the later Anita Blake books [...] have going for them [is that] Anita's relationship with her live-in partners Nathaniel and Micah is perhaps the most functional and sane of all the romance and sex going on in the book." Though Mandelo does not discuss Hamilton's *Merry Gentry* series, it should be noted that Hamilton es-tablishes a premise of consensual non-monogamy for Merry in the first novel, *A Kiss of Shadows* (2000), clearly establishing it as another non-mononormative narrative series.

Mandelo's critique of the lack of non-mononormativity within SFF is quick-ly rebutted by their readership, with many readers commenting on the article to mention over sixty different SFF texts that contain or center on non-mononormativity. Judging by the readership comments on Mandelo's "Queering SFF: Where's the Polyamory?," the questioning of mononormativity within the fantastic exists throughout its genres, modern to current, and is of interest to some of its readers and scholars. Perhaps the concept of mononormativity would be of some use in future academic discussions of a similar nature, for it seems unlikely that a subject of such import to those interested in liminal identities within the fantastic would stop being discussed. If nothing else, the label, "mononormativity," and its related terms, such as "non-mononormativity," pro-vide a clear and common lexicon for such examinations, as well as a variety of nuanced interpretations for various ethically non-monogamous inquiries found within narratives.

Indeed, Mandelo is not the only author, critic, and editor discussing non-monogamy within the context of fantastic literature on *Tor.com*. In her *Tor.com* article, "Five Books about Loving Everybody," Nisi Shawl discusses five texts that she describes as stories that are not about consensual non-monogamy as a specific ideology, but rather about "loving everybody" as a central tenet of the narratives (2016). "More accurately, these stories are around polyamory: loving everybody figures into what they're about in different ways [...] a thorough search would provide at least as many examples of ways of portraying poly-amory in SFF as there are of practicing it" (ibid). In her article, Shawl notes that by "[r]eversing the conventional interpretation of polygamy's power dynamic while keeping numbers and gender identical, Samuel R. Delany calls familiar readings of such relationships into question" (ibid) by having the singular husband be the 'property' of his many wives rather than the other way around in his *Tales of Nevèrÿon* (1979). Octavia Butler's *Fledgling* (2005) showcases a heroine who "spends the bulk of the book carefully constructing a polyamorous family for her own protection and nourishment. [...] On top of that, her species, which is called the Ina, mate with other Ina in groups, and they live communal yet sex-segregated lives" (ibid). Shawl finds that the polyamorous relationships in Kai Ashante Wilson's short story, "«Légendaire.»" (2015), to be a "given, background to a fantastic tale" and "not the focus of '«Légendaire.»' but its armature. In this case, the mundanity of multiply-partnered love." N.K. Jemisin's *The Fifth Season* (2015), the 2016 Hugo Award-winning novel which Shawl notes is the first novel in a planned trilogy, "brings together three major characters in a joyful male/female/male ménage à trois." Finally, Shawl describes Candas Jane Dorsey's *Black Wine* (1997) as featuring characters that "bond with one another in families of three or more. Five adults is the usual number, and these romantic, sexual, and domestic circles are called, unsurprisingly, 'hands,' with individual members known as 'fingers.'" While two of the above authors, Delany and Butler, appear in comments to Mandelo's "Queering SFF" column on polyamory in fantastic genres, Shawl's article further underscores the plurality of non-mononormative societies within the fantastic that Mandelo's readers are so quick to point out. Given the fundamental nature of estrangement within fantastic genres, it is clear upon deeper inspection that the three texts discussed in-depth earlier in this chapter are not exceptions, but rather examples of how fantastic texts inherently have the capacity to challenge the patriarchal ideology of mononormativity.

CONCLUSION: THE FUTURE OF FANTASTIC CRITICISM AND NON-MONONORMATIVE EXPLORATIONS

The above discussion prompts one to question where questioning mononormativity might lead, with respect to critical studies of fantastic texts. As shown, there is notable intersectionality between ethical non-monogamy and fantastic literature, particularly with respect to theories developed in queer studies. In their article "Whatever Happened to Non-Monogamies? Critical Reflections on Recent Research and Theory" (2014), Barker and Langdridge discuss a number of possible theories that have been or might be applied to social science critiques of mononormativity. Specifically, they note that "critiques of mononormativity

follow from the ways in which it can be located in a specific cultural and historical moment. Most position monogamy as inherently patriarchal and capitalist
and present feminist and/or Marxist arguments for alternative ways of relating"
(2010: 753). Barker and Langdridge also find, in the social sciences, "a number
of [...] critiques of monogamy notably informed by anarchist politics, queer theory and post-structuralism, which offer more radical challenges to concepts of
static, singular selves and relationships, the prioritizing of certain forms of love
and intimacy, and the potential for possession and ownership of others" (ibid:
753). In theoretical scholarly work within the social sciences, "new theoretical
perspectives also draw on anarchist, Buddhist and existentialist philosophies to
reimagine relationships" (ibid: 762). Most of these theories are commonly used
within the study of fantastic texts, and it seems natural that the very same theories used in the past to inform literary critiques of heteronormativity would be
appropriate theories to apply to critiques of mononormativity seen in fantastic
literature. While real-world scientists must "be cautious when criticizing and de-
constructing identities and practices [such as ethical non-monogamy] that occupy such a precarious position and have not yet reached any point of recognition
or rights – whilst maintaining caution over the kinds of normalization often used
as a basis for these –" the fantastic offers the safety of estrangement, which allows for critiques of mononormativity to occur in relative freedom (ibid: 756).
The above sentence could have easily been written about queer studies in the social sciences and in fantastic scholarship at an earlier point in time. It is a fitting
evolution in liminal studies within critical literature on the fantastic to begin to
include socially-borderline identities that are beginning to come under study in
the social sciences and the public sphere, such as ethical non-monogamists. It is
my hope that this chapter has provided a context for such studies, while proving
that non-monogamy has long been a part of the fantastic and continues to find its
way into fantastic texts for us to study, if we only look closely enough.

WORKS CITED

Banerjee, Suparno (2012): "An Alien Nation: Postcoloniality and the Alienated
Subject in Vandana Singh's Science Fiction." In: *Extrapolation* 53/3, pp.
283-306.
Barker, Meg/Darren Langdridge (2010): "Whatever Happened to Non-
Monogamies? Critical Reflections on Recent Research and Theory." In: *Sex-
ualities* 13/6, pp. 748-772.

Blackmore, Tim (1995): "Talking With Strangers: Interrogating the Many Texts That Became Heinlein's *Stranger in a Strange Land*." In: *Extrapolation* 36/2, pp. 136-150.

Easton, Dossie/Hardy, Janet W. (2009 [1997]): *The Ethical Slut: A Practical Guide to Polyamory, Open Relationships, and Other Adventures*, New York: Berkeley.

Heinlein, Robert A. (1991 [1961]): *Stranger in a Strange Land*, New York: Berkley.

Hollinger, Veronica (1999): "(Re)Reading Queerly: Science Fiction, Feminism, and the Defamiliarization of Gender." In: *Science Fiction Studies* 26/1, pp. 23-40.

Khazan, Olga (2014): "Multiple Lovers, Without Jealousy." In: *The Atlantic* July 21, (https://www.theatlantic.com/health/archive/2014/07/multiple-lovers-no-jealousy/374697/).

Le Guin, Ursula K. (2010 [1969]): *The Left Hand of Darkness*. New York: Berkley.

Lothian, Alexis (2006): "Grinding Axess and Balancing Oppositions: The Transformation of Feminism in Ursula K. Le Guin's Science Fiction." In: *Extrapolation* 47/3, pp. 348-395.

Mandelo, Brit (2010): "Queering SFF: Where's the Polyamory?" In: *Tor.com* August 31, (http://www.tor.com/2010/08/31/queering-sff-wheres-the-polyamory/).

Mandelo, Brit (2013): "Alternative Relationships in YA: Inheritance by Malinda Lo." In: *Tor.com* September 9, (http://www.tor.com/2013/09/24/book-review-inheritance-malinda-lo/).

Marcellino, William (2009): "Shadows to Walk: Ursula Le Guin's Transgressions in Utopia." In: *Journal of American Culture* 32/3, pp. 203-213.

Marcus, Stephanie (2015): "Jada Pinkett Smith Talks Open Marriage Rumors, Says She's Not Will Smith's 'Watcher.'" In: *HuffingtonPost.com* June 4, (https://www.huffingtonpost.com/2015/06/04/jada-pinkett-smith-open-marriage_n_7510392.html).

Reno, Shaun (1995): "The Zuni Indian Tribe: A Model for *Stranger in a Strange Land*'s Martian Culture." In: *Extrapolation* 36/2, pp. 151-158.

Roberts, Robin (1990): "Post-Modernism and Feminist Science Fiction." In: *Science Fiction Studies* 17/2, pp. 136-152.

Sartorius, Annina (2004): "Three and More in Love: Group Marriage or Integrating Commitment and Sexual Freedom." In: *Journal of Bisexuality* 4/3-4, pp. 79-98.

Shawl, Nisi (2016): "Five Books About Loving Everybody." In: *Tor.com* August 29, (http://www.tor.com/2016/08/29/five-books-about-loving-everybody/).

Sheff, Elisabeth/Hammers, Corie (2011): "The Privilege of Perversities: Race, Class and Education among Polyamorists and Kinksters." In: *Psychology & Sexuality* 2/3, pp.198-223.

Singh, Vandana (2008): *Distances*. Bellingham: Aqueduct Press.

Taormino, Tristan (2008): *Opening Up: A Guide to Creating and Sustaining Open Relationships*, San Francisco: Cleis Press.

Organic Fantasy and the Alien Archetype in Nnedi Okorafor's *Lagoon*

JOHANNA PUNDT

In a 2014 blog post, Nigerian-American author Nnedi Okorafor discusses the status of science fiction in Africa and argues that the genre is still relegated to the literary margins with regard to the limited number of publishers, writers, and readers devoted to it. Okorafor, whose science fiction and fantasy works have received widespread acclaim and won major prizes such as the Nebula and World Fantasy Award, mentions several reasons for this perceived unpopularity, but emphasizes specifically that science fiction tends to neglect the African continent, its people, and cultures. Okorafor writes: "Few science fiction classics and contemporary works feature main characters of African descent, African mythologies, African locales, or address issues endemic to Africa. And until recently, next to none were written by African writers" (2014a). A growing field of African science fiction counters these absences in mainstream science fiction by writing from a perspective that capitalizes on the genre's inherent counter-hegemonic potential. Okorafor elucidates this by referring to the anthology *AfroSF: Science Fiction by African Writers* (2012), Wanuri Kahiu's short film *Pumzi* (2009), and works by South African authors Lauren Beukes and Sarah Lotz, as well as her own writing. These authors subvert dominant Eurocentric notions of futurity and modernity by creating science fiction which is open to local mythologies and non-Western systems of knowledge.

However, the idea that the recent increase in African science fiction publications marks the emergence of a completely new aesthetic form of writing has been challenged. In "African Science Fiction 101," Mark Bould provides a more extensive list of science fiction published by authors situated across the African continent and its diasporas, explaining that "African sf is already at least a century old" (2015: 18), and thus turns the debate towards questions of visibility. This observation demands a critical reflection of the genre categories, which are used to market fantastic literature – including science fiction. In postcolonial contexts, for example, the prominence of the label "magical realism" becomes problematic in cases where it functions as a mere catchall term for fantastic fiction published in the even broader category of postcolonial literature. In cases where categories such as postcolonial science fiction or African science fiction might be useful alternatives, it is important to note that "African" and "postcolonial" are generalizations encompassing highly different forms of expression. Furthermore, as Bould illustrates, the label African science fiction

"runs significant risks: of homogenizing diversity; of creating a reified, monolithic image of what it might mean to be 'African'; of ghettoizing the sf of a continent as some kind of subset or marginal instance of a more 'proper' American or European version of the genre; of patronizing such sf as somehow not yet fully formed, 'developing' rather than 'developed'; of separating such fiction from the wider culture(s) of which it is part; of colonizing such cultural production by seeing it not through its own eyes but through those of Americans and Europeans." (ibid: 11)

Postcolonial science fiction undoubtedly faces similar problems. However, I agree with Bould's assertion that such labels are always indicative of a "strategic identity" (ibid: 11) and that genres need to remain open for change (ibid: 11). The potential of African, and by extension postcolonial, science fiction to counter representational practices of American and European science fiction does not mean that they necessarily oppose these established forms of the genre. Instead, they frequently reshape the narrative strategies, motifs, and themes of mainstream science fiction and expand the latter's range through a synthesis of local mythologies and alternative knowledge systems. Such interventions are to be understood as a contribution to a larger global transformation in science fiction. Istvan Csicsery-Ronay Jr. states:

"[A]s more and more models of the fantastic flow together from different artistic and folk traditions, what will be generally understood as sf will include more and more assemblages involving incongruous ontologies of motivation. Sf will be less a kind of text and more a specific attitude, which will often be merely one thread in a work's textual weave." (2012: 480-481)

Hence, postcolonial science fiction is less concerned with establishing new genre demarcations in which it would reside in opposition to mainstream science fiction, but through its creative reshaping of the tropes and themes of science fiction it attests to the general and necessary permeability of genre boundaries.

In the following, these interventions to science fiction will be discussed in relation to Nnedi Okorafor's 2014 novel *Lagoon*, which adapts the genre to envision a future Nigeria. Okorafor's novel constitutes an important contribution to alien encounter narratives, not only because of its setting in the metropolis Lagos and the resulting subversion of common representations of the West as the sole site of futurity, but also through its advocacy of an animist worldview as a counter-discourse to Eurocentric notions of modernity. *Lagoon* envisions how a country that has experienced colonial invasions would react to a spaceship landing in the waters of Lagos. However, this arrival of extraterrestrials is not a simple historical allegory. Instead the aliens are harbingers of change who seek to destroy the remains of colonialism, leading the country towards a future devoid of neo-colonial exploitation, oppressive socio-political structures, and environmental destruction. In order to bring about Nigeria's transformation, the aliens awake the spirit world and cooperate with figures from Igbo and Yoruba mythology. The novel imagines the future Lagos as a place where technoscience and futuristic aliens coexist with animist worldviews and mythological creatures. This use of animism is not an advocacy of idealized notions of precolonial cultural practices but shows the traditions' adaptability to futuristic changes. I thus argue that *Lagoon* radically deconstructs Eurocentric notions of development and modernity which are often conceptualized solely in relation to technological and capitalist advancement. The novel's emphasis on animism as a determining component of Nigerian futurity is above all discernible in Okorafor's technique of "organic fantasy" (2011), which subverts uniform representations of reality by demonstrating that the fantastic and magical are valid forms of perceiving the world. Based on Harry Garuba's notion of animism as a "re-enchantment of the world" (2003: 266),[1] I argue that organic fantasy can be understood as a defamiliarization strategy of postcolonial science fiction. In contrast to Darko Suvin's definition of science fiction as the genre of cognitive estrangement, which describes the process of rendering the familiar strange as one that is bound to rational and scientific frameworks of explanation (1972: 375), organic fantasy is concerned with re-enchanting the familiar. Hence, the novel illustrates how postcolonial

---

1   As I will show in the subsequent section, Garuba uses the term re-enchantment to describe an alternative to Max Weber's perception of modernity as a turn towards rationalization. Re-enchantment characterizes alternative modernities which are premised on the coexistence of magical and scientific worldviews.

science fiction challenges the monochrome, uniform voice with which science fiction narratives have often expressed their visions of the world.

1. SCIENCE FICTION AND/AS POSTCOLONIAL CRITIQUE

Recent postcolonial studies of science fiction have noted how mainstream texts of the genre perpetuate Western notions of technological advancement, industrialization, and modernity (cf. Langer 2011c: 129-130; Hoagland/Sarwal 2010: 9, 15). Despite the fact that stories may be set in alternative worlds and characters use technological devices which have not been developed as yet or will never come into existence, science fiction's imaginaries are predominantly scientific and rational. Adam Roberts elucidates this by reference to the recurring motif of faster-than-light travel, which is

"something that scientists assure us can never happen. Rather than abandon the rationale of science, though, SF stories that involve 'faster-than-light' travel slip into the idiom of 'pseudo-science', providing rationalisations of these impossible activities in terms that *sound like* scientific discourse. [...] [T]he important thing about the 'science' part of 'science fiction' is that it is a discourse built on certain logical principles that avoids self-contradiction; that it is *rational* rather than emotional or instinctual." (2000: 8-9 original emphasis)

As Darko Suvin argues, scientific reasoning is a central feature of the genre's creation of cognitive estrangement (1972: 381). Based on Bertolt Brecht's *Verfremdungseffekt* and Viktor Shklovsky's concept of *ostranenie*, Suvin describes science fiction's cognitive estrangement as a means to transform conventional reality and, in turn, to achieve a heightened perception of the familiar (ibid: 374-375). Suvin explains that "[t]he cognition gained may not be immediately applicable, it may be simply the enabling of the mind to receive new wavelengths, but it eventually contributes to the understanding of the most mundane matters." (ibid: 380) He continues by stating that the cognitive element in science fiction is "*in most cases strictly scientific*" (ibid: 381 original emphasis). Roberts even argues that Suvin's remarks suggest that cognitive is a synonym for scientific and, thus "it seems to embody a certain common-sense tautology, that science fiction is scientific fictionalising" (2000: 8). For Suvin this focus on the scientific dimensions of the genre is essential to distinguish it from related fantastic writing such as the myth or fairy tale (1972: 375).

Postcolonial approaches to science fiction have not only challenged such strict demarcations, but have also criticized the genre's exclusion of alternative knowledge systems that operate outside and beyond Western science. Jessica Langer, for example, refers to Grace L. Dillon's concept of indigenous scientific literacies to argue that postcolonial science fiction offers spaces to reconcile scientific with indigenous epistemologies and ontologies (2011c: 130). Langer insists that works of postcolonial science fiction

"function above all as vehement denials of the colonial claim that indigenous, colonized and postcolonial scientific literacies exist in the past and have no place in the future. [...] Their traditions and ways of knowing are relevant, applicable and necessary. They belong to the past, but also to the present and to the future." (ibid: 152)

Hence, in works of postcolonial science fiction, estrangement affirms the authority of magic, the supernatural and the mythological as relevant categories to make sense of this world and its future. I argue that Okorafor's notion of organic fantasy, as a defamiliarization strategy which is based on an animist worldview, functions as an alternative to the scientific premise of cognitive estrangement. Okorafor coined the term organic fantasy to describe that the magical and mythical elements in her novels are grounded in reality; her fiction "blooms directly from the soil of the real" (2011: 152).[2] She explains this magical, mythological engagement with the world as resulting from her "complex African experience, which on many levels has been a series of cultural mixes and clashes between being American and being Nigerian" (ibid: 150). As a second reason she refers to her perception of the world as "a magical place" (ibid: 150). According to Okorafor, the fantastic and magical are not categories which stand in opposition to reality. Thus, she uses an animist worldview to challenge the notion of "the real," suggesting that reality is a mere construct; a flexible, fluid concept which can also be understood as potentially fantastic. This is reminiscent of a statement made by Ursula K. Le Guin in her essay "From Elfland to Poughkeepsie," in

---

2 As Alice Curry notes, Okorafor does not explicitly mention an ecocritical dimension to organic fantasy (2014: 37-38). Nonetheless, Curry's analyses of Okorafor's young adult novels shows how the concept bears a particular potential to articulate ecocritical messages. In her essay, Curry also points to the relation between organic fantasy and animism in Okorafor's works, which "successfully deconstructs the human-environment or culture-nature dichotomy" (ibid: 38). A similar subversion is also represented in *Lagoon*'s depiction of an eco-conscious swordfish who takes revenge for the pollution of the ocean (see below).

which she describes fantasy as "a different approach to reality, an alternative technique for apprehending and coping with existence. It is not antirational, but pararational; not realistic, but surrealistic, superrealistic, a heightening of reality" (1979: 84). Such heightening of reality is achieved through processes of defamiliarization which organic fantasy uses "to make something familiar strange" (Okorafor 2011: 152). In doing so, the familiar is viewed from a new, in this case fantastic, mythical perspective, which can shed light on the unnoticed things of every-day life. This points to the empowering capacities of organic fantasy to counter and enrich representations of conventional reality. Okorafor understands such enchanted approaches to the world as "the most accurate way of describing reality" (ibid: 153).

Similarly, Harry Garuba interprets animism, which permeates many African cultural, literary, and social contexts, as a means to re-enchant the world (2003: 265). He contextualizes this re-enchantment as a counter-discourse to Western notions of modernity. Through an analysis of contemporary forms of animism, with a particular focus on Nigeria, Garuba argues that these beliefs are not necessarily indicative of a revival of traditionalism, but they rather express an alternative mode of being in the world which subverts Western notions of modernity (ibid: 265-266). The latter is understood in Weberian terms as a process in which societies witness a disenchantment due to capitalism and processes of technological advancement, whereby wonder, religion, and mythology lose currency and make way for a more scientifically-based worldview.[3] Garuba criticizes this common definition of modernity as a concept exclusively referring to social and scientific changes in the West and, as a result, unable or unwilling to consider different forms of modernity. He explains: "Based on the experience of a particular society, Weber's sociological theory could not account for the *different or alternative rationalizations* that are increasingly coming to the fore in the history of so-called Third World societies as they evolve or construct their own modernities." (ibid: 266-267, original emphasis) Garuba argues that animism can be understood as an alternative modernity which leads to "a *continual re-enchantment of the world*" (ibid: 265, original emphasis). He describes this re-enchantment as

---

3 Garuba does not reference a specific publication by Weber. In the essay "Science as a Vocation" (1917), Weber quotes Friedrich Schiller's prominent phrase "the disenchantment of the world" to describe modernity as an increasing replacement of magic with science and rationalization (Weber 2004 [1917]: 12-13). In colonial contexts, the construction of modernity as rational and scientific was equated with "civilization" and thus instrumentalized to justify European colonial endeavors.

"a process whereby 'magical elements of thought' are not displaced but, on the contrary, continually assimilate new developments in science, technology, and the organization of the world within a basically 'magical' worldview. Rather than 'disenchantment,' a persistent re-enchantment thus occurs, and the rational and scientific are appropriated and transformed into the mystical and magical." (ibid: 267)

As this quote shows, the prefix "re-" does not mark a reversal of process of disenchantment or the return to a notion of tradition which excludes science. Instead, re-enchantment suggests that disenchantment as a rationalization of thought is neither absolute nor a process which is a necessary condition of modernity. Thus, animism as a worldview which illustrates this re-enchantment does not exclude technology or science but it diffuses the hierarchical structures which position science/modernity above tradition/animism. Garuba explains: "What may be much closer to the reality [than the clash of tradition and modernity] is that animist logic subverts this binarism and destabilizes the hierarchy of science over magic and the secularist narrative of modernity by reabsorbing historical time into the matrices of myth and magic" (ibid: 270).

Though Garuba shows that animism influences all forms of social and cultural practices, his remarks on animism in literature are most relevant for the context of postcolonial science fiction. He introduces the term "animist realism" to describe how magic and spiritualism offer "techniques and strategies to construct a narrative universe in which transpositions and transgressions of boundaries and identities predominate" (ibid: 271). By reference to Brenda Cooper, Garuba names the inclusion of "spirit, ancestors and talking animals, [...] both adapted folktales and newly invented yarns" (Cooper in Garuba 2003: 272) as possible ways to express animism in literature. While his analysis indicates that magical realism is one of the most dominant literary modes to engage with animism, he emphasizes that other literary genres which challenge uniform conceptualizations of reality may also be subsumed under animist realism (ibid: 272, 275). Examples can be found in works of postcolonial science fiction, such as *Lagoon* or Hopkinson's *Brown Girl in the Ring* (1998), Ian McDonald's *River of Gods* (2004), Larissa Lai's *Salt Fish Girl* (2002), and Beukes's *Zoo City* (2010), to name but a few. These novels are set in worlds premised on the coexistence of the magical, mythical, and the scientific.[4]

---

4   Detailed analyses of this topic in relation to Hopkinson, McDonald, and Lai's works can, for example, be found in Jessica Langer's chapter on "Indigenous Knowledge and Western Science" (2011c). For a discussion which points to the entanglement of technology and indigenous knowledges in Lauren Beukes's novels *Zoo City* as well as

The examples named above elucidate how postcolonialism functions not merely as a critical reading practice that criticizes canonical science fiction's investments in colonialism, modernity, and technological advancement, but also exemplify postcolonialism's potentially empowering capacities as a writing strategy (Reid 2009). As Masood Ashraf Raja and Swaralipi Nandi argue, "[t]he connection between science fiction and postcolonial studies is almost natural: both these fields are deeply concerned with questions of temporality, space, and existence. Central also to both these fields of study are the questions of the 'other' – human, machine, cyborg – and the nature of multiple narratives of history and utopias of the future" (2011: 9). Before the overlaps of science fiction and postcolonialism are discussed more thoroughly, I will address some of the controversies around the latter's definition. My brief considerations focus on two central debates which were raised in the "notoriously problematic" (Langer 2011a: 4) attempts to define postcolonialisms: First, the disagreement about the temporal dimensions designated by the "post" and, second, the negotiations between materialist and discursive approaches in postcolonial criticism. As will be shown, both of these ongoing discussions are pivotal for an engagement with science fiction from a postcolonial perspective.

A key definitional problem of postcolonialism is related to questions of temporality, more specifically, to what period the "post" refers. Many critics have accused postcolonialism of assuming colonial dominance to be a phenomenon of a historical moment that has been overcome. Such interpretations translate the "post" as past and, hence, understand postcolonialism as a chronological term describing the period after independence. Proponents of this position have denounced the concept's failure to address the legacy of colonialism as well as its supposed ignorance towards ongoing (neo)colonialism (cf. Shohat/McClintock in Hall 1996: 242-243). In contrast to that, advocates of postcolonialism frame the concept as a continuous process, which encompasses not only the diverse forms and consequences of colonial dominance, but includes the decolonial struggles, the immediate phase after independence, as well as reflections of ongoing social, economic, and political power dynamics (Hall 1996: 246).

In postcolonial science fiction, a consideration of "the aftermath of the colonial" (Young 2009: 13) may reach beyond a reflection of the present moment to extrapolate potential future realities. Hence, the question "What if …?," which is at the heart of many works of science fiction, is closely related to my understanding of the postcolonial condition, which in light of current neocolonial

---

Moxyland (2008), see Brady Smith's article "SF, Infrastructure, and the Anthropocene: Reading *Moxyland* and *Zoo City*" (2016).

practices and racist social structures continues to be much more a utopian vision of the future than an established reality, sharing with science fiction its speculative potential to imagine the future. As Joshua Yu Burnett argues, "postcolonialism creates a space for us to think our way out of hegemonic neocolonial dead ends. [...] [I]t does advance the sort of counterhegemonic thinking that is a precondition for creating meaningful change" (2015: 138).

In the interrogation of colonialism and its legacies, postcolonial studies seek to acknowledge the specific local contexts in which relations of domination and subordination emerged and continue to exist (Langer 2011a: 4-5). This points to the second crucial issue within postcolonial studies, namely the balance between materialist approaches and discursive, i.e. theoretical or textual, analyses (ibid: 5). In his study on postcolonial science fiction, Eric D. Smith argues that most previous scholarly work in the field has engaged with the topic in form of discourse analyses, focusing on how central concepts of postcolonial studies such as hybridity, diaspora, racialization or representation can be applied to science fiction (2012: 14-15). Although Smith acknowledges the importance of such approaches, he states that the material realities which have led to the emergence of postcolonial science fiction and how this genre operates as a form of resistance need to be considered (ibid: 15). Jessica Langer, in turn, argues that "the materialist approach risks denying the real power of narrative and other discourse as catharsis and the real necessity of psychological as well as physical decolonization" (2011a: 6). The conflict between discursive and materialist approaches is probably best negotiated by trying to incorporate both in postcolonial science fiction and its potential contribution to decolonization processes. In this regard, postcolonialism's dual function as a reading strategy and a writing strategy needs to be emphasized (cf. Reid 2009).

As indicated above, writing postcolonial science fiction offers an active intervention to the representational practices of many canonical science fiction texts and hence constitutes a political act. In his introduction to the anthology *AfroSF: Science Fiction by African Writers* (2012), Ivor W. Hartmann explains this further by suggesting that "[i]f you can't see and relay an understandable vision of the future, your future will be co-opted by someone else's vision, one that will not necessarily have your best interests at heart. Thus, Science Fiction by African writers is of paramount importance to the development and future of our continent" (2012: 7). However, using the genre's empowering potential to radically imagine alternative realities, requires changing established genre tropes and techniques. This is also noted by Nalo Hopkinson, who states: "To be a person of colour writing science fiction is to be under suspicion of having internalized one's colonization" (2004: 7). Instead of discarding science fiction as a mode of expression, Hopkinson argues that it is pivotal to reshape the genre from within. Alluding to Audre Lorde, Hopkinson explains: "In my hands, massa's tools don't dismantle massa's house – and in fact, I don't want to destroy it so much as I want to undertake massive renovations – they build me a house of my own" (ibid: 8). Such reconfiguration of science fiction from postcolonial perspectives has materialized in various approaches. In Nnedi Okorafor's *Lagoon* the science fiction trope of an alien invasion as well as the genre's strategy of cognitive estrangement are appropriated in order to explore the future of Nigerian ontologies and epistemologies.

2. "THE WINDS OF CHANGE ARE BLOWING"[5]: ANTI-IMPERIAL RESISTANCE FROM OUTER SPACE

Set in 2010, *Lagoon* introduces Lagos as a city whose first contact with "aliens" dates back more than 500 years. As the narrator Udide Okwanka, the story-spinning spider from Igbo mythology, emphasizes in the novel's opening lines, "The Portuguese first landed on Lagos Island in the year 1472" (Okorafor 2014b: Epigraph). The ambiguity of the verb "landed" consciously plays with the novel's theme of an alien encounter in that an interpretation of colonialists as extraterrestrial invaders is evoked. According to Mark Dery, understanding colonial forces as "aliens" is crucial to explain why science fiction can speak particularly to readers and artists of African descent (1994: 179-180). In his definition of Afrofuturism, a cultural and political movement which can be broadly summarized as an engagement with the future from the perspective of people of color, Dery reinterprets the science fiction tropes of extraterrestrial invasions and abduction to metaphorize the transatlantic trade of enslaved Africans (ibid: 180). Simultaneously, he compares the status of the alien as other to the marginalized social position of African Americans, whose exposure to dehumanization, intolerance, racism, marginalization, and exploitation makes them "inhabit a sci-fi nightmare" (ibid: 180). While Dery's remarks refer to the U.S.-American context and, particularly, to the legacy of the trade of enslaved Africans, *Lagoon* represents the consequences of colonialism and neocolonial policies in Nigeria in the form of political, social, and ecological issues such as corruption, Christian big-

---

5   The alien ambassador Ayodele uses these words in her first public address to Lagos's human citizens (Okorafor 2014b: 112 original emphasis). Using her power to hack electronic devices, Ayodele contacts the Lagosians via television, mobile phones, and radios to proclaim the great transformation of the city.

otry, homophobia, the exploitation of the country's natural resources and the resulting environmental destruction.

Due to the country's history, the novel cannot be read as a classic alien invasion story because this would frame the encounter of the aliens and humans as one of first contact and consequently neglect the colonial intrusions of the past (O'Connell 2016: 294-295). The forceful European invasion and its legacy continue to haunt the Lagosian population of the novel. Hence, the majority of people react with panic and fear upon hearing that the strangers seek to bring change to Nigeria. A sense of intrusion is felt, not least because the aliens use their shapeshifting abilities to enter the city as humans, infiltrating the lives of the citizens. The alien ambassador contacts Lagos's human population as a woman who is described vaguely as a "dark-skinned African woman with long black braids" (Okorafor 2014b: 13). She is called Ayodele, a Yoruba name, which not only illustrates the novel's Nigerian setting but, since it is a name for both men and women, underlines the ambassador's shapeshifting ability.

On the one hand, the representation of Ayodele as a woman of color counters the tendency in science fiction to construct the world as white by default. Isiah Lavender III, who applies critical race theory to mainstream science fiction, elucidates how the genre tends to envision color-blind settings, while implicitly purporting suspiciously homogeneous worlds in which whiteness continues to serve as an unproblematized normative category (2009: 185). Lavender III thus considers "sf's supposed 'colorblindness' as an investment in whiteness as the norm" (ibid: 185). If works of science fiction are able to imagine the future but capitalize on the marginalized status or even absence of people of color in these scenarios, they imply that not all of humanity has a future. *Lagoon* subverts these white supremacist representational practices.

On the other hand, Ayodele's appearance as a woman of color is explained as a strategic necessity in order to gain trust, which elucidates the alien body's function as a central marker of alterity. Ayodele argues that "[h]uman beings have a hard time relating to that which does not resemble them" (ibid: 67). Since she merely adapts to humans in order to achieve her end, the status of 'the human' as an ideal life form is challenged. Furthermore, Ayodele's comment illustrates human inability to deal with otherness. This is also mirrored in the various descriptions of Ayodele as "the woman-thing" (Okorafor 2014b: 86) or "the woman who was not a woman" (ibid: 121). While Ayodele is not seen as completely human by many characters in the novel, the use of familiar categories suggests that otherness is engaged with from the vantage point of the self, to borrow and reverse Carl D. Malmgren's assertion that alien encounter narratives "explore the nature of selfhood from the vantage point of alterity" (1993: 16).

The designations used for Ayodele expose otherness as a mere construction of language in opposition to an equally constructed norm, in this case the human.

The normative status of the human is also subverted through the three human protagonists: Adaora, a marine biologist, the soldier Agu, and the Ghanaian rapper Anthony are chosen by Ayodele to support her mission. This group, initially strangers to each other, have more in common than just the first letter of their names. As is revealed towards the end of the novel, all three characters have superhuman powers which align with their professions: Adaora is able to breathe under water and swim like a fish (Okorafor 2014b: 257), Agu has extraordinary physical strength (ibid: 256-257) and Anthony can unleash a vibration he calls "the rhythm" which allows him to get in touch with all things in a three-mile radius (ibid: 167-168). The location of otherness, i.e. the protagonists' strange powers, within the human self, challenges any notion of a uniform conceptualization thereof and depicts alterity as part of the self. According to Patricia Kerslake, the "recurrent definition and location of self [in relation to its others] is a pervasive leitmotif in SF" (2007: 10). However, Kerslake draws attention to the vastly different understanding of the self/other opposition in science fiction and postcolonial theory and explains that "[p]ostcolonial thought accepts and embraces the concept of the Other, as it enables polyvalency and hybridity, but in SF the Other must forever remain a figure apart" (ibid: 11). Indicating that this marginalized position of the other is also evaluated in diverging ways, she continues: "[W]here postcolonial theory challenges the silencing and marginalisation of the Other, SF takes the stance that such marginalisation is a key element of self-identification" (ibid: 11). Acknowledging that the distinction between self /"us" and the other /"them" is an inevitable result of attempts to make sense of the world and one's position in it, postcolonialism scrutinizes this strict, seemingly absolute opposition and questions the attributes associated with these two poles, particularly the self's often unquestioned hierarchical status above the other. Similar to that, *Lagoon* challenges the hierarchical structures inherent in science fiction's representation of the other/self-relations by using Adaora, Agu, and Anthony as figures who combine human features and alterity in form of superhuman powers. While all three have suppressed their abilities for much of their life for fear of being stigmatized and excluded from society, Ayodele encourages them to embrace their otherness. As the novel progresses, all three learn to use their superhuman powers to contribute to the change of Lagos. The demarcations of the human are thus scrutinized, recalling those posthuman theories which center on "the conviction that 'the human' no longer is – if it ever was – a coherent and stable ontological category" (Hollinger 2009: 269). It is worth noting that *Lagoon's* approach towards the posthuman emphasizes the stability of ethnicity in transformations beyond the human, i.e. the aliens as well as the human protagonists are explicitly characterized as people of color, which is striking with regard to many posthumanist theories which tend to lack critical engagements with concepts of "race" and ethnicity. Based on Sylvia Wynter's criticism of Enlightenment conceptualizations of the human, Zakiyyah Iman Jackson states "that there is much humanity, and even humanism, that *post*humanist theory has yet to pass through" (2013: 676 original emphasis). Jackson asks whose humanism is actually transgressed and warns that posthumanism's intention to deconstruct Enlightenment notions of the human is not subverting the racist structures underlying its creation. Hence, these attempts might backfire in a perpetuation of the very concepts that they seek to destabilize and, as result, would fail to adequately acknowledge the humanity of people of color (Jackson 2015: 215).

Despite her outward appearance, Ayodele's status as beyond the human is marked by her technologized body. A blood sample reveals that she consists of tiny metal balls which enable her to shift shapes. Furthermore, she can manipulate technology and uses this power repeatedly in the novel to spread her message to avert social, political, and environmental challenges. According to Hugh Charles O'Connell it is precisely the aliens' embodiment of technology paired with their rhetoric of change which initially recalls (neo)imperialist myths of African countries as lacking development and as being dependent on outward benefactors. In his analysis of the novel, O'Connell categorizes *Lagoon* as a second contact story which necessarily complicates any reading of the aliens as mere benevolent harbingers of change (2016: 294-295). He states: "Despite the aliens not presenting themselves as colonizers, the enforced imposition of an outside definition of change and technology remains the neoimperial hallmark of neoliberal developmentalism" (ibid: 299). This turns the aliens into ambiguous figures "between technocratic neocolonialism and anticolonial awakening" (ibid: 308). O'Connell argues that the aliens signify a utopian transformation whose unknowable dimensions mirror the strangeness of Ayodele and her companions. Hence, he "consider[s] the aliens not as aliens, but conceptually as the placeholder of the event [i.e. the radical, anticolonial transformation of Nigeria], as that which is alien, unknowable, or unlocatable to the ideology of the contemporary world-system [...] [T]hey are represented as that which cannot be represented by the regulative state or its discourse" (ibid: 309). In this regard, it is worth noting that the aliens are unable to advance the transformation they preach on their own. Despite their advanced mastering of technology, they initially fail to convince the population that they "do not want to rule, colonize, conquer or take" (Okorafor 2014b: 220). When chaos begins to dominate the city, the aliens thus unleash capacities and enhance structures of resistance already existent before their arrival. Among these suppressed potentials that cooperate with the aliens are the mythological and fantastic figures which inhabit the spirit world. Although O'Connell similarly emphasizes that the aliens "reawaken and reveal the revolutionary possibilities that lie dormant within Nigeria and the people themselves" (2016: 309), he characterizes the change advocated by Ayodele and her companions as dependent on their technology. He explains:

"This 'change' is so thoroughly connected to the alien's technology in the novel and really to the aliens *as* technology, given their ability to radically transform themselves and anything else seemingly at the molecular level, such that 'change and technology' become an inseparable pairing. It is as the embodiment of change and technology, then, that they promise to transform Nigeria." (ibid: 298 original emphasis)

The transformation, however, is only able to materialize after the synthesis of the technological aliens and the city's spiritual dimensions. Rather than reading the technological aspects as the central element for the Nigerian transformation envisioned in the novel, I argue that *Lagoon* advocates an animist worldview in which the magical and supernatural are equally crucial for the country's empowerment. The novel mirrors this approach in its usage of "organic fantasy" (Okorafor 2011) as an alternative to Darko Suvin's cognitive estrangement.

3. "THERE'S MORE TO THIS CITY THAN YOU IMAGINED"[6]: RE-ENCHANTMENT AS DEFAMILIARIZATION

Throughout *Lagoon*, organic fantasy as a defamiliarization strategy based on animism is used to imagine a Nigeria in which the magical and mythological intersect with science. Though animism is a broad label for various beliefs and practices, many forms of animism are based on a spiritualized perception of the world. As Garuba explains, "animist thought spiritualizes the object world,

---

6 When Ayodele is attacked by a violent mob of people, Anthony uses his power to rescue her. The sonic waves he unleashes are not only able to control the angry masses, but allow him to "read" (2014b: 168) Lagos and its inhabitants. Despite the hate expressed by the mob, Anthony is convinced that the majority of Lagosians will welcome the change proclaimed by Ayodele. Thus, he assures the alien ambassador of Lagos's potential, stating that "[t]here's more to this city than you imagined" (2014b: 168).

thereby giving the spirit a local habitation" (2003: 267). *Lagoon's* depiction of the Lagos-Benin Expressway as being possessed by a spirit is a telling example in this context (Okorafor 2014b: 202-209). Due to the regular accidents occurring on the road connecting the country with the neighboring Benin, the motorway is considered to be the most dangerous road in Nigeria. In the novel, these incidents are attributed to the Bone Collector, a spirit figure Okorafor created to make sense of the otherwise seemingly unexplainable frequency and brutality with which the road has caused innumerous deaths. On her blog, Okorafor insists that in the light of the theories which try to explain the accidents, her animist interpretation might be equally possible (2015). Thus, the scene exemplifies Okorafor's notion of organic fantasy and its approach towards conventional reality from an animist perspective. Moreover, the motorway's possession by a spirit entity signifies the entanglement of the mythological and the technological, which is further emphasized through the eventual sacrifice of an alien to the road. Upon swallowing the extraterrestrial, i.e. the embodiment of technology, the spiritualized road comes to a rest again. Through this literal incorporation of technology, the spirit ceases to be a mere signifier of tradition.

Further examples can be found in episodes that make use of animal focalizers, a typical characteristic of animism in literature. One of these is a swordfish, who lives in the lagoon in which the aliens land their spaceship. The fish, thus, is the first creature on Earth whom the newcomers from space contact. Since most of the earth's surface consists of water, the subversion of humanity's status as the species entitled to welcome the aliens seems justified. As a symbol of change and a signifier of fluidity, the water is the only suitable terrain for the aliens to initiate the all-encompassing transformation of Nigeria. As indicated, the swordfish, who describes the pollution of "[h]er waters" (Okorafor 2014b: 3 original emphasis) caused by human oil mining, focalizes the scene. Through the insight into the animal's perspective, a heightened awareness of environmental issues is created. The swordfish, readers are told,

"is on a mission. She is angry. She will succeed and then they will leave for good. They brought the stench of dryness, then they brought the noise and made the world bleed black ooze that left poison rainbows on the water's surface. She often sees these rainbows whenever she leaps over the water to touch the sun. Inhaling them stings and burns her gills." (ibid: 3)

The parataxis at the beginning of the quote indicates the swordfish's determination to take revenge. Her anger is stressed through the description of her swift movements as she "slices through the water" (ibid: 3) towards the pipeline, ready to attack. According to the animal, the pipeline looks like a "giant dead snake" (ibid: 3) whose poison, the oil, appears in beautiful, though deadly layers on the water's surface. The use of these metaphors illustrates the destruction of nature as the rainbow no longer evokes positive connotations but signifies a life-threatening phenomenon. Human intrusion into nature is tremendous, affecting all senses of the swordfish: She hears the sound of the crude oil vessels and mining platforms, she sees the thick oil layers and she smells and tastes the poisonous natural resource in her gills. It is not the first time that the swordfish attacked a pipeline, but since her assaults were only able to stop the mining temporarily, she feels compelled to protect her home again (ibid: 3). As can be guessed from the repeated attempts at destruction, the animal alone is unable to stop the pollution. Thus, the aliens contact her and offer help by cleaning the ocean, making it taste "sweet, sweet, *sweet!*" (ibid: 4 original emphasis) again. The threefold repetition reinforces the change while the italicized last word illustrates the swordfish's increasing awareness of the cleaned atmosphere. After the oil layers have vanished, the newcomers transform the swordfish and the other creatures inhabiting the waters of the lagoon into powerful beings, which are now able to protect the ocean from any further human intrusion.

The inspiration for the eco-conscious swordfish is based on a report about a group of swordfish attacking an oil pipeline in Angola in 2010 (Okorafor 2015). Playing with the uncertainty as to what caused the swordfish attack in Angola, the scene – similar to the Bone Collector episode – exemplifies Okorafor's notion of organic fantasy as being rooted in reality. As can be seen in news reports covering the swordfish attack (cf. Kurahone 2010), the incident was merely discussed in terms of the financial losses suffered by mining companies. Through the swordfish's focalization, readers gain insight into the effects of nature's destruction from the perspective of the creatures most directly affected by it, thus potentially generating a heightened awareness for the environmental pollution caused by the oil companies. Moreover, this empowerment of oceanic lifeforms challenges and partially subverts human supremacy. The aliens redistribute power and shift agency, in this case from human to animal.

As can be seen from the empowerment of the water creatures in this episode, by subsequent chapters focalized through animals, as well as through the narrator, the spider Udide Okwanka, *Lagoon* embraces an animist worldview by pointing to the various life forms which inhabit the Nigerian metropolis. This is also expressed in the novel's dedication, which is addressed "to the diverse and dynamic people of Lagos, Nigeria – animals, plant and spirit" (Okorafor 2014b:

Dedication).[7] The spirits are crucial to advance the transformation of Nigeria. When the humans increasingly react with panic to the aliens, "*the powerful spirits and ancestors who dwelled in Lagos*" (ibid: 194 original emphasis) rise from the spirit world to help the aliens achieve their goal. In this cooperation between the aliens as signifiers of futurity and the mythological entities as representatives of tradition, the latter are not only positioned as leading figures in the country's transformation, but they are also defined as belonging in the future, illustrating how postcolonial science fiction represents animist worldviews as an integral part of its world-building. This is mirrored in a central scene of *Lagoon* in which the aliens and the Yoruba masquerade Ijele join forces to stop Internet fraud.[8] The episode is set in a cyber café in which the majority of guests are involved in so-called 419 scams.[9] The chapter opens with the words "I was there" (ibid: 195), which indicates that the following description is a first-person account. Since the narrator refers to himself only with his nickname Legba, and explains that he uses the name of the trickster god to disguise his identity in order to

---

7   The emphasis placed on the diverse inhabitants of Lagos not only in this dedication but also in the novel's usage of multiple focalization, might be read as a reaction to the one-dimensional, racist depiction of Nigerians in Neill Blomkamp's *District 9* (2009). Although the film raises important questions about the parallels between the alien invasion, South African apartheid and recent social resentments against immigration in South Africa (cf. Langer 2011b: 81-82), its demeaning depiction of Nigerians as criminal gang members led by Obesandjo, who practices dubious spirit worship and seeks to gain power by eating aliens, has caused severe criticism. As Okorafor explains in the novel's acknowledgements, *Lagoon* was initially written as a script for a Nollywood film countering Blomkamp's representation but eventually turned out to be "something else entirely" (Okorafor 2014: 301).

8   Masquerades are part of Nigerian culture and are recurring figures in Okorafor's novels. Okorafor explains that "masquerades are spirits and ancestors who visit the physical world by passing through anthills" (2011: 159). In this scene, Ijele, a huge Igbo masquerade, emerges from the spirit world. For further information on Ijele see Odekanyin/Aiibola (2008).

9   The term "419" refers to a form of internet fraud in which scammers claim that they are, for different reasons, in need of money. The recipients of fraud e-mails are offered generous financial compensation if they agree to lend money to the alleged person in need. In this scene, Legba claims to be a Nollywood director. Gaining his predominantly female victims' trust by feigning to be in love with them, he tries to convince the women to send him money. The number 419 refers to the section of the Nigerian law which defines such action as criminal.

commit fraud, the report initially appears untrustworthy. Legba, however, justi-
fies his activities and states:

"Seriously, the woman was an idiot. She really believed her Caucasian blood and money
made her irresistible to one of Nollywood's top film directors. She'd even told me these
things in those exact words. She had no clue that she sounded like a racist condescending
asshole. There was a *very* pure strain of White Privilege running through her. So why not
capitalize on her idiocy?" (ibid: 196 original emphasis)

In his comment, Legba argues that the roots of 419 scams do not lie in Nigeria
but in the predominantly white victims' self-conception as superior to their alleged lovers. Thus, Legba interprets his deeds as a justified means to react and
almost take "revenge" for the underlying racist sentiments of the women he contacts. The fact that the women never bother to question his nickname "Legba"
and thereby fail to realize that he is a trickster just like the name suggests, further
indicates their ignorance. Legba's honest description of his frauds reverses prior
perceptions of him being an unreliable narrator.

Just before he is able to fool his latest victim, the cyber café begins to shake
and a masquerade enters the room. Legba, who remembers theatrical versions of
masquerades from his childhood, immediately realizes that he is now for the first
time witnessing "the *real thing*" (ibid: 199 original emphasis). By choosing a
cyber café for the appearance of Ijele, "Chief of all Masquerades, Igbo royalty"
(ibid: 199-200), the centuries-old figure becomes no longer merely a signifier of
tradition but is instead reimagined in a new technological context. The combination of past and future is emphasized when Ijele literally merges with an alien
who is disguised as a man in a black caftan. The alien is referred to as "the man
in black" (ibid: 200), a description evoking Barry Sonnenfeld's film series
(1997-2012). In contrast to the cinematic Men in Black whose aim is to disguise
the presence of extraterrestrials on Earth, *Lagoon*'s man in black *is* an alien who,
together with Ijele, mysteriously transforms into gas and smoke which float into
one of the computers (ibid: 201). Through this animist spiritualization of the
technological object, the computer, Ijele changes into a technologized spiritual
figure which, in turn, transforms the digital sphere into a futuristic spirit world.
This scene exemplifies postcolonial science fiction's radical subversion of the
dichotomy between supposedly traditional mythology and technoscientific conceptualizations of modernity.

After entering the computer, Ijele and the alien erase Legba's contacts and
emails and consequently work together to fight against fraud, which does not fit
into the future Nigeria. Witnessing these strange occurrences, Legba renounces

his trickster personality and promises to never commit fraud again. In a passage that almost sounds like an oath, he explains:

"[T]his woke me up. The coming of Ijele. I am not being melodramatic and I am not crazy […] I will never practice fraud again. Never. I swear. As I cowered under that table and watched Ijele and the man whom I now believed was one of the aliens look at each other, I felt this great swell of pride and love for Nigeria. I felt patriotism. I would die for it. I would live for it. I would create for it. This was *real*. Tears were streaming down my face." (ibid: 200 original emphasis)

In this scene, the encounter of an alien with a mythological figure is described as the starting point for change and self-transformation. Although the initial justification for the fraud make it appear reasonable, Legba's final assertion indicates that 419 is criminal because it is unpatriotic, shedding a negative light on Nigeria. The scene thus imagines the future in a positive way.

The entanglement of the aliens with the country's diverse inhabitants culminates in Ayodele's transformation into smoke which is inhaled by every organism in Nigeria. Ayodele proclaims, "[y]ou'll all be a bit … alien" (ibid: 268). The episode is not a mere alien infestation in the sense of a forceful intrusion into other organisms. Instead the entire country inhales the abstract idea of change. Like breathing air, this change is necessary for survival in the novel's Nigeria which is characterized by oppressive and exploitative social and political structures. The scene reifies the novel's message that decolonization is not merely an outward, formal transformation, but includes the unchaining of the mind. As O'Connell puts it, the incorporation of Ayodele leads to "a sudden epistemological awakening and transformation within the populace itself that brings them together" (2016: 310). Following this climatic scene, the chaos which has emerged after the spaceship landed in the lagoon is replaced by a collective movement towards a future Nigeria.

4. THE FUTURE IS NOW

Lagoon closes with a speech by Udide Okwanka in which the spider explains that the transformations which have begun to take shape in the city will not go unnoticed. She states that "[o]*ther people in other parts of the world* […] *see what is happening here. And they fear it. They are agreed. Lagos is a cancer. They wish to cut the cancer out before it spreads*" (Okorafor 2014b: 292 original emphasis). Despite the comparison of this change to a spreading, potentially deadly disease, the spider implies that these are merely the perceptions of a world that is unwilling to grant Nigeria its empowerment. Referring to her memory of the colonial invasion of the country – "*I have seen people come from across the ocean. I have seen people sell people.* [...] *They came in boats that creaked a desperate song and brought something I'd never have created*" (ibid: 291 original emphasis) –, the story-spinning spider insists that the aliens are to be respected for their deeds and thus separates them from any association with the colonizers of the past (ibid: 292). In light of the imminent attacks, Udide Okwanka emphasizes that the aliens have revived sentiments of resistance among all creatures, including the spider. Thus, Udide Okwanka warns that "*spiders play dirty*" (ibid: 293 original emphasis), showing that she is ready to protect Nigeria from any attempts that seek to suppress the country's potential.

With regard to Udide Okwanka's prophecy, it is worth noting that *Lagoon* is set in 2010 (ibid: 7). Hence, the future the novel envisions is now, in the present moment. Therefore, the spider's comments might be understood in relation to continuing neocolonial interferences in Nigeria. Despite the fact that the social, political and ecological issues addressed in the novel continue to exist, *Lagoon*'s message is far from irrelevant. Instead, the use of organic fantasy as a postcolonial defamiliarization strategy which allows to reframe science fiction from an animist worldview remains a powerful intervention to those visions of the future that exclude non-Western epistemologies and ontologies. In *Lagoon*, the fusion of technology with the mythological and magical paves the way towards the future. This future is not brought to Nigeria from the outside, but the essential elements that shape and implement it, namely the diverse inhabitants of Lagos and their rich mythologies, are already there. Transformation is already underway – or, as one of the aliens in the novel puts it, "[w]e are doing what is already happening" (ibid: 179).

WORKS CITED

Blomkamp, Neill, director (2009): *District 9*, TriStar.

Bould, Mark (2015): "African Science Fiction 101." In: *SFRA Review* 311, pp. 11-18.

Burnett, Joshua Yu (2015): "The Great Change and the Great Book: Nnedi Okorafor's Postcolonial, Post-Apocalyptic Africa and the Promise of Black Speculative Fiction." In: *Research in African Literatures* 46/4, pp. 133-150.

Csicsery-Ronay Jr., Istvan (2012): "What Do We Mean When We Say 'Global Science Fiction'? Reflections on a New Nexus." In: *Science Fiction Studies* 39/3, pp. 478-494.

Curry, Alice (2014): "Traitorousness, Invisibility and Animism: An Ecocritical Reading of Nnedi Okorafor's West African Novels for Children." In: *International Research in Children's Literature* 7/1, pp. 37–47.

Dery, Mark (1994): "Black to the Future: Interviews with Samuel R. Delany, Greg Tate, and Tricia Rose." In: Mark Dery (ed.), *Flame Wars: The Discourse of Cyberculture*, Durham: Duke University Press, pp. 179-222.

Garuba, Harry (2003): "Explorations in Animist Materialism: Notes on Reading/Writing African Literature, Culture, and Society." In: *Public Culture* 15/2, pp. 261-285.

Hall, Stuart (1996): "When Was 'the Post-Colonial'? Thinking at the Limit." In: Iain Chambers/Lidia Curti (eds.), *The Post-Colonial Question: Common Skies, Divided Horizons*, London/New York: Routledge, pp. 242-260.

Hartmann, Ivor W. (2012): "Introduction." In: Ivor W. Hartmann (ed.), *AfroSF: Science Fiction by African Writers*, no place indicated: StoryTime, pp. 6-7.

Hoagland, Ericka/Sarwal, Reema (2010): "Introduction: Imperialism, the Third World, and Postcolonial Science Fiction." In: Ericka Hoagland/Reema Sarwal (eds.), *Science Fiction, Imperialism and the Third World: Essays on Postcolonial Literature and Film*, Jefferson, NC/London: McFarland, pp. 5-19.

Hollinger, Veronica (2009): "Posthumanism and Cyborg Theory." In: Mark Bould/Andrew M. Butler/Adam Roberts/Sherryl Vint (eds.), *The Routledge Companion to Science Fiction*, London/New York: Routledge, pp. 267-278.

Hopkinson, Nalo (2004): "Introduction." In: Nalo Hopkinson/Uppinder Mehan (eds.), *So Long Been Dreaming: Postcolonial Science Fiction & Fantasy*, Vancouver: Arsenal Pulp Press, pp. 7-9.

Jackson, Zakiyyah Iman (2013): "Animal: New Directions in the Theorization of Race and Posthumanism." In: *Feminist Studies* 39/3, pp. 669-685.

Jackson, Zakiyyah Iman (2015): "Outer Worlds: The Persistence of Race in Movement 'Beyond the Human'." In: *GLQ: A Journal of Lesbian and Gay Studies* 21/2-3, pp. 215-218.

Kerslake, Patricia (2007): "The Self and Representations of the Other in Science Fiction." In: *Science Fiction and Empire*, Liverpool: Liverpool University Press, pp. 8-24.

Kurahone, Ikuko (2010): "Swordfish Attack Angolan Oil Pipeline." In: *Reuters.com*, February 2, (http://www.reuters.com/article/oukoe-uk-angola-crude-idAFTRE6113BU20100202).

Langer, Jessica (2011a): "Introduction: Elephant-Shaped Holes." In: *Postcolonialism and Science Fiction*, Basingstoke/New York: Palgrave Macmillan, pp. 1-10.

Langer, Jessica (2011b): "Race, Culture, Identity and Alien/Nation." In: *Postcolonialism and Science Fiction*, Basingstoke/New York: Palgrave Macmillan, pp. 81-106.

Langer, Jessica (2011c): "Indigenous Knowledge and Western Science." In: *Postcolonialism and Science Fiction*, Basingstoke/New York: Palgrave Macmillan, pp. 127-152.

Lavender III, Isiah (2009): "Critical Race Theory." In: Mark Bould/Andrew M. Butler/Adam Roberts/Sherryl Vint (eds.), *The Routledge Companion to Science Fiction*, London/New York: Routledge, pp. 185-193.

Le Guin, Ursula K. (1979): "From Elfland to Poughkeepsie." In: Susan Wood (ed.), *The Language of the Night: Essays on Fantasy and Science Fiction*, New York: Perigee Books, pp. 83-96.

Malmgren, Carl D. (1993): "Self and Other in SF: Alien Encounters." In: *Science Fiction Studies* 20/1, pp. 15-33.

O'Connell, Hugh Charles (2016): "'We are change': The Novum as Event in Nnedi Okorafor's *Lagoon*." In: *Cambridge Journal of Postcolonial Literary Inquiry* 3/3, pp. 291-312.

Odekanyin, E. A./ Aiibola, D. Alahiya-A. B. (2008): "Ijele Masquerade." In: *UNESCO Intangible Heritage*, (http://www.unesco.org/archives/multimedia/?pg=33&s=films_details&id=355).

Okorafor, Nnedi (2011): "Organic Fantasy." In: Sandra Jackson/Julie Moody-Freeman (eds.), *The Black Imagination, Science Fiction and the Speculative*, Abindgon/New York: Routledge, pp. 149-160.

Okorafor, Nnedi (2014a): "African Science Fiction is Still Alien." In: *Nnedi's Wahala Zone Blog,* January 15, (http://nnedi.blogspot.de/2014/01/african-science-fiction-is-still-alien.html).

Okorafor, Nnedi (2014b): *Lagoon*, London: Hodder & Stoughton.

Okorafor, Nnedi (2015): "Insight into the Lagoon." In: *Nnedi's Wahala Zone Blog*, September 25, (http://nnedi.blogspot.de/2015/09/insight-into-lagoon.html).

Raja, Masood Ashraf /Nandi, Swaralipi (2011): "Introduction." In: Masood Ashraf Raja/Jason W. Ellis/Swaralipi Nandi (eds.), *The Postnational Fantasy: Essays on Postcolonialism, Cosmopolitics and Science Fiction*, Jefferson, NC/ London: McFarland, pp. 5-14.

Reid, Michelle (2009): "Postcolonialsm." In: Mark Bould/Andrew M. But-ler/Adam Roberts/Sherryl Vint (eds.), *The Routledge Companion to Science Fiction*, London/ New York: Routledge, pp. 256-266.

Roberts, Adam (2000): "Defining Science Fiction." In: *Science Fiction: The New Critical Idiom*. London/New York: Routledge, pp. 1-46.

Smith, Brady (2016): "SF, Infrastructure, and the Anthropocene: Reading *Moxyland* and *Zoo City*." In: *Cambridge Journal of Postcolonial Literary Inquiry* 3/3, pp. 345-359.

Smith, Eric D. (2012): "Introduction: The Desire Called Postcolonial Science Fiction." In: *Globalization, Utopia, and Postcolonial Science Fiction: New Maps of Hope*, Basingstoke/New York: Palgrave Macmillan, pp. 1-19.

Suvin, Darko (1972): "On the Poetics of the Science Fiction Genre." In: *College English* 34/3, pp. 372-382.

Weber, Max. (1917, 2004): "Science as a Vocation." In: David Owen/Tracy B. Strong (eds.), *Max Weber: The Vocation Lectures 'Science as a Vocation', 'Politics as a Vocation'*, Indianapolis: Hackett, pp. 1-31.

Young, Robert J. C. (2009): "What Is the Postcolonial?" In: *Ariel* 40/1, pp. 13-25.

Latino/a Magical Realism and American Superhero Fiction as Constitutive Agents in the Negotiation of Dominican-American Identity in Junot Díaz' *The Brief Wondrous Life of Oscar Wao*

Michael Giebel

1. Introduction

For over two centuries, the United States has been a seminal destination for immigration from various parts of Latin America (Kanellos 2011: 1). Arising from the region's colonial past, the proportion of Latinos/as[1] in the U.S. has climbed steadily in the decades following WWI and ascended further during the latter part of the 20th century as people from almost every Latin American country sought to evade the ravages of political and economic instability that had befallen their homelands by way of immigration to the United States.[2] On account of the attendant growth, the Hispanic community has spread in significant num-

---

1 Generally, the term "Latino/a" refers to a Latin American ancestry, whereas the term "Hispanic" denotes belongingness to a Spanish-speaking country. As this paper primarily focusses on the Hispanic part of Latin America, however, both terms will subsequently be used interchangeably.

2 In spite of the fact that during this period Latin America made gradual progress toward greater democracy, from the 1940s until well into the 1980s, large parts of the region witnessed the emergence of military regimes, political upheaval, and civil conflict, see Rodríguez (2008: 211).

bers to nearly every area of the nation and constitutes one of the most sizable and diverse ethnic populations in the U.S. today (Rodríguez 2008: 210–211).

Connected to this history, the experience and the reality of immigration represents an enduring and central theme within the landscape of U.S. Latino/a literature. Starting with the first Hispanic novel of immigration in 1914 (*Lucas Guevara* by Alirio Díaz Guerra), Latino/a immigration narratives have consistently served as important vehicles to express "what it means to be Hispanic in the United States" (Kanellos 2011: 1) and for negotiating fundamental notions of arrival, citizenship, and adjustment to American society (ibid: 1–2, 7–8).

Although Dominicans currently rank among the larger Latin American immigrant groups in the United States, owing to the impetuously restrictive emigration policies of infamous dictator Rafael Leónidas Trujillo, who ruled the Dominican Republic from 1930 to 1961, the Dominican presence in the U.S. is a relatively recent phenomenon, beginning with Trujillo's assassination in 1961 and greatly increasing during the period of political unrest that ensued thereafter (Bramen 1996: 207–208). Along these same lines, compared with the already well-established canons of Chicanos/as or Puerto Rican-Americans, Dominican-American immigrant literature can be regarded as an emergent tradition, pioneered during the 1990s by an upcoming stream of Dominican-American immigrant writers, who were born in the Dominican Republic and emigrated to the United States during their formative years (Caminero-Santangelo 2016: 235). In their writing, they brought particular attention to the narratives of what renowned Cuban sociologist Rubèn Rumbaut has eminently termed the 1.5-generation. This notion specifically captures the experience of individuals who arrived in the United States between infancy and adolescence, and who fall in between the interstices of the conventional genealogical groupings of first and second-generation immigrants (Rumbaut 2012: 982). As their socialization began in one country, but continued in another, they are likely to develop an identity that is trenchantly constituted from a dual cultural heritage (Pérez-Firmat 2012: 4). While this peculiar upbringing commonly enables them to avail themselves of the resources both cultures have to offer, however, their in-between status may also become an incisive source of anguish (ibid: 4). As such, being confronted with the competing forces of two cultural reference systems, they are particularly susceptible to encounter an abiding internal struggle for belonging, striving to find their place in both their indigenous and their adopted U.S. culture, but may never feel fully part of either of them (Boddy 2010: 129).

Put forward by works such as Julia Alvarez's *How the García Girls Lost Their Accents* (1991) and *In the Time of the Butterflies* (1994), or Loida Maritza Perez' *Geographies of Home* (1999), these challenging notions have since proven fundamental to Dominican-American writers in the negotiation of their cate-gorically hybridized identity/ies. Thoroughly contesting "prior paradigms of uni-directional immigration and assimilation to a new [U.S.] culture" (Caminero-Santangelo 2016: 231), their literary pursuits have instead offered an expressly nuanced perspective on the (equivocal) immigrant reality in the United States (ibid: 231-232), by exploring "the complex relationships that exist between two [separate] homeland identities" (Suárez 2016: 111) and distinctly seeking to ex-press the burdensome experience of being torn between loyalty toward their eth-nic tradition and the lure of American ideals (Boddy 2010: 129).

These accounts are prominently expanded by one of their most notable repre-sentatives, highly acclaimed Dominican-American author Junot Díaz, whose parents emigrated from Santo Domingo to Palin, New Jersey when he was at the age of seven (Irizarry 2016: 54). In his Pulitzer-prize winning novel *The Brief Wondrous Life of Oscar Wao* (2007), a multigenerational family chronicle, he similarly captures the contemporary 1.5-generation Dominican immigrant reality in the United States, but most prominently positions the identity negotiation that lies at the center of the works produced by writers of his generation in the do-main of the fantastic. As such, in order to render the encounter of Dominican and American culture accessible, Díaz craftily employs the literary genres of Lati-no/a magical realism and American superhero fiction, as distinct, albeit stereo-typical, regional or cultural commodities of the Dominican Republic and the United States, respectively. With this generic arrangement installed as a narra-tive framework, the history of the Cabral family is told through the perspective of narrator and family friend Yunior, who (in an informal, urban voice) shifts fo-cus among the four central protagonists and connects their personal stories that span from the 1940s throughout the 1990s, and encompass the gruesome history the Dominican Republic endured under the Trujillo regime as well as the strenu-ous reality of diaspora in the United States.

In light of these considerations, this article undertakes a comprehensive ex-amination of the deeper-lying implications arising from the incorporation of La-tino/a magical realism and American superhero fiction, arguing that Díaz astute-ly complicates their fusion, to stage an intriguing conflict that seeks to make pre-sent the cultural strife underlying the 1.5-generation Dominican-American im-migrant experience. While borrowing from both literary traditions, Díaz distinct-ly casts their respective fantastic elements as ominous, self-destructive, and tan-gibly antagonistic potencies, whereby effectively creating a haunted ground that aesthetically mirrors the pressures and ambiguities that are characteristic of the conflict between maintaining a Dominican cultural heritage while at the same time grappling with a new and potentially conflicting cultural reality in the United States. However, whereas on one hand tapping into the real-life struggle Díaz and his generation encounter, it will be shown that, on a further level, *The Brief Life* eventually works toward reconciling this struggle, which ultimately culminates in an emphatic assertion of Dominican-American identity that firmly resides within the (cultural) cross-currents of the Dominican Republic and the United States.

2. LATINO/A MAGICAL REALISM AS OVERBEARING HERITAGE

Of the generic choices *The Brief Life* takes, the invocation of the Latin American literary tradition of magical realism tenably holds the strongest presence within the novel's narrative frame. Widely regarded as a (literary) phenomenon that "introduces unrealistic elements or incredible events, in a matter-of-fact-way, into an apparently realist narrative" (Ormerod 1997: 216), the genre[3] of magical realism possesses a long-spanning history, originating in Europe (Bowers 2004: 7)[4] and prominently emerging as an archetypal mode of writing unique to, and inseparable from the particular realities of Latin America during the 1960s (Moses 2001: 108). Championed by its most recognized practitioners, novelists Gabriel García Marquéz and Carlos Fuentes, Latino/a magical realist accounts have traditionally provided a trenchant evocation of regional history and scenery while creating an intriguing amalgam of physical and preternatural landscapes in which indigenous myths, legends and cultural rites coexist alongside ordinary Western forms of reality (Faris 2002: 102–103). Moreover, in view of its proneness to enter into a dialog with Latin American history, the practice of magical realism is similarly regarded as "a central element of postcolonial literatures" (ibid: 102), where it notably aids in the depiction and the negotiation of the historical experience of imperial conquest, and in which case notions of traditional folklore are specifically employed to "demonstrate, capture and celebrate ways

---

3   While conscious to the fact that there remains a weighty issue of whether magical realism merely constitutes a literary mode rather than a distinguishable genre, subsequent accounts shall follow literary scholar Wendy Faris' classification of magical realism as a literary genre, see Faris (2002: 102).

4   The term "magical realism" was first coined within the field of art criticism by German critic Franz Roh in 1925 and only established as a literary category in the decades that followed, where it spread from Europe to Central and Latin America, see Bowers (2004: 7-9).

of being [...] that are uncontaminated by European domination" (Cooper 1998: 17).

Loosely following in these footsteps, Junot Díaz skillfully installs autochthonous Dominican folklore elements as driving forces and unifying threads among the characters and historical figures that appear throughout the story. Yet, in a way that ostensibly signifies the 1.5-generation Dominican-American immigrant experience and its arduous reality of grappling with the potentially overbearing influence of a Dominican cultural heritage, Díaz distinctly casts these elements as a perpetual source of anguish. In this sense, he decidedly differs from the narratives of the famed magical realists which have often been regarded as striving to express "a nostalgic longing for and an imaginary return to a [precolonial] world that is past, or passing away" (Moses 2001: 106). Instead, while similarly establishing a pertinent linkage with the island's colonial past and intriguingly fictionalizing the Dominican Republic as a magical space where the fantastic flourishes, Díaz brusquely emphasizes the malicious potential of the metaphysical phenomena he employs to create a site of excruciating peril, one that is beset by the malevolent curse fukú, which acts as a truculent inciter for calamity and seems to bring the unspeakable tribulations of the colonial conquest back to life again. Seemingly inspired by its real-life practice as a "referent to witchcraft and malignant spirits" (Boyd 2010: 5) in the Caribbean, Díaz ties the curse fukú to the unsettled history of the island, suggesting an ancient, mythical provenance, soundly inscribed in the iniquities of the Spanish colonization, where it was fleetingly "carried [forth] in the screams of the enslaved" (Díaz 2008: 1) and eventually found its worldly emissary in the figure of the nefarious Dominican ruler Trujillo. Accordingly, narrator Yunior readily introduces the dictator as the fukú's "high priest" (ibid: 2) and provides a terse rendition about the prevailing belief

"that anyone who plotted against [him] would incur a fukú most powerful, down to the seventh generation and beyond. If you even thought a bad thing about Trujillo, fuá, a hurricane would sweep your family out to sea, fuá, a boulder would fall out of a clear sky and squash you, fuá, the shrimp you ate today was the cramp that killed you tomorrow." (ibid: 3)

Against this backdrop, the reader is acquainted with the Cabral family as well as family patriarch, upstanding and respected surgeon Dr. Abelard Cabral. Set during the height of Trujillo's regime in the early 1940s, the family are considered prosperous members of the island's bourgeoisie, whose elect status numbers them among the "High of the Land" (ibid: 220), but places them in a precarious position as they are frequently invited to official state functions of the Trujillista. A circumstance that would prove to be gravely consequential for the Cabral family as Abelard's defiance to make his teenage daughter Jacquelyn sexually available to Trujillo prompts the ignoble dictator to "put a fukú on the family's ass" (ibid: 252). As Yunior relays, this fateful incident "[t]ripped, at some cosmic level, a lever against the family" (ibid: 257) and sets in motion the chimeric and unprecedented "Fall" (ibid: 257) of the Cabral lineage. Craftily configured as an apparent allegory for the ruinous weight of the Dominican past – bifurcated by the colonial period and the infernal rule of Trujillo – the curse fukú thus reverberates all throughout the novel and symbolically haunts the Cabral's for generations to come, wielding its powers on the island and parasitically expanding to the U.S., while turning the accounts of the family into a saga of unceasing trauma and tangibly imposing on them the harrowing fate thousands of African slaves endured on the island.

Shortly after the curse is cast, this sinister chain of events immediately takes root as Abelard is imprisoned by the regime's secret police and soon thereafter his wife Socorro and his two elder daughters die in mysterious and extraordinary circumstances. Born during Abelard's vexatious trial, Belicia, the youngest of the three Cabral sisters, conspicuously escapes this ominous sequence with her life, however, orphaned and rendered homeless through her family's tragic demise, the destructive vehemence of the fukú appears to live on in her and cruelly turn her existence into a horrid pattern of dispersancy and abuse. In a palpable allusion to the Dominican history of colonial slavery, the curse insidiously ingrains and sets forth Belicia's misfortune in her birth as, opposite to the family's heredity, she is born with an African phenotype in a region "famed for its resistance to blackness" (ibid: 80),[5] upon which she is cruelly abjured by her remaining relatives and sold to complete strangers in the poverty-stricken rural region of Outer Azua, where she is forced to endure a devastatingly traumatic existence as a "child laborer" (Perez 2013: 96) that would constitute the first nine years of her life. While she is eventually rescued by Abelard's estranged cousin La Inca and subsequently "reestablishe[d] as a Cabral" (ibid: 97), the family fukú grimly intervenes once more and throughout the years of her (early) adulthood beguilingly draws Belicia into a series of ill-fated relationships with men in the ranks of Trujillo's government, in the course of which the curse ostensibly

---

5   Stretching back to the colonial era, the Dominican Republic has long denied its African heritage and taken significant strides toward becoming a more Westernized nation, which particularly during Trujillo's reign has given rise to rigorous negrophobic sentiments, see Higman (2011: 241-242).

reveals its most truculent hand. As such, upon falling pregnant with a man merely referred to as the Gangster, in a morbid turn of events, it is revealed that he is
already married to Trujillo's (equally) maleficent sister, who callously arranges
for the unborn child to be forcibly aborted. Thereupon, Belicia is brutally abducted by the dictator's henchmen and taken to a sugar cane field in the
outskirts of Santo Domingo, where she receives a jarringly vicious, "near-fatal
beating" (Díaz 2008: 158) at the hands of her captors – a scene that intriguingly
evokes the symbolic weight of the sugar plantations as a historical site of oppression, where the enslaved were forced to labor under the threat of violence and
"where bare lives were brought to die at the arbitrary request of the law" (Perez
2013: 100). In a manner that tenably represents an excruciating re-enactment of
these atrocities, Belicia is "plunged 180 years into rolling fields of cane" (Díaz
2008: 152), where she is eventually left for dead, "beat[en] [...] like she was a
slave" (ibid: 153), with her fetus perishing in her womb. At this juncture, however, the bodeful clout of the fukú is tentatively broken by the magic spell zafa,
which is placed in stern juxtaposition to the family curse and congruously introduced by Yunior as the "only [...] way to prevent [its] disaster from coiling
around you" (ibid: 7). In an apparent reference to its roots as a verbal remedy of
Dominican folk medicine (Foley/Jermyn 2005: 92), the spell is configured as an
ancillary to La Inca, who functions as a traditional native healer and through her
"numinous power of prayer [is able to lay] an A-plus zafa on the Cabral family
fukú" (Díaz 2008: 162). Presumably invoked by her remedying spell, as Yunior
describes, "like the Hand of the Ancestors themselves" (ibid: 154), Belicia becomes witness to the mystical appearance (which is to become a recurrent trope
throughout the story) of a conceivably amiable, golden-eyed mongoose that
seems to act as "a totemic protector straight out of Afro-centric folklore" (Irr
2014: 36). Thus, just as she nears her death and "was set to disappear across that
event horizon" (Díaz 2008: 154) the spectral creature exhorts Belicia to rise and
guides her through the maze of the cane field, amid the promise of a propitious
future and "the son [and] the daughter [...] who await" (ibid: 155). However, despite being introduced as the fukú's "surefire counterspell" (ibid: 7), the protective power of the zafa charm, foremostly manifested through the benevolence of
the mongoose, appears to only momentarily be capable of averting the wrath of
the family curse, whose overarching and insidious (omni-)presence it is unable
to contain. While the unearthly creature first appears as a guardian presence that
might be able to countervail the downfall of the story's protagonists, its persistent and good-natured endeavors to obviate the ill-boding denouement of the
curse eventually prove to be unavailing and merely accomplish to prolong the
agony of the Cabral family, whose (coming) lives primarily remain left in devas-

tation. As such, following her transcendent redemption, Belicia meets the man who would become the father of her two children and together, they plan to find their heartsease by seeking exile in Paterson, New Jersey. Yet, in a preponderant manifestation of the fukú's iniquitous sway, her husband abandons her prematurely and leaves her with "the cold, the backbreaking drudgery of the factorías, the loneliness of Diaspora" (ibid: 171–172) and a blighted spirit pervaded by "a rage that will persist and poison Beli for the rest of her life" (Perez 2013: 97).

Arising from this starkly humbling relationship, however, another generation of the Cabrals is born, who gruelingly inherit the traumatic family lineage and in whose lives "the [colonial] violence and evil wrought by the family's curse" (Hanna 2010: 500) is mysteriously carried out anew. Thus, having found new, fertile ground on U.S. soil, the fukú's trail of devastation unremittingly expands to Belicia's children and slyly imbues their experiences with the fateful undertow of the Dominican history, in a way that establishes an eerie similitude to their mother's detriment. Belicia's son Oscar, lending the novel its title, comes to be particularly affected by the bad omen of the fukú, as his impassioned attempts to follow in the tradition of, and live up to the stereotypical (Afro-)Dominican masculine ideal of the philandering womanizer are bitterly hijacked and ultimately thwarted by the curse, relishing the "blessed days of his youth" (Díaz 2007: 11) he spends as a teenage Casanova, when suddenly, as Yunior relates, "[s]hazam!—his life started going down the tubes" (ibid: 17). Over the coming years, he enters a tremendous cycle of tribulation, torturously made to witness the mystifying divestment of his body as "he grew fatter and fatter," while his face is scrambled "into nothing you could call cute" (ibid: 17) and he breeds a social awkwardness that places "even a rudimentary love [...] beyond his reach" (Perez 2013: 105). Against these seemingly insurmountable odds, he embarks on a meandering quest for love, keenly making overtures to a myriad of girls during high school and college, but despite his travails, he remains condemned to a life of solitude "because at best they ignored him, at worst they shrieked" (Díaz 2008: 17). As a consequence, thoroughly "vacated of hope" (ibid: 194), Oscar appears to give in to the malice of the family fukú and wanders out toward the New Brunswick train bridge, staunchly entertaining thoughts of suicide, when another miraculous appearance of the mongoose occurs. Thus, while he is on the point of "[r]eviewing his miserable life" (ibid: 196) the magical creature is suddenly standing by his side. After staring at each other in a moment of pristine serenity, more on wondrous impulse than principle, Oscar leaps from the bridge and yet, through the intervention of the mongoose, he lands "on the freshly tilled loam of the divider" (ibid: 197) and survives. Despite this critical rescue and a renewed sense of optimism, in an episode that uncannily "echo[es] his mother's experience" (Perez 2013: 105) from thirty years before, Oscar's romantic pursuits are furtively drawn toward the Dominican Republic. There he becomes entangled in an ill-omened flirtation with the community prostitute Ybón, oblivious to the fact that she is the girlfriend of an army officer in the service of Balaguer's government,[6] who cruelly appears on the scene just as Oscar was about to receive "his first kiss ever" (Díaz 2008: 304), upon which he is taken to the historically charged site of the cane field by the captain's cronies and receives a similar, equally savage beating. Along the same line, while being on the verge of death, he also experiences a(-nother) benign, preternatural vision of the mongoose:

"What will it be, muchacho? it demanded. More or less? And for a moment he almost said less. So tired, and so much pain—Less! Less! Less!—but then in the back of his head he remembered his family. [...] More, he croaked. ———— ———— ————, said the Mongoose, and then the wind swept him back into darkness." (ibid: 312)

However, while the talismanic creature's protective spirit succeeds in saving his life for a second time, it cannot prevent the harrowing triumph of the fukú when, in the final chapter, Oscar is drawn back to the island by "the Ancient Powers" (ibid: 325) and eventually shot to death by his former tormentors, whereby the cycle of relived colonial repression eventually reaches a somber culmination as he dies in the "organized wildness of the cane field" (Perez 2013: 100). At length, Oscar's sister Lola, as Belicia's second child, also becomes bequeathed with the (historical) force of the family curse, which seemingly begins to work on her life implicitly as during her formative years she becomes the forlorn victim of her mother's unruly furor. Feasibly corrupted by the tormenting influence of the fukú, Belicia appears to turn the family household into a domestic site of oppression by keeping Lola "crushed under her heel" (Díaz 2008: 57) and vilely treating her as a "Dominican slave" (ibid: 58). Emerged from her maidenhood and largely leading a life apart from her family, however, the "Doom of the Cabrals" (ibid: 149) eventually seems to catch up with Lola with all its might as she is set to endure her own series of heartbreaks that is ominously reminiscent of her mother's (youthly) misfortunes. This begins with the death of her boyfriend Max, who tragically "ended up being mashed between a bus" (ibid: 216), and

---

6   Joaquín Balaguer assumed presidency during the aftermath of Trujillo's assassination and remained in power for over thirty years. As a former protégé of the Trujillista, his reign is largely regarded as a continuation of his predecessor's politics of patronage and corruption, see Liberato (2013: 1-2).

continues through her involvement with (narrator) Yunior, with whom, in "a real moment of excitement" (ibid: 279), she comes to expect a child of her own. However, she is begrudgingly compelled to have an abortion, because he turns out to be a wanton, suave playboy (arguably the kind that Oscar fails to become) who by his own admission "could not keep [his] rabo [dick, vulg.] in [his] pants [and] was cheating on her with some girl" (ibid: 279). In the end, having overcome these tragedies, alongside her husband Rubén, Lola appears to enjoy the most promising future out of the Cabral family circle, yet she remains acutely aware of the looming menace the fukú continues to represent.

In consequence, whereas Díaz follows in the Latin American tradition of magical realism, in light of the Dominican-American immigrant experience, he distinctly employs elements of Dominican folklore to cast the Dominican Republic as a haunted space presided over by the malevolent curse fukú. As a corollary, seemingly functioning as a chronotope and figural representation of the influence of a potentially overbearing Dominican cultural heritage, the eminently destructive force of the fukú symbolically ravages through the exemplary lives of the Cabral family, reevoking the unspeakable rigors of the island's colonial period, relentlessly abounding national borders, and finding a new habitat in the U.S., where it ultimately remains a perpetual (mortal) threat.

3. AMERICAN SUPERHERO FICTION AS NEW, CONFLICTING REALITY

The magical realist framework *The Brief Life* establishes is complemented by the U.S.-American-rooted genre of superhero fiction, a literary variant of the domain of science fiction that was initially brought into prominence as an instrument of wartime propaganda in the United States during the 1940s and famously popularized by Joe Simon and Jack Kirby's comic book hero Captain America[7] waging battle against German Nazi leader Adolf Hitler in an effort to advocate the U.S. entry into WWII. Since that time, through the prolific use of "fantastic powers, which may be internalized or externalized in high-tech paraphernalia" (Franklin 1998: 151), the figure of the American superhero has remained intimately tied to the nation's political endeavors and continuously featured popular

---

7   Although the superhero genre was established by the comic book adventures of Superman in 1938, Captain America was the first superhero character to become an acknowledged national figure and to effectively permeate the American socio-political landscape, see Costello (2009: 5).

iterations like *Superman*, *Iron Man*, and *The Amazing Spiderman* boldly defending the country against nuclear threats during the Cold War or battling terrorist
forces post-9/11 (Costello 2009: 63, 199). In this respect, the superhero fiction
has served as an important avenue to help construct and foster America's vision
of its role as a global superpower (Costello 2015: 125–126) and thus, in analogy
to magical realism's preeminence within Latin American and Dominican
spheres, can be considered as a literary genre that is deeply engrained in U.S.
(pop) culture and history.

Drawing from this tradition, the above-mentioned relevance of the superhero
fiction to *The Brief Life* is readily signaled in its opening epigraph, which makes
an explicit connection to the popular American comic book series *Fantastic
Four* (1961–present) as one of the novel's apparent narrative frames of reference. Apart from being directly credited, however, the series assumes a much
more prominent role within the general character structure the novel develops.
As such, during a public reading at UCLA's Armand Hammer Museum of Art in
2008, Junot Díaz revealed his aesthetic decision to purposely span an intriguing
pattern between the novel's main protagonists and the superhero team of the
Fantastic Four. Representing another brainchild of Simon and Kirby, the series
centers on a group of former astronauts who were bestowed with fantastic powers after their ship was inadvertently exposed to a cloud of cosmic rays during a
scientific mission to outer space (Krensky 2008: 58). With their lives irrevocably
upended, the group quickly learns to harness their newly acquired abilities and
determine to devote their lives to shielding the U.S. Government and its people
from harm. Team leader Dr. Reed Richards becomes Mister Fantastic, with the
power to convert his body into a highly malleable state, and greatly enhanced
mental abilities that turn him into a scientific mastermind. Jonathan Storm takes
on the moniker Human Torch when he discovers that he has attained the mental
capacity to transform his body into a living flame at will. Mission pilot Ben
Grimm, transformed into a rock-skinned, monster-like creature with superhuman
strength upon exposure, is dubbed the Thing, while Susan Storm christens herself the Invisible Woman, to reflect her ability to direct light rays around her
body and thus render herself invisible (Regalado 2015: 191). In their quest to
protect the nation, the *Fantastic Four* are frequently complemented by Uatu the
Watcher, a representative of an advanced extraterrestrial race that observe lesser
species and follow a vow to only guard but never to interfere. However,
throughout the series Uatu violates his pledge and crucially assists the group in
battle against their arch enemy Galactus, a God-like figure, who feeds by drain-
ing living planets of their energy and who is threatening to consume the Earth
(Alsford 2006: 135-136).

Though of slightly subtler nature then the Dominican folklore influences discussed, the principal members of the Cabral family share intriguing similarities with the characters of the *Fantastic Four*, yet with a similarly unfavorable bearing. In this sense, while Díaz follows into the tradition of the superhero fiction, contrary to the inherent principles of the superhero genre, he does not set up a (narrative) realm where the heroes' superpowers function as an operative metaphor for American superiority in moral fortitude, power, and ingenuity (Costello 2015: 128–129). Instead, in a way that ostensibly symbolizes an allegorical representation of the encounter of a new and conflicting cultural reality in the United States germane to the 1.5-generation Dominican-American immigrant reality, he perverts the conventional depiction of superpowers as a laureate of traditional American ideals and essentially strips the superhuman traits he adopts of their transcendent splendor. As such, in spite of the Cabral family bearing semblance to a group of superheroes in one form or another, their 'superpowers' are allegorically rendered ineffectual or even self-destructive, and the family members eventually succumb to the forces of evil.

In analogy to Mister Fantastic serving as the "father figure" (Regalado 2015: 192) and paragon of mental acuity to the team, as the head of the family, Abelard is configured in a congruent manner. Accordingly, being a "brilliant doctor," he also possesses a supreme intellect, is exceptionally well read and likewise described as "one of the most remarkable minds in the country" (Díaz 2008: 221). However, despite his preeminent intelligence, an errant slip of the tongue ironically becomes his downfall as a wrongheaded remark he makes about Trujillo's heinous practices of disposing of opposition party members presents the Trujillo regime with a convenient opportunity to incriminate him, and to convict him to an 18-year sentence for "[s]lander and gross calumny against the Person of the President" (ibid: 242). Eventually, during his confinement in Nigüa prison, he is beaten mercilessly with leather truncheons and subjected to the gruesome torture of La Corona,[8] until "[t]he proud flame of his intellect [is] extinguished," and for the (brief) remainder of his life he is left to exist in "an imbecilic stupor" (ibid: 261). In the same spirit, through her childhood experience, his daughter Belicia can be linked to the character of the Human Torch and the element of fire. Thus, during her direful chapter in Azua, as she kept skipping out on work to attend classes in the province's rural school to atone for her destitute condition, in a frenzied brawl thereupon, she was burned horribly when her "step father"

---

8   As Yunior reports, this procedure involves a wet rope cinched around the head of a manacled prisoner, who is placed in the scorching sun, causing the rope to tighten and inflict upon the recipient unbearable pain.

splashed a pan of hot oil on her naked body, leaving her severely scarred with a "monsterglove of festering ruination extending from the back of her neck to the base of her spine" (ibid: 268). In a similarly grievous sense, on account of his sudden "loss of physical control over the contours of his body" (Perez 2013: 103) and prodigious obesity, her son Oscar bears close resemblance to the mutated monstrosity of the Thing. Merely carrying a "zero combat rating" (Díaz 2008: 15), however, Oscar woefully lacks any of the redeeming attributes his superhero counterpart possesses. As a consequence, bereft of any superhuman strength and "weighing in at a whopping 245 (260 when he was depressed, which was often)" (ibid: 20), he is left to wallow in misery, perpetually lamenting over "[t]he miles of stretch marks [and the] tumescent horribleness of his proportions" (ibid: 30). Lastly, through her apparent restlessness, the figuration of his sister Lola reveals characteristics that are distinctly akin to those of the Invisible Woman. Thus, engendered by Belicia's emotional neglect, during her early youth, she is fueled with an incessant longing "for [her] own patch of world that had nothing to do with her [mother]" (ibid: 57). Consequently, throughout the story, she is resolutely driven by a constant urge to "disappear" (ibid: 63) and repeatedly experiences a "crazy feeling [...] that [...] takes hold of [her and that is] telling [her] to run away" (ibid: 74-75). Yet, despite having the inclination or at least the desire to disappear, her "powers" are also cast in tragic irony as they are explicitly directed against her family.

In a corresponding strain, Uatu's assistance to the group is noticeably reminiscent of the Cabral's association with narrator Yunior, who refers to himself directly as "your humble Watcher" (ibid: 4) and evidently occupies the role of his extraterrestrial analogon. Like Uatu, he first appears as a noninvolved observer – and seemingly heterodiegetic narrator – who merely chronicles the family history. Only halfway into the novel, he is gradually established as a character and comes to partake in the plot by sharing a dorm room with Oscar at Rutgers University. Being patently more adept and popular than him, Yunior diligently endeavors to steer him back onto the path of favorableness. However, unlike Uatu's crucial intervention to the superheroes' cause, his attempts are to no avail as he finds himself unable to alter Oscar's downward trajectory or to prevent his untimely death. In a similar way, his involvement with Lola also proves to be one born under a most auspicious star as his imprudent infidelity effectively prompts her misfortune and coerces her to have an abortion. At length, equivalent to the *Fantastic Four* being confronted with God-like villain Galactus, the Cabral family finds itself faced with the might of Trujillo, whose purported larger-than-life status is similarly reflected through a "linguistic pairing of God and the dictator" (Hanna 2010: 503) in what Yunior refers to as "[t]he national slogan[:] 'Dios y Trujillo' [God and Trujillo]" (Díaz 2008: 3). Consonant-ly, in the same manner Galactus consumes worlds, Trujillo cruelly wields his despotic powers to sap the country of its lifeblood by "changing ALL THE NAMES of ALL THE LANDMARKS in the Dominican Republic to honor him-self" (ibid: 3) and keeping the population under his lurid reign of tyranny. Nev-ertheless, to consummate the family's downfall, whereas comic book villain Galactus, much like his historical predecessor Hitler, can ultimately be over-come, Trujillo's evil sway is dourly permitted to prevail and he remains an om-nipotent figure that detrimentally affects every member of the Cabral's in the form of the fukú even long after his death.

As the above accounts demonstrate, by adopting common elements of super-hero fiction and symbolically corrupting the traditional portrayal of superpowers as a tangible proxy of the American spirit, Díaz essentially creates a similarly haunting experience that effectively rivals the evil wrought by the family fukú and that arguably echoes the Dominican-American reality of being confronted with a new and conflicting cultural reality in the United States. Concurrently, in a way that moves opposite to the genre's narrative principles, the members of the Cabral family are symbolically robbed of their alluded superpowers and are ul-timately subjected to tremendous spells of detriment in their toilful existence as impotent and defective superheroes.

Generic Battle as Identity Conflict

Apart from individually providing a source of affliction, there also seems to be a stringent interplay of inhibition and negation in place between the two fantastic genres of magical realism and superhero fiction that serves to express the identi-ty conflict inherent to the Dominican-American immigrant reality and conceiva-bly epitomizes the "heartbreaking ambivalence" (Valerio-Holguín 2007: 3) of being caught in between the competing forces, and the cultural referents, of two home nations. Thus, to an extent that seemingly captures this arduous reality, it appears reasonable to suggest that the fukú may also function as the potential ar-chitect behind the pernicious nature of the character's "superhero qualities," cru-elly preventing their empowering capacities from taking root and manifestly turning them into self-destructive aberrations. To this end, as the curse had al-ready been cast when Abelard experiences his tragic verbal lapse and inadvert-ently finds himself casting aspersion on Trujillo, this instance can presumably be determined as the fukú's incipient manifestation. Furthermore, as an immediate consequence of Abelard's incarceration, Belicia falls into the hands of her churl-ish foster parents, where she is dreadfully singed and eventually left with the horrid burns that will mar her for the rest of her life. In a similar vein, it also seems to be the malicious force of the fukú that is effectively responsible for Oscar's dramatic and ill-fated transmogrification, and which arguably instills in Lola the immutable desire to abandon her dysfunctional family. Moreover, the grounds for this palpably imbalanced struggle are arguably to be found in Trujillo's dual (miscreant) role as emissary of the fukú and supervillain Galactus, whose divalent thrust cruelly seems to thwart any tangible symptom of superheroism, and as such, may serve as a symbolic representation of the potentially conflicting influence of a Dominican heritage that might serve as an incessant impediment to a tenable Anglo-oriented, or Anglo-centric assimilation.

From these considerations, as has become evident throughout this section, Junot Díaz delicately interweaves the fantastic literary traditions of Latino/a magical realism and American superhero fiction, as distinct cultural artifacts of Dominican and U.S. American tradition, into the narrative frame of *The Brief Life*, but astutely problematizes their (mutual) inclusion as their respective supernatural elements are cast as troublesome and palpably menacing potencies that are entangled in a resolute conflict with one another. As a corollary, in a way that manifests the strenuous reality of grappling with the potentially overbearing influence of a Dominican cultural heritage as well as the encounter of a new and conflicting cultural reality in the United States, this expressly dissonant composition evidently makes present the real-life struggle Díaz and his generation are – or have been – subjected to and, as such, can be regarded as a literary manifestation of the cultural burden ingrained in the 1.5-generation Dominican-American immigrant reality.

4. RECONCILIATION OF GENERATIONAL STRUGGLE

While Junot Díaz adopts fantastic elements to conceivably signify the cultural struggle of a generation, at the same time, the imbrication of magical realism and superhero fiction also reveals another, more cooperative function that feasibly embraces the disparate facets of the 1.5-generation immigrant reality, pertaining to the (lack of) adherence toward the ideological precepts traditionally inscribed within both literary genres deployed.

To this end, as has already been alluded to, apart from being regarded as a denominator of Latin American culture, the genre of magical realism also possesses a rich history of being employed to represent a voice of resistance against Western hegemony in the southern hemisphere. Regarded as a European import and "the language of the colonizer" (Faris 2002: 103), the literary category of realism has traditionally purported to provide an accurate representation of the world, based on fidelity to empirical evidence (ibid: 103). In this sense, to introduce magical elements into a realist narrative has served to destabilize the authority of realism and ultimately question the dominant discourse of the colonizer (ibid: 112-113). From this perspective, magical realism can be considered to constitute "a kind of 'liberating poetics'" (ibid: 103), designated to counter the colonizer's usurpation of a land, and to revive, protect, and defend indigenous tradition (ibid: 102-103). However, while in former magical realist accounts the supernatural is firmly incorporated into the rationality of the text and presented as well as accepted as an uncontested reality (ibid: 102-103), Díaz' approach significantly differs from earlier works. Thus, rather than weaving elements of magic seamlessly into the narrative, Yunior's comments distinctly "cast a veil of vagueness" (Pifano 2014: 6) over the accounts. Claiming to provide the historical narratives as they were relayed to him, he still imparts significant doubt to undermine their reliability. In this manner, amid the inaugural appearance of the mongoose, before extensively recounting its conversation with Belicia, Yunior acutely distances himself from committing to the validity of this part of the scene: "And now we arrive at the strangest part of our tale. Whether what follows was a figment of Beli's wracked imagination or something else altogether I cannot say. Even your Watcher has his silences, his páginas en blanco." (Díaz 2008: 155)

In doing so, he markedly detracts from establishing the creature's genuineness, while at the same time undermining its further appearances. And despite recounting the protagonists' encounters with the mongoose in great detail, his accounts remain "fraught with skepticism" (Ostman 2017: 100) as he effectively leaves open the question whether the mongoose represents a phenomenon that has or has not occurred in reality. In a similar way, Yunior sternly reckons with the legitimacy of the family curse fukú. To this end, throughout the novel's opening paragraph, as he provides a lengthy digression about the history of the fukú, he distinctly diverges himself from its actual veracity by introducing and acknowledging it merely as "an imaginative feature of his parents' and ancestors' generation" (ibid: 100): "In my parents' day the fukú was real as shit, something your everyday person could believe in. Everybody knew someone who'd been eaten by a fukú, just like everybody knew somebody who worked up in the Palacio" (Díaz 2008: 2). Despite prefacing the bearing of the curse in this fashion, throughout his narration, he continuously attributes the malefic events the family members endure to the curse, yet never settling on the fact of its genuine existence in the story and subtly dismissing his own discernible dubiety by stating that "it's not like the fukú itself would leave a memoir or anything" (ibid:

253). Eventually, he includes the readership in his process of contemplation and readily invites the reader to come to his or her own conclusion: "So which was it? you ask. An accident, a conspiracy, or a fukú? The only answer I can give you is the least satisfying: you'll have to decide for yourself. What's certain is that nothing's certain" (ibid: 252–253).

To this extent, Yunior's accounts notably provide a curious blend of both belief and skepticism, oscillating between establishing the veracity of the supernatural and, at once, allowing for its dismissal. By employing autochthonous Dominican folklore elements as (mythical) driving forces of the story, Díaz effectively brings *The Brief Life* into dialog with the Latin American literary tradition of magical realism and readily invites comparisons to earlier magical realist texts. Yet, at the same time, he largely differentiates the novel from the genuinely mythologically invested accounts of previous writers of the magical realist tradition by having narrator Yunior report potential occurrences of magic with an "ironic and irreverent tone" (Bautista 2010: 46) and, as such, markedly retracts from the genre's historical and conventional principles.

With a similar bearing, since their inception, superhero narratives have been widely recognized as a site for the reproduction of American national identity, with the comic book superhero portraying the United States as a virtuous nation immaculately engaged in the earth's conflicts (Costello 2009: 3), bringing freedom and democracy to the world and along the way, perpetually championing over ideological or political deviants that must be defeated in the name, or in the defense of these treasured ideals (ibid: 5).

The *Fantastic Four*, however, are considered as a distinct turning point in the evolution of comic books as they represent the first superhero series to not purely aid in the propagation of American values, but to also take a stern inquiry into the validity of dominant U.S. ideology (Lippert 1994: 41). Thus, their inception in 1961 tapped into a period when the nation was ruptured into conflict over civil rights and the Vietnam War as many Americans were thrown into doubt whether their proudly-held national identity "was [based] more [on] myth than reality" (Costello 2009: 2). This proclivity is specifically exemplified through the character of the Thing and the physical transformation he endures, as in previous instalments of the comic-book superhero franchise, the division between heroes and villains was primarily contingent on their visual representations where the evil's ugliness[9] stood in stark contrast to the physical attractiveness of the super-

---

9   As a stylistic means to signify their corruptness and deviance, comic book villains commonly bore hideously deformations, oftentimes precipitated by their own hyperbolic voracity, see Costello (2009: 65).

heroes, reinforcing the premise that "the political economic system the villains represent is not only ideologically repulsive but morally bankrupt" (ibid: 63–65). Acknowledging this discursive convention, yet astutely reversing its basic suppositions, as a representation of the American hero, the Thing is distinctly beset with the negatively connoted condition of physical disfigurement. As such, while his superpowers may bestow him with physical might, his appearance threatens to render him a social outcast who is to suffer numerous episodes of feeling "marginalized, alienated, lonely, and misunderstood" (Regalado 2015: 193).

In choosing the *Fantastic Four* as a narrative frame of reference, Díaz thus ties in with the series' deviating approach, which is most aggressively played out in the titular character Oscar. As the main protagonist of the story (albeit his accounts do not receive more extensive consideration than those of his family), his character arc, as has been established in the preceding passages, runs parallel to the detriment the Thing endures. His plight, however, is greatly magnified as he is effectively robbed of the pathos that emerged from the Thing's condition. As a consequence, Oscar is set forth on his thoroughly futile life's journey, which culminates in a tragic (farewell) monolog mere moments before he is cold-bloodedly shot by the captain's men, musing on his hapless "loves" and imparting that in a potential afterlife, in a metaphysical reality that his worldly existence has denied him, "he wouldn't be no fatboy or dork or kid no girl had ever loved; over there he'd be a hero, an avenger. Because [on the other side,] anything you can dream (he put his hand up) you can be" (Díaz 2008: 332).

In this sense, in narrativizing the demise of the story's perceived hero and, with unrelenting puissance, carrying his predicament over to the entire Cabral family, Díaz effectively creates what Yunior refers to as a story of the "Great American Doom" (ibid: 5). Accordingly, the novel's trajectory seems to move opposite to the presumptions of the superhero fiction as a classical American (heroic) success story and arguably seeks to oppose and deconstruct the embrace of a (Great) American Dream narrative, notably departing from the national myth of the United States as the land of freedom, hope, and opportunity traditionally espoused by superhero comic books and distinctly casting it as a perpetuated illusion.

As a result, by drawing from the literary traditions of Latino/a magical realism and American superhero fiction, Díaz evocatively addresses both his Latin American mother and U.S.-American master canon, yet doing so in a way that mutually confronts and eventually transgresses the historical ideologies inscribed in both genres. With regard to *The Brief Life* as a work produced by an author of, and in the context of the Dominican-American 1.5-generation, this orchestrated ideological departure arguably signals a literary emancipation of the cultural burden their in between status entails as well as a veritable attempt to eventually reconcile the cultural strife that characterizes their immigrant reality in the United States.

5. Conclusion

As has been established throughout this paper, in his highly acclaimed novel *The Brief Wondrous Life of Oscar Wao*, Dominican-American author Junot Díaz distinctly places the identity negotiation that lies at the center of the works produced by writers of his generation in the domain of the fantastic. By incorporating the fantastic genres of Latino/a magical realism and American superhero fiction as narrative prisms through which the 1.5-generation Dominican-American immigrant reality is aesthetically reconstituted, Díaz stages a conflict firmly grounded in the ambivalent and challenging reality of his generation, yet demonstrates that it can eventually be overcome. As a consequence, through this pointed and eminently liberating expression of cultural multiplicity, *The Brief Life* conceivably lays claim to occupying an alternative position in-between the cultural referents of the Dominican Republic and the United States, through which it can be perceived as an ardent campaign for Díaz' generation, in all their distinctiveness, to be recognized as a fundamental fiber of American society and to carve their own discrete niche within the domains of U.S. (literary) history. An endeavor, which has been crowned with an award that propels authors and their respective works into the higher echelons of the American literary canon: The Pulitzer Prize.

Works Cited

Alsford, Mike (2006): Heroes and Villains, Waco: Baylor University Press.

Bautista, Daniel (2010): "Comic Book Realism: Form and Genre in Junot Díaz's *The Brief Wondrous Life of Oscar Wao*." In: *Journal of the Fantastic in the Arts* 21/1, pp. 41-53.

Boddy, Kasia (2010): *The American Short Story Since 1950*, Edinburgh: Edinburgh University Press.

Boyd, Antonio O. (2010): *The Latin American Identity and the African Diaspora: Ethnogenesis in Context*, Amherst: Cambria Press.

Bowers, Maggie A. (2004): *Magic(al) Realism*, London: Routledge.

Bramen, Carrie T. (1996) "Dominican-American Literature." In: Alpana S. Knippling (ed.), *New Immigrant Literatures in the United States: A Sourcebook to Our Multicultural Literary Heritage*, Westport: Greenwood, pp. 207-220.

Caminero-Santangelo, Marta (2016): "Historias Transfronterizas: Contemporary Latino/a Literature of Migration." In: John M. González (ed.), *The Cambridge Companion to Latina/o American Literature*, Austin: University of Texas Press, pp. 231-246.

Cooper, Brenda (1998): *Magical Realism in West African Fiction. Seeing With a Third Eye*, London: Routledge.

Costello, Matthew J. (2009): *Secret Identity Crisis. Comic Books and the Unmasking of Cold War America*, New York: Continuum.

Costello, Matthew J. (2015): "U.S. Superpower and Superpowered Americans in Science Fiction and Comic Books." In: Gerry Canavan/Eric C. Link (eds.), *The Cambridge Companion to American Science Fiction*, New York: Cambridge University Press, pp. 125-138.

Díaz, Junot (2008 [2007]): *The Brief Wondrous Life of Oscar Wao*, New York: Penguin.

Faris, Wendy B. (2002): "The Question of the Other: Cultural Critiques of Magical Realism." In: *Janus Head* 5/2, pp. 101-119.

Foley, Erin/Jermyn, Leslie (2005 [1995]): *Cultures of the World. Dominican Republic*, Tarrytown: Marshall Cavendish.

Franklin, Bruce H. (1998): "The Vietnam War as American Science Fiction." In: Brett Cooke/Jaume Martí-Olivella/George Edgar Slusser (eds.), *The Fantastic Other: An Interface of Perspectives*, Amsterdam: Rodopi, pp. 165-186.

Hanna, Monica (2010): "Reassembling the Fragments: Battling Historiographies, Caribbean Discourse, and Nerd Genres in Junot Díaz's *The Brief Wondrous Life of Oscar Wao*." In: *Callaloo* 33/2, pp. 498-520.

Higman, Barry W. (2011): *A Concise History of the Caribbean*, New York: Cambridge UP.

Irizarry, Ylce (2016): *Chicana/o and Latina/o Fiction: The New Memory of Latinidad*, Illinois: University of Illinois Press.

Irr, Caren (2014): *Toward the Geopolitical Novel: U.S. Fiction in the Twenty-First Century*, New York: Columbia University Press.

Kanellos, Nicolás (2011): *Hispanic Immigrant Literature: El Sueño del Retorno*, Austin: University of Texas Press.

Krensky, Stephen (2008): *Comic Book Century: The History of American Comic Books*, Minneapolis: Twenty-First Century Books.

Liberato, Ana S. Q. (2013): *Joaquín Balaguer, Memory, and Diaspora: The Lasting Political Legacies of an American Protégé*, Lanham: Lexington Books.

Lippert, David (1994): "Comics and Culture." In: *National Forum* 74/4, pp. 41-45.

Moses, Michael V. (2001): "Magical Realism at World's End." In: *Literary Imagination* 3/1, pp. 105-133.

Ormerod, Beverley (1997): "Magical Realism in Contemporary French Caribbean Literature: Ideology or Literary Diversion?" In: *Australian Journal of French Studies* 34/2, pp. 216-226.

Ostman, Heather (2017): *The Fiction of Junot Díaz: Reframing the Lens*, Lanham: Rowman & Littlefield.

Pérez-Firmat, Gustavo (2012 [1995]): *Life-on-the-Hyphen. The Cuban-American Way*, Austin: University of Texas Press.

Perez, Richard (2013 [2012]): "Flashes of Transgression: The Fukú, Negative Aesthetics, and the Future in *The Brief Wondrous Life of Oscar Wao* by Junot Díaz." In: Lyn Di Iorio Sandín/Richard Perez (eds.), *Moments of Magical Realism in US Ethnic Literatures*, New York: Palgrave Macmillan, pp. 91-108.

Pifano, Diana (2014): "Reinterpreting the Diaspora and the Political Violence of the Trujillo Regime: The Fantastic as a Tool for Cultural Mediation in *The Brief Wondrous Life of Oscar Wao*." In: *Belphégor: Littérature populaire et culture médiatique* 12/1, pp. 1-11.

Regalado, Aldo J. (2015): *Bending Steel: Modernity and the American Superhero*, Jackson: University Press of Mississippi.

Rodríguez, Ana P. (2008): "As the Latino/a World Turns: The Literary and Cultural Production of Transnational Latinidades." In: Havidan Rodriguez/Rogelio Saenz/Cecilia Menjivar (eds.), *Latinas/os in the United States: Changing the Face of América*, New York: Springer, pp. 210-224.

Rumbaut, Rubén G. (2012): "The Educational Experiences of Generation 1.5." In: James A. Banks (ed.), *Encyclopedia of Diversity in Education*, London: Sage, pp. 982-983.

Suárez, Lucía M. (2016): "Trans-American Latino/a Literature of the 1990s: Resisting Neoliberalism." In: John M. González (ed.), *The Cambridge Companion to Latina/o American Literature*, Austin: Universtiy of Texas Press, pp. 111-127.

UCLA: "Junot Diaz, Hammer Readings." Filmed [Mar. 2008]. YouTube video, March 2009, (http://www.youtube.com/watch?v=3iJWaO78jK0&t=16s).

Valerio-Holguín, Fernando (2007): "Dominican-American Writers: Hybridity and Ambivalence." In: *Forum on Public Policy: A Journal of the Oxford Round Table* 2/2, pp. 1-16.

Popular Culture

Flights of Fancy, Secondary Worlds and Blank Slates: Relations between the Fantastic and the Real

SARAH FABER

1. INTRODUCTION

Some fantastic genres deliberately take real-world places and history and inject them with fantastic elements.[1] Urban fantasy, steampunk, gothic and horror tales, as well as some subgenres of historical fiction, all spin out stories set in our world or a very similar alternative version thereof, and add a few key differences. From the magic-wielding inhabitants of Regency England in *Shades of Milk and Honey* to *Harry Potter*'s version of 20th-century Britain, from urban fantasy novels like Ilona Andrew's *Magic Bites*, to Sydney Padua's fictionalized account of *The Thrilling Adventures of Lovelace and Babbage* – starting out as loosely biographical and developing into alternative history –, to augmented reality games like *Pokémon GO*, the formula of adding a novel element to an otherwise familiar world has proven very popular. How these settings are connected to and influenced by the real world seems obvious: Reality – whether contemporary or historical – provides a basic context, into which the fantastic element intrudes.

However, other fantastic subgenres do not use our reality as a basis, but instead create whole new worlds. From Tolkien's Middle Earth to Pratchett's Disc World, fictional secondary worlds have become a well-known staple of fantastic narratives. In a secondary world, everything is possible. It need not be concerned

---

1 In a very broad sense, see 2.

with the known facts of history, social and cultural norms, anatomy, known species, or even the laws of nature. It is – theoretically – a blank slate, an exploration of the full extent of the human imagination. The question is, however: How great is that extent, really?

In spite of their theoretical freedom from reality, all fantastic narratives, including secondary world fantasy, frequently hark back to familiar concepts from our own history and culture. This chapter examines how and why this echoing of the real in the fantastic occurs, working with the thesis that real-world references are needed for the processes of understanding and contextualization, immersion, and critical engagement. After establishing the basic theoretical concepts used in this analysis, I will devote one chapter each to how reality impacts immersion, the audience's understanding and engagement with the narrative, and finally, how the fantastic can recontextualize aspects of reality to critically reflect on them.

2. THEORETICAL BACKGROUND

Before an investigation into the question of how far the human imagination really stretches can begin in earnest, it is necessary to untangle some of the definitional concerns at the heart of this matter. Specifically, what is meant, in this case, by the terms "fantastic," "reality," and (reference/primary/secondary/ story) "world" needs to be established.

This analysis uses a very broad working definition of "the fantastic," which is understood as the depiction of a fictional world that contains at least one element considered impossible in our primary reality. This includes the use of anachronisms – i.e., historical impossibilities, such as the technologically advanced 19th-century setting which is typical of steampunk – and implies, of course, that a work can change from "fantastic" to "realistic" and vice versa, depending on the current consensus on reality. For example, ghost stories could be re-classified if, in the future, scientific studies were to prove that ghosts actually exist and have always existed. On the other hand, it is important to distinguish between "unreal" and "impossible in our reality;" the former merely differentiates fiction and non-fiction, while the latter is a marker of the fantastic. The specific protagonist of a historical novel may have never existed, so they are unreal, but as long as their existence at the time is theoretically possible and plausible, it is an instance of the fictional, but not the fantastic. While the present analysis focuses on fantastic narratives, this definition includes the possibility of non-narrative fantastic works, e.g. paintings. The fantastic in this sense can be embodied in and transcend different media – whether they tell a story or not –, as long as they are able to depict an impossible world.[2] Media with a capability for expressing the fantastic include, but are not limited to: literature, film, TV, comic books, videogames, tabletop games, drama, and the visual arts. This is a decidedly maximalist approach, a perspective on the fantastic which has been increasingly employed over the last decades, but also, for instance, by H. P. Lovecraft, Harald Fricke and Theodor Adorno (cf. Durst 2010: 29-30). The present approach also spans the oft-cited chasm between systemic and historical/pragmatic definitions, blending systemic ("at least one impossible element") and historical criteria ("considered impossible at present"), which goes back mainly to the definition of "reality" employed here (see below). This conceptualisation of "the fantastic" is one of a multitude of definitions that have been suggested and hotly contested over the years (cf. ibid: 17-69; Spiegel 2015).

In order to determine what is impossible in our reality, it must, of course, be clarified what "reality" means, in the first place. This daunting question has occupied philosophers for centuries (cf. Descartes 1978 [1637]; Locke 1975 [1690]; Heidegger 2006 [1927]; Watzlawick 2005 [1978], to name just a very small selection), so it will come as no surprise that there will be no comprehensive attempt to answer it here. This chapter will content itself with a very basic definition in the general vein of critical realism (cf. Bräuer 2003: 583): "Reality" is understood as a temporally and spatially situated world which exists outside subjective experience; which can, to a certain degree, be perceived adequately by the senses; and on which, thus, a basic consensus can be formed. Some aspects of this consensus may be shaped by subjective or cultural notions and may or may not adequately represent inter-subjective reality, and some aspects may be

---

2   I would argue that real-world architecture, for example, is not able to do this, since its material and referential dimensions are more tightly interwoven than they are in many other media. A canvas may feature an image of a fairy, but one would no more speak of a "fantastic canvas" than a "fantastic building." The canvas merely supports a fantastic painting, meaning, a painting with a fantastic subject. Architecture is usually less representational (or, if it is, it mainly achieves this effect by incorporating representational media, such as mosaic or sculpture); it does not depict so much as it just is, making the differentiation between form and content more difficult. If the form is real and cannot be differentiated satisfactorily from the content, then the content is also real, and hence, not impossible. Karl R. Kegler mentions the possibility that fictional buildings, or real buildings with additional fictional properties, may be considered fantastic architecture, however (cf. Kegler 2013: 227).

revised over time, as accepted models of explaining the world change.[3] "Our reality" (or "primary reality," which this paper uses synonymously) is, thus, a cultural construct which may contain flaws (incorrect assumptions about the factual, autonomous, "actual" reality), which definitely contains blind spots where our knowledge is insufficient, and of which there exist several cultural and individual variations. For judging whether a text is fantastic or not, the cultural context thus indirectly plays a significant role.

The reality which we, the creators and recipients of the narratives under discussion here, inhabit is considered the primary world or "reference world" (Ryan 2014: 33), while various narratives create fictional worlds that we cannot directly access, but imagine based on their medial representation. This chapter uses "world" and "reality" synonymously, and considers a "secondary world" as a fictional world that does not claim to share any history or geography with the reference world. For example, *Harry Potter*'s magical Britain, post-apocalyptic narratives like *Mad Max: Fury Road*, or even fairy-tales introduced by the formula "Once upon a time ..." are, in this sense, fantastic narratives, but take place in a fictionalised version of our world. *The Lord of the Rings* or *A Song of Ice and Fire*, on the other hand, are very clearly set in worlds that have their own history and geography. These narratives do not take place on any version of planet Earth, as the maps which are conveniently included with the novels unambiguously clarify.

Given that the following analysis hinges on the difference between reality and fiction, their interplay, and an understanding of "the fantastic" as essentially a reference to an unreal world, it makes sense to mention the concept of storyworlds at this point. Storyworlds are a subset of fictional worlds, or more specifically, as the term implies, fictional worlds in which a story takes place. Herman uses the term to describe "the world evoked implicitly as well as explicitly by a narrative" (Herman: 2009: 106) and clarifies that "narrative artifacts provide blueprints for the creation and modification of such mentally configured storyworlds" (ibid: 107). A storyworld is a flexible construct that develops over time: it is "more than a static container for the objects mentioned in a story; it is a dynamic model of evolving situations, and its representation in the recipient's mind is a simulation of the changes that are caused by the events of the plot" (Ryan: 2014: 33). Herman's and Ryan's insistence on storyworlds as a construction in

---

3   This may be even more arguable than the definition of "the fantastic," but the objective here is not to find a true and comprehensive explanation of existence – a daunting task indeed –, but, rather, to present one way of looking at the matter that will provide a reasonable basis for conducting the following analysis.

the individual recipient's mind is important: The concept acknowledges that, while the clues or elements that prompt the construction of a storyworld can be pinpointed in the narration, the storyworld as a whole spans more than the narrative can show – other places and people, mundane moments, and so on – which are constructed by the audience, and which may vary from one recipient to the next. In their constructions of the storyworld, audiences fill in many of the explicit and implicit gaps in the narrative and just assume that certain things exist and happen even though the narrative does not mention them.

3. IMMERSION

When investigating how the real impacts the fictional and, more specifically, the fantastic, it is necessary to discuss immersion – the state in which audiences largely forget, for a limited time, their own reality and accept a storyworld as a possible alternative. This sensation is one of the main reasons why people enjoy narratives; not just fantastic narratives, but narratives in general.[4] Of course, not all narratives aim to be entirely immersive. Some forms, like Brechtian theater and many pop-cultural narratives, acknowledge and play with their own artificiality. For instance, the *Deadpool* film (2016) includes, just like the comics it is based on, several fourth wall-breaking moments, in which the main character addresses the audience directly. Nevertheless, immersion represents a "source of satisfaction" derived from the consumption of narrative media (Ryan/Thon 2014:12) and, for that reason, it is an effect that most pop-cultural narratives try to evoke.

This pleasant immersion requires the fictional world to seem potentially real, i.e., realistic. This is achieved primarily by a storyworld's including enough fa-

---

4   I very consciously say "one of the reasons," as the general insistence on immersion's paramount role in entertainment and its close ties to narrativity has prompted some very reasonable criticism (cf. Calleja 2011: 17-34). The gist of that criticism is that people enjoy media and entertainment for different reasons, and that immersion is not always related to narration, but can also be induced by intense engagement on other levels, such as captivating gameplay mechanics in a non-narrative game like Tetris (cf. Salen/Zimmermann 2003: 451-2); this specific kind of immersion is characterised by an intense state of focus that is more about forgetting reality than about substituting it with a fictional world. To clearly situate the present analysis: I do focus on narrative immersion, or more specifically, what Calleja terms "immersion as transportation" (Calleja 2011: 32), but recognise that it is not the only kind of immersion in existence.

miliar aspects to enable the audience to imagine and understand the fictional world, and by the narrative's avoiding any (too glaring) logical contradictions. Under these conditions, audiences can suspend their disbelief and become immersed. Mary-Laure Ryan elaborates on how this process works:

"Through their act of make-believe, readers, spectators, or players transport themselves in imagination from the world they regard as actual toward an alternative possible world – a virtual reality – which they regard as actual for the duration of their involvement in the text, game, or spectacle. Once transported into this world, they either enter the body of a specific individual (dramatic acting, playing big bad wolf; controlling an avatar in a computer game) or they pretend to be an anonymous member of the fictional world who receives the narration or observes the unfolding of fictionally real events (reading a novel, watching a play). I call this projection into a virtual body an imaginative recentering [...] and I regard it as the precondition of the experience of immersion." (Ryan 2007: 251)

The "projection into a virtual body" (ibid: 251) is common to many immersive activities, whether reading, acting, watching a play or film, or playing a video game. During all of these activities, disbelief is suspended in favor of the pretense of being an inhabitant of the same fictional world as the characters in the story – possibly, of even being one of these characters themselves. This "recentering," an act of combined empathy and make-believe, allows us to experience immersion. In this sense, being immersed is, essentially, shifting the focal point, the center of one's experience of the world, away from one's real self for a limited time, in order to privately pretend to be somebody else and imagine how that person would think and feel.

Against this backdrop, it becomes apparent that fantastic narratives and narratives set in secondary worlds, in particular, perform a balancing act in order to enable their audiences to become immersed: While the genre contains, per definition, unrealistic elements and non-existent places – elements which directly contradict our knowledge of how the world works and what it is like –, the narrative must yet seem life-like, realistic, believable enough for the audience to suspend their disbelief and pretend to inhabit the fictional world. This difficulty is eased somewhat by the fact that most fantastic concepts are actually recombinations of familiar elements, which means they can often be integrated with relative ease into an otherwise "realistic" perspective.

What is considered "realistic" by the audience is not necessarily real or even familiar as a fictional concept; it mainly needs to be plausible within the rest of the framework of assumptions and regularities which the storyworld provides. Where the storyworld does not explicitly spell out this framework, however, we do revert to the familiar: Mary-Laure Ryan's principle of minimal departure suggests that we "conceive fictional storyworlds on the model of the real world, and [...] will import knowledge from the real world to fill out incomplete descriptions," unless (or until) told otherwise by the narrative (Ryan/Thon 2014: 35). Ryan adds that in genres where storyworlds typically diverge relatively far from our reality, such as the fantastic, "MD [minimal departure] will be superseded by a 'generic landscape,' or a landscape constructed on the basis of other texts" (Ryan/Thon 2014: 45). Whether based on reality or fiction, however, the audience always makes silent assumptions about the laws governing a fictional world. For example, unless told otherwise, recipients will assume that any fictional world has gravity. If this assumption is violated by an event in the narrative, but not invalidated – for example, if a character takes a leap that seems to contradict other intradiegetic evidence of how gravity works –, audiences begin to consider the narrative implausible and unrealistic, which can disrupt their immersion in the fictional world. It becomes more difficult to maintain the imaginative recentering, i.e. to temporarily pretend the storyworld is real, if one notices logical contradictions that should not exist in any potentially real world. If, on the other hand, the conflicting assumptions are reconciled – for example, by attributing the unusual leap to special boots – the storyworld remains plausible and the audience's immersion largely intact.

4. Understanding and Engagement

On a different level, all narratives, including stories set in secondary worlds, require a minimum share of elements from our own primary reality for the audience to be able to make sense of the narrative at all. Reality provides a basis, context and frame of reference for all that we can imagine. Real elements within fictional narratives help us not only to understand the narrative in the first place, but also to make out patterns, form expectations on this basis, recognize intertextual references and engage critically with the narrative.

Narrative Essentials

First and obviously, some elements we know from our primary reality keep coming up in fantastic stories simply because they are an integral part of how we understand the world. Basic concepts such as personhood, needs and desires, an existence that is situated within and dependent on perceptible space and time, and communicating with others are just some of these basic structures that are integral to any kind of world that we can imagine and in which a narrative can still take place.

This becomes apparent in all of the – diverse and sometimes even contradictive – definitions of "narrative" which narratology offers. Though these definitions are very different from each other in some respects, they all agree, on a basic level, that narratives need concepts such as "events," "chronology," and "agents." Indeed, the term "narrative" itself already implies that stories are told, so there must be a person to do the telling, a chronological context in which the telling can occur, an audience for whose benefit the telling takes place, and a means of communication between audience and storyteller. Definitions of "narrative" rely heavily on these concepts. H. Porter Abbott, for example, states that, "[s]imply put, narrative is the representation of an event or a series of events" (2008: 13); David Herman postulates in a similar vein that "stories are accounts of what happened to particular people – and of what it was like for them to experience what happened" (2009: 1).

Although narratology originates in the field of literary studies, the discipline has expanded in recent decades, as the notion of "text" expanded, into a much broader, more inclusive field, venturing beyond literature and traditional texts to consider storytelling in all shapes and sizes, and narratology's more recent definitions hold true for stories in a broad variety of narrative media. For example, Egenfeldt-Nielsen et al. note in their introduction to video game studies, quite similarly, that "[n]arratives are made of events, and usually contain settings and characters" (2008: 174), and inter- and transmedial narrative scholar Marie-Laure Ryan stresses the importance of familiar concepts to the understanding of narratives when she describes narrative as "not something that is perceived by the senses: it is constructed by the mind, either out of data provided by life or out of invented materials" (Ryan 2009: 270).

Essentially, some aspects of the real world are so hard-wired into our ways of thinking that they limit the possibilities within the theoretically boundless imaginative space of secondary worlds. Some stories fight hard against these constraints and push the boundaries of fantastic worlds we can still conceive of. The well-known 19th-century novella *Flatland: A Romance of Many Dimensions*, for instance, is set in one- and two-dimensional spaces, and its characters are dots, lines and geometrical shapes. The resulting storyworld seems bizarre, and some effort to imagine such a narrative space is required, as well as some recourse to past geometry lessons:

"Imagine a vast sheet of paper on which straight Lines, Triangles, Squares, Pentagons, Hexagons, and other figures, instead of remaining fixed in their places, move freely about, on or in the surface, but without the power of rising above or sinking below it, very much like shadows—only hard and with luminous edges [...] and you will then have a pretty correct notion of my country and countrymen. Alas, a few years ago, I should have said 'my universe': but now my mind has been opened to higher views of things. [...] I dare say you will suppose that we could at least distinguish by sight the Triangles, Squares, and other figures, moving about as I have described them. On the contrary, we could see nothing of the kind, not at least so as to distinguish one figure from another. Nothing was visible, nor could be visible, to us, except Straight Lines; and the necessity of this I will speedily demonstrate.

Place a penny on the middle of one of your tables in Space; and leaning over it, look down upon it. It will appear a circle.

But now, drawing back to the edge of the table, gradually lower your eye (thus bringing yourself more and more into the condition of the inhabitants of Flatland), and you will find the penny becoming more and more oval to your view; and at last when you have placed your eye exactly on the edge of the table (so that you are, as it were, actually a Flatlander) the penny will then have ceased to appear oval at all, and will have become, so far as you can see, a straight line." (Abbott 1998 [1884]: 7-8)

Flatland acknowledges the difficulties most readers face when trying to follow and imagine a story set in non-three-dimensional space, not only by providing a number of illustrations to go with the text, but also by employing a narrator who knows three-dimensional space, though he is not native to it, and can, thus, describe Flatland (and Pointland) in terms that we denizens of three-dimensional space can understand, as the example of the penny demonstrates. Even though its characters are geometrical shapes, *Flatland* also retains the basic concepts which the definitions of "narrative" imply – personhood, communication, and a temporal and spatial context, even though the space of this narrative is an unusual one. The result is not really so much a mathematical thought experiment in narrative form as, in fact, social criticism: Abbott combines familiar, everyday-concepts with the highly unusual setting and characters in order to highlight and satirize the absurdities of Victorian England's social structures.

Other stories, most famously many of H.P. Lovecraft's writings, actively recognize and engage with the limitations of human thought, by postulating the hypothesis that things which go too far beyond human understanding would bend and break our minds if we encountered them. The now iconic "Call of Cthulhu," for example, begins with: "The most merciful thing in the world, I think, is the inability of the human mind to correlate all its contents. We live on a placid island of ignorance in the midst of black seas of infinity, and it was not meant that we should voyage far" (Lovecraft 1999b [1928]: 139). Nevertheless, this is exactly the space into which Lovecraft's stories venture – only to run up against the boundaries which the above passage describes. Lovecraft's protagonists set out from perfectly ordinary, real-world surroundings and stumble into encounters with the strange, otherworldly creatures of the Cthulhu mythos; encounters which are steeped in vague, fragmentary descriptions, only half-recognized sensory input and tinted by the confused, sometimes outright mad perspective of Lovecraft's narrators, who share their stories even though they frequently profess an urgent wish to forget the experiences they describe. "I must have forgetfulness or death" states the narrator of "Dagon" bluntly (Lovecraft 1999a [1919]: 1), before relating his encounter with a strange horror on the high seas in these bewildered terms:

"When at last I awakened, it was to discover myself half sucked into a slimy expanse of hellish black mire which extended about me in monotonous undulations as far as I could see, and in which my boat lay grounded some distance away. [...]
I was in reality more horrified than astonished; for there was in the air and in the rotting soil a sinister quality which chilled me to the very core. The region was putrid with the carcasses of decaying fish, and of other less describable things which I saw protruding from the nasty mud of the unending plain. Perhaps I should not hope to convey in mere words the unutterable hideousness that can dwell in absolute silence and barren immensity." (ibid: 1-2)

As the narrator struggles for words and finds them insufficient to describe his perceptions, he presents the audience with a perplexing duality: His description, so deceptively simplistic, portrays a scene that does not seem very threatening. The protagonist, previously disoriented and adrift in a small boat, has apparently found land, and it is merely a vaguely swamp-like space, characterized by nothing other than its blackish soil and unpleasant, fishy smell. Yet, the narrator insistently stresses that the place creates an instinctual, unspeakable terror in him, a statement that does not seem to match his description of the landscape and suggests an unknown – unknowable – missing link beneath the surface, beyond understanding. Many of Lovecraft's works derive their suspense and unsettling effect out of this tension between ostensible knowledge and the vague, contradictory sense of immense, threatening, potentially fatal ignorance. This struggle with the boundaries of understanding and expression prevails through the rest of "Dagon": The narrator feels himself "[u]rged on by an impulse which I cannot definitely analyse" (ibid: 3) and "filled [...] with sensations I cannot express" (ibid: 4), vaguely mentions "marine things which are unknown to the modern world" (ibid: 4) and an ancient civilization of whose "faces and forms I dare not speak in detail; for the mere remembrance makes me grow faint" (ibid: 4). He finally observes an unnamed "thing," "[v]ast, Polyphemus-like, and loathsome," with "gigantic scaly arms," and a "hideous head," and concludes: "I think I went mad then" (ibid: 5).

Lovecraft's strategy for describing truly unreal, unknown creatures is, essentially, to *not* describe them, to stress how insufficient our words and concepts are to capture something genuinely alien, to rely merely on partial impressions and the feelings these unnamed horrors inspire. His choice of perspective underscores the fact that we need familiar elements of the real to make sense of stories at all: Lovecraft's narrators are always human – bewildered, terrified, insane, but always human –, since the concept of the strange, ancient creatures in itself is mutually exclusive with taking their perspective or making them the narrator of a human story; no understanding, no translation of language or concepts is possible beyond this boundary.

Fantastic Recombinations

As the analysis so far and the examples from *Flatland* and Lovecraft's fiction suggest, the human mind needs real and familiar concepts in narratives for them to be comprehensible, and when stories attempt to leave this familiar space, they find themselves either struggling to describe the completely unknown in comprehensible (i.e., known) terms, or resorting to metaphors and comparisons which relate the strange and unusual to ordinary concepts. Why, then, do fantastic narratives still work, even though the genre's very premise is ignoring reality and introducing wildly unrealistic ideas such as dragons, ghosts, or new worlds on distant planets? Perhaps because all these fantastic elements are not really that far removed from our everyday reality. In their entirety, they may be unknown or even unheard of in the real world, but they can be broken down into components that relate to our reality easily, and become fantastic only through recombination or inversion.

To give an example: Our reality does not include dragons. However, lizards, winged, flying animals, and even fire breathing are sufficiently well-known. A combination of these normally unrelated elements puts an interesting new spin on the whole, while keeping it comfortably within the boundaries of human imagination. Lovecraft's creatures are not indescribable because they are unreal; they are indescribable because Lovecraft refuses to rely on familiar elements and insistently stresses the component of a completely unknown, unnamable other.

Gary Alan Fine, writing on fantasy tabletop role-playing games, also observes this influence of real elements in the creative processes of imagination and invention, suggesting that expectations and emotional satisfaction also play a role in this observable need for real aspects in fantasy narratives:

"Since fantasy is the free play of a creative imagination, the limits of fantasy should be as broad as the limits of one's mind. This is not the case, as each fantasy world is a fairly tight transformation by the players of their mundane, shared realities. While players can, in theory, create anything, they in fact create only those things that are engrossing and emotionally satisfying. Fantasy is constrained by the social expectations of players and of their world." (Fine 2002 [1983]: 3)

Faced with the challenge to create something new, we still revert to what we know, sorting through our experiences and knowledge for buildings blocks. This process is aided and our imaginations slowly expanded through the sharing of fantastic narratives, which can lead to concepts that once needed a little stretch of the imagination, some straining to think of what a dragon might look like, being firmly established in the cultural mainstream. Over time, imaginative creations that once were new can become known as concepts of their own. When they are, they can act as shorthand or components in the process of creating new, more complex fantastic ideas. Once the ideas of "dragon" and "ghost" become as widely-known as they are now, it becomes easy to imagine the ghost of a dragon. The same feat would be a little more difficult without the solid establishment of these components in our minds, simply due to the sheer number of recombinations needed to imagine a "huge, fire-breathing, winged lizard that has passed away and left behind its body, but continues to exist in the ethereal shape of its soul." "Ghost of a dragon" is essentially the same thing, but that shorthand makes the mental task of recombining the known into a new unknown much easier.[5]

Repertoire and Genre

Beyond the issue of grasping a narrative's meaning on the level of plot, including elements from the real world in any fictional world is also vital for the purpose of creating a setting that is accessible and understandable in a wider sense. Fantastic narratives, in particular, create representations of worlds with which the audience can have no first-hand experience, because they are – at least in

---

5 This process essentially mirrors the way language in general gradually introduces new words to act as shorthand for longer descriptions, thus allowing us to express more and more complex thoughts with comparative ease.

some respect – fundamentally different from our own world. Perhaps it is just one or two crucial elements such as the existence of magic, or perhaps it is a whole new, secondary world with its own geography, fauna and flora, history, nations and customs. To make these fantastic worlds relatable, believable and interesting, the audience needs references beyond basic concepts such as the ones inherently required by any narrative (as laid out above: time, personhood, communication, chronology and space) to evoke a more distinct notion of the fictional worlds and to enable the audience to fill in some of the inevitable gaps.

Gary Alan Fine notes the importance of providing enough context for the successful portrayal of a fictional world: "Both [realism and logic] are somewhat paradoxical for the social construction of fantasy, since fantasy is said to be neither realistic nor logical. However, [...] a common frame of reference is necessary" (Fine 2002 [1983]: 80). He relates this need for a shared context especially to the communicative nature of storytelling, stating that "communication is only possible when a shared set of references exist for the key images" (ibid: 3).

The imaginary world forming the setting and backdrop for any story is inevitably incomplete, glanced by the recipient only in fragments. As outlined above, explicit and implicit gaps in the narrative are usually filled in with knowledge from either the real world (minimal departure) or other narratives. But how does the audience know which of these fields of knowledge to reference? In order to avoid confusion, the narrative must give clues; it is essential that the fragmentary representation of the storyworld be enough for the recipient to identify a fitting repertoire. In 1978, Wolfgang Iser formulated the concept of the repertoire as follows: "The repertoire consists of all the familiar territory within the text. This may be in the form of references to earlier works, or to social and historical norms, or to the whole culture from which the text has emerged – reality" (Iser 1978: 69). Though Iser was working with traditional, literary texts, his concept of the repertoire also applies to "text" in its wider sense of "narration in general," regardless of the medium. It is noted and expanded upon by contemporary scholars in different media including, for example, Henry Jenkins, who touches on the same idea in his discussion of video game narratives. He describes "evocative spaces," which "draw upon our previously existing narrative competencies. They can paint their worlds in fairly broad outlines and count on the visitor/player to do the rest" (Jenkins 2002: 123).

The concept of the repertoire is also picked up in an analysis of transmedial worlds conducted by Lisbeth Klastrup and Susana Pajares Tosca, who clarify that there is more than one repertoire and highlight the connection between repertoire and genre (cf. Klastrup/Tosca 2004: 2). Each repertoire is a set of information, conventions and norms, and while several of them may be activated by one story, a few of them are mutually exclusive. The audience picks up on familiar elements within the unfamiliar world of the narrative, and uses these clues to piece together an idea of which repertoire is applicable to the fictional world in question.

Repertoires often overlap significantly with genre conventions, i.e., recipients know what to expect of a story that identifies as romance, crime fiction, or fairy tale, as well as certain "setting-specific" labels, such as western, space opera, steampunk, or high fantasy. These labels form "specific systems of expectations and hypothesis" which present "a means of recognition and understanding" for the audience (Neale 1990: 179). By matching the clues they have been given about the imaginary world against their knowledge of the real world and other stories, cross-referencing tropes and common elements, audiences can identify the appropriate genre and repertoire(s), and apply this information to the narrative to fill in some of the gaps and form expectations about the further development of the plot, as well as of dramatic and stylistic conventions that will probably be used.[6] With a few well-placed clues, a narrative can swiftly create a background that seems rich and plausible, because calling on genre expectations allows it to imply much more than it directly shows: "The fictional world is immediately recognizable, and thus believable, because it is similar to many stories we have seen and read before" (Egenfeldt-Nielsen et al. 2008: 173).[7]

Although this process theoretically allows for great efficiency, many narratives keep mentioning pointers and clues towards the appropriate repertoire throughout, partly because it provides continued orientation to the audience, and partly because these elements are, of course, clues for a certain repertoire for a reason – they are common or even necessary in these stories. Unless a story is intentionally disorienting, such clues are usually introduced as early as possible, to let the reader form an idea of what the narrative will be like and whether or not they wish to continue investing their time in it. Take, for example, this first paragraph of *Soulless*, a contemporary novel:

"Miss Alexia Tarabotti was not enjoying her evening. Private balls were never more than middling amusements for spinsters, and Miss Tarabotti was not the kind of spinster who could garner even that much pleasure from the event. To put the pudding in the puff: she

---

6   For example, a film exhibiting markers of the horror category will lead audiences who are familiar with that repertoire to expect jump scares.

7   Here, Egenfeldt-Nielsen et al. also point out the connection between what is familiar and what seems believable, i.e. realistic.

had retreated to the library, her favorite sanctuary in any house, only to happen upon an unexpected vampire." (Carriger 2009: 1)

The words "private ball" and "spinster" clearly convey that the reader should expect not a contemporary, but a historical setting. If the recipient has the required intertextual knowledge, the term "private balls" may remind them of a certain passage in *Pride and Prejudice*[8] and narrow down the historical context a little further to late 18th- or 19th-century England. "To put the pudding in the puff" evokes a vague notion of quaint Englishness and supports the Austenesque flair. The paragraph thus builds a distinct impression, only to serve up a surprising twist at the end: The intruding element of the vampire gives an immediate and unmistakable clue that the world of this text cannot be appropriately described by the historical repertoire that seemed fitting up to this point. Instead, the text now presents itself as possessing a historical setting that is blended with paranormal occurrences – some of which clearly cancel out or overwrite known historical facts. At the same time, the introduction of the paranormal puts the reader on edge with this first unexpected element, prompting the expectation of further subversive strategies in the same vein.

Obviously, text-external information and practices such as branding, blurbs, certain conventions regarding the look of book covers in different genres, as well as the name of the author help with the process of contextualization. In the present example, the cover gives some clear hints as to the specific genre by depicting a young woman wearing 19th-century fashion combined with goggles and a slightly strange-looking parasol featuring cogwheels; both goggles and gears are central elements of the steampunk aesthetic. The background is comparatively muted, showing a photorealistic foggy public square with pedestrians, which contrasts with the book's title and author's name written in a modern, sanserif font and styled in loud neon colors that would not typically be used for a historical novel. The blurb on the cover says "A novel of vampires, werewolves, and parasols," unambiguously identifying the presence of supernatural elements in the novel, as well as hinting at the pointedly absurd humor. Furthermore, Gail Carriger has established herself as a quite well-known author of steampunk novels by now, meaning that her name alone may hold plenty of information for some readers. In spite of all these external clues, however, a book can hardly rely exclusively on its cover to identify the setting and genre; the text itself must also supply internal clues, as discussed above.

---

8   "Perhaps by and by I may observe that private balls are much pleasanter than public ones" (Austen 2004 [1813]: 69).

Intertextuality

The example from *Soulless* already hints at another meaning-making strategy for which real-world contexts are indispensable. The workings of intertextuality have received much attention in academic circles during the past decades[9] and are sufficiently well-known, so they shall not be explained in great detail here. For the purpose at hand, it suffices to employ a basic understanding of intertextuality as concerned with the "relations between texts" (Allen 2000: 209). Different texts – in the wider sense – mostly situate themselves in different storyworlds, but they are created and consumed in our primary reality, which functions as a "central hub," from which different textual realities can be accessed. These other realities almost inevitably inform and provide a background for new texts, which leads to pointers, allusions, and similarities to previously published works in any text (cf. Berndt/Tonger-Erk 2013: 7). The audience can recognize these connections and, by drawing comparisons between the two works suggested, derive further meaning from these intertextual pointers. During this process, intertextual connections represent an intrusion of the real into the fictional narrative in three respects: They point out either real occurrences in the audience's own culture, or the audience's real knowledge about other stories, and they draw attention to the artificiality of the whole narrative situation.

First, intertextual clues may refer to our primary reality itself – its history, customs, pop-culture or urban legends – and widely-known non-fiction texts or media products. Drawing from many references of this kind, Terry Pratchett's Discworld novels *Soul Music* and *Moving Pictures*, for example, derive many of their comical as well as critical moments from references to real-world music and cinema, respectively. Among many other references to real musicians and their songs, *Soul Music* mentions bands called "The Whom" and "Lead Balloon" (Pratchett 1994: 215), clearly referring to The Who and Led Zeppelin.

Second, intertextual references to other works of fiction can still be considered as a prompt to refer to "real" knowledge, which audiences assimilate from the fictions they engage with. Intertextual references often make no sense from the point of view the audience takes during imaginative recentering, since the object of the referral often exists outside the fictional world the reference is made in. Thus, the audience must leave the intradiegetic point of view for a moment and refer to their real selves' knowledge to understand the reference. For example, *Moving Pictures* mentions dwarves singing a "'hiho' song" (Pratchett 1990: 73), which is of no particular significance to the inhabitants of Discworld,

---

9   For a summary, cf. Allen (2000); Berndt/Tonger-Erk (2013).

but, to the audience, a fairly transparent reference to Disney's *Snow White and the Seven Dwarves* (1937), in which the dwarves indeed sing a now well-known song that repeats the phrase "heigh-ho, heigh-ho."

Third, as a result, the imaginative recentering and suspension of disbelief is slightly interrupted by such references, reminding the recipient that they are engaging with an artificial narrative construct, which was created in and with which the audience engages from our primary reality. For example, *Pride and Prejudice and Zombies*, a recent re-writing of Austen's classic by Seth Grahame-Smith, theoretically works on its own as a historical novel with fantastic elements, but unfolds greater meaning when considered in comparison to Austen's original novel. Grahame-Smith actually incorporates much of the original text and retains Austen's light, playful tone, but often evokes new meanings by changing a single word in a sentence, or attributing a line of dialogue to a different character. Much of the novel's humor is derived from the comparison between Grahame-Smith's and Austen's version of the text: Without the comparison, zombie-infested Hertfordshire is mainly a bleak and brutal alternative historical scenario, narrated in a slightly incongruous, conversational manner; it makes more sense and unfolds a rather amusing dimension when these unrelentingly gory elements appear in places in the text where an informed intertextual reader is used to finding gentle quips about etiquette and manners. For example, in the original, Mr. Bennet remarks that "Lizzy has something more of quickness than her sisters" (Austen 2004 [1813]: 2), whereas the same passage in Grahame-Smith mentions "Lizzy, who has something more of the killer instinct than her sisters" (Grahame-Smith 2009: 8). Similarly, the first meeting with Lady Catherine de Bourgh undergoes an interesting re-contextualization. In Austen, the introduction proceeds like this: "Her Ladyship, with great condescension, arose to receive them; and as Mrs. Collins had settled it with her husband that the office of introduction should be hers, it was performed in a proper manner, without any of those apologies and thanks which he would have thought necessary" (Austen 2004 [1813]: 124). Grahame-Smith copies the entire first part of the sentence, but in his version, Charlotte has meanwhile been infected with the zombie plague, and the sentence concludes thus: "should be hers, it was performed with no shortage of difficulty as she struggled to speak in a manner comprehensible to others" (Grahame-Smith 2009: 124). Charlotte's original eloquence and good manners turn into embarrassing clumsiness. The moment initially evokes a grotesquely funny image, but also has an underlying sinister quality – Charlotte is, after all, slowly losing her humanity –, which emerges all the more starkly in contrast to the original scene, which is a) much more frivolous in comparison and b) ends well on the social level, whereas Grahame-Smith's version ends in embarrassment. This technique constantly keeps the reader stepping outside of their immersed, intradiegetic point of view to remember Austen's novel and compare the two texts. It is essentially a trade-off: The pleasure of immersion is diminished, but a different kind of stimulation is gained from following the intertextual connection.

5. RE-CONTEXTUALIZATION

Fictional worlds may also echo aspects of the real world to encourage critical reflection, by alienating the otherwise "normal" from its usual context or giving an exactly inverse portrayal. The previously mentioned novella *Flatland* does this by presenting common Victorian attitudes and social norms in a wildly alien context. Matriarchal societies or species knowing more or less than two biological sexes are other examples of secondary worlds using this strategy, in this case to highlight and question real-world preconceptions about sex and gender. Similarly, stories with non-human protagonists (such as animals, aliens, robots or digital entities) raise questions about the definition of personhood.

Sometimes, these issues go hand in hand with the repertoire of the story, which implies further information on the world's cultural background. For example, the Middle Ages, which are used as a rough outline and repertoire for many fantasy worlds, are typically associated with sexism, racism, violence, and less enlightened attitudes towards the sciences. In secondary world fantasy, these aspects may be either included to further contribute to the audience's identification of the repertoire, or may be subverted in order to highlight and critically reflect on them. Similarly, stories may utilize the pointed absence of something we understand as a basic, everyday concept. For example, the film *Equilibrium* (2002) portrays a dystopian society in which human emotions have been abolished because of their potential for violent conflict. This absence, striking and in itself almost painful to the viewer, draws attention to the central role emotion plays in our everyday lives, and their integral part in our concepts of identity and freedom.

In contrast, the *A Song of Ice and Fire* novels (1996-) and their TV adaptation, *Game of Thrones* (2011-), employ the confirmation strategy. They depict a violent, sexist, quasi-medieval society, which mirrors its historical model in most aspects and which many fans appreciate and defend as appropriate and realistic. However, the series does include non-realistic elements such as magic and dragons, a fictional geography, fictional nations and languages, and both the novels and their TV adaptation employ the common narrative convention of tacitly "translating" the standard language of the fictional world into perfectly comprehensible, non-medieval English. These non-historical elements, as well as the existence of other fantasy narratives which are based on medieval Europe, but reject the "realistic" elements of sexism and racism,[10] highlight the fact that – while effective as a narrative strategy – incorporating these historical elements into a fantasy narrative is an optional, authorial choice. *A Song of Ice and Fire* uses this confirmation strategy very successfully. However, there is no strict narrative necessity for it.

In contrast, *Merlin* (2008-12), a BBC series about the youth of the mythical sorcerer and many other prominent figures of the Arthurian legend, employs the subversion strategy. Though clearly set in medieval England, the TV series has its male characters treat the female characters much more respectfully and equitably than would historically have been the case. This holds true not only for Morgana, a white noblewoman, but also for her servant Gwen (Guinevere), who is, in this adaptation, not only female and lower-class, but also a woman of color. Regardless of their differences, Arthur, Merlin, Gwen, and Morgana become friends in a very modern, egalitarian sense of the word. More generally, the social relationships and conventions shown in *Merlin* present some quite decided subversions of medieval social standards, but the series shows enough markers of "medievality," mostly in its set and costume design, to nevertheless enable its audience to identify the medieval repertoire with ease. The subversion of historical reality, in this case, does not work to undermine comprehension of the setting, but merely highlights the deviations from expected norms and prompts the audience to critically reflect on why these aspects were changed.

Jane Fletcher's novel *The Exile and the Sorcerer* employs a similar strategy, though it centers the narrative around its political issue more pointedly. In many ways, the novel is a typical high-fantasy adventure story: Its protagonist, trained as a swordfighter, leaves her native island, travels the world, slays a basilisk and meets a magically gifted woman (the titular sorcerer). Its setting is a low-tech world bearing certain similarities to the European Middle Ages. The novel imposes one central twist on our key perception of the historical model, however: It erases the patriarchy. Instead, Fletcher explores questions about sex, gender, and identity by contrasting two different types of societies: one matriarchal culture (which is otherwise strongly reminiscent of Viking society) and one in which the sexes enjoy perfect equality. Situations and constellations which are well-known to the reader thus appear in a new context, highlighting the often absurd signifi-

---

10 E.g., *Merlin* (2008-12, see below), Neil Gaiman's *Stardust*, or Cornelia Funke's *Igraine Ohnefurcht*.

cance we attach to sex and gender. The following scene, which takes place on the protagonist Tevi's native island with its matriarchal society, illustrates this effect well:

"[T]he coming feast had disrupted the daily schedule. Little real work was being done. The men still cleaned and cooked, but older women gathered to discuss the prospect of war while younger ones practiced swordplay and archery with even more zeal than usual. Outside the storeroom, three men were struggling with a large cider barrel. Brec marched over and put out a restraining hand. The men—Brec's brother, Sparrow, and two of Tevi's cousins—immediately stood back.

'Is this for the feast?' Brec asked.

'Grandmother told us to get it,' Sparrow answered defensively.

'You were shaking up all the dregs.'

'We were trying to keep it steady.'

Brec relented and smiled. 'Tevi and I will carry it.'

'We'll cope.'

'I'd rather not take the chance. I'm hoping to drink some tonight.'

'They'll be alright without us.' Tevi said, hoping to spare her knee.

'We can't leave the boys to lug this around. It must weigh twice as much as them,' Brec argued.

Tevi gave in. The full barrel was clearly too heavy for the men, but thanks to Abrak's potion, it presented no problem for Brec and Tevi, apart from Tevi's knee complaining with each step. They wove their way to the main square while Brec directed a stream of banter at the men.

'You don't want to pull a muscle, else you'll be no fun at the feast and even less fun afterwards. Although the fun thing to pull then doesn't have a muscle in it.'

Tevi's cousins giggled and blushed above their beards. Sparrow walked beside Tevi, smiling at her shyly." (Fletcher 2006: 30-1)

In this excerpt, the men are associated with traits and activities which we identify as stereotypically feminine – domestic work, physical inferiority, giggling, blushing and shyness. They defer to female authority and are clearly at a disadvantage in this conversation, taking a defensive stance. The women, meanwhile, are clearly designated as leaders and fighters, act decisively, make lewd jokes and offer help to the weaker sex in a stance that conflates chivalry and patronization – a situation that is quite familiar to the inhabitants of patriarchal Western societies, except that here, the roles are reversed. Tevi, the queer main character, expresses mild criticism of this pecking order and feels uncomfortable with the behavior that is expected of her – "They'll be alright without us" (ibid: 30) –, but

submits to it, nevertheless, hinting at the role of peer-pressure in the establishment of social norms.

This passage also mentions one important concession Fletcher makes to "realism" and illustrates the importance of a cohesive set of rules governing the way
a secondary world functions to its credibility in the eyes of the audience. As described above, conflicts between events within the fictional world and the (explicit or implicit) rules of this world make the narrative seem unrealistic. To
avoid this jarring effect, Fletcher's novel introduces a potion, "[a] magic brew
that gave the women their strength. Without it, they would be even weaker than
men" (ibid: 14). Against the backdrop of current developments in the field of
gender studies, we should be prepared to question how far differences in physical strength between men and women might not actually be the result of nurture
rather than nature; after all, different socialization structures for boys and girls
exist from early childhood on, imparting different, gendered values and beauty
standards right from the start[11]. Strength and bulk are painted as desirable for
boys and men, while delicate skinniness is the ideal girls are encouraged to aspire to, and expressions such as "throwing like a girl" make sure that exhibiting
characteristics of the "wrong" gender is socially punished and made undesirable.
It seems only plausible that this consistent shaping and reinforcement of body
images and behavioral norms would result in measurably shaping the bodies
themselves. However, Fletcher seems to consider the physical disparity between
men and women as so immovable a fact – or, at least, something the majority of
her readership would think of as such – that the reversal of physical strength in
men and women requires an explanation; and not just any explanation, but the
one that trumps all others: magic. The text does not simply portray a society in
which women are naturally (or perhaps due to cultural norms and practices)
stronger than men, but in which a magical potion serves to justify women's
greater physical strength and offers a reason why we should suspend our disbelief and suppose, for the moment, that this ostensibly anatomically impossible
society might exist. This narrative strategy is problematic insofar as it undermines Fletcher's feminist point, but also telling with regard to how much our reality is actually subject to negotiations, opinions, cultural norms, and democratic
processes.

Throughout Fletcher's novel, the reversal of gendered concepts and attributes
we know from our primary reality is so consistent and striking that the reader
cannot help but notice. The expression "blushed above their beards" (ibid: 31) in

---

11 For example, a study by Connolly et al. finds that "the thin ideal, as seen in older girls
and women, is present from an early age" (2004: 5).

particular captures the essence of this strategy: a (supposedly) female trait like shy blushing, a passive response rather than an action, is combined with the (supposedly) exclusively masculine trait of facial hair, which we associate with power, rugged strength, and confidence. This combination produces a strong, unsettling effect. The almost inevitable, knee-jerk rejection such scenes provoke draws attention to the absurdity of gender stereotypes; if it is normal for a girl to blush shyly, why is the same behavior bizarre as soon as facial hair becomes involved? The consistent inversion of a patriarchal society which is depicted in the first chapters of Fletcher's novel highlights gender stereotypes, and, by placing familiar norms and behaviors in a new context, invites the audience to engage critically with their own gendered expectations.

6. CONCLUSION

It has been shown that all narratives, even and especially pop-cultural fantastic narratives, rely heavily on the inclusion of elements from and references to our primary reality. Elements of the real form a necessary basis for all human thought and comprehension, are inseparably connected to the nature of storytelling itself, and provide necessary further context. This context serves to help audiences recognize patterns and identify the appropriate repertoire(s) to apply to a given narrative, a process which enables them to form expectations and fill in some of the gaps in the portrayal of the fictional world. The real also enters fantastic narratives through intertextual references, inversion and pointed absence, creating a recontextualization which parodies or challenges common ideas and practices. While we enjoy wild flights of fancy and new, original ideas, we can only understand and appreciate them in relation to pre-existent concepts; it is, in this regard, unsurprising that what is imaginable is 'merely' a recombination or reconfiguration of elements that are actually real.

This last point suggests that, if all fantastic ideas are made up of known concepts and can themselves turn into known concepts over time, which serve as the building blocks of new imaginative creations, then it should be possible to trace this genesis of fantastic ideas, at least in some instances, throughout popular storytelling. Some such diachronic studies of fantastic concepts have already been conducted, e.g. in Sandra Martina Schwab's 2013 study, *Of Dragons, Knights, and Virgin Maidens*, but there are many fantastic concepts whose origins are still shrouded in relative mystery. It might, furthermore, be interesting to consolidate several such studies in a greater structural analysis in order to shed some light on underlying shared features in the evolution of fantastic concepts.

The present analysis has shown that all narratives depend strongly on elements of the real. This includes fantastic narratives, whose incorporation of impossible elements is the genre's defining quality, and, more particularly, even stories set in secondary worlds, which are empty canvasses for the free play of the imagination only in theory. In practice, there is no such thing as a blank slate.

Works Cited

Abbott, Edwin A. (1998 [1884]): *Flatland: A Romance of Many Dimensions*, London: Penguin.

Abbott, H. Porter (2008): *The Cambridge Introduction to Narrative* (2nd ed.), Cambridge: Cambridge University Press.

Allen, Graham (2000): *Intertextuality*, London/New York: Routledge.

Austen, Jane (2004 [1813]): *Pride and Prejudice*, Oxford: Oxford World Classics.

Austen, Jane/Grahame-Smith, Seth (2009): *Pride and Prejudice and Zombies*, Philadelphia: Quirk Books.

Game of Thrones (2011-): Benioff, David/Weiss, D.B. (Prod.), HBO, Warner Bros. Television.

Berndt, Frauke/Tonger-Erk, Lily (2013): *Intertextualität: Eine Einführung*, Berlin: Erich Schmidt.

Bräuer, Holm (2003): "Realismus." In: Wulff D. Rehfus (ed.), *Handwörterbuch Philosophie*, Göttingen: Vandenhoeck & Ruprecht, pp. 581-5.

Calleja, Gordon (2011): *In-Game: From Immersion to Incorporation*, Cambridge, MA: MIT Press.

Carriger, Gail (2009): *Soulless*, New York/London: Orbit.

Connolly, Jennifer M./Mealey, Linda/Slaughter, Virginia (2004): "The Development of Preferences for Specific Body Shapes." In: *The Journal of Sex Research* 41/1, pp. 5-15.

Descartes, René (1978 [1637]): *Discours de la Méthode*, Paris: Hachette.

Durst, Uwe (2010): *Theorie der phantastischen Literatur* (2nd, rev. ed.), Münster: LIT.

Egenfeldt-Nielsen, Simon/Heide Smith, Jonas/Tosca Pajares, Susana (2008): *Understanding Video Games: The Essential Introduction*, New York/London: Routledge.

Fine, Gary Alan (2002 [1983]): *Shared Fantasy: Role-Playing Games as Social Worlds*, Chicago: University of Chicago Press.

Fletcher, Jane (2006): *The Exile and the Sorcerer*, Philadelphia: Bold Strokes.

Funke, Cornelia (1998): *Igraine Ohnefurcht*, Hamburg: Cecilie Dressler.

Gaiman, Neil (2008 [1999]): *Stardust*, New York: Harper Collins.

Heidegger, Martin (2006 [1927]): *Sein und Zeit*, Tübingen: Max Niemeyer.

Herman, David (2009): *Basic Elements of Narrative*, Hoboken, NJ: Wiley-Blackwell.

Iser, Wolfgang (1978): *The Act of Reading*, Baltimore: Johns Hopkins University Press.

Jenkins, Henry (2002): "Game Design as Narrative Architecture." In: Pat Harrington/Noah Waldrop-Fruin (eds.), *First Person*, Cambridge: MIT Press, pp. 118-30.

Merlin (2008-12): Jones, Julian/Gardner, Bethan (Prod.), BBC One: Fremantle-Media.

Kegler, Karl R. (2013): "Architektur." In: Hans Richard Brittnacher/Markus May (eds.), *Phantastik. Ein interdisziplinäres Handbuch*, Stuttgart/Weimar: J.B. Metzler, pp. 226-32.

Klastrup, Lisbeth/Tosca, Susana Pajares (2004): "Transmedial Worlds: Rethinking Cyberworld Design." In: *Proceedings International Conference on Cyberworlds* 2004, August 12, (http://www.itu.dk/people/klastrup/klastruptosca_transworlds.pdf).

Kowal, Mary Robinette (2010): *Shades of Milk and Honey*, New York: TOR.

Locke, John (1975 [1690]): *An Essay Concerning Humane Understanding*, Oxford: Clarendon.

Lovecraft, H.P (1999a [1919]): "Dagon." In: *The Call of Cthulhu and Other Weird Stories*, London: Penguin, pp. 1-6.

Lovecraft, H.P (1999b [1928]): "The Call of Cthulhu." In: *The Call of Cthulhu and Other Weird Stories*, S.T. Joshi (ed.), London: Penguin, pp. 139-69.

Mad Max: Fury Road (2015): Miller, George (Dir.), Warner Bros. Pictures.

Deadpool (2016): Miller, Tim (Dir.), 20th Century Fox.

Neale, Steve (1990): "Questions of Genre." In: Barry Keith Grant (ed.), *Film Genre Reader IV*, Austin: Texas University Press, pp. 178-202.

Padua, Sydney (2015): *The Thrilling Adventures of Lovelace and Babbage: The (Mostly) True Story of the First Computer*, New York: Pantheon.

Pratchett, Terry (1990): *Moving Pictures*, London: Gollancz.

Pratchett, Terry (1994): *Soul Music*, London: Gollancz.

Rowling, J.K. (1997): *Harry Potter and the Philosopher's Stone*, London: Bloomsbury.

Ryan, Marie-Laure (2007): "Fictional Worlds in the Digital Age." In: Ray Siemens/Susan Schreibman (eds.), *A Companion to Digital Literary Studies*, Hoboken, NJ: Blackwell, pp. 250-66.

Ryan, Marie-Laure (2009): "Narration in Various Media." In: Peter Hühn/John Pier/Wolf Schmid/Jörg Schönert (eds.), *Handbook of Narratology*, Berlin/New York: de Gruyter, pp. 263-81.

Ryan, Marie Laure/Thon, Jan-Noël (2014): "Introduction." In: *Storyworlds across Media: Towards a Media-Conscious Narratology*, Lincoln, NE/London: University of Nebraska Press, pp.1-21.

Salen, Katie/Zimmermann, Eric (2003): *Rules of Play: Game Design Fundamentals*, Cambridge, MA: MIT Press.

Schwab, Sandra Martina, (2013): *Of Dragons, Knights, and Virgin Maidens: Dragonslaying and gender roles from Richard Johnson to Modern Popular Fiction*, Trier: WVT.

Spiegel, Simon (2015): "Wovon wir sprechen, wenn wir von Phantastik sprechen." In: *Zeitschrift für Fantastikforschung* 1/2015, pp. 3-25.

Tolkien, J.R.R. (2013 [1954]): *The Fellowship of the Ring*, London: Harper Collins.

Watzlawick, Paul (2005 [1978]): *Wie wirklich ist die Wirklichkeit? Wahn, Täuschung, Verstehen*, München: Piper.

Equilibrium (2002) Wimmer, Kurt (Dir.), Miramax Films.

Creepypastas: How Counterterrorist Fantasies (Re-)Create Horror Traditions for Today's Digital Communities

ATALIE GERHARD

1. INTRODUCTION: DIGITAL HORROR STORYTELLING BETWEEN CONTROVERSY AND COMMODITY

May 31, 2014: After the 12-year old Payton "Bella" Leutner is brutally stabbed by her friends following a sleepover party at her house in the suburbs of Waukesha, Wisconsin and almost dies, media coverage of the incident quickly turns to the girls' motives. Morgan Geyser and Anissa Weier, who are also pre-teens, explain to the police and psychiatrics that the mythical online character Slender Man made them do it (cf. O'Keefe 2017). They claim to have discovered the character, who originated as a creepypasta Internet meme[1] created by Eric Knudsen in 2009, online and been followed by him as well as threatened that they must either sacrifice someone to become his proxies or be killed by him (cf. Cambridge/Christodoulou). Following the crime, articles such as "Slenderman,

---

1   Limor Shifman defines "Internet memes" as "units of popular culture that are circulat-ed, imitated, and transformed by individual Internet users, creating a shared cultural experience in the process" (2013: 367); as data packages, Internet memes are re-created and/or "repackaged" in participatory processes of dissemination that can quickly catapult the pop-cultural snippets to the heart of current social phenomena (cf. Shifman 2014: 18). Especially the aspects of creativity and independent self-expression within an online collective, which Shifman stresses in her definition of "In-ternet memes," have a direct impact on my notion of creepypasta storytelling.

Creepypasta and Your Children: The Dangers of Internet Folklore" (Levine 2015) suggested that the girls' consumption of online fantasy fiction is to blame for their violence. Others, such as scholars Shira Chess (mass media studies) or Andrew Peck (communication arts), defended creepypastas to U.S. journalists. This article seeks to explore the fantastic phenomenon of creepypastas by, firstly, defining them, and, secondly, explaining their popularity with respect to the cultural climate in which they emerge.

The creepypastas (to be pronounced: [kɹ'ipɪ'p'eɪstəz]) that will be looked at more closely in this article all revolve around the memes of Slender Man and Black Eyed Kids whose relation to traditional horror figures and origins in digital communities will be explained in more detail in the following. These texts are pieces of fiction created online for story-telling and -reading forums dedicated particularly to paranormal phenomena. They imagine encounters with monsters in postings that range from formulaic prose narratives emulating oral speech to digital art in the form of photomontages or drawings. Creepypastas either aim to strengthen a reader's faith in the existence of the monsters when they are framed as evidence,[2] or are instances of fan art that participates in defining the features of the creatures as outlined in previous texts. When consumers accumulate these fragments over time and then use them as inspiration for their own productions by copying, re-pasting, and expanding existing texts, a communication process is initiated across space and time with the result of building myths akin to folkloric practices.[3] Creepypastas establish their relevance for digital communities

---

2   One of Victor Surge's original images of Slender Man can be said to participate in this category of creepypasta-related digital art parodying official evidence to the extent that an alleged photograph of him looming behind children on a playground contains a false archive stamp (cf. June 10, 2009).

3   In his thematic essay for the *Harvard Encyclopedia of American Ethnic Groups*, Roger D. Abrahams provides a broad definition of folkloric practices to include any kinds of oral narratives and traditional behaviors that the members of small groups acquire through intimate contact with each other and that distinguish them within larger, pluralistic societies (cf. 1981 [1980]: 370-1). He shares this general concept with the American Folklore Society, whose objects of study range from the first Native American to contemporary U.S.-American migrant cultures and often chart acculturation by the ways that original, indigenous traditions are used to devise group-specific self-images (cf. ibid: 371-3). I suggest a comparison of individuals' performances within online communities to revisit the concept of folklore for global internet societies in order to determine what role digital communication possibilities also play for ethnic traditions of performing identity. When I compare creepypasta narratives to folklore

through both their participatory modes of production and the implication that somehow these stories will become meaningful to their readers who are threatened to be haunted by Slender Man or the Black Eyed Kids once they have read about them. Thereby, these readers are then encouraged to imagine an encounter of their own which they can recount in the creepypasta forums, too, thus endlessly perpetuating the circulation of the subject-matter and its formulas.

Given the nature of their production that I briefly outlined above, typical creepypastas about Slender Man or Black Eyed Kids are highly generic texts (prose and/or video or sound recordings) involving individuals who recite having sighted or apprehended the presence of these figures but were able to escape the situation. In forums dedicated to paranormal storytelling, other contributors will then add their speculations about these scenes in the comments' sections, where they will discuss what the intentions of the entities may be, for example, to devour their victims like vampires or zombies, or possess their souls like demons. Of course, different websites have different guidelines, as can be observed when considering the differences between *Creepypasta.com*, which is dedicated to practicing storytelling (cf. Sloshedtrain 2014), and *Reddit/No Sleep*, where users are explicitly asked not to question the truthfulness of the narrated incidents (cf. ObliviousHippie 2015). What all these digital texts share, however, is the fact that they develop contemporary horror figures in interactive and collaborative online communities in contrast to past stock figures like vampires or zombies whose lore is elaborated in closed narratives like novels or films.

Especially since so-called "sightings" of such recurring figures as Slender Man or the Black Eyed Kids in online group forums can be both staged as a fact by collaborative authors' recounting and commenting, as well as debunked by skeptics, it is also important to understand how social networks allow for and foster the creative variation of digital storytelling and, thus, the dissolution of an author-centered, closed notion of a generic text. In this sense, I am not only interested in outlining the genre conventions of creepypastas as the digital age's outstanding contribution to the fantastical literary mode of horror writing, but also in understanding the cultural, historical, and social circumstances that contributed to the phenomenon of internet users collectively weaving legend cycles. Yet, there is no theoretical way of determining the contributors' exact motives, which may range from a desire to improve their narrative writing skills to an obsession with memes of otherworldly power as a way to cope with and/or escape

---

in my article, however, I must limit myself to analyzing the ways in which writers and readers construct their sense of "us" exclusively within forums for fantastical storytelling for the sake of simplicity.

everyday struggles and hardships. My analysis of two specific and very well-known creepypasta memes, Slender Man and Black Eyed Kids, predetermines my focus on a contemporary Western socio-cultural framework, since stories about both are usually written in English and are directly inspired by classic European horror literature and Hollywood films. Moreover, I propose to study the pop-cultural significance of creepypastas as a relatively new genre of horrific storytelling in the historical framework provided by the War on Terror. Since the attacks of September 11, 2001, this initially U.S. political enterprise came to range from military occupations such as Operation Iraqi Freedom to the foundation of the Department of Homeland Security in the pursuit of preventing terroristic attacks in the future. At the same time, single preemptive measures such as the Patriot Act continue to face massive criticism worldwide for expanding the legal possibilities of U.S. intelligence agencies to monitor the digital behavior of individuals with the goal of detecting radical agents who threaten national security. In this article, I suggest that the important frameworks of counterterrorist culture and virtual espionage both derive from and inspire a diverse set of social fears; at the same time, however, the innovative utilization of digital technologies inspires and fuels the contemporary creation and dissemination of cyber legends and fantastical narratives in digital communities. This framework will render comprehensible how the complex interrelation of digital communication and social media communities with the War on Terror and its establishment of counterterrorist practices vis-à-vis a paranoid fear of a terrorist "other" has inspired the evolution of horror storytelling into Anglophone creepypastas.

Digital Storytelling and the War on Terror

As early as 2006, Peter N. Stearns assumed that there is a causal link between the ready availability of countless platforms for citizens to read news and express themselves on the internet and the fact that, when interviewed in the years following September 11, 2001, U.S.-Americans reported higher levels of fear than at any other time in their historical past (cf. 2006: 14-5). He argues that the George W. Bush administration and the Western media promoted responses to so-called "Islamic" terrorism that led to a shift in the U.S. patriotic self-image away from ideals of stoic bravery toward a sense of vulnerability, perpetual threat, and high anxiety (cf. ibid: 19, 44). The outcome of such counterterrorist self-defense strategies as color-coding threat levels on a daily basis, he continues, led to citizens incorporating the fear of terrorism into their lives and conceiving of the War on Terror on personal levels, so that they would support their government's military campaigns in the Middle East in the hope that it would directly and immediately remove their innermost fears (cf. ibid: 17-8, 36). Stearns' approach to a contemporary cultural phenomenon is useful to me in my readings of creepypastas, because they share their basic features with mainstream media warnings of terrorist threats: they all personalize the danger of mysterious "others" whose intrusions into the placid everyday world of relatable subjects are repeatedly narrated. Additionally, both creepypastas and counterterrorist propaganda are created from the perspective of an inherently vulnerable and fragile collective who cannot imagine actually overcoming the source of threat, be it a monster or global terrorism,[4] but continues to reiterate past encounters with a focus on the emotional sensation of fear.

It will also be posited that acts of collaboratively developing fear-inspiring characters are means of uniting and engaging diverse audiences by mimicking external discourses that capitalize on fear. One example for this general tendency can be found in the U.S. Department of Homeland Security's National Terrorism Advisory System campaign, "If You See Something Say Something," which Joseph Masco discusses (cf. 2014: 28-9) by referring to Michel Foucault's notion of social discourse as a structure of knowledge production, but criticizing how during the War on Terror, social bonds are fashioned from shared fears rather than democratic ideals (cf. Masco 2014: 138). I argue that on a discursive micro-level, creepypasta forums reflect such a community that is guided by anti-rational fantasies of "others," who represent everything the narrators are not. In greater detail, Slavoj Žižek further concludes that Hollywood-style fantasies of collective threat and disaster have always been required for social cohesion in the U.S. because their liberal democracy fashions itself as the world's only, uncontestable provider of civil liberties, but betrays its mission while fighting fundamentalist Arab regimes on the grounds of its own totalitarian ideological self-construction (cf. 2002: 2.3, 17). However, it is important to note that creepypastas – unlike counterterrorist paranoid clichés of omnipresent threats – are produced for entertainment, and that online users have a greater amount of

---

4   In this sense, Vice President Dick Cheney claimed in 2002 that the people living today will probably never see an end to War on Terror (cf. Žižek 2002: 57). On the flipside of this statement, the singular aspect of the threatening "other's" immunity to the passing of time can also be found in creepypastas that construct evidence for Slender Man's or the Black Eyed Kids' existence in previous historical periods. Some examples are *The Slender Man Files.org*'s tracing of the monster to 16th-century German woodcuts (2008) or Smokescreenzwei's alleged repetition of their grandfather's recollection of a visit from Black Eyed Kids in 1918 (2014).

choice to let themselves be terrified or not by the characters or subject matters of their stories.

Therefore, Austin Considine, who first wrote about the emerging genre of creepypastas in his *New York Times* article, "Bored at Work? Try Creepypasta, or Web Scares," points out their potential to fascinate office workers whose relative comfort is contrasted by the stories they consume (cf. 2010). But while his rather vague observation is limited to the entertainment value of creepypastas as horror fiction that is available *en masse*, I want to raise the question how these consumers' fervent desire for evermore digital scares relates to larger Western cultural contexts of (politically-inspired) paranoia. In fact, the emphasis he places on typical creepypastas' staging of authenticity, which underlies his comparison of early examples with previous pop-cultural products like the film *The Blair Witch Project* (1999) or chainmail that have also experienced mass distribution, necessitates a discussion on why consumers especially desire their *frisson* from horror fantasy fiction to be delivered in the guise of mundane amateur narratives. This phenomenon that politically and economically comparatively privileged audiences (like the U.S. majority) fantasize about the destruction of their reality is also noted by Žižek in his interpretation of statements made by 9/11 witnesses, who compared the sight of the collapsing Twin Towers to the Hollywood disaster films that previsioned such attacks (cf. 2002: 16-7). In a similar, albeit more philosophical line of argument than Considine, he diagnoses an underlying craving of U.S.-Americans for sensations of a postmodern Real that clashes with their dominantly sheltered situation in a democratic, capitalistic nation which, in the course of history, has become accustomed to conceive of horrific scenarios like wars as always located beyond their borders (cf. ibid: 9-11). Cultural producers thus have to stage their community's power to survive in masochistic fantasies in lieu of genuine proof of an ability to liberate themselves from oppression (cf. 2003: 286).

Given their nature of collaborative development, and their situation in the virtual world of online forums, I suggest that creepypasta memes are particularly suitable to meet this desire of large audiences for sensation although one can of course also imagine them to offer distraction to readers or writers trying to escape their emotionally devastating reality regardless of where they live. This potential of creepypasta circulation to appeal to participants with such a diverse range of motivations calls for a reconsideration of this genre's name, which is a neologism derived from the words "copy" and "paste" and was coined in reference to the possibility of producing these stories by copying and pasting narrative elements from earlier texts. However, this expression predated the popularity of entire creepypasta forums where particular memes like Slender Man or the

Black Eyed Kids do not figure in only one story to excite a *frisson* in readers because of their novelty alone, but continue to be woven into new narratives that compete with each other in terms of their storytelling techniques, so that the authors' focus lies as much on ingenuity as it does on imitation.

Considering the fact that certain tropes continue to be repeated in creepypastas, such as the thus staged elusive origins and motivations of Slender Man and the Black Eyed Kids or their apparitions in commonplace settings, it is possible to assume that readers and writers hold these aspects to be the most important. Of course, certain narrative elements have also come to characterize classic horror fiction, as John G. Cawelti points out with respect to the vampire novels, which originally condensed and mirrored the moral anxieties of the 19th-century European societies they originated from by inviting readers to associate at once familiar and taboo characteristics with the monsters but survived precisely because they create this conflict in the consumers' imagination (cf. 2004 [1999]: 346-7). While it is yet unclear how long Slender Man and the Black Eyed Kids will fascinate their fans through their opacity, the point can be made that they allow a discussion of insecurities their society represses and that the perpetual imitation of these tropes amounting to a competition between writers who all want to realize these fantastical aspects of "otherness" to draw the largest audiences further attests their cultural relevance within Anglophone digital communities. Drawing on the observation of Masco that the counterterrorist state forges its bonds among global citizens from the paranoia that mainstream media and government propaganda instill (cf. 2014: 28-31), I argue in the following analyses of selected Slender Man and Black Eyed Kids creepypastas that these stories fabricate terrifying specters designed to be impossible to defeat and who derive their basic structures from their circulation within communities geared toward imaging common sources of maximal fear. When reading creepypastas comparatively to study their representation of their genres, this approach makes it possible to take into account the historical background of the War on Terror and global surveillance that accompanied the rise of this mode of storytelling and inspires its memes, as well as to determine the general trajectory of these stories (to inspire fear). In the following subchapters, I will use this historico-cultural framework to analyze two of the most well-known examples of contemporary creepypasta storytelling: Slender Man and the Black Eyed Kids.

2. SLENDER IS THE HORROR BEYOND THE DIGITAL CAMPFIRE

In the introduction, I tried to trace the defining features of creepypasta to promote paranoid fantasies and creatively engage diverse digital communities to
both the historical background of the global War on Terror as well as to their
formulas as contemporary horror fiction. One such principle characterizing popular creepypasta memes is their elusiveness inside narratives, where humans
claiming to have encountered them say it is impossible to ever fully know where
they are from, how to defeat them, or even why they are threatening. In counterterrorist propaganda, this idea that a threat's elusive nature multiplies its potential to terrify can be found in a 2002 speech by Secretary of Defense Donald
Rumsfeld, where he states that "unknown unknowns" are to be feared more than
"known unknowns" (cf. Masco 2014: 16-7). Although it will be shown that
Slender Man's origins in cyberspace can actually be found very easily, he can be
studied as a particularly suitable allegory for narrative mechanisms of counterterrorist figures of threat that necessitate repetition within a community in order
to gain substance in the imaginations of individuals. Žižek similarly points out
that precisely because historical traumas stem from missed opportunities for
communities to process their recollections of (forced) passivity, they need to be
remembered frequently by all witnesses before they can be forgotten. This repetitive reworking of trauma through a communal testimonial practice must happen
regardless of how fragmentary the testimonies may be and how little factual evidence supports them (cf. 2002: 22).

So, at the first glance, accounts of Slender Man indeed require followers to
produce highly similar narratives as a means of promoting his popularity and en-
forcing a particular image of him as "unknow-able" in a process that seemingly
demands less creativity than writing a closed narrative about his fictional origins,
weaknesses, and overcoming would. However, as Andrew Peck points out, stories about Slender Man rather advance creative fantasizing in vernacular discussions on the internet, because their *vraisemblance*, which continues to draw in
devotees, is created by negotiations about what makes the described situations
seem even more likely. He references comments criticizing an early photomontage by Victor Surge where Slender Man's tentacles are visible at a distance for
not generating enough suspense (cf. 2015: 342, 346). For this reason, he sees
digital horror writing as the future of legends which always serve the function to
challenge the boundaries of a society through narratives that are relatable to most
of the members, but deal with extraordinary or taboo themes (cf. ibid: 335).
Through the creative work of fans, Slender Man creepypastas can be seen to re-

alize this principle of negotiating their communities' concept of knowledge at the crossroads of the familiar and the unknown, because these stories aspire toward establishing *vraisemblance* in their relatable aesthetics and vernacular narrative style, while exclusively projecting the illusion of fantastical elusiveness and "un-knowability" upon Slender Man. But because it is actually easy to trace the origins of the Slender Man meme to Victor Surge's (a.k.a. Eric Knudsen's) contribution to a *Something Awful.com* Photoshop contest on June 10, 2009, this central dichotomy reflects a complex parallel to the notion of the subjective imagination as a viable alternative to factual knowledge. This is especially palpable in situations that are defined by the perception of being personally threatened, that is also in situations, in which citizens are demanded to trust their intuition and report suspicious "others" to counterterrorist forces. On a symbolical level, both creepypastas and counterterrorist advisory campaigns thus require subjects to manifest fear and discourage them from interrogating the truth value of thus treated "classified" information (cf. Masco 2014: 128-30), so that the vaguely defined speech figure of the terrorist with a weapon of mass destruction (cf. ibid: 37-9) remains as faceless as Slender Man in the following image which shows the final form in which he is known today:

Image 1: "New HBO Slender Man Trailer Offers up Horrifying Look"

Source: http://moviecreedlive.com/entertainment/2671338-slender-man-trailer-horrifying-look-hbo/ (November 11, 2016)

This photomontage advertises the documentary *Beware the Slenderman* (2016) about Geyser's and Weier's attempt to murder their 12-year-old classmate in order to appease the Slender Man, who they claim, would have otherwise killed them and their families. Released two years after the tragedy, the documentary addresses an audience already familiar with the stabbing incident from the press and notably features interviews with the families of the girls who lament their belief that the meme is real, but the film title still suggests that he is to be feared, at least in terms of his potential influence on young fans. Moreover, rather than supporting the message that Slender Man is a work of fiction and thus urging viewers to attribute less belief to creepypasta lore, the chosen image of his face as lacking features functions to proliferate the illusion that he is in fact a mystery beyond "know-ability," while at the same time consolidating those characteristic features that defined his appearance by repeatedly occurring in creepypasta online forums into a "final" representative form. In this sense, Shira Chess recognizes how Slender Man's creation process depended on voluntary efforts of worldwide forum users made possible by the free availability of digital media before a closed narrative about him could appear in the form of the web series *Marble Hornets* (2009-14), which needed a final version of the figure to have crystallized, so that it could further establish this form as the definitive norm that, by now, resists being altered (cf. 2012: 375-6, 385-7).

Of course, both Chess' and Peck's approaches are very useful in terms of studying how users gather in online forums to collaborate creatively on folkloric horror figures even before there is a definitive form that these monsters take. My focus as an American Studies researcher is, however, on why this mode of horror writing emerges precisely at this historical moment and is so popular in Anglophone web spaces with most of the sightings of Slender Man located in the United States. While the simplest answer would be that only by the beginning of the 21st century, the technological possibilities were available to broad masses of users to engage in such past-times as pasting Slender Man into vintage photographs of children in lonesome forest settings, it is still possible to argue that non-digital media also allows the production of such collages and that magazines could have featured such contributions. Therefore, I prefer to turn to Masco to understand on which premises communities form in the digital spaces that are so typical for this moment in time. The following post about a subject's encounter with Slender Man on *Reddit/NoSleep* will be shown to reflect counterterrorist communal communication processes, because (most of) the commentators collaborate to highlight the message that this phantom figure is terrifying, while discouraging debate about why he is or whether he should be so at all:

"What happened next was a little too much for me to comprehend. In the split-second it took me to open my eyes, he had suddenly crossed the street, came into the tiny strip I was standing in and stood only inches from me. In my coiled state, I was mildly surprised after turning this over that I didn't jump backward. Still, there he was, hunched over, face level with mine. The weight of his eyeless gaze had me locked in place it seemed. I was so scared that I could feel a lump of vomit rising in my throat... I think I tried to move, but I'm not entirely sure. Then it happened. My eyes were drawn to a bit of motion near the lower right of my vision. A pale, thin hand drew up... His icy fingers grazed downward across my face... The feeling was one I could only describe as 'cold'. Mind you, it's April in Tampa Florida. What I felt was definatly [sic!] his fingers, for it was too warm out to be anything else... I closed my eyes tight, expecting to wake up to the sight of the Pearly Gates, but when I opened them all I saw was the light across the street." (BiohazardBunny 2012; comment added)

In the comments section of this representative instance of an online narrative portraying an encounter with Slender Man, the (majority of) readers significantly enforce the depiction of this figure in a mundane setting as terrifying although he did nothing to physically harm the narrator.[5] Unlike with mainstream media warnings of upcoming threats, the readers could creatively channel their disbelief and thus still comply with the creepypasta forum's guidelines.

Further, the narrator of this text is an Anglophone everyman who lacks distinctive features and therefore invites audiences to identify with him and also with his self-description as vulnerable, powerless, and confused in this situation – qualities which link him with the image that (especially) the United States have begun to promote when struck by a terrorist attack since 9/11, despite the nation's ongoing diplomatic, military, and economic power around the world (cf. Stearns 2006: 17; Žižek 2002: 44-7; Masco 2014: 2-3). Indeed, in the forum there are also a few comments speculating about whether Slender Man might ac-

---

5   This pattern of reinforcing a fearful impression of Slender Man begins when the narrator of the encounter, BiohazardBunny, dispels Naruhinagirl's suggestion that he might simply be a mouthless mutant who developed the superhuman power to teleport (cf. Naruhinagirl 2012). Until the end of the thread, he then continues to ask users experiencing "Slender Sickness," that is, the nauseous apprehension of the monster's presence, to message him, thus exemplifying the forum rule of credibly performing belief. Finally, the latest thread lends a voice to Slender Man (--SlenderMan--2012: "SO GLAD YOU TOOK THE TIME TO MENTION ME NOW WITH ME AROUND, YOU'LL NEVER BE IN HARMONY"; emphasis in original) to at once solidify the illusion that he is dangerous and omnipresent and, moreover, that he is aware of his treatment as a fictional creepypasta meme when the contributor impersonating him rejects BiohazardBunny's applause of this novel type of comment (cf. ibid: "NOVELTY? WHO SAYS IM [sic!] NOVELTY?", emphasis in original, comment added).

tually be a sympathetic character because his gesture of trailing his finger down the narrator's face could also be interpreted as a caress.[6] Yet, the majority of narratives about Slender Man reflect the prevailing view of him as inherently malevolent and thus the ensuing community consolidates itself through manifestations of fear. These are akin to manifestations of fear in the face of vague threats of violence invoked by Western politicians that, according to Masco (cf. 2014: 14, 20, 24-5), become the central criteria of belonging for members of a counterterrorist nation. So, it does not have to matter whether all forum users are really terrified by Slender Man or not, since the simple fact that they encourage each other to engage with him as if they were terrified signifies that collectively performing fear and conjuring new aspects about him to fear is an important part of creepypasta users' creative practices. This is also of central importance in the following text:

"The eeriness of Slender Man is, essentially, his seeming normality. You're walking, it's a normal day. Maybe you're done with classes, maybe you're getting lunch, but you see him, in the distance. A tall bald man in a suit, standing perfectly still. It's weird, but maybe he's going to a job interview or something. You're sure there's a reasonable explanation. So you keep going. Your own business is, of course, your own business. You keep walking and, after ten minutes, see him again, standing beyond the crowd. You have a moment of disorientation, have you been here before? Is this deja vu [sic!]? No way he could've gotten around you. You write it off as a coincidence.

But all the while, there's something off about him, something you can't place and the way that no matter what, he's always facing you, sends shivers down your spine. So you keep going, maybe you get back to your house, maybe the restaurant or classroom of your choice. Still nervous, you glance back and you see him, still in the distance, but closer now, always closer and you know. You know that somehow, he's seen you as you've seen him. Somehow, he's followed and beat you here. And you know, that he's going to keep getting closer." (Solias 2013; comment added)

This scenario was posted in a Reddit forum dedicated to Slender Man as the response to a forum user asking what the most terrifying aspect of Slender Man is and was soon met with enthusiastic demonstrations of agreement on the side of other contributors. In their answers, readers could identify with the experience described by the narrator, who recounted noticing Slender Man in an urban

---

6   For instance, Hogwing states: "Seriously, the dude has no mouth to talk with, and people go spreading rumors that he's such a creep. If I ever met this man and am not dead afterward, I'll know he's a pretty cool guy" (2012).

crowd and already presented this exemplary sighting as a universally relatable occurrence by using the second person pronoun in a singular, direct address.[7] If we apply Masco's ideas on how counterterrorist communities unite in manifestations of fear, we can now see how the content of the text, that is Slender Man appearing in a crowd for no apparent reason, is less important in gathering an audience than the fact that he is presented as inspiring fear, which is alluded to by new contributors on the Reddit threat: subsequent contributors confirm this quality and then collaboratively add examples of their own imaginations, which also capitalize on feelings more than any precise warnings as to why he is to be feared – much like early government prognoses on terror threats.[8] In Western political discourse, this mechanism of shrouding the source of fear, that is so-called "Islamic" terrorism in mystery allows leaders to hyperbolically emphasize threats to their nations' lifestyles in order to justify military campaigns in the Middle East in the public eye as the only way to prevent otherwise unavoidable attacks from unknown "others," who target complete strangers without discrimination (cf. Masco 2014: 21, 26, 43, 122-4) – a narrative pattern of representing terrorism that finds a cultural pendant in discussions about Slender Man such as the thread cited above. However, engagement with creepypastas, unlike statements on real-life terrorism, are not obliged to position themselves in support or opposition to the subject matter discussed, as they can playfully sublimate social problems into horror tropes.

---

7   For instance, Knife7's answer continues to construct Slender Man as a genuine figure and expand the scope of readers affected by his terror by speaking in the first-person plural in a generalizing statement: "I believe it's because Slender Man's motivations, emotions and intentions are unclear. We don't know what he wants, why he wants it or if he even wants anything at all but for whatever reason he's following us and torturing us for reasons we can't possibly understand" (2013).

8   An example that can be cited here is U.S. Homeland Security Secretary Tom Ridge's prediction in December 2003 that further terrorist attacks are imminent and more than likely, but that citizens should continue their holiday plans (cf. Masco 2014: 22), thereby withholding precise information from them as if they were anyway incapable of reducing their odds of being affected. Also, the Department of Homeland Security installed a color-coded chart designed to indicate the probability of an upcoming terrorist attack but, from 2002 to 2011, never set the threat level below Code Yellow meaning "elevated" (cf. ibid: 22). Masco discusses these instances of counterterrorist propaganda as mechanisms to disseminate fear, without providing substantial information to individuals that would make it possible for them to participate in public discourses on actually fighting terrorism at its roots (cf. ibid: 22-4).

Given this last quality, it can be seen how Slender Man creepypastas also reflect the traditional feature of mystery literature, which, as Cawelti argues, often projects historical insecurities upon fantastical monsters (cf. 2004 [1999]: 338, 349, 355-6). These works of fiction further exemplify the potential for multiple meanings that characterizes older horror figures such as vampires, who embody the social fear of deviance against the cultural background of their creators, along with a desire to transgress moral boundaries (cf. ibid: 342). In digital spaces of the counterterrorist age, Slender Man equally encapsulates the unknown that is at the core of discourses on the terrorist "other" with unpredictable plans and motives that early counterterrorist speeches by, for example, the U.S. Secretary of Defense Donald Rumsfeld already addressed (cf. Masco 2014: 16-7). In this sense, the fact that fans of this creepypasta meme can engage with each other in both passive and creative ways may mean that they are either rehearsing the practice of paranoid speculation that Western counterterrorist public discourses strive to promote (cf. ibid: 20-2, 27, 37), or that they are artistically inverting this threat. After all, when anonymous internet users each add another fragment to Victor Surge's original Slender Man figure that enshrouds him in more mystery rather than giving clarity, they convert the discursive practice of generating sources of threat and fear into entertainment in virtual spaces.

3. BEHIND THE BLACK EYES OF A CYBERSPACE LEGEND

After the last chapter dealt with the pop-cultural significance of Slender Man in the historical counterterrorist setting and interrogated how he meets the desires of horror fans to envision mechanisms of coping with their social anxieties in creative ways akin to the way that classic monsters do, the following part will seek to shed light on the popularity of Black Eyed Kids creepypastas. The texts selected will serve as examples of how these memes, too, parallel public discourses related to "unknow-ability" in ways universal enough to appeal to creepypasta fans from around the world. Their projection of this trope upon children, who appear to be normal with the exception of their opaque black eyes, will further illustrate how the theme of threatening "otherness" is constructed as both omnipresent and mysterious.

When considering the engagement of digital audiences with Black Eyed Kids, it is first of all important to note that their first documented mention was posted in a Google Group forum by the journalist Brian Bethel on August 28, 1997, well before the internet was being used as a tool for detecting and reporting terrorist threats. In addition to this aspect – or perhaps precisely because of it –

these figures remained the same over time, unlike Slender Man, whose appearance underwent multiple modifications by several developers since his inception, which were partly incorporated into the text as it is known today and partly rejected. Moreover, creepypastas of Black Eyed Kids are met with performances of genuine belief on the side of readers, who may receive compliments on their particular narration of an encounter, but still claim to the truthfulness of their stories and follow in the footsteps of Brian Bethel, who continued to relate alleged facts about these monsters on the reality TV show *Monsters and Mysteries in America* in 2012, among other formats, and to re-confirm his experience in an article about them in the *Abilene Reporter News* as late as 2013. This comparable resistance to modification and lack of creativity that characterizes Black Eyed Kids creepypastas from the start can be shown to align them with a classical definition of traditional folktales to an even greater extent than Slender Man lore.[9]

However, the fact remains that when creepypastas about Black Eyed Kids in virtual communities warn of their own consumption, they, unlike urban legends in cities that caution against moral transgressions actually generate more of the *frisson* in fans that Considine claimed they are seeking in their online forums (in contrast to, for example, "The Hook," where a teenage couple venturing into a lonesome lover's lane to engage in illicit sexual activities is attacked by a serial killer with a hook replacing one of his hands (cf. Brunvand 2003 [1981]: 48-51). So, how do creepypastas about Black Eyed Kids still negotiate this original function of orally repeated horror stories and is this even a reason for their distribution? I agree that, on the one hand, these Black Eyed Kids creepypastas stylistically emulate oral storytelling in digital spaces to form communities of fans in the way that Peck sees Slender Man narratives as a continuation of folkloric practices that predated printed horror literature. But, on the other hand, when Black Eyed Kids creepypastas threaten the reader with the possibility of encountering these creatures in the near future,[10] they do not caution against such activi-

---

9   In his comprehensive *Encyclopedia of Urban Legends*, Jan Harold Brunvand delineates the scope of his objects of analyses to include stories that are orally circulated within communities with cautionary intentions, however subtle (2012: 245). When one considers that many Black Eyed Kids creepypastas warn readers of consuming them, claiming that then these monsters would intrude into the real lives of their audiences, as well the vernacular tone these narratives are usually set in, Brunvand's definition can also be taken to fit these stories.

10 For instance, in the comments section on the report "Encounter…?" by Xurichs (2016) which will be cited later in this article, WonderlandWhit wonders whether the

ties as parking in a secluded lover's lane (cf. ibid: 48-51). Instead, these creepy-pastas playfully subvert the formal aspect of urban legends to caution listeners, by automatically taking readers who clicked on the stories beyond the point of their transgressive behavior of seeking knowledge about Black Eyed Kids and proclaiming that these will now unavoidably appear on the doorstep of the curious consumer.

Thereby, this acquisition of knowledge in itself can be framed as the beginning of a horrific climax within the story. Characteristically, Bethel's eye witness account is focused exclusively on his own perceptions and thoughts as he is driving home from work one night and is addressed by two teenagers outside a cinema who beg for a ride home in his car so they can get their money to watch *Mortal Kombat* (1995) until the following realization takes place:

"For the first time, I noticed their eyes. They were coal black. No pupil. No iris. Just two staring orbs reflecting the red and white light of the marquee. At that point, I know my expression betrayed me. The silent one had a look of horror on his face in a combination that seemed to indicate: A) The impossible had just happened and B) 'We've been found out!' The spokesman, on the other hand, wore a mask of anger. His eyes glittered brightly in the half-light. 'Cmon [sic!], mister,' he said. 'We won't hurt you. You have to LET US IN. We don't have a gun …'." (cf. Bethel 1997, emphasis in original, comment added)

Significantly, the narrator's sense of uneasiness around the two male teenagers predates his realization of their black eyes and thus encourages readers to follow their instincts during an encounter with strangers and potentially forget the principle of stopping to help wandering children that is universal to societies who claim to be civilized and guided by morals. In this sense, the particular cultural relevance of the legend of Black Eyed Kids lies in its reflection on how the Internet actually allows two threats to materialize simultaneously: Firstly, users might read a horror story online but the monsters haunt their imaginations in the non-virtual world, and secondly, practices of discrimination and egoism that contradict the values of a democratic society might be unleashed when forum visitors unite to confirm each others' instincts without inquiring why exactly Black Eyed Kids should be avoided.

---

narrator had read or thought a lot about Black Eyed Kids previously to apprehending their presence on the other side of their door, since a common trope in stories about them is that they become attached to humans in a parasitic manner by first invading their thoughts and then physically appearing in order to beg for permission to enter their homes (cf. 2016).

Therefore, Cawelti's observation that horror fiction reveals the tacit morals of the community it originates from, as in the case of late 19th-century vampire fiction, which thematizes the taboo of cannibalism (cf. 2004 [1999]: 342), holds true for creepypastas, too. But to me, the fact that Brian Bethel chose to organize his new horror figure around the trope of unknown children asking for help in the late 1990s rather than any other paranormal phenomenon, signifies that this popular legend connects to a historical moment where encounters with strangers came to be connoted with both irresistibility (reflected by the Black Eyed Kids' hypnotic powers) and terror. Especially because children traditionally symbolize innocence, I suggest that firstly, these creatures' transformation into black-eyed monsters illustrates the uncanny nature of an ever-expanding globalized world order where the vulnerable narrator is left to her/his subjective judgment, and that secondly, the Black Eyed Kids' continued popularity is reflective of current social threats, too. After all, Masco describes a central project of the War on Terror within the United States and its associated ever-expanding digital territories to be the distribution of paranoia among its citizens, so that reason is suspended when authorities suggest the existence of classified information about an imminent threat (cf. 2014: 1-3, 6, 26-7). When Black Eyed Kids are discussed in online forums, users still rehearse the same act of tuning into this affect for the thrill of speculating about who or what these monsters might actually be, with every repetition re-enforcing their representation as evil in the early counterterrorist discourse's logic that Brian Massumi also criticizes in George W. Bush's retrospective legitimation of Operation Iraqi Freedom as a necessary means to prevent a hypothetical threat (cf. 2010: 53-4).[11]

---

11 Massumi's example is from a 2004 speech where Bush stated that the fact that U.S. intelligence suspected Iraq to be a national threat was enough to justify the preemptive removal of its regime in the following words (cf. 2010: 53-5): "Although we have not found stockpiles of weapons of mass destruction, we were right to go into Iraq. And America is safer today because we did. We removed a declared enemy of America who had the capability of producing weapons of mass destruction and could have passed that capability to terrorists bent on acquiring them. In the world after September the 11th, that was a risk we could not afford to take" (Bush 2007: 1298). What underlies Bush's argumentation is a circular logic that equates the effect of U.S. subjects' fear of Iraqi military violence with factual evidence to support an enterprise like Operation Iraqi Freedom against a significantly poorer and less resourceful country. This structure of thought can also be seen to underwrite the reactions narrators report to encountering Black Eyed Kids: they avoided them, because they were terrified, alt-

So, the question must be asked if it is also possible to imagine Black Eyed Kids in a sympathetic fashion which would link them to horror literature in print and distance them from the practice of urban legends by providing more freedom to the creativity of individual writers and no longer exclusively performing a socially cohesive function. Indeed, one example of a representation of Black Eyed Kids as sympathetic can be found in Sgt_Hydroxide's multi-part short story on */r/Humanity Fuck You*, where an adult Black Eyed Kid seeks out the narrator in a bar to aid him in defeating a demon called the Goat Man, who is persecuting him. In this narrative, the principal Black Eyed Kid figure is designed to challenge previous imaginations of his kind with the encounter less recreating the *frisson* of Brian Bethel's first reported sighting than providing explanations for the terrifying aspects of these creatures that range from the pseudo-scientific to the melodramatic:

"'The urban legends get it wrong. We're not demons or aliens. We're human. Or at least, we *were*.' He cleans the tobacco bits from his nails. 'Black-eyed children are all orphans. Usually, sole survivors of some traumatic event involving the paranormal. It makes us more susceptible. More in tune with things normal people don't see. I can't remember how I was recruited. Not many memories of my time before the agency.' He pauses, staring off into the distance. 'Probably better that way.'

He rolls up his sleeve. Points to a dark spot in the curve of his elbow. 'They inject us with a compound. Supposedly a two thousand-year old formula with a few modern molecular adjustments. Hurts like hell. Burns for days. Most of us go into a coma. Some of us don't come out. But when we do – that's when the change starts.'

He spreads his fingers, as if studying them. They're as pale as he is. Nearly bloodless. 'Pallor and cold skin. Faster reflexes. Better stamina. Heightened senses. Accelerated healing, both physical and psychic. We can function with a fraction of the food, water, or sleep a normal human being needs. And, of course,' he taps the side of his face, 'the *eyes*. Always the eyes. The first change that indicates the process is successful.'

He continues. 'We start off as spotters. Two-person teams, one boy, one girl, like I just said. We do recon on areas where repeated paranormal sightings have been reported over a three-day period. Relatively low-risk, gives us a chance to learn the territory. Get our feet wet. Still remember my first house.'" (Sgt_Hydroxide 2016; italics in original)

---

hough the circumstance that they are children should mean that they are *per se* more vulnerable and might actually be in need of help.

These explanations that Black Eyed Kids, who are ghost-hunters for a paranormal investigations agency, gain their uncanny appearance as a result of a chemical transformation process that elevates them from the victims of tragedies to the defenders of unsuspecting humans against truly evil demons, all focus on their typical features but revise their perception by adding information. In this sense, this story proves that on the one hand, any encounter with one of these figures is invariably a horror trope in a fantastical narrative, but on the other hand, it is also possible for the writers to shift their focus from this climactic moment itself by embedding the latter within a multi-part story – a practice that is facilitated by the technical possibilities of digital storytelling, to regularly post another section and at the same time engage with readers whose suggestions might be included in the creative production process.

This way, it becomes an option to challenge readers' static perceptions of Black Eyed Kids as inherently evil, since followers can be invited to speculate on which direction this more complex plotline could take and thus add new mythical elements to the subject-matter itself rather than merely reiterating it in a generic rehearsal of creepypasta storytelling practices.[12] Although it is also possible that readers could have participated in this narrative process if the story was print-based and had appeared, for instance, in a periodical, there is no doubt that its publication on the internet allows for it to engage an even broader and more diverse audience. Additionally, this writer's serial dissemination of his reports of paranormal experiences at the side of a former Black Eyed Kid increases their capacity to captivate readers by engaging them on both an affective level through suspense as well as a speculative level by challenging them to question their perception of the monster as evil.

As this revision takes place along the course of the five different fragments of the story, the arrival of the Black Eyed Kid can encourage fans of these memes to join into the narrative process based on the evocation of another secret threat that they respond to collectively, emulating their affective conditioning by counterterrorist press announcements. While political speeches occasioned by real-life attacks (such as the Pulse Nightclub Shooting in 2016, to cite a more recent example) and fictive horror tropes proliferated in creepypasta forums are

---

12 In addition to the general enthusiasm and praise that Sgt_Hydroxide received, Ssilversmith further proclaims an end to the fascination of creepypastas when compared to a serial narrative whose plot is more influenced by the individual creativity of the writer rather than the repetition of conventions (cf. 2016). S/he especially underlines how lucrative this new type of deploying the established memes of Black Eyed Kids in closed narratives could be for the writer.

entirely different entities, their narrative strategies may be eerily similar, as they highlight the unavoidability of further threats and therefore function to naturalize an exceptional state that demands the constant expectation of such attacks.

However, the particularity of creepypastas such as those about Black Eyed Kids is that they allow flexible usage within fantastical storytelling. The trope of the encounter can be both repeated in structure and content akin to the practice of urban legends, or further developed like the meme of Slender Man in order to transcend the communal narrative framework in which it originated. Parallel to this last process where the stories' key features are solidified with every retelling, consumers of Black Eyed Kids creepypastas might also claim that the figures materialize beyond the digital space where they first encountered information about them, as in the following example:

"But this weird feeling suddenly hit me & said 'There is a goddamn BEK outside. Don't go near the door.' And now I'm holed up, filled with absolute terror. It could just as easily be a robber trying to find a victim, but there are several cars outside and lights on inside. I'm terrified. This was an hour ago. I know they can't hurt me if I don't let them in, much less even look at them, but my anxiety ramps up at the mere thought of peeking out the door. I hate that I ever learned about them & increased my chances of attracting one, or whatever it is." (Xurichs 2016)

Here, the narrator describes being tortured by fear during a solitary evening at home while believing to apprehend the presence of a Black Eyed Kid outside as a result of reading about them. The narrator also experiences panic at the thought of an encounter where s/he would feel the typical anxiety about their intentions and the difficulty to resist their pleas as described by Brian Bethel. Thus, this creepypasta illustrates another common element of the digital storytelling about Black Eyed Kids: fear of the unknown as a source of fear in itself despite the impossibility to know whether any threat is actually materializing. Finally, it is this possibility for creepypasta narrative practices to aesthetically comment on the contemporary trope of the unknown that makes them such an appropriate form of entertainment for users who can thus allegorically challenge their self-perception as victims of impending terrorist attacks that counterterrorist propaganda promotes and instead return to the Western cultural view of fear as the primary threat to reasonable judgment that Stearns highlights in President Franklin Roosevelt's famous phrase, "The only thing we have to fear is fear itself" – an attitude which he claims has been replaced by the normalization of social performances of being terrified in political War on Terror discourses (cf. 2006: 14-5).

4. CONCLUSION: THE HORRIFIC NOW – POP-CULTURAL EXIGENCIES AND DIGITAL TALES OF TERROR

While the last two sections sought to explain the relationship of two popular memes of contemporary creepypastas, Slender Man and the Black Eyed Kids, to established forms of horror storytelling, especially oral urban legends, I would like to conclude my analysis by briefly suggesting a few alternative starting points for a discussion on the relevance of creepypasta memes today. After all, as Chess remarks, the development of these figures requires a great deal of voluntary creative labor on the side of creepypasta forum users (cf. 2012: 382, 384, 388), and does fulfil a very basic communicative function for the communities it unites, which is why Peck compares the genre to folkloric narratives (2015: 334, 346-7). As a matter of fact, one must wonder what it is that creepypasta provides readers and writers with that other kinds of fantastic fiction do not. Throughout this article, the answer I have provided to this question is that these stories allow participants to project their cultural and historical anxieties on figures like Slender Man or the Black Eyed Kids and render manifest narrative patterns of reasoning from public discourses, for example, on the dangers of the Internet and, more importantly, the omnipresence of terrorist suspects in a potentially subversive form of entertainment.

Indeed, by performing the same communicative tactics employed by counter-terrorist propaganda in the seemingly unpolitical context of creepypasta forums, writers who report an encounter with monsters parody the meaning of news in the paranoid culture of the global War on Terror, where citizens are asked to surveil each other. However, by inventing evasive sources of threat, even more vague than the specters of terrorism perpetuated throughout the mass media, creepypasta distributors also allow a pose of submission to structure their creations that may connote as much an acceptance and commodification of this discursive practice as a subversive use of its rhetorical patterns when removed from an official context. It can hence be said that creepypastas offer a creative outlet to writers who are inspired by the narrative practice of transforming mystical figures into the basis for self-proclaimed cautionary or informative posts and by the accompanying possibility of authoring paranoid subject positions. But it can equally be assumed that in so doing, these cultural producers are incorporating the threatening allure of their monsters in an empowering symbolical gesture of self-elevation, since their identities, like the fictional origins of their creatures, remain concealed to the point that anybody anywhere could be creating and disseminating creepypastas. Finally, it is this impossibility to certainly know the intentions of the writers of horror stories from their publications and predict the reception by their readers which are typically centered on the mystical "otherness" of a particular kind of subject-matter, for example vampirism, zombie-ism, hauntings, or monstrous apparitions or transformations, which is at the core of the diversity and fascination of the many genres of horror writing.

But in addition to the two functions that Cawelti attributes to horror figures – to serve as examples of amorality necessitating punishment to fans or as empowering symbols of moral transgression who challenge social conventions (cf. 2004 [1999]: 342) –, creative imaginations of terrorism-related "otherness" reveal yet another quality. Ilka Saal reads Don DeLillo's novel *Mao II* (1991) with a focus on the characteristics that make the elusive antagonist Abu Rashid, an Oriental terrorist the truly central point of the story as opposed to the protagonist Bill Gray, who aspires to influence his time through his novels but eventually must recognize his limits (cf. 2006: 250-2, 264). She determines that this fictional story illustrates the demise of the solitary writer as a historical force because their isolation no longer simulates the effect of the postmodern Real in consumers like the anonymous terrorist does (cf. ibid: 262-4). Therefore, she identifies DeLillo to pronounce the end to the Western ideal of the individual writer's imagination as the source of the single affect that Edmund Burke most likened to the experience of divine omnipotence during natural disasters when the subject becomes aware of her/his personal insignificance to the world around her/him (cf. ibid: 262). Given that Cawelti echoes Tzvetan Todorov's claim that fantastic literature (including horror) in the West bridged the romantic and the realist eras (cf. 2004 [1999]: 336-7, 347-8), one could now speculate about their monsters' capacity to create a Burkian sublime moment today, in which the human subject feels both vulnerable and unable to understand why these figures appear, yet continuously revisits them in contemporary (creepypasta) narratives.

The difference between the horror classics that are usually analyzed by cultural and literary studies and the newer digital format of creepypastas is, however, that the latter typically do not include a moment of victory of the relatable narrating subject over the mysterious entity at the root of her/his terror. Instead of constructing the plot around the two poles of a rational but threatened human and a monster whose supernatural powers can be understood and challenged toward the end of the story, creepypastas capitalize on the single moment of the confrontation between an unspecified narrator and a paranormal creature, which cannot be overwhelmed, but of whom others can only be warned. Each posting of a creepypasta perpetuates this pattern and invites new audiences to join into the consumption and continuation of the static tropes of absolute vulnerability and schematic evil where the only victory for the narrator of the text is to have survived the encounter to tell others about it. In this article, I consider the nor-

malization of such a state of being vulnerable to an elusive paranormal appari-
tion without the possibility to know its motives or defeat it, which creepypastas
produce through repetition, both an artistic mediation of contemporary clichés of
virtual worlds and a subversive gesture akin to parody.

Still, the reasons why audiences prefer to perform this gesture especially in
the form of fantastical narratives about monsters are difficult to estimate when
considering only the texts but not asking individual readers what exactly they
mean to them in particular. Therefore, the focus in this article could only limit itself to the cultural significance of selected creepypastas in the historical framework they can be linked to through their uses of literary effects through which
concerns of the digital spaces united in counterterrorist vulnerability are manifested in the aesthetic of horror. But aside from pointing out that Slender Man
and the Black Eyed Kids demonstrate traits that ground their emergence in the
late 20th- to early 21st-century Anglophone setting of the global Internet, I have
also put into perspective how such an indirect approach can mask issues like the
impossibility to know who is making which claims on which basis in virtual
communities. On the one hand, this versatility of creepypasta texts allows developers to fuse their diverse inspirations with subject-specific storytelling formulas
and engage in creative labor independently of their motivation. On the other
hand, narrative conventions that arise as a result of the collaborative nature of
creepypasta forums are also policed by the community. Potential aberrations
from the subject matter can also instantly be dismissed. Pyric_lancaster received
the discouraging response "So you *can* escape. Hmm…" (Cok3 2012; italics in
original)[13] to a story in which he claimed that his girlfriend fought back against
Black Eyed Kids with a katana once he let them into his home only to be at-

---

13 Interestingly, pyric_lancaster's post explicitly encourages the counterterrorist cultural
practice of xenophobia and the ideal of a militarized citizenry because the writer
chooses not to speculate on the motives of the Black Eyed Kids in this particular situation or the possibility of a dialogue with them and announces that he will acquire a
concealed firearms license as a consequence of the encounter (cf. 2012). The fact that
ZombieLloyd offers him the position of co-moderator in the comments section of this
creepypasta here proves that this story can be considered a particularly suitable example of its genre with its central opposition of the unknowing, vulnerable human victim
and the mysterious Black Eyed Kids who appear unthreatening to the narrator just before s/he notices their elusive difference (cf. ZombieLloyd 2012). In turn, the efficiency of this trope of both familiarity and monstrosity that Black Eyed Kids incorporate
is attested by the following addition to ZombieLloyd's name "Founder. I might be a
BEK" which invites further fantastical speculations among followers.

tacked. Such responses suggest that only particular styles of imagining are "correct" as they conform to the established norm.

Indeed, a dismissive reaction can also be found in the comments section on *Crappypasta.com* to Em's account of her romance with Slender Man where she transforms from his stalking-victim to a monster that feasts on children just like him after their wedding (cf. 2013). The fact that the criticism inherent in the dismissive statements[14] is directed at the author's imagination of the monster as a sympathetic figure here reveals the extent to which communal storytelling practices can promote static conceptions of fantastical "otherness," which result in peer censorship as much as in dissemination and creative collaboration. When exclusively considering their formulaic patterns, creepypastas seem to limit their monsters' capacity to symbolize deviance from social norms in both positive, inspirational, and negative, threatening ways. However, this rigorous abidance by narrative conventions of creepypasta writers and readers can also be interpreted as dedication to the intended effect of the original short, detailed evidence of encounters with Slender Man or the Black Eyed Kids posted online that is aimed at producing a momentary *frisson*. Rather than slowly guiding the consumer to a narrative climax by building up suspense, it is a recurrent pattern in creepypastas to instantly deliver the peak of possible affects narrators claim to experience during an encounter with a monster and not speculate upon a cathartic moment in the aftermath or a rational explanation for why precisely this subject and not another was targeted.

Because Slender Man and Black Eyed Kids creepypastas focus the readerly attention so profoundly on the feeling of being threatened by fantastic evil rather

---

14 Indeed, the posting of Em's story on *Crappypasta.com* already signifies that it is categorized as a poor example of its genre, because this website especially allows creepypastas that were rejected by *Creepypasta.com* to still be viewed publicly, so that the authors can receive reviews on their texts, which can also be "up-voted" to the original site by readers. However, Potato absolutely rejects the possibility that Slender Man could even possess a face that can only be seen by his beloved (cf. 2013), and Blank questions Em's mental health because she shared an erotic fantasy with the monster (cf. 2015). Mr. Destluer states that this meme is exclusively designed to inspire fear and no romantic feelings (cf. 2014). While partly personally offensive and thus testifying to the possibilities that creepypasta forums provide spaces not only for artistic collaboration, but also for bullying and harassment, these statements importantly reveal how the underlying practices of communal storytelling impose limits on the development of its subject-matter after consumers have established definitive narrative formulas.

than, for example, on the origin stories of the subjects involved, I have focused on connections between these contemporary mass-produced online horror narratives and the current global counterterrorist culture that capitalizes on the affects of citizens all over the world. Analogously to the way Masco considers paranoia to be both an operative tool to be deployed and a condition of life under omnipresent government surveillance since September 11, 2001 (cf. 2014: 1-2, 18, 26-7), I read creepypastas as pop-cultural artefacts that address an arbitrary threat while negotiating a historically specific fantasy of absolute, mysterious evil. After all, creepypastas share a capacity to involve fans by imagining situations to be feared and by developing monsters to embody even more tropes of mystery but refuse to provide rational advice for overcoming the apparitions and possibly uncovering their definitive motives or origins in the logic of their respective genres. Much like late 20th- and early 21st-century media tropes of all-consuming virtual realities or the terrorist with an unspecified weapon of mass destruction, these texts thus blur the lines between fantastical and seemingly real extra-textual discourses of their time, and illustrate practices of group formation that can be likened to oral storytelling traditions from folklore to urban legends. Finally, I hope to have inspired readers of this article to consider some of the particularities of a relatively recent kind of fantastical writing that has the potential to simultaneously expose and challenge the imaginative basis on which digital communities weave new tales of terror that will prove as enduring as they are relevant.

WORKS CITED

--SlenderMan-- (2012): Comment on "He... Touched Me... (X-Post from /R/Slender_Man)." In: *Reddit.com* August 31, (https://www.reddit.com/r/nosleep/comments/s6s0k/he_touched_me_xpost_f rom_rslender_man/?sort=old).

Abrahams, Roger D. (1981 [1980]): "Folklore." In: Stephan Thernstrom/Ann Orlov/Oscar Handlin (eds.), *Harvard Encyclopedia of American Ethnic Groups*, Cambridge/London: The Belknap Press of Harvard University Press, pp. 370-9.

Bethel, Brian (1997): "Black-Eyed Children." In: *alt.folklore.ghost-stories* August 28, (https://groups.google.com/forum/#!topic/alt.folklore.ghost-stories /HFXkIXeq9ec).

BiohazardBunny (2012): "He…Touched Me…(X-Post from /R/Slender_Man)." In: *reddit.com* April 12, (https://www.reddit.com/r/nosleep/comments/s6s0k /he_touched_me_xpost_from_rslender_man/).

Blank (2015): Comment on "Slender: My Personal Account." In: crappypasta.com October 29, (http://www.crappypasta.com/slender-my-personal-account/).

Brunvand, Jan Harold (2003 [1981]): *The Vanishing Hitchhiker. American Urban Legends and Their Meanings*, New York/London: W.W. Norton & Company.

Brunvand, Jan Harold (2012): *Encyclopedia of Urban Legends. Updated and Expanded Edition. Vol. 1*, Santa Barbara: ABC-CLIO.

Bush, George W. (2007): Public Papers of the Presidents of the United States. George W. Bush. 2004. Vol. 2. Washington: United States Government Printing Office.

Cambridge, Ellie/Holly Christodoulou (2017): "Slender Man Stabbers. What Is the Slender Man Stabbing Case, Who Are Morgan Geyser Anissa Weier and Why Did They Attack Payton Leutner? Two Teenage Girls Held Down and Stabbed a 12-Year-Old Classmate, Inspired by An Online Horror Meme." In: thesun.co.uk October 8, (https://www.thesun.co.uk/news/2643061/slender-man-stabbing-case-anissa-weier-morgan-geyser-payton-leutner/).

Cawelti, John G. (2004 [1999]): "The Literature of Mystery: Some Reconsiderations." In: Ray B. Browne/Pat Browne (eds.), *Mystery, Violence, and Popular Culture: Essays by John G. Cawelti*, Madison: Wisconsin University Press, pp. 328-56.

Chess, Shira (2012): "Open-Sourcing Horror. The Slender Man, *Marble Hornets*, and Genre Negotiations." In: *Information, Communication & Society* 15/3, pp. 374-93.

Cok3 (2012): Comment on "I Help Them, Almost Died." In: reddit.com March 27, (https://www.reddit.com/r/BlackEyedKidsStories/comments/rfp15/i_help _them_almost_died/).

Considine, Austin (2010): "Bored at Work? Try Creepypasta, or Web Scares." In: nytimes.com November 12, (http://www.nytimes.com/2010/11/14/fashion/14noticed.html?_r=0).

Em (2013): "Slender: My Personal Account." In: crappypasta.com May 3, (http://www.crappypasta.com/slender-my-personal-account/).

Hogwing (2012): Comment on "He…Touched Me… (X-Post from /R/Slender_Man)." In: reddit.com April 14, (https://www.reddit.com/r/nosleep/comments/s6s0k/he_touched_me_xpost_f rom_rslender_man/?sort=old).

Knife7 (2013): Comment on "What Is the Scariest Aspect of the Slender Man?" In: reddit.com April 23, (https://www.reddit.com/r/Slender_Man/comments/1cv6jh/what_is_the_scari est_aspect_of_the_slender_man/?st=j1u7xont&sh=6323ab47).

Levine, Gary (2015): "Slenderman, Creepypasta and Your Children: The Dangers of Internet Folklore." In: naplesherald.com February 26, (http://naplesherald.com/2015/02/26/slenderman-creepypasta-and-your-children-the-dangers-of-internet-folklore/).

Masco, Joseph (2014): *The Theater of Operations. National Security Affect from the Cold War to the War on Terror*, Durham and London: Duke University Press.

Massumi, Brian (2010): "The Birth of the Affective Fact. The Political Ontology of Threat." In: Melissa Gregg/Gregory J. Seigworth (eds.): *The Affect Theory Reader*, Durham/London: Durham University Press, pp. 52-70.

Mr. Destluer (2014): Comment on "Slender: My Personal Account." In: crappypasta.com April 11, (http://www.crappypasta.com/slender-my-personal-account/).

Naruhinagirl (2012): Comment on "He...Touched Me...(X-Post from /r/Slender_Man)." In: reddit.com April 12, (https://www.reddit.com/r/nosleep/comments/s6s0k/he_touched_me_xpost_f rom_rslender_man/?sort=old).

ObliviousHippie (2015): "What Is NoSleep? Don't Be the Jerk in the Movie Theater?" In: reddit.com November 17, (https://www.reddit.com/r/nosleep/wiki/nosleep).

O'Keefe, Jack (2017): "Why Are Anissa Weier & Morgan Geyser Being Tried as Adults? The Slenderman Case Is Complicated." In: bustle.com January 23, (https://www.bustle.com/p/why-are-anissa-weier-morgan-geyser-being-tried-as-adultsthe-slenderman-case-is-complicated-323609).

Peck, Andrew (2015): "Tall, Dark, and Loathsome: The Emergence of a Legend Cycle in the Digital Age." In: *Journal of American Folklore* 128/509, pp. 333-48.

Potato (2013): Comment on "Slender: My Personal Account." In: crappypasta.com May 3, (http://www.crappypasta.com/slender-my-personal-account/).

Pyric_lancaster (2012): "I Help Them, Almost Died." In: reddit.com March 27, (https://www.reddit.com/r/BlackEyedKidsStories/comments/rfp15/i_help_th em_almost_died/).

Saal, Ilka (2006): "'The Only Possible Heroes for Our Time': Imagining Terrorism in Postmodern Art." In: Heike Schaefer (ed.), *America and the Orient.* Heidelberg: Universitätsverlag Winter, pp. 249-66.

Sgt_Hydroxide (2016): "I Had Never Been More Frightened… The Story of Black-Eyed Children in the Night." In: reddit.com March 16, (https://www.reddit.com/r/HFY/comments/4apqzm/i_had_never_been_more _frightenedthe_story_of/).

Shifman, Limor (2013): "Memes in a Digital World: Reconciling with a Conceptual Troublemaker." In: *Journal of Computer-Mediated Communication* 18/3, pp. 362-377.

Shifman, Limor (2014): *Memes in Digital Culture*, Cambridge/ London: MIT Press.

Sloshedtrain (2014): "Statement on the Wisconsin Stabbing." In: creepypasta.com June 3, (http://www.creepypasta.com/statement-wisconsin-stabbing/).

Solias (2013): Comment on "What Is the Scariest Aspect of the Slender Man?" In: reddit.com April 22, (https://www.reddit.com/r/Slender_Man/comments/1cv6jh/what_is_the_scari est_aspect_of_the_slender_man/?st=j1u7xont&sh=6323ab47).

Smokescreenzwei (2014): "BEK Indecent in 1918 from My Grandfather. (FACT)." In: reddit.com July 7, (https://www.reddit.com/r/BlackEyedKidsStories/comments/2a1zxw/bek_in decent_in_1918_from_my_grandfather_fact/).

Ssilversmith (2016): Comment on "I Had Never Been More Frightened… The Story of Black-Eyed Children in the Night." In: reddit.com March 17, (https://www.reddit.com/r/HFY/comments/4apqzm/i_had_never_been_more _frightenedthe_story_of/).

Stearns, Peter N. (2006): *American Fear. The Causes and Consequences of High Anxiety*, New York/London: Routledge.

Surge, Victor (2009): Comment on "Create Paranormal Images." In: web.archive.org June 10, (https://web.archive.org/web/20120120074129/http://forums.somethingawful .com/showthread.php?threadid=3150591&userid=0&perpage=40&pagenum ber=3).

The Slender Man Files (2008): "16th Century German Woodcuts." In: slendermanfiles.org, (http://www.slendermanfiles.org/home/16th-century-german-woodcuts).

WonderlandWhit_ (2016): Comment on "Encounter...?" In: reddit.com December 1, (https://www.reddit.com/r/BlackEyedKidsStories/comments/5f3l17/en counter/).

Xurichs (2016): "Encounter...?" In: reddit.com November 27, (https://www.reddit.com/r/BlackEyedKidsStories/comments/5f3l17/encounte r/).

Žižek, Slavoj (2002): *Welcome to the Desert of the Real! Five Essays on September 11 and Related Dates*, London/New York: Verso.

Žižek, Slavoj (2003): "The Violence of the Fantasy." In: *The Communication Review* 6/4, pp. 275-88.

"All the Better to Eat You With": The Eroticization of the Werewolf and the Rise of Monster Porn in the Digital Age

ALEXANDRA LEONZINI

1. INTRODUCTION

In the past few years, much attention has been paid to the transformation of the werewolf concept in contemporary popular culture. Authors such as Kimberley McMahon-Coleman, Roslyn Weaver, Chantal Bourgault du Coudray, and Rosalind Sibielski have analyzed how the werewolf has, over the past two centuries, transcended the limits of genre and transitioned from a creature of folk narrative, to monster of gothic horror, to hero of urban fantasy. They argue that whereas the werewolf was once emblematic of a despised other – a creature we feared becoming – today, it has emerged as an empowering emblem of the disenfranchised self, a vehicle through which to discuss and highlight cultural norms as they pertain to class, race, gender, sexuality, control of self, and the body.[1] While this may be true of the sympathetically constructed Daniel "Oz" Osbourne of Joss Whedon's *Buffy the Vampire Slayer* series, Remus Lupine of J.K. Rowling's *Harry Potter* series, and Scott Howard of Rod Daniel's 1985 fantasy-comedy *Teen Wolf*, it cannot be said for the hyper-masculine Alpha male heroes that prowl the pages of the paranormal erotic romance, nor the monstrous beasts of "monster porn" e-books today. Characterized by Harlequin Mills and Boon as "a force to contend with" (Mills & Boon), the 'heroes' of these print and digital stories are every bit as dangerous to the heroines of their tales as the villain of

---

1 Cf. Bougault du Coudry 2006; McMahon-Coleman/Weaver 2012.

Charles Perrault's 1697 *Le Petit Chaperon Rouge*, for much like the wolf that devours Little Red Riding Hood in her grandmother's bed, the 'wicked' were-wolf hero of the paranormal erotic romance,[2] and the out-of-control creature of "monster porn" desire nothing more than to fall upon their prey and eat her up (Lang 1889: 53).

It is the contention of this chapter that the recent emergence of "monster porn," i.e. self-published erotic stories depicting graphic scenes of sexual violence between humans and mythical creatures, is the result of the normalization and eroticization of sexual violence in popular paranormal erotic romance fiction. While traditional publishing houses now have strict terms and conditions forbidding the publication of stories with overt depictions of sexual violence, the violent sexual dynamics of the "bodice ripper," a non-paranormal sexually explicit romantic novel with a historical setting,[3] has been romanticized by authors of paranormal erotica since the late-1970s, and has found new life online where authors are no longer constrained by social, sexual, or legal norms. Enabled by reading and writing platforms like Wattpad and Literotica, and informed by the dark, violent, and highly idealized paranormal romances of the 1990s and early 2000s, the inherent violence of the werewolf concept has become increasingly eroticized in digital paranormal content, while the werewolf figure itself has undergone a dramatic reconceptualization, becoming more domineering and sexually aggressive than ever before.

While hypersexuality has often been associated with the werewolf concept, from the frightening seductions of the *She-Wolves of Jülich* (1591) to the "smooth-tongued, smooth-pelted wolves" Perrault warns his readers to avoid (Carter 2008: 3), it was the popularization of the erotic romance and revisionist horror fictions of the 1970s that enabled the werewolf to emerge as a credible romantic lead by the early 1990s (Crawford 2014: 5-6). This chapter will first examine how the emergence of the bodice ripper in 1972, described by Pamela Rosenthal as "the sexual radical fringe of romance," opened a "conversation in the romance world about sexuality and its complexities," particularly the intersection "of power and pleasure" (Rosenthal 2010). It will then highlight the significant backlash the "bodice-ripper" received from feminist critics who decried

---

2 Paranormal erotic romance is a subgenre of both romance fiction and speculative fiction. These stories focus on romantic love and feature graphically depicted sex scenes between humans and vampires, shapeshifters, ghosts, and other entities of a fantastic or otherworldly nature. Plot, rather than sex, drives the narrative, and every story must end with a "Happily Ever After."

3 Cf. Jensen 1984, 66-67; Zidel 1999.

the genre as normalizing sexual violence, and detail how one such critic, Angela Carter, embraced the erotic and didactic potential of the dominant paranormal lover by transforming the "demon lover" (Lutz 2006: 6) of the bodice ripper into a literal monster in "The Company of Wolves" (1979) to demonstrate the violence of the "forced seduction" trope popularized by the genre. This chapter will then outline how Carter's seemingly sympathetic portrayal of the werewolf found an appreciative audience, enabling the genre to gain popularity throughout the "boom years" of horror publishing in the 1980s (Frost 2003: 187), attain a distinctive generic identity of its own in the early 1990s, and rise to prominence in the first years of the 21st century, with the appearance of Stephenie Meyer's highly polarizing *Twilight* series. The problematic sexual dynamics normalized in the *Twilight* series will be discussed, as will the roles that online fan-cultures and the rise of the e-book have played in the continued development of the genre.

Indeed, since 2007, digital content has been the primary engine driving the creation, production, and critical apparatus of paranormal erotic fiction. Companies such as Amazon's Kindle Direct Publishing, an online platform for self-publishing with a 70 per cent royalty rate for authors, make it possible for any author to self-publish an e-book and distribute it through a global platform without an agent. Romance fiction accounts for the majority of e-book sales, and of all romance subgenres to choose from, paranormal romance is the fifth most lucrative category as of 2016, with stories featuring werewolves and animal-shifter heroes the most popular among readers.[4] This rapid rise of the e-book has enabled a democratization of digital literary content, freeing authors to write the stories they wish to without being constrained by the terms and conditions of traditional publishing houses. As such, they have become increasingly daring in their depiction of paranormal couplings, pushing the boundaries of acceptability, taste, and legality. Often depicted as more animal than man, the viral, dangerous, and uncontrolled werewolf of 21st century online fiction presents a stark contrast to the "more effeminate and 'devirilized' vampire" figure popular in the horror paperbacks of the 1970s and 80s (Duclos 1998: 83). Undisputedly masculine – "primitive, almost mythical in their macho power" (Tobin-McClain 2000: 301) – paranormal erotic romances featuring werewolf heroes driven by biologically de-

---

4   Amazon is the principle means of e-book distribution, accounting for 74 per cent of all US e-book purchases and 71 per cent of all US consumer dollars spent on e-books in 2015 (Authorearnings). Romance fiction accounts for 45 per cent of these sales (approximately 174 million Kindle e-books annually), with an additional 61 million sales coming from Apple, Nook, Kobo and Google e-books annually (Data Guy 2016).

termined instincts serve to renaturalize sexual violence as part of men's biological makeup, resulting in sexual couplings in which the consent of the heroine is, at best, dubious (Deffenbacher 2014: 926); a damaging sexual dynamic replicated in the monster porn stories readily available online today.

2. FRIGHTENING BUT FASCINATING: THE DEMON LOVER OF THE BODICE RIPPER

While mass-market romances (erotic or otherwise) have largely been ignored by critics, dismissed as "high literature's Other, a negative icon, what not, what never to be" (Curthoys/Docker 1990), they are nonetheless "a dynamic cultural form, and publishers and writers respond to reader interests and cultural changes in a way that is unmatched by most other types of publishing and popular media" (Lee 2008: 54, cf. Thurston 1987: 6-7).[5] A consequence of the Sexual Revolution of the 1960s, 70s and 80s, the erotic romance genre, despite its commercial success, was heavily criticized by second-wave feminists as threatening female autonomy and romanticizing sexual violence (McKnight-Trontz 2001: 23). Romance novelist Violet Winspear, for example, received hate mail after stating the following during the BBC current affairs television program *Man Alive* in 1970:

"Most of my heroes, well all of them really [...] frighten but fascinate. They must be the sort of men who are capable of rape: men it's dangerous to be alone in the room with [...] I put all these cruel manly words into these men's mouths [...] and then work so as he makes a grab for the girl. And then she's half fainting, you know what I mean, with a burning desire, which she doesn't even understand herself. And then he's bruising her mouth with his urgent, demanding kisses, and he's got this strange steely light in his eyes. And I get it so the girl says to herself, 'What does it mean, what does it mean?'" (Parkin 1970: 51)

In her correspondence with her publisher, Alan Boon of Mills & Boon, Winspear repeatedly tried to explain that rather than meaning to suggest that women were inherently drawn to potential rapists who felt entitled to a woman's body and

---

5   An incredibly profitable genre, the Romance Writers of America (RWA) estimated in 2013 that sales of romance novels amounted to $1.08 billion, and accounted for 13 per cent of adult fiction consumed that year, outselling science-fiction, mystery and literary novels. In the five years up until 2015 in Britain alone, romance and erotic fiction sold 39.8 million physical books worth £178.09 million.

sexuality, she only meant to say that her heroes were masterful, "would fall un-
controllably for her heroines, would brush aside their hesitation, sweep them off
their feet, and – ultimately – would love and cherish them forever" (qtd. in Dyhouse 2017: 158-159). Despite this, however, Winspear's comments saw her
disgraced and made a laughing stock of by journalist Molly Parkin, who depicted
Winspear, as "mad on men" and suffering from "man mania" (Parkin 1970: 51).

Two years later, however, Winspear would be vindicated when Kathleen E.
Woodiwiss' *The Flame and the Flower* (1972), the first modern bodice ripper,
was published by Avon Books, finding immense commercial success and revolu-
tionizing the romance industry. Depicting graphic encounters of pre-marital sex
and featuring a more active, independent heroine than was traditionally found in
mass-produced romances, the plot of *The Flame and the Flower* is nonetheless
built upon an act of rape depicted as an "erotic fantasy" of subjugation rather
than an act of sexual violence (Lutz 2006: 6). Brandon Birmingham, the hero of
the piece, emanates cruelty and darkness from the offset – "[t]all and powerful
he stood, garmented regally in black velvet and flawless white. He was Satan to
her. Handsome. Ruthless. Evil. He could draw her soul from her body and never
feel remorse" (Woodiwiss 1972: 92) –, and his violent control over Heather
Simmons, a penniless orphan whom he rapes, impregnates, and eventually mar-
ries, drives the story. Believing her to be a prostitute, Brandon feels entitled to
exert absolute control over Heather at their first meeting, dismissing her cries of
protest as a sophisticated sex game and overpowering her to achieve the sexual
release he craves. Predatory, possessive, tortured, and overly attached to anach-
ronistic, aristocratic values, Brandon is "characterised by spectacular masculinity" (Radway 1984: 128), sharing many traits with the villainous rakes of the
19th-century Gothic romance; "a man proud, moody, cynical, with defiance on
his brow, and misery in his heart, a scorner of his kind, implacable in revenge,
yet capable of deep and strong affection" (Cross 1835: 393). Despite this, however, Brandon is depicted by Woodiwiss, and accepted by her audience, as a figure of desire, "a damaged but noble soul yearning for redemption through romantic love" (Crawford 2014: 52). This redemption is granted at the novel's
conclusion, as Brandon comes to both respect and love Heather, the realization
and expression of which transforms him from dangerous demon lover to "pale"
and "trembling" suitor (Woodiwiss 1972: 152). After fighting his deepening
feelings for her throughout the novel, Brandon's verbal expression of his love for
Heather is her "most significant victory," for while he continually uses his superior strength to abuse and intimidate her, between them, only she has the strength
to endure and the power to save him from himself (Puney 1992: 23).

The novel became an immense success, selling over 4.5 million copies by 1978 and becoming the model upon which subsequent erotic romances were based (Putney 1992: 5, 56; Frum 2000: 193). By the late-1970s, however, as the feminist movement continued to evolve and the Sex Wars waged, such graphic depictions of sexual violence were increasingly rejected by mainstream audiences who demanded sexual encounters built on equality, and the celebration of women's sexuality (cf. Thurston 1987).

3. FROM DEMONIC TO MONSTROUS: THE FEMINIST CRITIQUE OF THE BODICE RIPPER AND THE EROTIC POTENTIAL OF THE PARANORMAL PARAMOUR

Critical of the dominant demon lover of the bodice ripper, feminist authors appropriated the archetype, highlighting the inherent violence of the dominant Alpha hero through retellings of fables and fairytales in which the domineering lover is depicted as a literal monster. Of these works, Angela Carter's short story "The Company of Wolves," published in *The Bloody Chamber* in 1979, is by far the best known, depicting the werewolf paramour as more sympathetic and seductive, yet no less dangerous, than the Big Bad Wolf of Perrault's tale.

Comprised of several mini stories, "The Company of Wolves" depicts the werewolf as a "beast [that] would love to be less beastly if only [it] knew how" (Carter 2013: 112). Celebrated by some as "boldly transform[ing]" the Little Red Riding Hood narrative from one of "victimization and voyeurism into opportunities for female empowerment" (Lappas 1996: 115-116; cf. Zipes 1989: 232), the story is nonetheless "a horror tale about a trapped, abused girl who goes to her fate with a resignation she rewrites as acceptance" (Bidisha 2016).[6] Recounting the girl's encounter with a charming stranger in the woods while on her way to visit her grandmother, "The Company of Wolves" replicates much of Perrault's *Le Petit Chaperon Rouge* but ends quite differently. After having wagered a kiss with a mysterious stranger in a bet that she can get to her grandmother's cottage before him, the girl dawdles, wishing to kiss him. Little does she know that he is a werewolf who kills her grandmother once reaching the cottage and hides the body under the bed to avoid detection. While initially elated that the stranger has reached the cottage before her, a "wise child," the girl's behavior immediately changes when she sees "a tuft of white hair" belonging to her grandmother poking out from under the bed. Trapped, she seduces the wolf "to save her own

---

6   Cf. Duncker 1984; Clark 1987; Lewallen 1988.

life." Pressing "hard on the disturbing line between fear and submission, choice and force, humiliation and annihilation, self-sacrifice and self-preservation," (Bidisha 2016) it becomes a story depicting the entrapment and sexual assault of a young woman coerced. Despite the implied violence of the piece, however, the idea of sleeping "sweet and sound [...] between the paws of the tender wolf" (Carter 2013: 80) proved temping to some who, like Lappas, read mutual consent in the girl's seductions, interpreting the actions of the wolf as sensual, romantic, and desirable.[7]

4. IN THE ARMS OF A BEAST: THE RISE OF THE PARANORMAL EROTIC ROMANCE

By the late 1980s, the once firm cultural divide between the desirable and the monstrous was destabilized by the increasingly sympathetic treatment of the monsters of Gothic fiction in popular culture, enabling the rise of the paranormal erotic romance (Frost 2003: 187). In contrast to the bloodthirsty and unpredictable beasts of horror, the werewolf heroes of paranormal erotic romances were dark, broody, and driven by an overwhelming biological need to find their fated mate, their only chance of redemption. In Susan Krinard's 1994 debut novel, *Prince of Wolves*, for example, Luke Gevaudan, one of the last survivors of an ancient race of werewolves, explains the nature of the werewolf mate-bond to his human mate, Joelle; "among my kind, there can be only one true mate. Once we have found that mate, the bond is for life. It is life, to us" (1994: 166). Like Brandon in *The Flame and the Flower*, Luke is demanding and domineering but unlike him, he is unable to deny his need for Joelle, for as his mate, only she can fill the "empty void of heart and soul" (ibid: 169) within him. As Joseph Crawford has observed, in paranormal romances, traditional genre conventions are elevated to natural laws as the werewolf hero is "biologically pre-programmed to behave like the hero of a traditional romance novel" (2014: 140). As such, plot devices traditionally used by authors of mainstream contemporary romances to inject conflict into their narratives and test the relationships of their protagonists, such as an unplanned pregnancy or the heroine's uncertainty of the hero's feelings for her, cease to function because the hero's love for the heroine is undeniable; the biologically determined mating bond simply will not allow him to love another.

---

7   Cf. Jowett 2012; Reid 2014

Instead, authors of werewolf romances most commonly create narrative conflict via a malignant third party who threaten the couple's future happiness. Weary of the danger to himself and to his mate, and incapable of losing her, the werewolf hero's possessiveness is reframed as protectiveness, for whereas once the heroine felt threatened by his domineering nature earlier in the narrative, she eventually submits to his control, seeing it as proof of his devotion to her. The inherent duality of the werewolf concept is highlighted in the hero's nature as a lover; as both possessive and protective, emotionally distant and loving, violent and gentle. At the beginning of these stories, the werewolf hero is always more animal than man, struggling against himself for control over his inner beast. It is only through the 'domesticating' love of the heroine that he is able to gain control over his baser instincts and become the civil, respectful, loving partner she needs him to be. Her love is transformative, far stronger than the anger within him, and, as Carol Dyhouse has stated, "softens male brutishness, and ultimately [...] empowers [the heroine]" (2017: 160).

Nowhere is this more clearly demonstrated than in Christine Feehan's award-winning *Dark* Series, which began in 1999 and has seen the publishing of the 31st book in the series, *Dark Legacy*, in September 2017. Her debut novel, *Dark Prince* (1999), won three Paranormal Excellence Awards for Romance Literature (PEARL) in 1999 and features Mikhail Dubrinsky, Prince of the Carpathians, a race of noble, vampiric, shapeshifting immortals who, without their lifemates, are doomed to degenerate into rage-filled monsters with no control over themselves or their actions. Although more vampire then werewolf, the popularity of the Carpathian hero shaped the werewolf hero in the years that followed, domesticating the monster figure and transforming it from a figure of terror "into a figure of traditional patriarchal conservatism [...] tightly wedded to their social role within their community [and] to their responsibilities as leader, guardian, father and husband" (Crawford 2014: 142-143).

At the opening of *Dark Prince*, Mikhail, having lost the ability to feel emotions and see color in the absence of his mate, expresses the need to find her, "his missing half, the life mate that would bring him forever into the light" (Feehan 2006: 2). After a chance encounter with Raven Whitney, a human psychic and telepath, restores his ability to see color, Mikhail recognizes her as his life mate and doggedly pursues her, invading her dreams and attempting to control her movements through the power of suggestion. From the offset, he is possessive, becoming enraged when he sees her embrace a faceless human lover in a dream:

"'*Has another man touched you like this?*' He whispered the words in her mind, dark, deadly sensuality.

'*Damn you, stop!*' Tears glittered like jewels in her lashes, in her mind. '*All I wanted to do was help you. I said I was sorry.*'

His hand moved higher because he had to, found heat and silk, tiny curls guarding treasure. His palm covered the triangle possessively, pushed into the moist heat. '*You will answer me, little one. There is still time for me to come to you, to put my mark on you, for me to own you,*' he warned silkily. '*Answer me.*'

'*Why are you doing this?*'

'*Do not defy me.*' His voice was husky now, raw with need. His fingers moved, probed, found her most sensitive spot. '*I am being exceptionally gentle with you.*'

'*You already know the answer is no,*' she whispered in defeat.

He closed his eyes, was able to calm the raging demons knifing pain through his body. '*Sleep, little one, no one will harm you tonight.*' He broke contact and found his body hard, heavy, bathed in perspiration. It was far too late to stop the beast in him from breaking free. He was burning with hunger, consumed with it, jackhammers beating at his skull, flames licking along his skin and nerve endings. The beast was unleashed, deadly, hungry. He had been more than gentle. She had inadvertently released the monster. He hoped she was as strong as he believed her to be." (Feehan 2006: 8)

Dangerous, possessive, controlling, and volatile, were Mikhail a human, his actions throughout the book would be read as abusive. Instead, as a non-human driven by instinct, his overwhelming need to control his mate is accepted as a consequence of his race, transforming him from terrifying beast of lore into an alpha male hero worthy of love and redemption. Heather Schell observes that, by constructing their heroes as non-humans, contemporary romance authors "retain the domineering hero of bygone days while simultaneously updating the heroine to reflect the sensibilities of modern women" (Schell 2007: 118). While the heroines of erotic romances became increasingly self-assured and driven in the 1980s as a response to feminist criticisms that their earlier shy submissiveness perpetuated rape culture and sexualized abuse, so did their non-human paramours, becoming ever more desirous of their mate's total submission. Such can be seen in Feehan's characterization of the hugely popular[8] hero of her novel *Dark Magic* (2000), Gregori:

---

8 *Dark Magic* won "Best Overall Paranormal Romance" at the 2000 PEARL Awards, and was a 2001 RITA finalist, while Gregori was voted "Best Hero" at the 2000 Awards Romance Books and Readers, "Favorite Hero" at the 2000 RBL Hughie Book

"[He] was one of the ancients, the most powerful, the most knowledgeable [...]The centuries had not softened his macho attitudes or changed his beliefs. He believed absolutely in his right to her, believed she belonged to him. He would protect her with his life from all harm, see to her every need and comfort. But he would rule her absolutely." (Feehan 2000: 46)

In these paranormal erotic romances, the blurring of the line between affection and violence is a consequence of the hero's nonhuman nature, justifying rape as evidence of his biologically determined need to claim his mate. As such, scenes of romanticized sexual violence are the norm, feeding into "cultural assumptions about unequal power relations in heterosexual relationships" (Modleski 2008: 34) wherein "women being the gender in touch with caring emotions [...] give men love, and in return men, being in touch with power and aggression [...] provide and protect" (hooks 2000: 101). The hero's inability to control himself in the presence of his mate, however, is central to the reading of these stories by female supporters of the genre as empowering. Susan Elizabeth Phillips, for example, suggests that "the domineering male becomes the catalyst that makes the empowerment fantasy work" (1992: 56) for the confrontation between the hero and heroine enables her to appropriate his power and save him from himself. Speaking of the genre's appeal to women, Karen Bethke states:

"Women love stories that reaffirm the idea that deep down, they have the power to tame even the wildest animal and redeem even the worst man. That, I think, is the core appeal of the paranormal romance. We are talking about bad boys who are so bad that even God has given up on them. But *we* [...] have the power to save them, if we just love them enough." (quoted in Crawford 2014: 82)

Even prolonged psychological and physical abuse can be excused as foreplay by the reader, who, aware of the formulaic nature of the category romance and its guaranteed happy ending, knows that the story will conclude with a passionate declaration of love and a happily ever after. Winning RWA's RITA Award for Best Paranormal Romance in 2007, Kresley Cole's *A Hunger Like No Other* (2006), for example, opens with a violent exchange been the hero and heroine when the protagonist, werewolf Alpha Lachlain MacRieve, scents "his mate, the one woman made for him alone," and hunts her down, forcing himself upon her:

Awards, and was a finalist in the "Most Tortured Hero" category of the 2000 All About Romance Awards (Feehan 2017).

"A vicious growl sounded. Her eyes widened, but she didn't turn back, just sprinted across the field. She felt claws sink into her ankle a second before she was dragged to the muddy ground and thrown onto her back. A hand covered her mouth, though she'd been trained not to scream. 'Never run from one such as me.' Her attacker didn't sound human. 'You will no' get away. *And we like it.*' [...] 'Don't do this! Please...' When her last word ended with a whimper, he seemed to come out of a trance, his brows drawing together as his eyes met hers, but he didn't release her hands. [...] She struggled, but it was useless against his strength." (Cole 2006: 9-11)

Taking his fated mate, half-vampire, half-Valkyrie Emmaline Troy, hostage, Lachlain blackmails her into staying with him by threating her family's safety, deceiving her, stealing her credit cards, and forcing her to perform sex acts against her will. The abuse is so bad that at one point she threatens to jump off a balcony to escape him. Despite this, however, Emmaline eventually comes to accept Lachlain as her fated mate, falling in love with him despite his deplorable treatment of her, and healing the wounds of his past. Lutz credits postfeminism as an important factor in enabling such narratives to be read as empowering in the 21st century, stating, "postfeminism, while recognizing the advances of the feminists that have come before it, loosens some of the tight holds of early feminism and is willing to appropriate certain paradigms that were earlier deemed dangerous to feminism, such as the attraction of the demon lover" (ibid: 12). Thus, accepted as an expectation of the genre, by the beginning of the 21st century, scenes of sexual violence began to appear in works of paranormal fiction aimed at increasingly younger audiences. The most prominent example of this is the *Twilight* series, which "wrenched the vampire genre out of dark obscurity into blinding publicity" (Brown 2009), capturing the imaginations of a young and active fan base, and drawing heavy criticism for, among other things, "robbing [teen girls] of agency and normalizing stalking and abusive behavior" (Butler 2009).

5. "TEAMJACOB4LYF": THE *TWILIGHT* PHENOMENON, ONLINE FAN-CULTURE, AND THE NORMALIZATION OF SEXUAL VIOLENCE

One does not have to search far to find academic studies and opinion pieces which criticize *Twilight* as promoting unhealthy relationship models.[9] The vam-

---

9   Cf. Housel 2009; Ames 2010; Durham, 2012; Michel 2011; Kendal and Kendal 2015.

pire protagonist Edward Cullen's treatment of human Bella Swan throughout the book (2005-2008) and film series' (2008-2012), is regarded as particularly problematic as his stalking, kidnapping and manipulative control of the heroine is romanticized throughout, reminiscent of the actions and reception of the demon lover of the bodice ripper. Responding to these concerns, Meyer has asserted that the series "is not even realistic fiction, [as] it is a fantasy with vampires and werewolves, so no one could ever make [Bella's] exact choices" (Meyer 2017a). Nonetheless, her work depicts or describes multiple scenes of eroticized sexual violence, much of which is perpetrated by werewolf characters. When, for example, Jacob Black, a friend of Bella's family and wolf-shapeshifter, declares his love for her in *Eclipse* (2009), he does so by forcing himself upon her:

"He still had my chin – his fingers holding too tight, till it hurt – and I saw the resolve in his eyes.

'N – ' I started to object, but it was too late.

His lips crushed mine, stopping my protest. He kissed me angrily, roughly, his other hand gripping tight around the back of my neck, making escape impossible. I shoved against his chest with all my strength, but he didn't even seem to notice. His mouth was soft, despite the anger, his lips molding mine in a warm, unfamiliar way.

I grabbed at his face, trying to push it away, failing again. He seemed to notice this time, though, and it aggravated him. His lips forced mine open, and I could feel his hot breath in my mouth.

Acting on instinct, I let my hands drop to my side, and shut down. I opened my eyes and didn't fight, didn't feel... just waited for him to stop." (Meyer 2009: 300-301)

While this scene ends with Bella punching him hard enough to break her hand, Jacob is unscathed by the blow and is unapologetic. When Bella, for example, tells him that she hates him, he responds, "[t]hat's good. Hate is a passionate emotion," quipping, "Oh, c'mon... that had to be better than kissing a rock" (ibid: 302). Despite attracting criticism for Jacob's use of force in this scene, Meyer defended his actions as those of a "16-year-old boy," stating, "those who are upset by some of his tactics should consider his youth and the fact that he is, after all, right. Bella is in love with him" (Meyer 2017b).

Many readers enjoyed Jacob's heavy-handed seduction, and felt him a better fit for Bella than Edward, beginning a now infamous[10] "Team Edward" vs "Team Jacob" public debate, which resulted in the sale of merchandise allowing the wearer to announce to the world on which side of the debate they fell: vam-

---

10 Cf. Martens 2010; Schau and Buchanan-Oliver 2012: 39.

pire or werewolf. This only increased the popularity of the series and paranormal content in general, with *Breaking Dawn* selling 1.3 million copies in its first day alone (Crawford 2014: 181).[11] This *Twilight* craze, however, attracted heavy backlash, and, amplified by the Internet, critics dismissed fans of *Twilight*, dubbed "Twihards" and "Twitards" (Schau/ Buchanan-Oliver 2012: 40) as juvenile, uneducated, and unsophisticated (cf. Donelan 2015).

Seeking an environment in which to openly discuss their love for the series, fans turned to the Internet and established online clubs and forums dedicated to the discussion of the *Twilight* books and films. These sites, such as *Twilifers*, *Twilight vef France*, and *Twihards4evar*, allowed readers from all over the world to share their ideas and experiences in a supportive environment. More than just a place to interact with fellow fans, this digital scene also served as an incubator for talent, providing "a powerful and new distribution channel for amateur cultural production" (Jenkins 2006: 135-136), which enabled aspiring authors to contribute to the exponential growth of digital literary content, creating a culture of participation rather than simple consumerism, and enabling a shift "from the mass-mediated public sphere to a networked public sphere" (Benkler 135-136). The stories they wrote replicated and explored the violence of *Twilight*'s sexual dynamics, detailing hardcore sex scenes the abstinence-promoting original lacked.[12] Encouraged by their communities, some fans began publishing pieces on sites not affiliated with the series, such as *fanfiction.net*, leading to a rapid proliferation of hardcore and graphic *Twilight* fanfiction. By the middle of 2007, thousands of *Twilight*-inspired stories appeared, with twenty to thirty new works

---

11 Aware that they needed to capitalize on the public's immense appetite for paranormal content, traditional romance publishing houses who had long abandoned the subgenre began to establish lines of their own. Harlequin, for example, launched their Silhouette Nocturne lines devoted exclusively to paranormal content in October 2006, one month after the release of the second novel in the *Twilight* series, *New Moon*. Like traditional romance publishers, established authors of paranormal romance, such as Feehan, also rode the wave of Meyer's success, seeing a dramatic increase in their book sales and growth in their fan bases. As such, between 2005 and 2010, nearly 30 per cent of the romances that appeared on the *New York Times* bestseller list were in the paranormal subgenre.

12 The most prominent example of this E. L. James' *Fifty Shades of Grey* series, which was developed from a *Twilight* fan fiction series she wrote under the name "Snowqueen's Icedragon." Originally titled *Master of the Universe*, James' *Twilight* fanfiction reimagined Bella as an innocent college student and Edward as a billionaire playboy with a penchant for BDSM sex.

added to the site every day (Crawford 2014: 187). *LiveJournal, Archive Of Our Own* (ao3.com), Facebook, Twitter, Tumblr, and Tickld all provided platforms for the distribution of fanfiction, allowing members of different fandoms to meet and exchange ideas which lead to interplay between media and a redefinition of core concepts. This is particularly true of the conceptualization of the werewolf, which, unleashed online, became the paranormal embodiment of a violent, animalistic, and dominant sexuality.

Growing out of the *Supernatural* (2005-present) and *Teen Wolf* (2011-present) fandoms, the werewolves of Alpha/Beta/Omega (A/B/O) stories are a prime example of this. Set within what has been dubbed the "Omegaverse," A/B/O stories posit societies in which biological imperatives divide people into wolf-pack based hierarchies. Replicating the central tropes of the paranormal erotic romance, the werewolf Alpha's primal need to mate is romanticized in often brutal scenes of sexual domination. Traditionally featuring homosexual couples, A/B/O stories incorporate concepts from a multitude of fandoms including "Pon Farr," *Star Trek*'s Vulcan mating cycle, first introduced in the episode "Amok Time" in 1967. Written by Theodore Sturgeon, the episode details how Vulcans must mate with someone with whom they are empathically bonded or suffer excruciating pain, insanity, and possible death, not unlike Feehan's Carpathians (Bryson/Holly/Moxey 1994: 311-312). Often labeled "fod" or "mod" ("fuck or die" or "mate or die" respectively), the A/B/O stories featuring "Pon Farr" depict the event as animalistic, violent, and uncontrolled. A common trope is for the Omega male to go into heat and release pheromones, driving the Alpha wild. They then mate violently, and, at the moment of climax, the Alpha wolf's penis forms a 'knot' at its base, like that of a canine's, resulting in the impregnation of the submissive male (Busse 2013: 316). More sexually aggressive and biologically "animal" than the heroes of print paranormal erotic romance, the werewolf Alphas of A/B/O stories push the werewolf concept well past mainstream tastes, skirting on the edges of social, sexual and legal norms in order to titillate their readers.

6. In the Arms of a Beast: Bestiality, the E-Book, and the Rise of Monster Porn

As the werewolves of paranormal erotic romance and fanfiction have become more aggressive in their sexuality and animalistic in demeanor, the question as to whether sexual activity between a human and a werewolf constitutes bestiality has been raised by publishers, book distributors and legal bodies alike, going as far as the San Francisco Court of Appeal in 2013. After Andres Martinez, an inmate at Pelican Bay State Prison, had his copy of Mathilde Madden's paranormal erotic romance *The Silver Crown* confiscated in 2011, the court was asked to determine whether paranormal erotic fiction was too obscene to be given to prisoners, yet it was unable to reach a definitive ruling (Pahle 2013). In their assessment of the novel, the court highlighted the "great number of graphic sexual encounters" between the human heroine and werewolf paramour, listing "detailed descriptions of intercourse, sodomy, oral-genital contact, oral-anal contact, voyeurism, exhibitionism, and *ménage à trois*," adding "no bestiality is portrayed [unless werewolves count]" (Berkowitz, 2015: 199). Ruling that access to werewolf-erotica was Martinez's constitutional right, the novel was returned to him, yet the question, ultimately, remained unanswered. Today, most publishing houses explicitly forbid the publication of scenes in which humans engage in sexual acts with naturally-occurring animals, yet fantastic creatures such as werewolves fall outside these parameters. Amazon Kindle Direct Publishing's own terms and conditions are open for interpretation, simply stating, "[w]e don't accept pornography or offensive depictions of graphic sexual acts. What we deem offensive is probably about what you would expect" (Kindle Direct Publishing). As such, it is not uncommon to find stories depicting bestial themes available online for purchase.

An example of this is the work of Christin Morgan, who first started uploading stories to *Literotica* under the name "Sabledrake" in 2002. With 158,254 views to date, and a rate of 4.73 stars out of 5 for "Hotness," her short story "Hairy Men," published on 29 May 2004, depicts the seduction of a human woman by hyper-masculine Alpha-male werewolf twins. Her description of the heroes is typical of the genre:

"He was a big man, broad through the shoulders and chest, with arms like a lumberjack's. His hair was so black that the sun struck indigo highlights from it, and it was worn long, almost to his shoulders. A dusky bristle of beard-shadow covered his cheeks, chin, and upper lip. He had darkly tanned skin, and startling, vivid green eyes." (Sabledrake 2004)

The werewolf heroes are rugged, outdoorsy, and undeniably masculine. What is atypical about the story, however, is that the heroine engages in multiple sex acts with the brothers while they are in wolf form, something that is not depicted in the works of major publishing houses due to its potential to be read as obscene and illegal.

"She started to sit up, and immediately the wolf growled again, cowing her into motion-less submission. Its nose pressed to her leg, sniffing, moving up from her knee and over her thigh. Its tongue made a few more swipes, tickling and slippery. She could see its head in clear detail, the way its ears angled back, the pelt forming a ruff around the neck and down onto the broad chest…

It was strange, it was wrong. Trapped here, flat on her back on the forest floor being threatened by a gigantic wolf, she should have been scared to death. And she *was* scared… but she was turned on, too. Sick though it was, she liked the helpless feeling of having her clothes violently stripped from her body, of being unable to move for fear of being bitten." (Sabledrake 2004)

The sex is violent, animalistic, and unconventional, yet after the act, the "terrify-ing, fierce wolf of earlier" is gone, domesticated by the heroine, "replaced by an oversized puppy giving her a hopeful, head-tilted, yearning gaze with big win-some eyes" (ibid). Considered a "fun" and "humorous" tale by her readers, Mor-gan published the story in 2013 under the title "Moon Mates" in *Kink*, a compila-tion of stories previously published by One Handed Reads, an independent pub-lisher founded in 2011 "to meet an exponentially growing demand for cheap, filthy ebooks" (Fictophilia).

Enabling readers to discreetly download erotica from the privacy of their own homes, the "e-book revolution" (Herald/Orr 2013: 304) ignited by the in-troduction of the Kindle in 2007 saw a dramatic diversification of the romance market, allowing authors to directly distribute content which, for one reason or another, was considered unpublishable by traditional houses. Paranormal ro-mances, hardcore erotica, and stories with strong BDSM themes all found devot-ed audiences online, where anonymity enabled many to experiment and explore their sexuality. As such, by the late 2000s, independent e-book publishing began to seriously impact the margins and influence of traditional publishing houses. At the time of the e-reader's release, traditional publishers, such as Harlequin Mills & Boon and Avon Books in the romance sector, completely controlled the means of book production, distribution and sales, dictating, rather than serving, the tastes of their audiences. "It was a print-centric world," states Mark Coker, Founder of Smashwords, an e-book distributor, "where print books accounted for 99.8 percent of book sales, and where publishers were the bouncers at the pearly gates of authordom" (2016). Due to the fierce competition for shelf space in brick and mortar book retailers, publishers were reluctant to stray from main-stream tastes, and the primary challenge that faced writers of stigmatized genres, such as romance and erotica, was access to retail distribution. In the words of Raelene Gorlinsky of Ellora's Cave, an e-publisher specializing in romance novels with a high graphic sex index trademarked as "Romantica," "[i]t was very difficult to sell erotic romance through the chains [...] they were wary of what they put on their shelves" (Greenfield 2011). As such, seeking a way to overcome these difficulties, romance authors and their readers were the "first to embrace indie e-book publishing, the first to achieve significant commercial success as indies, and the first to pioneer many of today's best practices for e-book publishing and promotion" (Coker 2016). Enabled by the rise of independent e-book publishing houses and self-publishing tools like Kindle Direct Publishing, hardcore shifter erotic romances became a staple of the scene, and as the digital presence of paranormal erotic stories has become more pronounced, they have also become increasingly extreme, facilitating the rise of monster porn.

In December 2011, *Cum for Bigfoot,* a 12,000-word novella, was published via Amazon's Kindle Direct Publishing, changing the landscape of paranormal erotica forever. Labelled "cryptozoological erotica," "erotic horror" or monster porn, author Virginia Wade's work details the kidnapping and repeated sexual assault of a group of women at the hands of Bigfoot, a simian-like cryptid with "a huge cock" (Wade 2011). Unlike the werewolf romances previously discussed, these stories are not by any stretch of the imagination romantic; sex propels the narrative and there's no guarantee of a Happy Ever After. Instead, they are the most extreme manifestation of the desired animalism of the werewolf hero: savage and unrelenting. Downloaded from Amazon over 100,000 times in 2012 alone, *Cum for Bigfoot*, which was also distributed by iTunes and Barnes & Noble, netted Wade between $6,000 to $30,000 a month, prompting her to turn the story into a 16-part series (Spitznagel 2013). She is not alone in making a living from the genre, with over 11,334 titles categorized as monster porn on Amazon.com at the time of writing. Of these, over 1000 feature werewolf characters raping or "forcefully seducing," female humans, with werebears, yetis, dragons, aliens, minotaurs, goblins, and dinosaurs also proving popular. On the appeal of such couplings, Clarissa Smith, editor of the journal *Porn Studies,* states, "[t]he idea of having sex with [a mythical creature] is outside the realms of possibility. It's a bit like 'magic', where all rules become suspended, and for that reason it may well allow... for kinds of imaginative risk-taking impossible in more standard couplings" (qtd. in Hartley 2015). She further suggests that an element of fear and the permission to think about non-human sexual pleasures may help explain interest in the genre: "I think this is perhaps the appeal of monsters – that it is the very impossibility of such scenarios that are fascinating and arousing, allowing the possibility of joining in with the game of imagining such outrageous couplings with other people" (ibid). With provocative titles, such as Hunter Fox's *Pterodactyl Turned Me Gay* (2015), and Cameron Pierce's *Ass Goblins of*

Auschwitz (2009), these stories are designed to amuse as well as titillate, and have amassed a large and dedicated audience.

One of the most prolific and popular proponents of "cryptozoological eroti-ca" is the pseudonymous Dr. Chuck Tingle, who was nominated for a Hugo Award in 2016 for his short story *Space Raptor Butt Invasion.*[13] Beginning his career by writing monster porn, Tingle has since become the most recognized author of gay niche erotica today. Dubbed tinglers, Tingle describes his own sto-ries as "so sensual, so erotic, and so powerfully gay that it will change the whole way you look at erotic romance literature" (Jones 2015). Blurring the lines be-tween erotica, post-modernism, and meta-fiction, Tingle's tinglers often explicit-ly engage with politics, with recent titles including, *Fake News, Real Boners* (2016), *Redacted In The Butt By Redacted Under The Tromp Administra-tion* (2017), and *Domald Tromp Pounded In The Butt By The Handsome Russian T-Rex Who Also Peed On His Butt And Then Blackmailed Him With The Videos Of His Butt Getting Peed On* (2017). Though humorously titled, they nonetheless portray human men being forcefully taken by monstrous beasts and sentient ob-jects. Despite the subgenre being largely out of the public eye in 2013, concern about the content of self-published erotic titles available to purchase on Amazon via Kindle Direct Publishing spiked when an incendiary article called "An Epi-demic of Filth" was published on *The Kernel*, claiming that online bookstores like Amazon, Barnes & Noble, and WHSmith, were selling self-published e-books that featured "rape fantasies, incest porn and graphic descriptions of besti-ality and child abuse" (Wilson 2013). "Unlike the bookshelves in physical stores," Wilson wrote, "online bookstores appear to be a Wild West of depraved content sure to horrify every parent and book-lover. Some of Britain and Ameri-ca's most treasured brands are profiting from paperbacks, e-books and audio

---

13 Largely considered a laughingstock by the small audience who knew of his work be-fore his first Hugo nomination, Tingle was thrust into the public eye after his nomina-tion was secured by the coordinated bloc voting of two racist neo-reactionary groups called the Sad Puppies and the Rabid Puppies in 2016, which sought to delegitimize the Hugos by nominating joke candidates and "Make Science Fiction Not Diverse Again" (Hathaway 2016). Refusing to be used by these groups to further their regres-sive political agendas, Tingle instead used the platform his controversial nomination provided to demean the actions of the Sad and Rabid Puppies, making a mockery of them on Twitter and drawing attention to his own work in the process. In addition to amassing a cult of loyal followers (dubbed "buckaroos" by Tingle), the publicity sur-rounding this drama lead to an increase in the sales of cryptozoological erotic titles and an explosion of interest in the subgenre.

books stuffed with deeply repellant material that skirts the boundaries of illegality" (ibid).

Dubbed "erotica-gate" by Michael Tamblyn of Kobo, the e-book publisher at the center of the controversy, the story received significant attention, with major news outlets like the *Daily Mail* adding their voices to the calls for the "vile trade" in "sick ebooks" to cease for the good of society (Ellery/Gallagher 2013). While some retailers responded to this outrage with public apologies, WHSmith took the unprecedented move of shutting down its website completely until "all self-published eBooks [were] removed and [they were] totally sure that there [were] no offending titles available" (Wyatt 2013). Amazon's response was somewhat more muted, addressing the scandal by quietly pulling thousands of titles from their shelves, deleting "not just the questionable erotica but [also] [...] any e-books that might even hint at violating cultural norms," including monster porn (Hoffelder 2013). As such, popular tiles, such as Wade's *Cum for Bigfoot*, disappeared from the site, found to be in violation of Amazon's content guidelines. In response, Wade, who says she lost 60 per cent of her work in the Amazon purge and has decided to abandon the genre, republished *Cum for Bigfoot* as *Moan for Bigfoot* in order to work around Amazon's restrictions. Despite this, however, thousands of paranormal erotic e-books and stories continue to be published today as authors compete to be the next Stephenie Meyer, E. L. James, or Chuck Tingle.

7. CONCLUSION

While the uncertainty surrounding Amazon's crackdown on monster porn has led some authors, like Wade, to abandon the genre and target a more mainstream audience, it continues to be a commercial success. With the knowledge that traditional publishing houses, constrained as much by self-imposed codes of conduct as the law, refuse to publish content depicting graphic scenes of sexual violence, readers who favor the sexually domineering, violent lovers of the bodice ripper and the paranormal erotic romance know to turn to the self- and indie-published content available online. As such, the advent of the internet has led to a significant shift in power between traditional and indie-publishers, with digital content becoming the primary engine driving the creation, production, and critical apparatus of paranormal erotic fiction. Today, the work of popular authors like Chuck Tingle, whose careers would have been impossible ten years ago, is directly sourced and distributed to global audiences online. This democratization of literary content, by which all tastes in erotica content can potentially be met, is the reason that stories produced today continue to contain the same romanticized acts of sexual violence that second-wave feminists decried in the 1970s. Unfettered by social, cultural, or legal norms, and emboldened by the destabilization of the once firm cultural divide between the desirable and the monstrous, authors of monster porn will continue to push the limits of the genre to meet the expectations of an audience who are increasingly unsatisfied by the 'domesticated' Alpha male heroes favored by traditional publishing houses: "Regular male characters in romance books tend to be over-the-top perfect glistening warriors and knights," writes Bonnie Burton, host of the monthly YouTube webseries *Vaginal Fantasy Book Club*. "I want an imperfect monster who needs love to show that he can be just as sweet as his human competition" (Burton 2013). Despite this demand, however, since the "erotica-gate" scandal, Amazon content managers have become quick to remove any titles they find to be in breach of the company's guidelines, guidelines that remain confusing to authors and indie publishers alike. While independent authors and e-book distributors have celebrated the freedom self-publishing has granted them, in the wake of Amazon's content censorship many are now asking if it is worth it and have started to question the very foundations of the genre; "[i]s a werewolf an animal? What about a minotaur? Where do you draw the line? Sex with beasts is a common theme in paranormal romance. Do dinosaurs need to be a protected class of animal? What about a Sasquatch? When are they real, when are they not, when can you have sex with them and when can you not?" (Coker qtd. in Spitznagel 2013). While Amazon has been slow to clarify its position, authors of monster porn have continued to produce the violent sexual content at the center of this scandal, frequently meeting in Amazon's Kindle Direct Publishing support forums to discuss the nuances of sex with a mythical creature, and sharing tips as to how to evade Amazon's censors (Amazon KDP Support). While they acknowledge that they are playing a dangerous game, many consider the potential rewards to outweigh the possible consequences of their deception, and are mindful that their audiences do not care about the legal ambiguity of the stories they love as long as they can be the stars of their own paranormal erotic adventures and sleep "sweet and sound… between the paws of the tender wolf" (Carter 2013: 80).

WORKS CITED

Amazon KDP Support (2012): "Thread: are werewolves considered bestiality? + mythical creatures." In: amazon.com July 11,
(https://kdp.amazon.com/community/thread.jspa?threadID=41860).

Authorearnings (2015): "Apple, B&N, Kobo, and Google: a Look at the Rest of the Ebook Market." In: authorearnings.com October 2015,
(http://authorearnings.com/report/october-2015-apple-bn-kobo-and-google-a-look-at-the-rest-of-the-ebook-market/).

Benkler, Yochai (2006): *The Wealth of Networks: How Social Production Transforms Markets and Freedom*, New Haven: Yale University Press.

Berkowitz, Eric (2015): *The Boundaries of Desire: A Century of Bad Laws, Good Sex, and Changing Identities*, Berkeley: Counterpoint.

Bidisha (2016): "Angela Carter's wolf tales ('The Werewolf', 'The Company of Wolves' and 'Wolf-Alice')." *In: British Library, Discovering Literature: 20th Century* May 25,
(https://www.bl.uk/20th-century-literature/arti-cles/angela-carters-wolf-tales).

Bougault du Coudray, Chantal (2006): *The Curse of the Werewolf: Fantasy, Horror and the Beast Within*, London: I.B. Tauris.

Brown, Caitlin (2009): "Feminism in the Vampire Novel," In: *The F Word* September 8, (http://www.thefword.org.uk/features/2009/09/feminism_and_th).

Bryson, Norman/Michael, Holly Ann/Moxey, Keith P. F. (1994): *Visual Culture: Images and Interpretations*, Middletown, CT: Wesleyan University Press.

Burton, Bonnie (2013): "Sexy beasts: Why 'monster porn' needs love too." In: cnet.com December 30,
(https://www.cnet.com/news/sexy-beasts-why-monster-porn-needs-love-too/).

Busse, Kristina (2013): "Pon Farr, Mpreg, and the rise of the Omegaverse." In: Anne Jamison (ed.) *Fic: Why Fanfiction Is Taking Over the World*, Dallas: Smart Pop.

Butler, L. Lee (2009): "Twilight and Abusive Relationships." In: *YALSA Blog* November 24,
(http://yalsa.ala.org/blog/2009/11/24/twilight-and-abusive-relation-ships/).

Carter, Angela (2008): *The Fairy Tales of Charles Perrault*, London: Penguin Classics.

Carter, Angela (2013): "The Company of Wolves." In: *Ecotone* 9/1, pp. 72-80.

Clark, Robert (1987): "Angels Carter's Desire Machine." In: *Women's Studies* 14/2, pp. 147-161.

Coker, Mark (2016): "2017 Book Industry Predictions: Intrigue and Angst amid Boundless Opportunity." In: Smashwords December 31. (http://blog.smashwords.com/2016/).

Cole, Kresley (2006): *A Hunger Like No Other,* New York et al.: Pocket Books.

Crawford, Joseph (2014): *The Twilight of the Gothic?: Vampire Fiction and the Paranormal Romance*, Chicago: University of Chicago Press.

Cross, Maurice (1835): *Selections from the Selections from the Edinburgh Review Comprising the Best Articles in that Journal from Its Commencement to the Present Time*, Paris: Baudry's European Library.

Curthoys, Ann/Docker, John (1990): "Popular Romance in the Postmodern Age. And an Unknown Australian Author." In: *Continuum: The Australian Journal of Media & Culture* 4/1, (https://wwwmcc.murdoch.edu.au/ReadingRoom/4.1/Curthoys.html).

Data Guy (2016): "2016 Romance Writers of America RWA PAN Presentation" In: authorearnings.com July 15, (http://authorearnings.com/2016-rwa-pan-presentation/).

Deffenbacher, Kristina (2014): "Rape Myths' Twilight and Women's Paranormal Revenge in Romantic and Urban Fantasy Fiction." In: *The Journal of Popular Culture* 47/1, pp. 923-936.

Donelan, Carol (2015): "Vampires Suck! Twihards Rule!!! Myth and Meaning in the Twilight Saga Franchise." In: *Quarterly Review of Film and Video* 32:3, 240-250.

Duclos, Denis (1998): *Werewolf Complex: America's Fascination with Violence*, London: Bloomsbury.

Duncker, Patricia (1984): "Re-imagining the Fairy Tales: Angela Carter's Bloody Chambers." In *Literature and History* 10, pp. 3-14.

Durham, Meenakshi (2012): "Blood, Lust, and Love: Interrogating gender violence in the Twilight." In: *Journal of Media and Culture* 6/3, pp. 281-299.

Dyhouse, Carol (2017), *Heartthrobs: A History of Women and Desire*, Oxford: Oxford University Press.

Ellery, Ben/Gallagher, Ian (2013): "WHSmith's vile trade in online rape porn: Bookseller apologises after sales of sick ebooks are revealed." In: dailymail.co.uk October 12, (http://www.dailymail.co.uk/news/article-2456651/WHSmiths-vile-trade-online-rape-porn-Bookseller-apologises-sales-sick-ebooks-revealed.html).

Feehan, Christine (2000): *Dark Magic*, New York: Love Spell.

Feehan, Christine (2006): *Dark Prince*, London: Piatkus.

Feehan, Christine (2017): "Dark Magic Awards & Honors." In: christinefeehan.com October 24,
(http://christinefeehan.com/dark_magic/index.php).

Fictophilia (2012-2017) "One Handed Reads,"
(https://fictophilia.ecwid.com/#!/One-Handed-Reads/c/19306080).

Frost, Brian J. (2003): *The Essential Guide to Werewolf Literature*, Madison: The University of Wisconsin Press.

Frum, David (2000): *How We Got Here: The '70s, the Decade That Brought You Modern Life - For Better or Worse*, New York: Basic Books.

Greenfield, Jerry (2011): "DBW Profiles: Raelene Gorlinsky, Publisher, Ellora's Cave Publishing Inc." In: *Digital Book World: Digital Publishing News for the 21st Century* October 27, (http://www.digitalbookworld.com/2011/dbw-profiles-raelene-gorlinsky-publisher-elloras-cave-publishing-inc/).

Hartley, Emma (2015): "Rex Appeal: the Literary Attraction of Dinosaur Erotica." In: theguardian.com February 13,
(https://www.theguardian.com/books/booksblog/2015/feb/13/rex-appeal-literary-attraction-dinosaur-erotica).

Hathaway, Jay (2016): "Chuck Tingle counter-trolls the Gamergaters who nominated his erotica for a Hugo Award." In: dailydot.com May 5,
(https://www.dailydot.com/unclick/chuck-tingle-trolling-hugo-zoe-quinn-genius/).

Hoffelder, Nate (2013): "Self-Published Erotica is Being Singled Out For Sweeping Deletions From Major eBookstores." In: the-digital-reader.com October 13, (http://the-digital-reader.com/2013/10/13/amazon-bn-whsmith-now/).

hooks, bell (2000): *Feminism is for Everybody: Passionate Politics*, Cambridge, MA: South End Press.

Housel, Rebecca (2009): "The 'real' danger: fact vs. fiction for the girl audience." In: Rebecca Housel/J. Jeremy Wisnewski/William Irwin (eds.), *Twilight and Philosophy*, London: John Blackwell and Sons.

Jenkins, Henry (2006): *Convergence Culture: Where Old and New Media Collide*, New York: New York University Press.

Jensen, Margret Ann (1984): *Love's $weet Return: The Harlequin Story*, Bowling Green: Bowling Green State University Popular Press.

Jones, Ralph (2015): "I Got Erotica Master Chuck Tingle to Workshop My Dinosaur Erotica." In: jezebel.com May 1, (https://jezebel.com/i-got-erotica-master-chuck-tingle-to-workshop-my-dinosa-1700057882).

Jowett, Lorna (2012): "Between the Paws of the Tender Wolf: Authorship, Adaption and Audience." In: Sonya Andermahr and Lawrence Phillips (eds.) *Angela Carter: New Critical Readings*, London: Continuum, pp. 33-43.

Kendal, Evie and Kendal, Zachary (2015): "Consent is Sexy: Gender, Sexual Identity and Sex Positivism in MTV's Young Adult Television Series Teen Wolf (2011-)." In: *Colloquy: Text Theory Critique* 30, pp. 26-39.

Lang, Andrew (1889): *The Blue Fairy Book,* London, Longmans Green & Co.

Lappas, Catherine (1996): "'Seeing is believing but touching is the truth': Female Spectatorship and Sexuality in The Company of Wolves." In: *Women's Studies* 25, pp. 115-135.

Lee, Linda J. (2008): "Guilty Pleasures: Reading Romance Novels as Reworked Fairy Tales." In: *Marvels and Tales* 22/1, pp. 52-66.

Lewallen, Avis (1988): "Wayward Girls but Wicked Women?" In: Gary Day and Clive Bloom (eds.) *Perspectives on Pornography: Sexuality in Film and Literature*, Basingstoke: Macmillan, pp. 144-58.

Lutz, Deborah (2006): *The Dangerous Lover: Gothic Villains, Byronism, and the Nineteenth-Century Seduction Narrative*, Columbus: Ohio State University Press.

Martens, Marianne (2010): "Consumed by Twilight: The Commodification of Young Adult Literature." In: Melissa A. Click/Jennifer Stevens Aubrey/Elizabeth Behm-Morawitz (eds.), *Bitten by Twilight: Youth Culture, Media, & the Vampire Franchise*, New York: Peter Lang, pp. 243-260.

McMahon-Coleman, Kimberley/Weaver, Roslyn (2012): *Werewolves and Other Shapeshifters in Popular Culture*, Jefferson, NC: McFarland.

McKnight-Trontz, Jennifer (2001): *The Look of Love: The Art of the Romance Novel*, New York: Princeton Architectural Press.

Meyer, Stephenie (2007): *Eclipse*, London: Atom.

Meyer, Stephenie (2017a), "Frequently asked Questions: Breaking Dawn," (https://stepheniemeyer.com/the-books/breaking-dawn/frequently-asked-questions-breaking-dawn/#feminist).

Meyer, Stephenie (2017b), "Frequently asked Questions: Eclipse." (https://stepheniemeyer.com/frequently-asked-questions-eclipse/#flaws).

Mills & Boon, "Series Guidelines: Mills & Boon Nocturne," (https://www.millsandboon.com.au/author-guidelines#nocturne).

Modleski, Tania (2008): *Loving with a Vengeance: Mass-produced Fantasies for Women*, New York: Routledge.

Orr, Cynthia/ Herald, Diana Tixier (2013): *Genreflecting: A Guide to Popular Reading Interests*, Exeter: Libraries Unlimited.

Pahle, Rebecca, "California Court Finally Decides It's OK for Prisoners to Read Werewolf Erotica." In: themarysue.com June 12, (https://www.themarysue.com/california-prison-werewolf-erotica/).

Parkin, Molly (1970) *Radio Times* 188, p. 51.

Phillips, Susan Elizabeth (1992). "The Romance and the Empowerment of Women." In: Jayne Ann Krentz (ed.) *Dangerous Men and Adventurous Women: Romance Writers on the Appeal of the Romance*, Philadelphia: University of Pennsylvania Press, pp. 53-60.

Putney, Mary Jo (1992): "Welcome to the Dark Side." In: Jayne Ann Krentz (ed.) *Dangerous Men and Adventurous Women: Romance Writers on the Appeal of the Romance*, Philadelphia: University of Pennsylvania Press, pp. 99-105.

Radway, Janice A. (1984). Reading the Romance: Women, Patriarchy, and Popular Literature. Chapel Hill: University of North Caroline Press.

Reid, Jennifer (2014): "Wolves in Sheep's Clothing: Transgressive Sexualities in 'Little Red Riding Hood' and Angela Carter." In: *Postgraduate English* 29, pp. 2-25.

Rosenthal, Pam (2010): "A Generation of Erotic Romance." In: *History Hoydens* November 5, (http://historyhoydens.blogspot.com/2010/11/generation-of-erotic- romance.html).

Sabledrake (2004): "Hairy Men." In: literotica.com April 29, (https://www.literotica.com/s/hairy-men).

Schau, Hope Jensen/Buchanan-Oliver, Margo (2012): "'The Creation of Inspired Lives': Female Fan Engagement With the Twilight Saga." In: Cele C. Otnes/Linda Tuncay Zayer (eds.) *Gender, Culture, and Consumer Behavior*, New York: Routledge, pp. 33-62

Schell, Heather (2007): "The Big Bad Wolf: Masculinity and Genetics in Popular Culture." In: *Literature and Medicine* 26/1, pp. 109-125.

Spitznagel, Eric (2013): "MONSTER PORN: Amazon Cracks Down On America's Latest Sex Fantasy." In: businessinsider.com December 21, (http://www.businessinsider.com/monster-porn-amazon-crackdown-sex-fantasy-bigfoot-2013-12?IR=T).

Tamblyn, Michael (2013): "Infinite Shades of Grey: The Promise and Peril of Self-Publishing" On: youtube.com November 27, (https://www.youtube.com/watch?v=4kfV8c7ibDc).

Thurston, Carol (1987): *Romance Revolution: Erotic Novels for Women and the Quest for a New Sexual Identity*, Chicago: University of Illinois Press.

Tobin-McClain, Lee (2000): "Paranormal Romance: Secrets of the Female Fantastic." In: *Journal of the Fantastic in the Arts* 11/3, pp. 294-306.

Wade, Virginia (2011): *Cum For Bigfoot*, I Love Stacy, Smashwords Edition.

Wilson, Jeremy (2013): "An Epidemic of Filth." In: thedailydot October 11, (http://kernelmag.dailydot.com/features/report/exclusive/6016/an-epidemic-of-filth/).

Wyatt, Daisy (2013): "WH Smith takes website offline after porn ebook scandal." In: independent.co.uk October 14, (http://www.independent.co.uk/arts-entertainment/books /news/wh-smith-takes-website-offline-after-porn-ebook-scandal-8879241.html).

Woodiwiss, Kathleen E. (1972), *The Flame and the Flower*, New York: Avon.

Zipes, Jack (1989): "A Second Gaze at Little Red Riding Hood's Trials and Tribulations." In: Jack Zipes (ed.) *Don't Bet on the Prince: Contemporary Fairy Tales in North America and England*, New York: Routledge.

About the Authors

Brandy Eileen Allatt earned her Master of Arts degree in Literature from Texas State University, USA, in 2015, after successfully defending her thesis about "Lies and Individuation: External and Internal Authority in the Politics and Anima of *Dune*." Her current research interests include liminal identities in literature, dystopian futures written for young adults, and Frank Herbert's works. She is a regular participant and presenter at The International Conference for the Fantastic in the Arts (ICFA).

Fred Botting is a professor of English Literature and Creative Writing at Kingston University London, UK. He is an internationally renowned expert in Gothic fiction and cultural theory and has written extensively on Gothic theory, literature, film, and cultural forms. Currently, he works on figures of horror fiction and film generally, and on zombies in particular, and focuses on spectrality, the uncanny, and sexuality.

Sarah Faber is a research and teaching associate in the Department of English and Linguistics at Johannes Gutenberg University, Mainz. Her doctoral thesis formulates an interdisciplinary approach to narration in multiplayer environments. Other research interests include fantastic narratives, constructions of gender, and 19th-century Britain.

Atalie Gerhard is currently a doctoral candidate at the Friedrich-Alexander University of Erlangen-Nuremberg, Germany, where she also received her B.A. and M.A. degrees in English and American Studies, as well as in French Romantic Studies. In her research, she focuses on the visual art accompanying U.S. American minority resistance, and on counterterrorist popular culture. Her volunteer integration work with refugees in Germany has received official recognition and been featured in the press.

Michael Giebel is a Bachelor student of German and English Studies at the University of Münster. Prior to his current studies, he earned a B.A. degree in Psychology at the Freie Universität Berlin. He has a marked interest in the intersection between psychological discourse and literary narratives of German and Anglophone origin, specifically regarding the notions of pathology and identity. His other research interests are socio- and cognitive linguistics as well as media and cultural studies.

Irina Golovacheva is a professor of the Philological Faculty at St. Petersburg State University in Russia. She is the author of three books: *Science and Literature: The Archeology of Scientific Knowledge of Aldous Huxley* (St. Petersburg Univ. Press, 2008), *Fantastika and the Fantastic* (St. Petersburg: Petropolis, 2013), and *A Guide to "Brave New World" and Around* (Moscow: LRC Publishing House, to be released in December 2017). She has also published numerous papers on the fantastic, Aldous Huxley, Henry James, mass culture, and mathematical methods in literary criticism.

Alfons Gregori is Assistant Professor at the Adam Mickiewicz University in Poznan, Poland, and the Head of the Centre for Catalan Studies. He is the author of numerous journal articles and book chapters about fantastic literature, gender studies, contemporary popular music and criticism of literary translation. He also was the lead researcher for the grant project "The ideological element in fantastic literature" (2011-2015), financed by the Polish National Science Centre (Narodowe Centrum Nauki).

Larissa Lai is Associate Professor and Canada Research Chair in Creative Writing at the University of Calgary, Canada. Her most recent critical book, *Slanting I, Imagining We: Asian Canadian Literary Production in the 1980s and 1990s* (Ontario, Canada: Wilfrid Laurier UP, 2014), presents a compelling reappraisal of the formation of Asian Canadian literature. She is also the author of two novels, *When Fox Is a Thousand* and *Salt Fish Girl*, and two books of poetry, *sybil unrest* (with Rita Wong) and *Automaton Biographies*.

Alexandra Leonzini is a joint Masters in Global History student at the Freie Universität Berlin and the Humboldt Universität zu Berlin, and former Global Humanities Junior Fellow for the Thematic Network Principles of Cultural Dynamics at l'École des Hautes Études en Sciences Sociales (Paris, Fance). Her research interests include the history of the werewolf, the gendering of the werewolf concept in popular literature, and the construction of masculinity in contemporary romance and erotic literature.

Johanna Pundt is a research assistant at the University of Augsburg, where she teaches courses on representations of slavery in film, Orientalism, indigenous science fiction and postcolonial studies. She received her M.A. in English Studies and a Master of Education in English and Ethics from the Carl von Ossietzky University Oldenburg in 2014. Her PhD project traces notions of the "speculative" in Indian Anglophone literature, sequential art, and film. Her research interests include postcolonial theory and literatures, speculative fiction, adaptations and rewritings of the Ramayana as well as Indian cinema.

Daniel Scott is a lecturer in American Studies at the Johannes Gutenberg University, Mainz. His research interests include theology, ethics as well as religious and Fantasy fiction. He is currently working on his doctoral thesis, which deals with atheism and theism in contemporary Fantasy fiction.

Social Sciences and Cultural Studies

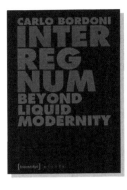

Carlo Bordoni
Interregnum
Beyond Liquid Modernity

2016, 136 p., pb.
19,99 € (DE), 978-3-8376-3515-7
E-Book
PDF: 17,99 € (DE), ISBN 978-3-8394-3515-1
EPUB: 17,99€ (DE), ISBN 978-3-7328-3515-7

Alexander Schellinger, Philipp Steinberg (eds.)
The Future of the Eurozone
How to Keep Europe Together:
A Progressive Perspective from Germany

October 2017, 202 p., pb.
29,99 € (DE), 978-3-8376-4081-6
E-Book
PDF: 26,99 € (DE), ISBN 978-3-8394-4081-0
EPUB: 26,99€ (DE), ISBN 978-3-7328-4081-6

European Alternatives, Daphne Büllesbach,
Marta Cillero, Lukas Stolz (eds.)
Shifting Baselines of Europe
New Perspectives beyond Neoliberalism and Nationalism

May 2017, 212 p., pb.
19,99 € (DE), 978-3-8376-3954-4
E-Book: available as free open access publication
ISBN 978-3-8394-3954-8

**All print, e-book and open access versions of the titles in our list
are available in our online shop www.transcript-verlag.de/en!**

Social Sciences and Cultural Studies

Ramón Reichert, Annika Richterich, Pablo Abend,
Mathias Fuchs, Karin Wenz (eds.)
Digital Culture & Society (DCS)
Vol. 1, Issue 1 – Digital Material/ism

2015, 242 p., pb.
29,99 € (DE), 978-3-8376-3153-1
E-Book: 29,99 € (DE), ISBN 978-3-8394-3153-5

Ilker Ataç, Gerda Heck, Sabine Hess, Zeyrep Kasli,
Philipp Ratfisch, Cavidan Soykan, Bediz Yilmaz (eds.)
**movements. Journal for Critical Migration and
Border Regime Studies**
Vol. 3, Issue 2/2017: Turkey's Changing Migration Regime
and its Global and Regional Dynamics

November 2017, 230 p., pb.
24,99 € (DE), 978-3-8376-3719-9

Annika Richterich, Karin Wenz, Pablo Abend,
Mathias Fuchs, Ramón Reichert (eds.)
Digital Culture & Society (DCS)
Vol. 3, Issue 1/2017 – Making and Hacking

June 2017, 198 p., pb.
29,99 € (DE), 978-3-8376-3820-2
E-Book: 29,99 € (DE), ISBN 978-3-8394-3820-6

**All print, e-book and open access versions of the titles in our list
are available in our online shop www.transcript-verlag.de/en!**